FIELDING'S
NEW ZEALAND

Other Fielding Titles

Fielding's Alaska Cruises and the Inside Passage
Fielding's America West
Fielding's Asia's Top Dive Sites
Fielding's Australia
Fielding's Bahamas
Fielding's Baja California
Fielding's Bermuda
Fielding's Best and Worst — The surprising results of the Plog Survey
Fielding's Birding Indonesia
Fielding's Borneo
Fielding's Budget Europe
Fielding's Caribbean
Fielding's Caribbean Cruises
Fielding's Caribbean on a Budget
Fielding's Diving Australia
Fielding's Diving Indonesia
Fielding's Eastern Caribbean
Fielding's England including Ireland, Scotland & Wales
Fielding's Europe
Fielding's Europe 50th Anniversary
Fielding's European Cruises
Fielding's Far East
Fielding's France
Fielding's France: Loire Valley, Burgundy & the Best of French Culture
Fielding's France: Normandy & Brittany
Fielding's France: Provence and the Mediterranean
Fielding's Freewheelin' USA
Fielding's Hawaii
Fielding's Hot Spots: Travel in Harm's Way
Fielding's Indiana Jones Adventure and Survival Guide™
Fielding's Italy
Fielding's Kenya
Fielding's Las Vegas Agenda
Fielding's London Agenda
Fielding's Los Angeles Agenda
Fielding's Mexico
Fielding's New Orleans Agenda
Fielding's New York Agenda
Fielding's New Zealand
Fielding's Paradors, Pousadas and Charming Villages of Spain and Portugal
Fielding's Paris Agenda
Fielding's Portugal
Fielding's Rome Agenda
Fielding's San Diego Agenda
Fielding's Southeast Asia
Fielding's Southern California Theme Parks
Fielding's Southern Vietnam on Two Wheels
Fielding's Spain
Fielding's Surfing Australia
Fielding's Surfing Indonesia
Fielding's Sydney Agenda
Fielding's Thailand, Cambodia, Laos and Myanmar
Fielding's Travel Tool™
Fielding's Vietnam, including Cambodia and Laos
Fielding's Walt Disney World and Orlando Area Theme Parks
Fielding's Western Caribbean
Fielding's The World's Most Dangerous Places™
Fielding's Worldwide Cruises

FIELDING'S
NEW ZEALAND

by
Zeke Wigglesworth
and
Joan Wigglesworth

Fielding Worldwide, Inc.
308 South Catalina Avenue
Redondo Beach, California 90277 U.S.A.

Fielding's New Zealand

Published by Fielding Worldwide, Inc.

Text Copyright ©1997 Zeke Wigglesworth and Joan Wigglesworth

Icons & Illustrations Copyright ©1997 FWI

Photo Copyrights ©1997 to Individual Photographers

FIELDING WORLDWIDE INC.

PUBLISHER AND CEO **Robert Young Pelton**
GENERAL MANAGER **John Guillebeaux**
OPERATIONS DIRECTOR **George Posanke**
ELECTRONIC PUBLISHING DIRECTOR **Larry E. Hart**
PUBLIC RELATIONS DIRECTOR **Beverly Riess**
ACCOUNT SERVICES MANAGER **Cindy Henrichon**
PROJECT MANAGER **Chris Snyder**
MANAGING EDITOR **Amanda K. Knoles**

PRODUCTION

Martin Mancha   **Reed Parsell**
Ramses Reynoso   **Craig South**

COVER DESIGNED BY **Digital Artists, Inc.**
COVER PHOTOGRAPHERS — Front Cover **Walter Bibikow/FPG**
Back Cover **Mt. Cook, South Island - James L. Amos**
INSIDE PHOTOS **Courtesy of the New Zealand Tourism Board, Corel Professional Photos**

Inquiries should be addressed to: Fielding Worldwide, Inc., 308 South Catalina Ave., Redondo Beach, California 90277 U.S.A., ☎ *(310) 372-4474*, Facsimile *(310) 376-8064*, 8:30 a.m.–5:30 p.m. Pacific Standard Time.
Website: http://www.fieldingtravel.com
e-mail: fielding@fieldingtravel.com

ISBN 1-56952-152-2

Printed in the United States of America

Letter from the Publisher

In 1946, Temple Fielding began the first of what would be a remarkable new series of well-written, highly personalized guidebooks for independent travelers. Temple's opinionated, witty and oft-imitated books have now guided travelers for almost a half-century. More important to some was Fielding's humorous and direct method of steering travelers away from the dull and the insipid. Today, Fielding's travel guides are still written by experienced travelers for experienced travelers. Our authors carry on Fielding's reputation for creating travel experiences that deliver insight with a sense of discovery and style.

Zeke and Joan Wigglesworth spent 12 years laying the painstaking foundations for this entertaining and informative guide to the "other" land down under. They've traveled to all the undiscovered treasures that this panoramic island nation has to offer. They've also done a superb job of guiding the adventurous traveler to the country's natural wonders. The Wigglesworths' delightful intimacy with New Zealand's history, people and culture will make your trip to the land of the kiwi unforgettable.

The concept of independent travel has never been bigger. Our policy of *brutal honesty* and a highly personal point of view has never changed; it just seems the travel world has caught up with us.

Enjoy your New Zealand adventure with the Wigglesworths and Fielding.

R Y P

Robert Young Pelton
Publisher and CEO
Fielding Worldwide, Inc.

Dedication

For Toots and Eldon, always there when we needed them, even if it meant worms in the chili.

Fielding Rating Icons

The Fielding Rating Icons are highly personal and awarded to help the besieged traveler choose from among the dizzying array of activities, attractions, hotels, restaurants and sights. The awarding of an icon denotes unusual or exceptional qualities in the relevant category.

RATINGS

Fielding Award	Author Selection	Money Saver	Expensive	Quality	Warning	Danger	Inexpensive
Spacious	Cramped	Mild Disapproval	Timesaving				

CULTURAL

Museum/ Art	Interesting Architecture	History	Book Reference	Artistically Important	Musically Interesting	Cultural Archeology	Crafts
Theatre	Festivals						

SIGHTS

Picturesque	Great Scenery	Market	Beaches/ Resorts	Cultural	Fortress	Castles	Church

WHERE TO STAY

Simple	Luxurious	Cottage	Bed & Breakfast	Scenic	Business	Honeymoon	Chateau

TRAVEL TIPS

Arrival/ Departure	By Air	By Water	By Train	By Car	Bus/Local Transit	Barge	River Boat
Calendar	Itinerary	Compass	Kids				

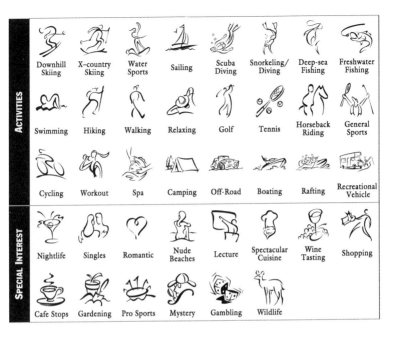

Map Legend

Essentials

- Hotel
- Youth Hostel
- Restaurant
- Bank
- Telephone
- Tourist Info.
- Hospital
- Pub / Bar
- Music Club
- Post Office
- Parking
- Taxi
- Subway
- Metro
- Market
- Shopping
- Cinema
- Theater
- Int'l Airport
- Regional Airport
- Police Station
- Courthouse
- Gov't. Building
- Attraction

- Military Airbase
- Army Base
- Naval base
- Fort
- University
- School

Activities

- Beach
- Campground
- Picnic Area
- Golf Course
- Boat Launch
- Diving
- Fishing
- Water Skiing
- Snow Skiing
- Bird Sanctuary
- Wildlife Sanctuary
- Park
- Park Headquarters
- Mine
- Lighthouse
- Windmill

- Cruise Port
- View
- Stadium
- Building
- Zoo
- Garden

Historical

- Archeological Site
- Battleground
- Castle
- Monument
- Museum
- Ruin
- Shipwreck

Religious

- Church
- Buddhist Temple
- Hindu Temple
- Mosque
- Pagoda
- Synagogue
- Cemetery
- Hebrew Cemetery
- Muslim Cemetery

Physical

- — — — — · International Boundary
- — · — — · County / Regional Boundary
- **PARIS** ⊙ National Capital
- **Montego Bay** • State / Parish Capital
- **Los Angeles** ● Major City
- **Quy Nhon** ○ Town / Village
- = = (5) = = Motorway / Freeway
- (163) Highway
- **1AB** Freeway Exit
- Primary Road
- Secondary Road
- — — — — Subway
- Trolley / Street Car

- Biking Routed
- Hiking Trail
- Dirt Road
- Railroad
- **RR** Railroad Station
- Ferry Route
- ▲ Mountain Peak
- Lake
- River
- Cave
- Coral Reef
- Waterfall
- Hot Spring

©FWI

TABLE OF CONTENTS

LIST OF MAPS

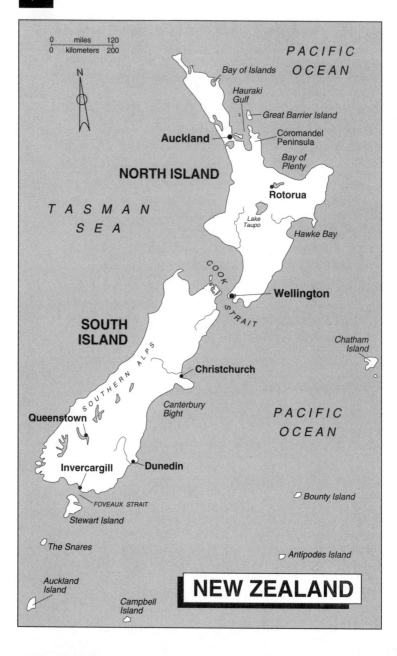

0 miles 120
0 kilometers 200

N

PACIFIC
OCEAN

Bay of Islands

Hauraki
Gulf

Great Barrier Island

Auckland

Coromandel
Peninsula

NORTH ISLAND

Bay of
Plenty

Rotorua

*TASMAN
SEA*

Lake
Taupo

Hawke Bay

COOK

Wellington

STRAIT

**SOUTH
ISLAND**

Chatham
Island

SOUTHERN ALPS

Christchurch

Canterbury
Bight

PACIFIC
OCEAN

Queenstown

Invercargill

Dunedin

Bounty Island

FOVEAUX STRAIT

Stewart Island

The Snares

Antipodes Island

Auckland
Island

Campbell
Island

NEW ZEALAND

INTRODUCTION

The Lady Bowen cruise boat is a pleasant way to see Milford Sound.

Mother England had two children Down Under, one boisterous and often uncouth, the other more gentlemanly and decorous. In many ways the two—Australia and New Zealand—are very similar.

They are both countries situated far out in the Southwest Pacific. They both have a mostly Anglo-Scottish-Irish culture superimposed on an older indigenous population. They are both former colonies of the British Empire, and thus are culturally, politically and philosophically attuned to Great Britain. They play the same games, enjoy the same cultural events, tell the same jokes, have roughly the same accent (at least to a North American ear). They are economically intertwined; if the Australia market gets a cold, New Zealand gets pneumonia. The citizens of both countries migrate back and forth continually, depending on which society seems to have the most jobs or the most promise at any given moment. They fight wars together, and they die far from home together.

The scenic Dart Valley can be seen from the Rees-Dart Track.

Green and Pastoral

There are vast differences between Australia and New Zealand as well. The major one is attitude, probably created by the differences in geography. Most of the population of Australia clings to the southeastern coast because most of the interior of the country is relentless desert. This huge area, the same size as the United States, gives Aussies a decided frontier outlook in many ways. On the other hand, New Zealand is a gentle country, even in the South Island where there are extremes of cold and heat. There is a famous poem in Australia, written by Dorothea Mackellar, that says: "I love a sun-burnt country." But in New Zealand, like Ireland, the overwhelming image is green—paddocks filled with sheep and deer, green bushlands clinging to the sides of green fjords, green rainforests swathing the bases of glacier-covered mountains. *The green of New Zealand has made the Kiwis more pastoral, more tranquil, less involved with taming a rugged landscape.* They seem, on the whole, to be quieter and less strident than their Australian brothers and sisters, a bit more sedate and at ease with themselves. The New Zealanders, after all, had nothing to prove to the English—unlike the first colonists to Australia, taken to Sydney in chains, the Kiwis came to their land as free citizens, on an equal footing with Great Britain from the first.

Culture

There are also some profound cultural differences. Modern-day Australia, while it has come a long way since the days when the official government policy was "Whites Only," still carries the burdens of a racist society. Part of the reason is historical. It is estimated that only 300,000 Aboriginals lived in the vast expanse of Australia when the Europeans arrived. They were primitive hunter-gatherers, totally unprepared for the incursion of a technically superior society. The fate of the Aboriginals was never in doubt from the first. Today they comprise only about one percent of the total population and have little political power.

Maoris enjoy teasing tourists with the Maori challenge.

The Maoris

In New Zealand, it has been a different story. Europeans encountered a well-organized (if violent) Polynesian society when they landed in the 1820s. The Maoris, as they are called, were more than a match for the Europeans, and despite numerous bloody clashes between the two societies, New Zealand has been a dualistic nation for more than a hundred years. In truth, this does not mean the two peoples have lived in complete harmony or that racial biases are unknown. But compared to Australia, New Zealand is a well-integrated and tolerant society. Part of the reason, of course, is that the Maoris are not the same subjugated people as the Australian Aboriginals. The Maoris have political clout and growing land rights and make up a third of the population.

INTRODUCTION

Australia and New Zealand

Too often, visitors to the antipodes link Australia and New Zealand closer than they really are. They are unique cultures, both worthy of attention, both worthy of examination. And, too often, because of money or time constraints, the two are linked together on a whirlwind tour that does justice to neither. It's much like somebody coming to North America and trying to see Canada and the United States on one trip. There is also a common assumption that the two countries are right next to each other. They are close, but not that close—*1300* miles of ocean separate them.

We urge those with the time and the wherewithal to allow enough time on a single trip to do both countries properly, or lacking that, do them one at a time. Having said that, and knowing the realities of travel, we have tried in this book to offer our thoughts about how to get the most out of a trip to New Zealand. We first arrived here thinking the country was just another state of Australia, another Tasmania, perhaps—off the beaten path from Sydney and a long way from Los Angeles. What we found is a society that clings to what we in the United States used to call "old-fashioned values." *Some observers think New Zealand is in a time warp, a society living 50 years in the past.* But this is a misconception. For all its isolation, New Zealand is a progressive and contemporary country, with a flair for food and excellent wines, for sports and outdoor activities and for gung-ho political activism. What is obvious is that the country is a vacationer's dream. Every possible activity is available, and the range of choices is from international, five-star quality down to mom-and-pop shoestring. We know of no country that surpasses New Zealand in its ability to take care of tourists, especially middle-income travelers and those who see the sights from beneath a backpack. Many hotels, and even some international-class hotels, have baby-sitting services, something unheard of in most places. There are special backpackers' passes, there is excellent, modestly priced bus and train service, and there are also lodges where you can blow US$500 a night—without meals.

About Us

Zeke and Joan Wigglesworth

We think, to judge the observations contained in this book, you should know a bit about us. This is our second guidebook (*Fielding's Australia* was the first). Travel journalism is not new to us, however, nor is travel. The male member of the outfit is the travel editor for a well-respected newspaper in the Bay Area of California. The female half has been his research assistant, fellow writer and traveling companion for more than 30 years. Together or separately, we have been all over the world, from Tehran to Casablanca to Prague to Khabarovsk to Vietnam to the Greek Islands—and the list goes on. We say this not to dazzle you with our expertise, but to alert you to the fact that we have made just about every stupid mistake you can make and still live to tell (or write) about it. We have been confused and lost in so many places so many times we lost count, and the number of fights we've had about directions, plans, hotel choices and menu translations make Divorce Court look like a kindergarten class.

What to Expect

Travel books, like any form of journalism, carry with them the biases of their creators, some subtle, some obvious. Over the years and over the miles, we have developed habits and patterns of enjoyment and methods of criticism that we apply to our travels, our selection of accommodations, our fancies in food, our methods of conveyance. There is nothing wrong with this, certainly, as long as these biases are made plain—which we have tried to do here.

We are, first and foremost, Americans, which designation carries with it hordes of prejudices concerning clean toilets, potable water supplies and legal rights. But more, we are Northern Californians, which means we have certain outlooks normally found only on the West Coast, including a tendency to scoff at wines not produced in Napa or Sonoma counties, coupled with an irresistible urge to devour tons of fresh artichokes and eat tons of fresh garlic. (There is no such thing as too much garlic.)

We are both Greenies, having seen examples all over our planet of our species slowly fouling its own nest, and we have little regard for societies that forget that people are the first order of business, not political or monetary agendas.

We like isolation and wildernesses, and camped more than our share back when the kids were small and even a Motel 6 was financially impossible. But we also like cities and have a real fondness for paved streets and flush toilets. While we are not reluctant to sup with strangers when necessity or instant friendship arises, and have been known to take bus tours and actually enjoy them, we prefer doing things on our own. We have learned to be patient and flexible, having discovered early on that Murphy was indeed an optimist.

Given a choice, we ignore timetables, try not to adhere too closely to itineraries. Trains have their place; so do buses and guided tours. But for our tastes, the only way to travel is by personal vehicle, be it camper van or car—we are too lazy for bikes, too conventional for motorcycles. Money and time often make such independent travel impossible, but whenever possible, we are on the road, enjoying the freedom of being able to stop where and when we want, of taking any back route that comes along, of making our days as long or as short as we choose. We think this is essential to your enjoyment of New Zealand. On the one hand, the country is small enough to easily allow such freedom. And on the other, and more important hand, the New Zealanders make it very easy to travel independently —in fact, they encourage it.

A few things about how to use this book: *Because New Zealand is on the decimal system using dollars and cents, there can be confusion when discussing prices. In almost all cases, we have quoted prices in New Zealand dollars so you can use current exchange rates to estimate expenses.* The rate over recent years has hovered around 60–70 U.S. cents to the Kiwi dollar.

What's in the Stars

Fielding's Five-Star Rating System

★★★★★ Exceptionally outstanding hotels, resorts, restaurants and attractions.

★★★★ Excellent in most respects.

★★★ Very good quality and superior value.

★★ Meritorious and worth considering.

★ Modest or better than average.

Restaurants are star-rated and classified by dollar signs as:

$	Budget	$NZ15–40
$$	Moderate	$NZ40–90
$$$	Expensive	$NZ90 and up

Prices are for two people.

A NOTE TO OUR READERS:

If you have had an extraordinary, mediocre or horrific experience, we want to hear about it. If something has changed since we have gone to press, please let us know. If you would like to send information for review in next year's edition, send it to:

Fielding's New Zealand
308 South Catalina Avenue
Redondo Beach, CA 90277
FAX: (310) 376-8064
Website: http://www.fieldingtravel.com

THE EXPLORERS

Captain Cook's Statue and Young Nick's Head

The two Lands Down Under—Australia and New Zealand—primarily owe their discovery by European explorers to a philosophic quest for balance. By the beginning of the 17th century, most of the major land masses on the planet had been outlined by the Europeans, although vast interior areas were still unexplored. But it seemed to European philosophers and cartographers that such an ideal form as a sphere required an equally ideal balance of masses. Europe, North America, India, Cathay, the lands of the Near East—all lay to the north of the equator. There were the masses of subequatorial Africa and South America, to be sure, but a sense of harmony insisted that there should be at least one more great continent in the south, a mythical land mass that came to be called *terra australis incognita* in Latin, "the unknown southern land."

The island continent of Australia had been nibbled at for centuries, but was thought to be just an extension of New Guinea, not the mythical missing land, so the search for the great southern land mass continued well into the 18th century.

The First European Discovery

The credit for the first European investigations of any part of Australia fell to the Dutch, who had by the beginning of the 17th century taken firm hold of Indonesia. Ships sailing south and east from Batavia—modern Jakarta—chanced upon the mostly inhospitable west, south and north coasts of Australia. Throughout the 1600s, Dutch traders and explorers flushed out their charts of Australia but sailed past, seeing little to attract colonization or trade.

In the slow process of wooden-ship exploration, Dutch sailors apparently were the first westerners to discover one of the southern hemisphere's little gifts to navigators: the Roaring Forties. From the tip of Cape Horn, east past the Cape of Good Hope, south past Australia, great winds blow almost constantly around and around the planet, like a giant merry-go-round. If you catch a ride between 40 degrees and 50 degrees south latitude, you can sail the vast stretches between land masses with a constant, predictable, strong west wind at your back.

The Agrodome, Rotorua, is the site of sheepshearing competitions.

The Dutch

One of the most successful of the Dutch explorers—at least in terms of discoveries—was Abel Janszoon Tasman, a Dutch East India Company captain. In

1642, he was given orders to sail well south of the East Indies to near the Antarctic Circle to look for that elusive and as yet undiscovered great southern continent. He sailed August 14, and by October was far to the southwest of Australia at about 49 degrees south latitude, a record at the time. He never found land, only fog and heavy seas, so he decided to sail back to about 45 degrees south, then head east until he reached the approximate longitude of New Guinea, then head north. It was a route that almost guaranteed he would hit land.

On November 24, he sighted what would later become Australia's main penal colony and only island state, naming it Van Diemen's Land in honor of Anthoonij van Dieman, governor-general of the East Indies. It would be well into the 19th century before the island would be known by its modern name: Tasmania. He sailed north along the island, but storms forced him east before he got to what would later be named the Bass Strait, the often turbulent stretch of water separating mainland Australia from Tasmania. After leaving the island, he sailed across the waters east of Australia (now called the Tasman Sea) until December 13, when he ran into a big landmass sitting right square on top of the Roaring Forties.

New Zealand had been discovered again—but this time by a European sea power, 1000 years after the Polynesians. Tasman apparently first sighted New Zealand, which he named "Staten Landt," in the vicinity of modern Hokitika on the west coast of the South Island. He sailed north in an effort to determine if the landmass was an island, and actually sailed into the narrow strait separating the two islands. Bad sea conditions forced him back, so he continued on north, passing and naming Three King Islands, where the South Pacific and the Tasman Sea meet.

In all, he spent less than a month in New Zealand waters. He had less than a pleasant experience with the locals, who killed several of his crew and were not at all hospitable. Winds carried him to the northeast, where he eventually made landfall in Tonga. After puttering around in the Solomon Islands and the Bismarck archipelago, he returned to Batavia in June 1643 after sailing about 5000 miles. The Dutch East India Company was not much taken with his performance (no trade possibilities had arisen), but the voyage did prove Australia/New Guinea was not connected to any missing landmass. The Dutch started calling Australia "Nieuw Holland," and Tasman's "Staten Landt" eventually became listed on naval charts as "Nieuw Zeeland," named after Zeeland, the maritime province of the Netherlands west of Antwerp.

Captain James Cook

For reasons best left to Dutch historians, none of their bold sailors ever made thorough enough investigations of the east coast of Australia or New Zealand to recommend colonial establishments. It would be more than 125 years before Europeans showed any interest in the two lands beneath the Southern Cross. It again fell to a single naval captain to write the next chapters. But the captain who arrived off New Zealand in 1769 was no Abel Tasman—he was James Cook, without doubt one of the most successful mariners in the history of Pacific Ocean exploration.

A camper enjoys afternoon tea.

In the summer of 1769, there was to be a transit of the planet Venus—Venus would pass between the earth and the sun—which was an astronomical event of some importance. The Royal Navy, also still concerned about *terra australis incognita* (and rumors that the Spanish and French were sniffing around), decided to kill two birds with one stone and dispatch a ship to watch the heavens and also look for the missing continent.

Their Lordships had a spare ship—a beamy, bulky, shallow-draft former coal ship named the *Endeavor*—and they had a spare naval lieutenant, one James Cook. The *Endeavor*, about 100 feet long, carried a crew of 94. In addition to Cook, there were several scientists, including an astronomer and two botanists, Joseph Banks, a fellow of the Royal Society, and Daniel Carl Solander, a pupil of the great Swedish botanist, Carolus Linnaeus. Cook was ordered to go as far south as 40 degrees latitude, then sail around until he either found the missing continent or reached New Zealand, which, as we have noted, had been ignored for more than a century following Tasman's discovery. Cook did his Venus-transit job while enjoying the attractions of Tahiti, then headed south for the second part of his duties. In Tahiti, he was joined by a local chief, Tupaia, who came along for the ride and to help translate. Cook sailed 1500 miles southwest from Tahiti, failing to find anything faintly resembling a continent. He then headed for New Zealand. *At about 2 o'clock on October 7, 1769, one of the ship's boys, 13-year-old Nicholas Young, spied land—what is now called Young Nick's Head near Muriwai on the north-central coast of New Zealand's North Island.*

Cook's orders from the Admiralty also instructed him to parley with any New Zealand natives he met and see if he could work out a real estate deal of some benefit to His Majesty's Government. Cook exceeded that brief somewhat by simply claiming the whole thing for good King George III. He had also been given orders to survey New Zealand and chart its waters. *Cook, with his usual careful attention to detail, spent almost six months charting almost 2500 miles of Kiwi coastline, a survey job that to this day is a marvel of accuracy and detail.*

Wild thyme in Cromwell Gorge

A Violent Introduction

Cook made landfall October 9 in a bay lying north of Young Nick's Head, near the modern-day city of Gisborne. It was not a good beginning. Cook went ashore hoping to get water and fresh food. He also took Tupaia, who, to Cook's delight, was able to converse with the local residents. Despite the conversations, violence broke out, resulting in one Maori being shot and killed. When a war canoe filled with irate Maoris tried to attack the *Endeavor*, the crew shot and killed four more warriors. The harbor soon was full of very irate New Zealanders, and Cook, who abhorred violence and was dispirited by the deaths, decided to avoid further bloodshed and sailed October 11, naming the harbor Poverty Bay, because, he said, "it afforded us no one thing we wanted." (These days, Poverty Bay might be more to Cook's tastes—it's a major wine-growing and agricultural area.)

He sailed south, but finding no good anchorages—or friendly locals—changed his course back north at a point he called Cape Turnagain. He continued north to a harbor he called Mercury Bay (he observed a transit of Mercury there), then went north around North Cape, sighted Tasman's Three Kings Islands, then passed down the west coast. Along the way, he sighted and named Mount Egmont, the 8261-foot dormant volcano that serves as New Zealand's Mount Fuji. He then sailed through the strait, named after him, that separates the North and South Islands. He went north again as far as Cape Turnagain to prove North Island was indeed an island, then sailed south to circumnavigate the South Island. He passed by the Southern Alps, but clouds obscured the 12,350-foot mountain later named after him—just as clouds had obscured Tasman's view of 11,470-foot Mount Tasman the century before. The Maori name for New Zealand—*Aotearoa: the Land of the Long White Cloud*—was living up to its name.

Cook's survey proved that New Zealand was two islands, not part of any great southern continent. He left New Zealand on March 31, 1770, and sailed for home—via Australia and some very hairy experiences on the Great Barrier Reef. He reached Batavia October 10, 1770, where many of his crew—including Tupaia, his Tahitian translator—died of land-based diseases. He finally returned to England on July 13, 1771.

The Missing Continent

The admiralty was greatly pleased by Cook's accomplishments; so much so, that within months, he was presented to George III at court, promoted and given orders to return to the South Pacific to continue his search for the missing continent—and while he was at it, stake a claim to whatever he could because the French and Spanish were apparently still muddling around out there, as well. He left England again in July 1772, this time with two ships, his own *Resolution* and the *Adventure*, commanded by Captain Tobias Furneaux. The old *Endeavor*, battered but not beaten, had been sent off to the Falkland Islands as a supply ship.

Hunting on the Coromandel Peninsula

Cook's strategy for his second voyage was simple: sail to a point as far south of 40 degrees latitude as possible, then sail east in a giant circle from south of the Cape of Good Hope to New Zealand, then to Cape Horn and back around to the Indian Ocean. This way, he figured if there was a great missing continent down there, he should find it. He planned to try his great circle route during two southern summers, spending the winters exploring in the vicinity of Tahiti.

The "Filthy Fifties"

By December, he was near 57 degrees in what folks in the navy trade call the "Filthy Fifties," where he encountered storms, fog, icebergs—and no land. One startling discovery was made—iceberg ice, melted, became fresh water; the notion that icebergs came from freshwater glaciers was apparently unknown at that time.

Crossing the Antarctic Circle

On January 17, 1773, Cook and Furneaux crossed 66.33 degrees south latitude, becoming the first men to cross the Antarctic Circle. A few days later, they reached 67.15 degrees south, 39.35 east, a point just 75 miles north of present-day Enderby Land and the closest they ever came to Antarctica. Early in February, the two ships were separated in a fog, but Cook and Furneaux had made arrangements to rendezvous at Queen Charlotte Sound, the beautiful fjordlike harbor on the northeast tip of the South Island, now used by *interisland* ferries.

Cook and *Resolution*, having sailed almost 11,000 miles without seeing land, hauled into Dusky Sound, one of the isolated fjords on the southwestern coast of the South Island, on March 27. Cook and crew rested for about six weeks, then went on to their meeting with Furneaux at Queen Charlotte Harbour. After a winter of fun in the sun (including a relaxed visit with the good folks in Tonga), the two captains headed for the Antarctic again, intending to stop at Queen Charlotte. On the way, the ships became separated again in a storm. Cook stayed at the harbor until November 1773, then left, leaving a note to Furneaux in a bottle (plus a sign on a tree: "Look underneath"). Furneaux and crew, battered by the storm, arrived a few days later and met with a disaster. (See the discussion of cannibalism in "The Maori" chapter.)

Cook, meanwhile, was heading toward the ice again. On January 30, 1774, he and his crew became the first recorded humans to pass south of 70 degrees, but he was still far from land—where he was, the Antarctic landmass lies at about 75 degrees. Having by this point had his fill of ice and storms, he sailed north to Easter Island, then to Tahiti. He returned to Queen Charlotte Sound in October (after charting Easter Island, New Caledonia, the New Hebrides and the Marquesas), then sailed for England, having circumnavigated (but never seen) Antarctica.

Manuka shrubs and beach are part of the beauty of Stewart Island.

Cook's Last Voyage

He visited Queen Charlotte Sound one more time, on his third and last great voyage of exploration. He arrived in mid-January 1777, and left at the end of March. The intent of this voyage was to find a northwest passage between the Pacific and the Atlantic somewhere in the Arctic. Cook sailed north, discovered the Hawaiian Islands, mapped the coast of Alaska and Siberia, then returned to the Hawaiian Islands in October 1778. In February 1779, on the Big Island of Hawaii, Cook was killed by the islanders. He was 50.

War and Progress

In the years following James Cook's explorations, New Zealand was visited by a mob of explorers, English and French, and growing numbers of seamen came to hunt seals, and later, sperm whales. By the 1820s, one of the first European settlements had been started at a place called Kororareka in the Bay of Islands on the North Island. Today, the settlement is called Russell, and is a quaint little tourist and fishing town. But in the whaling days, it was known as the "Hellhole of the Pacific," an epithet used with glee today by tourism boosters. It was made the first capital of the fledgling colony in 1840, an honor that lasted less than a year.

By as early as 1830, things were pretty raunchy in some parts of New Zealand, which was getting a bad reputation in sailing circles and government offices, especially back in England. The general view was that law and order were virtually nonexistent; many of the country's resources were being pillaged, Maoris were being killed and exploited. Protests began, from missionaries in New Zealand as well as social activists in England, insisting that something had to be done to protect the Maoris and their land rights—as well, of course, to Anglicize the country so that colonists could live in some sort of peace.

And what better way to protect the Maoris than by simply taking control of the country? Although Cook had claimed New Zealand for the British crown on his first voyage, the islands had for the most part been ignored in the years following. The English seemed to be more intent on making Australia a working proposition than paying attention to the colonization of New Zealand.

Treaty with the Maoris

In 1840, an English representative, William Hobson, met with about 50 Maori chiefs at a place called Waitangi, not far from Russell in the Bay of Islands. In the treaty signed there February 6, the Maoris recognized the sovereignty of Queen Victoria, and the queen in return recognized Maori rights to land, fishing, forests and other property. Further, it was agreed that only the crown could purchase Maori land. Not all the Maoris, including several major chiefs, were willing to sign the document. But in the end, about 500 or so chiefs accepted the treaty. The Treaty of Waitangi officially opened the doors to English colonization, which was sporadic. At first, colonists were vastly outnumbered by the Maoris, and for the first years of their history, colonial New Zealanders were, as one historian put it, living in "mere encampments on the fringe of Polynesia." February 6 is now a national holiday in New Zealand.

The Maori Arts and Crafts Institute in Rotorua honors Maori culture.

Until 1852, New Zealand was directly governed by the crown—or at least the ministers working for the crown. In that year, a constitution for New Zealand was approved by the British Parliament. The document set up a governor appointed by the British, plus an upper house appointed by the governor and a locally elected lower house. Final veto over legislation passed in New Zealand remained in London, even if it had been approved by the governor. That system lasted, with a few changes, until 1947, when New Zealand was given the final legal powers to amend its own constitution and thus become a fully independent nation.

A Model for Change

In the late 19th century, New Zealand became internationally famous among political theoreticians as a sort of modern test tube for social change. In the 1880s, the country had a severe depression, resulting in a movement toward left-wing political parties and welfare legislation. In 1890, the Liberal Party took control, a tenure that lasted until 1912. During those two decades, universal suffrage was introduced—women got the vote in 1893—and compulsory arbitration of labor disputes was enacted, land reform was introduced, minimum wage laws were passed, old age pensions were begun.

In 1935, after a period of conservative control, the Labour Party, philosophic heirs to the Liberals, took control again and ushered in New Zealand's modern welfare state. The country soon had free health care, free education, welfare benefits, low-cost housing, the 40-hour week and many socialized industries. In recent years, there has been a trend toward decentralized government, with some backlash against government ownership and control of industries and utilities. Some industries have been sold to private companies, and some New Zealanders feel the only way to get the economy bubbling again is to get into a free market system.

In mid-1994, to the disgust of those New Zealanders who like to distance themselves from Australia, Prime Minister Jim Bolger flew a trial balloon suggesting that by the year 2000, New Zealand should toss off the shackles of the British Commonwealth and become a republic—the same scenario advanced several years earlier by Australian Prime Minister Paul Keating. Within a day, a Wellington newspaper conducted a national poll that found the general reaction to the idea of a New Zealand republic was mostly unpopular with the Kiwi people. Most political observers were not betting on any change soon. But stay tuned. New Zealand, always experimenting with government, is still at it.

An outcrop at Abel Tasman National Park

World War II

From the time the country was colonized, until after World War II, the Kiwis, like their cousins in Australia, constantly rallied to the defense of Mother England, sending troops to die in wars thought essential by London. And like the Australians, they paid dearly for the privilege. Something like 3000 Kiwis died in the mismanaged, ill-advised Gallipoli campaign in 1915. They were part of the Australia–New Zealand Army Corps—the Anzacs. Like in Australia, April 25, the day the troops landed in 1915, is celebrated as a national holiday. In all, about 100,000 New Zealanders went off to World War I. Casualties were staggering: 45,000 wounded, 16,000 killed.

World War II was a great blow to New Zealand–Great Britain ties. The mighty British navy, supposedly the backbone of the Empire's defenses, was knocked out of the Pacific war early, and the attack at Pearl Harbor meant the Kiwis and the Aussies were all alone and virtually unprotected against the Japanese. In the end, of course, the reborn U.S. Pacific fleet prevailed, and after the Japanese surrender, New Zealand, like Australia, formed attachments with the new Pacific power, the United States. About 28,000 Kiwis were killed or injured in the war.

This tramping hut at Nelson Lakes National Park provides hikers a rest stop.

Antinuclear Pioneers

Ties with the United States were so strong following the war, in fact, that New Zealand joined with Australia to form ANZUS, one of the Cold War–spawned mutual defense treaties. That lasted until the early 1980s, when New Zealand again made international headlines with a bold antinuclear stance. It refused to allow any ships with nuclear weapons to enter New Zealand waters, which immediately caused Washington to dump the Kiwis from the ANZUS organization. A decade of chill settled over New Zealand–U.S. relations, not helped by America's refusal to confirm or deny if its ships were carrying nukes. Things have thawed a bit, but remember, New Zealand is still "Clean, Green and Nuclear Free." Most New Zealanders seem to genuinely like Americans—U.S. military and foreign policies, on the other hand, are not much accepted. And no American head of state or secretary of state has visited New Zealand in recent years. Relations between France and New Zealand are even icier, however.

The French, for reasons not understood by anyone in the South Pacific, continue nuclear tests in the area. Greenpeace, which has been trying to stop these tests for years, sent one of its protest ships, the *Rainbow Warrior*, to Auckland harbor in 1985. The French, in a truly stupid move, sent secret agents down to blow it up. The sinking of the *Warrior* caused an international scandal and, to this day, the French are less than welcome in New Zealand. The *Rainbow Warrior* is still in New Zealand—it was towed to a spot near the Bay of Islands and scuttled to make an artificial reef. It's popular with scuba divers.

The French–New Zealand wars are not over. In the middle of 1995, the French, ignoring international protests, began a series of below-ground nuclear tests in the Pacific. The Kiwis, followed by Australia, began an intense anti-French campaign, including Greenpeace flotillas at the bomb-test site and boycotts of French goods, including wine. There is little love lost between the two countries.

THE MAORI

Waka Huia Patu Haka is a Maori ceremony at Ngaruawahia.

Imagine a huge triangle cut into the surface of the Pacific Ocean, with the base running roughly north-south from the Hawaiian Islands to New Zealand, its sides running east to Easter Island. This is the great Polynesian Triangle, a huge expanse larger than several of the continents—more than 5000 miles on each side, a total area of something like 14 million square miles. It has been the site of one of the boldest migrations in human history. Among the societies contained within the boundaries of the triangle, in addition to Hawaii, Easter Island and New Zealand, are the Cook Islands, the Marquesas, Tonga, Tahiti and the Samoas.

It seems strange now, looking at the snowcapped Southern Alps, or driving by the carefully cropped sheep paddocks of modern New Zealand, to remember that until the late 18th century, this mostly Caucasian nation was Polynesian. The usual concept of a Polynesian island is palm trees, warm breezes, bananas, tropical coral lagoons—a far cry, indeed, from the temperate to chilly climate found in New Zealand. But Polynesian it was, the southern territorial limit of the peoples who began their immense migration east across the Pacific more than 2000 years before Europeans came calling. In fact, 95 percent of all the landmass in Polynesia is that of New Zealand.

The Great Migration

There seems to be general agreement that the ancestors of the Polynesians who discovered New Zealand began their great migration from Southeast Asia maybe 4000 or 5000 years ago. By around 1500 B.C., they had expanded through Indonesia to New Guinea, and by 1000 B.C. were in Tonga and Samoa. During the next 1000 years, the societies in what is now called Western Polynesia thrived, evolved a distinct culture and set of languages and began expanding east. The last great discovery for these wide-ranging peoples was the two major (and one minor) islands that are now called New Zealand.

It was, by any measure, an incredible expansion of humans. Indeed, until the explosive European migrations that followed the discovery and eventual domestication of the New World, no peoples on earth were as widespread as the Polynesians.

The ability of the Polynesians to travel great distances across open oceans and establish permanent colonies was greatly aided by their ability to construct large, seagoing canoes, sometimes more than 60 feet long. Using such craft, often double-hulled, they were able to carry along the tools, animals, plants and equipment they needed to become self-sufficient on strange new islands. As they slowly made their way eastward, these great explorers discovered many islands basically void of food supplies, so they lived on the staples they brought with them—coconut, taro, sweet potatoes, breadfruit, bananas, plus domesticated pigs, dogs and chickens.

Arrival in New Zealand

Some paleontologists think the first Polynesians arrived in New Zealand between 700 and 1100 A.D. The consensus seems to be that these Polynesians—today called the Maori—are descendents of a group that almost certainly came from Eastern Polynesia—likely candidates being Tahiti, the Marquesas or the Cook, Society or Austral islands. On the island of Rarotonga in the Cook Islands, at a place called Ngatangiia Harbour, is a monument commemorating a group of seven Maori canoes that left in 1350 A.D. to make the trek to New Zealand. (New Zealand Maoris do not necessarily accept the Cook Island version of the voyage.) At any rate, several sites in New Zealand have revealed artifacts similar to those found in Eastern Polynesia. Some historians believe that the island-hopping explorations by the Polynesians were accidents, that canoes were caught in storms or blown off course. Others believe that the exploration was intentional, a sort of Pacific manifest destiny, and that the degree of expertise exhibited by Polynesian navigators was nothing less than phenomenal. Current theory lumps all of Maori history in New Zealand into a single millennium-long event, but divides it into two distinct eras, the Archaic (hunter/gatherer) and the Classic.

Maori costumes and customs are seen in numerous festivals.

When the first Polynesians arrived in New Zealand, they found a climate unlike anything they had come across on their oceanic travels: often cold, blustery, highly changeable, ranging from subtropical to sub-Antarctic. Their traditional food trees could not survive in most parts of the islands, and even the normally hardy taro plants were at risk. But unlike many other Pacific islands, New Zealand was full of stuff to eat—the forests were filled with birds, and the shores and river estuaries were rife with seals, shellfish and other seafood. Several native plants turned out to be good food sources, and after some experimentation, the Maori discovered ways of keeping *kumara* (sweet potatoes) sheltered during the harsh winters.

The Archaic Period

The major settlements during the Archaic period seem to have been along the northeastern shore of the South Island. At the time of the first settlements, the climate in New Zealand was warmer, and the South Island was not as intemperate as it can become these days. The abundance of nonagricultural food allowed the early Maori to migrate with the seasons, and apparently it wasn't until the climate cooled and population pressures built that the Maori were forced north and began establishing the semipermanent farming and fortlike *pa* sites that were a hallmark of the Classic period.

The Maori were not always kind to their adopted land. Because of their isolation, the islands of New Zealand evolved a huge variety of birds that thrived until human contact. Because there were no predators on the islands, many species of birds were flightless, fulfilling the evolutionary niche filled elsewhere by foraging animals. Because of their lack of mobility, these birds were easy targets for hungry hunters—thus, it is estimated that the bulk of the 13 known moa species (large flightless birds similar to emu and ostriches) had been hunted to extinction by 1300, as were perhaps 20 species of flying birds. Maori hunters also made massive dents in the seal population, and thousands of acres of forests were stripped, causing erosion and loss of wildlife. (By 1700, for example, breeding colonies of seals had been completely wiped out in the Cook Strait area.)

The Classic Period

The shift between the Archaic and Classic periods was not abrupt; the transition came faster in some parts of the islands than others. There is also evidence that agriculture was practiced to some degree during the Archaic period.

At any rate, by the time of the **first European contact** (Tasman in 1642, Cook in 1769), the Maori had evolved a complex, warlike society. One of the main hallmarks of the Classic period was the construction of fortified defensive positions called *pas*, and intertribal wars and skirmishes, fought in hand-to-hand combat, were common. Almost 6000 *pa* sites have been discovered in New Zealand, the bulk of which are on the North Island. By the late 18th century, the greatest number of Maori lived on the coastal fringes of the North Island. Most of the peoples living on the South Island and the isolated Chatham Islands (500 miles southwest of Christchurch) were fishers and birders. The total Maori population in 1770 is estimated to have been between 100,000 and 150,000.

By Pacific standards, the Maori were quite advanced. They had evolved intricate houses, finely carved and utilitarian, with internal hearths, windows, sliding doors and porches. Special birthing and funereal houses were constructed, as were separate cooking quarters, storehouses and tribal meeting houses.

Facial tattooing was common, as it was in a few other Pacific societies. For men, it was extensive on cheeks, nose and foreheads and showed warrior status; women normally only tattooed their chins. In Maori society, women were the main food gatherers and crop tenders. Men were thus free to build houses and boats, carve sculptures and make war. The concept of *utu*, or revenge, was central to Maori society, and almost any insult could lead to warfare. Usually, such wars of revenge took place in the nonplanting season when there was free time for outdoor activities.

Maori waka paddling at Turangawaewae

The Maori Mythology

Maori creation beliefs and tribal lore are complex and similar to those of other Polynesian societies. In the Maori version of discovery, a bold navigator named Kupe sailed from the homeland, a place called Hawaiki, and found New Zealand. He returned to Hawaiki (now thought perhaps to be Tahiti), and gave the people instructions about how to get to the two large islands he had discovered far to the southwest. Some centuries later, because of wars and population pressure, the ancestors of the Maori set sail to find New Zealand. They arrived in the islands in a series of great canoes, and modern Maori tribes trace their ancestors back to one of those specific canoes. It is generally conceded in most Maori accounts that the first landfall was at the **Bay of Plenty** on the North Island, usually Whangaparaoa in the East Cape region. While this seems logical if the first settlers came from Eastern Polynesia, there is also some evidence to suggest that the first settlements were on the South Island, but that northern Maoris conveniently forgot this later and changed the location to fit in with their own tribal lore. One of the Maori legends tells of the creation of New Zealand. Maui, fishing with his brothers, made his nose bleed and baited a hook with the blood. Something hit the line, and after a horrific battle, he pulled up a huge fish that turned into the North Island.

Cannibalism

It turned out that the often-brutal Maori were also cannibalistic, as apparently were the residents of the Marquesas, the islands where they might have come from. The first evidence that the New Zealanders dined on one another was gathered by Cook during his first voyage, 1769–1771. His favorite anchorage in New Zealand was Queen Charlotte Sound at the northern tip of the South Island. Here he made friendly contact with the locals, who were not reluctant to discuss their food habits with Cook and his scientists. One day, in a cove near his anchorage, Cook saw Maoris cooking up a stew and recognized human arm bones. He named the place **Cannibal Cove**. Also on this trip, he bought a gnawed-on arm bone to prove to the outside world that cannibalism did exist; Joseph Banks, one of the scientists on the trip, bought a preserved head. Banks thus apparently became the first tourist to snap up that particular type of New Zealand souvenir. The next century, so many whalers, sealers and passers-by were buying preserved heads that local chiefs were hard put to keep up with the demand. There's a combination museum/tattoo parlor in the red light district of Amsterdam, for example, where one of the most popular exhibits is a heavily tattooed, preserved Maori head, brought back, no doubt, by one of those early travelers. The Maoris told Cook that enemies were eaten to absorb the courage and spirit of the fallen.

Maori cannibalism became personal for Cook on his **second voyage**, 1772–1775. With him was a second ship, the *Adventure*, commanded by Captain Tobias Furneaux. During their explorations, the two ships became separated, and in November 1773, Cook sailed on, leaving instructions for Furneaux at the Queen Charlotte Sound anchorage.

When Furneaux finally arrived, battered and soaked from a storm, he decided to rest awhile before sailing on to join Cook. He sent a party of 10 men out for food; they never returned. A second party came upon the remains of the first—the head of a ship's servant, the tattooed hands of two seamen, five shoes and several baskets filled with human flesh ready for cooking. Figuring enough was bloody enough, Furneaux decided not to rendezvous with Cook, but instead sailed off to Cape Horn and then to England via the Cape of Good Hope, becoming the first man to go around the world west to east. He arrived back in England in 1774, and was promptly sent off to America to deal with the uppity Yankees.

In another incident on the second voyage, Cook grossed out his whole crew. Noting a freshly killed Maori corpse ashore, he decided, for the sake of science, to see the thing done up close. He was, he said, "filled with indignation against these Cannibals," but ordered a piece of the flesh roasted and brought on board, whereupon one of the Maoris aboard "eat it with a seeming good relish before the whole ships company [and it had] such an effect on some of them as to cause them to vomit. That the New Zealanders are Cannibals can no longer be doubted."

On Cook's third voyage, a Queen Charlotte area chief named **Kahoura** came aboard ship and confessed he had been in charge of the Maoris who had killed the Furneaux party. Apparently, the incident occurred when a trigger-happy crewman shot and killed two Maoris in a scuffle over some ship's biscuits. Cook, who by this time in his career was taking an anthropologist's approach to cannibalism, took no action. In fact, Kahoura asked for, and was granted, permission to sit for a portrait by John Webber, an expedition artist. The portrait still exists.

A Fierce Tribe

The Maori were, in all, a daunting people. Not only were they fierce—they looked fierce, with tattooed faces, colorfully decorated nose holes, vivid feathered cloaks and large hand weapons.

They further disconcerted the English with a bizarre dance-greeting for both friend and foe—they rolled their eyes and stuck out their tongues in an effort to terrify their intended victims, which they did. This display (dancing, tongues, rolling of eyes) is called a *haka* and not only serves to rattle the opposition, but limbers up the body for the forthcoming warfare. There is a tale, probably true, that during World War II, a Maori battalion decided to stage a *haka* on Crete prior to a bayonet attack. The Wermacht troops took one look at this horde of crazy New Zealanders sticking out their tongues and generally acting like Maori warriors and took off for the hills.

It took less than a generation for the effects of European contact to shatter much of traditional Maori society. Like other islanders throughout the Pacific, the Maori paid dearly for being discovered. European diseases killed them by the thousands. Maoris who resisted incursions by greedy whalers were shot and killed. Alcohol and prostitution took their toll. And, perhaps worst of all, Maoris were introduced to modern weapons of war, especially the musket. A series of intertribal wars began, and where once such combat was fought hand to hand with relatively light losses, muskets brought whole-sale slaughter. Some estimates say as many as 60,000 Maoris died in such clashes in the 1820s.

Missionaries

As in other cases throughout the Pacific Rim, missionaries came to tell the locals that most of their culture was wrong. Clothing styles, artwork, the basic beliefs of a long oral tradition, all wrong. And also, as in other parts of Polynesia, the missionaries were quite successful. Christianity has planted deep roots in contemporary Maori society.

One fascinating thing about this period in English colonial history is the contrast between treatment of the Maoris in New Zealand and the Aboriginal peoples of Australia. In Australia, there was never very much concern shown for the land rights of the Aboriginals. In fact, the English simply declared that Australia was a vacant land, and as such, was wide open to colonization.

In New Zealand, faced with a much more advanced indigenous popula-tion—as well as a native population that had shown itself capable of forceful-ly dealing with strangers—the tack was entirely different. Most everyone involved, including some Maoris, thought the only way to preserve Maori land rights and culture was for England to take control of things. This was good imperialistic logic, which served the English well around the world during the heady days of the Raj.

A Clash of Cultures

It was probably inevitable, given the two divergent cultures suddenly thrust together, that violence would break out. The English colonists, for their part, saw the open stretches of land around the islands as fertile farm and ranch land just waiting for the plow and cattle. The Maoris, whose con-cept of life held that many areas were *tapu*, or off-limits because of religious reasons, thought in the beginning that when they signed the Treaty of Wait-angi ceding control of New Zealand to the British crown, they were simply giving Queen Victoria the "shadow of the land," a sort of long-term lease, and that full ownership would always remain in their hands. In addition, of course, there was the European notion that treaties signed with non-Euro-pean peoples were just so much hot air and didn't really count, anyway. It was an outlook accepted by the French, English and Americans in North America, and by the British in Australia and New Zealand.

Fighting broke out in the early 1840s, beginning what is called in New Zealand history the "**Land Wars**." English settlers would move into lands owned by the Maori; the Maori would fight back. The end result of the wars, which lasted off and on until the 1870s, was that the Maori lost and the colonists became the dominant culture in New Zealand. Part of the problem was that the colonists were more or less unified, but the Maori, traditionally a tribal culture, had no countrywide, unifying force. Indeed, during the wars, Maoris fought Maoris to the benefit of the English. Some of the lands taken by force or deceit in those days are at the heart of present-day Maori land claims.

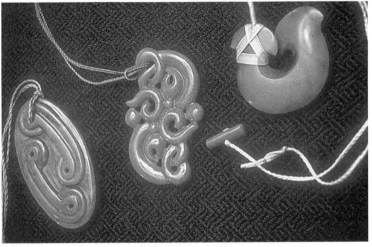

Maori arts at Art Centre in Christchurch

Maori Art

During their millennium-long development before arrival of the Europeans, Maori artists created a distinct form of Polynesian art, primarily in wood carvings, but also in their use of "**greenstone**" or nephrite and bowenite, two forms of jade mined in the valleys of the Taramakau and Arahura rivers on the west coast of the South Island.

Some of the finest wood carving was reserved for meeting houses, called *whare runanga*, with intricate interlacings and decorations and typical grotesque masks with abalone-shell eyes and huge distended tongues. In the later Classic period, extensive carving was also done on the interior panels of the meeting houses. Excellent carvings were also done on the prows of war canoes, treasure boxes and other household items. A definitive look at the greenstone and wood-carving skills of the Maori is offered in the book, *Te Maori*, written in 1984 and published by Harry N. Abrams Inc. in association with the American Federation of Arts. (In Maori, *te* means "the," a word you'll see all over the country in town and city names.) Greenstone was highly prized and used for ceremonial adzes, figures, pendants and war clubs. Some of the pieces are delightfully intricate works of art. Some anthropologists thought it would not have been possible for the Maori to develop such sophisticated art by themselves, and that the islands must have been visited by peoples who taught them the art forms. This view is pretty well ignored today.

Compared to Australia, which has had, over its 200-year history, many periods of overt, government-sponsored racial prejudice against the dark-black Aboriginal people, the lighter-skinned Maoris have in the main been treated much better in New Zealand. Racial harmony is part of the country's ethic; indeed, when 5000 or so American troops came to train and recuperate during World War II, the many incidents of G.I. and Marine Corps bigotry toward Maoris appalled New Zealanders, both Maori and *pakeha*, or non-Maori. There has been enough intermarriage, in fact, that there are few full-blooded Maoris today, and something like 10 percent of all New Zealanders have some Maori blood.

Preservation of Tradition

Again in contrast to the Australian Aboriginals, the Maoris were able to preserve much of their oral tradition and history in written form. Due to efforts of some early missionaries, especially a ne'er-do-well named Thomas Kendall, the Maori language was given a written form, and much of the oral traditions were retained and are available for 21st-century Maoris. The Treaty of Waitangi, for example, was written in English and Maori. In Australia, even today, almost all of the ancient tribal customs and mores are passed on orally.

This is not to say that Maori-*pakeha* relations have been all roses. Maoris have been cheated out of their lands and properties, relegated in many instances to second-class citizenship and pushed out of the mainstream, their 1000-year culture suppressed and ignored. But, like the Aboriginals in Australia, there is growing awareness of native rights and heritage, as well as growing political pressure to address what many Maoris see as a long record of mistreatment and dishonesty. Today, the once-vilified Maori language is protected, and "language nests" have been set up to teach and preserve the Maori tongue, much the same as the Irish have set up "gaeltecs" in Ireland to preserve Irish Gaelic. These pre-school language nests, called *Te kohanga reo* in Maori, are used in conjunction with a dozen or so elementary schools around the country where Maori language and customs are taught. About 15,000 children are presently enrolled in the language nests.

Maori women have close family ties.

Still, even with the progress of recent years, the race divisions in New Zealand are not yet healed. In a blistering report issued early in 1997 by the Ministry of Maori Affairs, officials warned of potential trouble ahead:

"New Zealand is in danger of creating a racial situation which will have serious consequences. It is particularly important that the disparities in education, health, employment and justice are eliminated," the report said. "Maoris earn less, die sooner and are imprisoned far more than pakehas...the three priorities for the government should be to bridge the economic gap, settle Treaty of Waitangi claims and look at constitutional arrangements that would ensure the Maori way of life survived."

One result of the increasing Maori militance: The traditional evening ceremonies at Whangarei on Waitangi Day have, for the moment, been abandoned, partially to remove a favorite target of Maori protesters. One Maori leader said it was a sensible thing to do because it would deny the protesters a chance to "make a big song and dance about nothing."

In addition, the Treaty of Waitangi, never completely implemented and often simply ignored, has been reaffirmed, with major land rights ceded back to the Maoris. In 1975, the government set up the Waitangi Tribunal to examine Maori land claims and violations of the treaty. As a result, Maoris have been given 10 percent of the national fishing quota and major mineral rights. If treaty rights are fully implemented, the Maoris could end up owning more than three-quarters of the South Island—a vast acreage that contains six national parks and such lucrative tourist properties as the world-famous Milford Track. Unlike Australia, where vast chunks of land have been ceded back to the Aboriginals—and then been closed to the white majority—the prevailing attitude among the Maoris seems not to be an attempt to shut off public access to their lands or create a separate Polynesian country. But they make no bones about wanting the income that such lands generate. The fishing quota alone, which Maori tribes can sell to private companies, is worth millions of dollars. The hope is that the additional income realized from control of their treaty lands will enable many Maoris to break the poverty cycle, and as a result, eventually bring Maoris and *pakehas* to an economic and racial balance, which is what New Zealand is supposed to be all about to begin with.

"Go Home Queenie"

Like any other group of humans, however, there is not complete agreement about the progress of Maori affairs in New Zealand, as Queen Elizabeth discovers every time she makes a visit. In 1990, she and Philip came to Waitangi in February to celebrate the 150th anniversary of the treaty signed by her great-great-grandmother, Victoria. As the royals stepped ashore, a group of Maori protestors shouted, "Go home, Queenie," and heckled her during a speech: "You already have everything. What more do you want, Elizabeth?" The ultimate insult came as the queen's motorcade passed. A young Maori student threw a wet black T-shirt at the queen's car as a symbolic gesture to protest New Zealand's treatment of the Maoris. The shirt did not hit the queen, but she looked startled as it landed in her car. (The girl was arrested and sentenced to several months of public service.)

But the queen was also given a friendly Maori greeting by warriors with temporarily tattooed faces who said howdy by dancing forward, jabbing the air with spears, rolling their eyes and sticking out their tongues in the traditional *haka*. Also, an estimated 100,000 Maoris took part in building or restoring 21 giant war canoes for the occasion. The canoes, built and navigated using traditional Maori methods, commemorated the Maori discovery of New Zealand.

The queen, for her part, said that she acknowledged that the treaty stipulations had not always been followed. Later, she met with some of the descendants of the original chiefs who had signed the treaty. All seemed sweetness and light.

Maori demonstrates the haka.

She came again in 1995, this time to personally approve a major Maori land rights bill called the Tainui Settlement, which gave back about 40,000 acres of land and $115 million to the Maori. Part of the legislation read: "The crown expresses its profound regret and apologizes unreservedly for the loss of lives because of the hostilities arising from the invasion, and at the devastation of property and social life which resulted." Note that "the Crown" is a reference not to the queen, but to the New Zealand government. Many Maori felt the queen's personal appearance to approve the bill was a matter of honor on her part, especially because her great-great-grandmother was the first English sovereign responsible for protecting Maori rights.

The process of Maori participation in modern New Zealand is not completely smooth, of course, despite Maoris being in Parliament, in seats of power, in the arts, in business, in all walks of life. A Maori, for the first time, was a member of the New Zealand downhill ski team at the Lillehammer Olympics: He finished 20th. There are scandals yet today in the way Maori affairs are being handled, and the dragging economy of New Zealand is making progress—for all New Zealanders—sometimes slow and painful. It does seem, however, that some sort of line has been drawn for Maori rights that cannot easily be erased. In the late 1990s, some Maori protests have turned violent. Buildings have been burned, scuffles have broken out. After a historic Maori schoolhouse was occupied, then torched during a Maori protest, several of the more radical leaders of the Maori community warned white New Zealand that things could get worse. "These children are fighting for our sovereignty," one leader said of the kids who helped burn the school. "They're the warriors of our people. We're fighting a protracted war." Many younger and militant Maori insist that the spirit of the Waitangi Treaty—the "shadow of the land" philosophy—be fully implemented, giving control of the country to the Maori. There is natural reluctance on the part of the majority population to cede everything to the original inhabitants, so the whole issue of land ownership and Maori rights is far from settled. There have even been calls for scrapping New Zealand's present constitution and replacing it with one based on the original 1840 treaty, thus giving the Maori a much larger voice in the government.

The New Zealand government recognizes the potential tourist interest in Maori culture, and has put together a brochure listing companies in the country that specialize in tours to important Maori sites, plus shopping excursions for Maori art and cultural performances. The guide is available from the **New Zealand Tourism Board**, *501 Santa Monica Boulevard, Suite 300, Santa Monica, CA 90401;* ☎ *(800) 388-5494 or* ☎ *(310) 395-7480.*

THE LAND

Lake Matheson, Westland, is typical of New Zealand's natural beauty.

Geology

As we write this, we are sitting about a three-iron shot from two major California earthquake faults: one, the infamous San Andreas, and the other, the lesser known but no less dangerous Calavaras Fault. From time to time, the faults around San Francisco Bay let go with a shaker of some size, reminding us always that our planet is still very much alive and kicking. We mention this only to show that some Americans have this, at least, in common with the folks in New Zealand. The tectonic activity that gives the coast of California its reputation—justified—for the shakes, is the very process that has created New Zealand.

New Zealand sits on the southwestern edge of a huge floating piece of earthly crust called the Pacific Plate, which is slowly grinding against another piece of crust called the Indian-Australian Plate. California sits at the northeastern edge of that same Pacific Plate, grinding against the American Plate. As the residents of either Wellington or Santa Cruz can tell you, all that grinding results in constant earthquakes, most small, some deadly. Both the Pacific Coast and New Zealand are part of the so-called "Ring of Fire," the vast area of tectonic activity that circles the Pacific Basin. New Zealand, geologically young and active, has little in common with Australia, an ancient, weathered continent that sits in the middle of the Australian Plate, relatively free of tectonic troubles.

Where Plates Collide

The present shape of New Zealand is about 5 million years old. *As Pacific islands go, New Zealand is unusual.* Most Polynesian islands are basaltic rock extruded from ancient volcanoes. New Zealand, however, is mostly the result of the earth's crust being heaved up higher and higher as the two plates collide. Much of the base rock of the New Zealand islands is sedimentary, left over from the ancient proto-continent called Gondwanaland. It is estimated that the flat lowland mass of New Zealand separated from Australia and Antarctica about 80 million years ago, then began its uplifting by tectonic forces about 5 million years ago. The North Island is the youngest of the two; rocks on the South Island date to between 400 and 600 million years old, twice as ancient as those of the North Island.

The fault lines that mark the meeting of the two crustal plates in New Zealand run through the heart of both islands. In the north, they have created the **Taupo Volcanic Zone**, which runs from the Bay of Plenty to the Tasman Sea, a belt that has created the popular thermal tourist resorts around Rotorua and Lake Taupo. *The North Island is also full of volcanoes,* from the west coast (dormant and lovely Mt. Egmont), to the active volcanoes of Tongariro National Park in the center and White Island, an active volcano about 30 miles north of Whakatane in the Bay of Plenty. This belt of volcanoes continues north all the way to Tonga and Samoa. White Island, privately owned, is a popular day-trip area. The government has recently warned tour operators that volcanic activity seems to be increasing on the island, and thought should be given to having emergency equipment and evacuation procedures in place. The longest and most violent eruption at the island was from 1976–1982. The Tongariro volcanoes erupt periodically, scattering ash as far south as Wellington. No better proof of the tectonic nature of the country was needed than the current activity of Mount Ruapehu, the most vigorous of the Tongariro volcanoes. Spectacular blasts over the last few years have sent *lahar* (mud slides) down the mountain, hurled dust and debris into the air, and forced the evacuation of nearby ski villages. *Earthquakes, too, are common in New Zealand, especially near the fault zones.* This century, there have been some biggies (7 or 8 on the Richter scale). One, on the North Island in 1931, raised a huge chunk of the harbor at Napier above sea level, creating 15 square miles of new land and killing about 160 people. In September 1995, a near-biggy, about 6.4 on the Richter, hit near the southwest tip of the North Island, rattling a huge chunk of the country. There was little damage. New Zealanders seem to have adopted the same fatalistic attitude about earthquakes as residents of California. They're just waiting for "the Big One." *In an official earthquake preparedness brochure issued by the New Zealand government, we have this nice bit of shaky logic: "The best answer for when the next major earthquake will occur in New Zealand is 'eventually.' "*

Mt. Cook National Park rivals any scenery you'll see in the European Alps.

The Mountains

It's no problem figuring out where the plates are meeting in the South Island: Just take a look at the Southern Alps. The fault lines run basically from near Picton south along the west coast, and the 400-mile-long row of mountains is the boldest evidence of the continental masses being thrust upward; *there are more than 15 mountains in the range that are at least 10,000 feet high.* The Alps are not volcanic—instead, ancient seabeds have become towering peaks buried beneath a permanent cover of snow. The mountains of the South Island have a long history of glaciation. Several large glaciers remain today, and the evidence of ice at work in the past can be seen all along the fjord-cut southwestern coast, which looks much like southern Norway. Here you find New Zealand's most famous fjord: Milford Sound.

The mountains split the South Island into three climatic zones. Prevailing weather patterns run west-east (remember the Roaring Forties), which make the west coast wet and windy. *It's not unusual for the coast to get 160–170 inches of rain a year, and gale-force winds can whip up any time.* The mountains themselves offer a true alpine ecosphere, with glaciers, hanging valleys, ice-melt rivers and stands of firs and other alpine plants. To the east of the mountains are the broad plains that comprise the South Island's agricultural zone. Warmer and dryer, the east coast is cut in many places by wide river valleys that have carried millions of tons of gravel down from the mountains. *Some of the gravel river plains in New Zealand are among the largest in the world.*

The climate in the North Island tends to be warmer in general than the South Island, although snow still covers the tops of the volcanic mountains and it can rain heavily at times. Auckland is usually warmer than Wellington, which has the advantage (or disadvantage) of sitting on the Cook Strait. *The strait acts as a funnel for the westerlies roaring through, and if a really serious blow comes along, the ferry trip from Wellington to the South Island can be very rough, sometimes impossible.*

Plants

New Zealand seems to be very keen on protecting its most valuable natural resource—trees. You'll see this almost anywhere you travel in the country. On one hill, you'll see evidence of clear-cutting through a forest, which is the timber industry's equivalent of an A-bomb, but just around the corner, you'll see another hill that has been completely replanted. They do harvest trees in New Zealand, but they also have a vigorous program of reforestation. It's a delicate balance —on the one hand, you have one of the most environmentally sensitive populations in the world. And on the other hand, you have a struggling timber industry in a country beset by economic problems. We read in a local newspaper of a woman, almost 80, who stepped in front of a bulldozer that was mistakenly clearing native bush from the wrong parcel of land. And in the same paper was an appeal for more people to invest in forestry industries.

Clean and Very Green

New Zealanders, like most everybody else in the world, have not always been sensitive to the environment and long-range problems caused by short-term goals. When the European settlers started arriving in number after 1840, they were less than pleased by the land—thorny shrublands, bleak grasslands, dense forests. Their solution was twofold: first, introduction of many species of European plants and animals (so they felt more at home), and, worse, a process they called "winning the land." This meant clearing large areas of land to make room for sheep and cattle. Often, that led to disaster as soil erosion set in. The land in many places in New Zealand is steep, so when it rains on unprotected soil, the result is predictable. Early settlers, either ignorant or uncaring, burned the native brush and planted grass—along came heavy rains, good-bye grass and soil. The denuded land also contributed to the loss of bird species and insects.

After World War II, New Zealanders decided enough was enough, and have become very protective of their lands and forests, something we cannot say about the Australians, who still haven't caught on that even renewable resources must be handled with care.

There are still many chunks of subtropical forests in New Zealand—which, if you're a plant freak, is the place to hang out. *There are 150 species of ferns, from two centimeters across to 50-foot-high man-ferns.* The country's national symbol is the **silver fern**, which is the emblem their beloved rugby team, the All Blacks, wear on their jerseys. Another species, the bracken fern, was used by the Maoris as a food source.

Trampers hike to McKellar Saddle for the incredible view.

Despite massive harvesting in the 19th century, there are still more than 100 species of native trees, mostly conifers and flowering hardwoods. The trees are more similar to species found in South Africa, Malaysia and South America than the next-door neighbor, Australia. But like Australia, New Zealand was cut off from the rest of the world, resulting in some species of plants found nowhere else. Some of the real treasures are the vast beech forests, dense and dark, which you can see around the big lakes of the South Island. Also abundant are **podocarps**, species of broadleaf trees with a thick ground cover of pines, ferns, mosses and orchids.

One of the great ecological disasters in New Zealand was the wanton destruction of the islands' *kauri forests*. **Kauris** *(Agathis australis)* are the redwoods of the Southern Hemisphere. Once these great trees covered vast areas of the country, but their very nature spelled their doom. They grow slowly, maturing over centuries, and grow tall and straight. The Maoris used the kauris to build their long war canoes. *As they grow, kauris shed their lower branches, meaning they make perfect masts for sailing ships.* The whalers first recognized their worth, and later the lumbermen moved in. In the space of about 40 years, most of the forests had been destroyed. In addition, at the base of the trees, large deposits of resinous sap gathered, which turned out to be an excellent source of varnishes. Between the lumbermen and the hordes who came to harvest the resin, the result was disastrous, leaving barren, eroded land in their wake. It was only in the late 1950s that the last stands of kauri were protected by legislation. The oldest tree in the country is thought to be more than 2000 years old. Kauris are also found in Queensland, and have suffered much the same fate. In New Zealand, they only grow above 38 to 39 degrees latitude, so *the best place to see them is in one of the protected forest parks on the North Island.*

Two of the more common plants you'll see touring around New Zealand are flax and cabbage trees.

Flax was to the Maori what the yucca was to the tribes of the southwestern United States. It's actually a lily, not a member of the linen flax plants found elsewhere. They used it to make clothing and to braid strong ropes. At one time, there were about 50 varieties. Californians, never a group to miss a trick, are now using several species of imported Kiwi flax plants as landscaping plants. When first imported, they carried such names as Maori Maiden, Maori Sunrise and Maori Queen. Sensitivity to Maori concerns has changed the names, however. Now you look for species with "rainbow" names—Rainbow Maiden, Rainbow Sunrise, etc.

If they hadn't picked the silver fern as the national plant, the Kiwis might have picked the **cabbage tree**, a ubiquitous member of the agave family. Maoris used it for food (edible taproots, stems and leaf-shots). It produces large, scented flowers in the spring when it blooms, and the leaves grow in tufts, giving it a distinctive shape. They look a lot like giant palmettos, usually growing up to about 40 feet high.

Another plant you can't avoid seeing is the **tussock**, for lack of a better comparison, the Kiwi equivalent of sagebrush or Australian spinifex. It's actually a grass that grows in clumps, and various species are found from alpine areas to the lowlands. The biggest tussock plants can grow up to three feet high.

New Zealand is a flower lover's paradise, with some 500 species of alpine flowers found nowhere else in the world. There are, for example, more than 60 species of **mountain daisies**, one of which produces a bloom 10 centimeters (about four inches) across. There is also a **New Zealand edelweiss**, not a close relation but similar in bloom. You'll also see 40 species of **buttercup**, including the Mount Cook lily. We were also pleased to see **ice plant**, which graces the dunes along the California coast. New Zealand even has its own version of Spanish moss called Old Man's Beard, a parasitic plant you'll see all over trees in the Milford Sound area.

Count on also seeing lots of introduced plants—**oaks**, **eucalyptus**, **cedars**, **redwoods**, **elms** and that most noxious of plants—and a real menace to farmers—**gorse**, a native of Scotland.

If you want to get a close-up view of New Zealand's special native plants, check out the **Otari Native Plant Museum** in Wellington, which raises and preserves 1200 species of indigenous plants. While you're out on the road, stop at the offices of national parks and preserves around the country which usually have a supply of local plant guides for sale.

Animals

Whale watching off Kaikoura is spectacular.

If you were a bird, and worried about getting through life without becoming some other animal's dinner, for millions of years, New Zealand was the place to be. No predators, no mammalian or reptilian egg-snatchers. It was a great

THE LAND

life—that is, until humans arrived. What happened after that, for birds, was an ecological disaster. When the Maoris populated New Zealand about 1000 years ago, they brought pigs, dogs and rats, none of whom were kind to the original residents. Because of the lack of native predators, many species of New Zealand birds had lost the ability to fly, and were easy targets for hungry Maori hunters. In fact, several types of flightless birds were hunted to extinction, including the **moa**, the New Zealand equivalent of the ostrich or emu. One type of moa stood 10 feet tall.

European Imports

As if the Maoris weren't bad enough, European settlers completed the destructive process by bringing along a whole cast of nasties, including **stoats**, **possums**, **cats** and **ferrets**. One of the first callers, Captain James Cook, a far-sighted sort, often left pigs behind at anchorages where he was likely to return. *That's what they call feral pigs in New Zealand these days: Cap'n Cookers.* Not, of course, that he's responsible for all the wild pigs running around. But with one thing and another, it is estimated that 70 percent of the original bird species have been wiped out. Not satisfied with killing off all the birds, the settlers also brought along rabbits, deer and chamois, which chewed the country into severe ecological problems. *All the introduced animals, especially rats, stoats, possums, ferrets and feral cats, continue to be a major threat to New Zealand birdlife.*

Mammals...

Fur seals have been legally protected in New Zealand since 1894.

The only mammals "native" to New Zealand are bats, seals and sea lions. By native, we mean prehuman, because it is generally agreed that almost all of

THE LAND

the original bird species in the country flew in from somewhere else, as did the bats. The seals and sea lions migrated in, as well. There are two species of bats—the short-tailed and the long-tailed. The seals and sea lions are the fur seal and Hooker's sea lions, a very rare species found only in the southern islands of New Zealand. The country is home to the a species of fur seal only found in New Zealand and the sub-Antarctic islands to the south. They have been legally protected in New Zealand since 1894, and the numbers have increased well beyond the endangered species status. There are dozens of spots around both islands to see the seals. The best time to see large numbers is during the breeding season, November–January. The females come ashore to give birth in December and mate shortly thereafter.

Living Fossils...

One of the more fascinating true native animals is a small reptile, an actual living fossil called the **tuatara**. *Here's an animal that can trace its family tree back 200 million years to the Lower Triassic. They are extremely rare, and can live to at least 150 years of age. They mate when they're 20, stop growing when they're 50.* They eat insects, shed their skins once a year, hibernate when it gets cold and can swim easily. Up close, if you're lucky to see one in captivity, tuataras look like small iguanas. It is thought they arrived in New Zealand in the Jurassic Period about 130 million years ago when the islands were still part of Gondwanaland. They once roamed all over New Zealand, but because of human intervention and introduced predators, have retreated to a few islands in the Cook Strait and northeast of the North Island.

The best place to see a tuatara is at the tuatarium at the Southland Museum and Art Gallery in Invercargill. The big draw at the museum used to be George, a tuatara who was, by tuatara standards, a giant—about 600 millimeters long (nearly 24 inches). He died in 1969 at the tender age of 150. Some of the new kids on the tuatara block at the Invercargill facility are Henry (he's 100 years old); Albert, 45; Lucy, 35, and Mildred, 30. We saw Henry, a rare treat. He ignored us. Admission to the museum and tuatarium is free, but donations are welcome.

New Zealand has three species of native frogs, unique in the world because they have no ears, do not vocalize and do not have a tadpole stage—they are born without hatching from an egg as miniature mirrors of their parents. And the New Zealand form of the **gecko**, unlike geckos in other parts of the world, is also born without hatching from an egg. The 17 species of geckos live throughout the country, including higher mountain elevations.

Giant Insects...

Three species of animals worth a mention are the **katipo**, the **glowworm** and the **weta**. Katipos are spiders, related to North American black widows or **Australian redbacks**. They are found mostly on the west coast of the north is-

THE LAND

land, and on dune formations on the South Island coast. They are the only animals in New Zealand that are a threat to humans. **Glowworms** are the larval stage of a fly or gnat found most commonly in limestone caves on the North Island, but can be found all over the country. They have chemical body lights, very much like our fireflies. They are a big tourist attraction, drawing visitors to caves at Te Anau and Waitomo. The insects coat the ceilings of caves, then drop long sticky filaments to catch flying insects, mostly mosquitoes. They stay in the larval stage about nine months. The weta is a primitive beastie, very rare, found in mountainous areas. One type, the **giant weta**, *is one of the heaviest insects in the world, weighing as much as a small bird.* They look like big, nasty versions of a cricket. They have jaws that can pierce skin, spikes and spines and, all in all, are not very social. Wetas often have a tough time surviving because they are eaten by rats. They are one of the country's most primitive creatures, dating back about 190 million years.

Four-Foot Eels...

The country is also home to a fish called the New Zealand **long-finned eel**, found in freshwater rivers and lakes. The three- to four-foot-long eels can live up to 80 or 90 years and weigh up to 50 pounds. Some New Zealanders feed the eels in an effort to make pets of them. The eels return to the ocean to spawn. You'll notice that menus all over the country often feature "whitebait," which are the juvenile form of a fish called the *"short-jawed kokupu."* Seeing an adult is very rare; recently on the west coast of the South Island, an adult was hauled up in an eel net. It was about 35 centimeters long and was probably about 20 years old.

The Kiwi is flightless and omnivorous.

Strange and Beautiful Birds...

*The most famous animal in New Zealand is also the national symbol and the national nickname—***the kiwi**. Kiwis are flightless, nocturnal, very shy and omnivorous. Their bodies are round and they have spiky feathers that resemble fur—they look, in fact, like giant Chinese gooseberries, a tasty morsel known in most countries as the kiwi fruit. They have enormously long, sensitive beaks they use to snuff through ground debris, lousy eyesight and a great sense of smell. The male can make an ungodly shriek called the "kiwi call," but mostly they're quiet and elusive. *Your chances of seeing one in the wild are almost nil*, but there are plenty of zoos and nocturnal displays around the country. There are three species of kiwis, the largest being maybe two feet long. Some Americans will recall a brand of shoe polish named Kiwi: it was invented by an Australian, and named after his wife, a New Zealander. Another bird, the **weka**, is sometimes confused with kiwis. It's brown, about the same size as a kiwi, and is common on the west coast of the South Island.

The native New Zealand wood pigeon can be found in several of the country's national parks.

One bird you probably won't have any trouble seeing at all is the **kea**, a pesky alpine parrot that fills the New Zealand niche reserved for uppity North American blue jays. They are curious and sneaky birds, and no tour bus is safe from them. They hang around tourist areas and mooch food and generally raise hell. There are signs here and there imploring you not to feed the keas, which is not only bad for them, but just encourages them to further mischief. You only find them in the wild in the South Island in areas between forests and alpine meadows. Keas are fairly large birds, growing up to 20 inches high, with strong beaks and brownish-green feathers. They were once hunted because farmers thought they attacked and killed small sheep. They will eat carrion, but there is no solid evidence proving that they will attack a healthy sheep. The birds are partially protected by law.

The tui bird, native to New Zealand, is a forest dweller.

Not satisfied with having one of the peskiest parrots around, *the New Zealanders also claim the world's largest parrot,* the extremely rare, very noisy **kakapo**, which is also the world's only flightless parrot and the world's heaviest parrot, weighing in as much as seven pounds. About the size of a small owl, the kakapo is on the verge of extinction in New Zealand, with only six known fertile females left. Naturalists have undertaken a vigorous breeding program, only partially successful. *Another extremely rare bird is the colorful* **takahe**, *another flightless animal. It was believed to have been extinct by 1898, but a small colony was found in 1948 near Lake Te Anau.* Takahes have been bred in captivity, but the numbers are still very small. Their decline, as with other native birds, was mostly due to introduced predators. The most endangered wading bird in the world, the New Zealand black stilt, it found almost exclusively in the Mackemzie Basin area near Twizel in the South Island. There is a viewing area (called a "hide") just south of Twizel. (See information later in the South Island section.)

All in all, the combination of surviving New Zealand species plus the many types introduced by the settlers makes New Zealand a birdwatcher's delight. Some of the rarer birds are in aviaries, but many of the really endangered ones exist only in the wild and are heavily protected. But among the many birds you'll see while you're driving around, in addition to the keas, are **black swans** (imported from Australia); **pukekos**, which look something like a takahe but aren't as rare; the **Australian harrier**; the **New Zealand gray duck** (looks like a female mallard); the **paradise shelduck**, seen all over the country; **oystercatchers** (almost any beach); **magpies** (another Aussie immigrant), the **Indian myna bird**; the **tui**, a white-wattled, very noisy forest dweller, and **shags**, a cousin to the North American cormorant. The smallest bird in the country is the New Zealand riflebird, only about three inches long.

Several popular species of birds are found only at certain locations around the country. For example:

The **royal albatross**, a huge seabird, nests in a colony at Taiaroa Head, about 20 miles from Dunedin on the South Island. Tours are available; the nesting season starts in November.

Yellow-eyed penguins are also found near Taiaroa Head, as are fur seals. The penguins come ashore to tend their nests in the afternoon; they are best seen June–August.

There is a **white heron** sanctuary near Whataroa on the west coast of the South Island near Franz Josef. The nesting season is November–February.

Gannets mate for life and can live 20 years.

The only onshore rookery for **gannets** in the southern hemisphere is located at Cape Kidnappers near Napier on the North Island. The males arrive in July to claim nesting sites. The birds mate for life and may live up to 20 years. The cape was named by Captain Cook because the Maoris tried to kidnap a Tahitian on board his boat.

Yellow-eyed penguin poses on the Otago Peninsula.

...And, of Course, Sheep

Sheepshearing

Lastly, but certainly not leastly, there is no way you will avoid seeing that most ubiquitous of New Zealand critters, the **sheep**.

New Zealand is the largest wool, lamb and mutton exporting nation in the world because of the huge flocks of sheep, which are found from island tip to island tip. In the spring, when it's lambing time, the total sheep population might reach 100 million. We remember driving from Queenstown to Te Anau once and losing count of the number of being-born and just-born lambs in paddocks we passed. It seemed like every sheep in New Zealand was pregnant. That's when we found out that sheep are born with long tails, which are cropped when they are babies. Being city folk, we never knew that. But then a week or two in New Zealand will teach you all sorts of things about sheep.

For instance, most ewes have multiple births; two are usual, but quads or even quints are not unusual. If a ewe only gives birth to one lamb at a time, she's soon off to the knackers—the abattoir. Among the many breeds, you see mostly **merinos** (the sheep that made Australia), **Romneys, Corriedales, English Leicester** and **Drysdales**. It will not be uncommon to see a sea of sheep moving up and down the hills being pushed and prodded by one or two sheepdogs, a marvelous sight. One term you're likely to run into is *"hogget,"* which is a one-year-old sheep, which the Kiwis prefer eating to spring lamb.

When the United Kingdom joined the European Economic Community in the early 1970s, one of New Zealand's major meat markets was severely restricted. As much as half of all New Zealand's exports were going to Great Britain—within a decade, it was down to just over 10 percent. Much of the country's mutton and sheep output is now going to the Near East, and to a certain degree, North America. The first sheep in New Zealand were introduced by—who else—James Cook on one of his stops at Queen Charlotte Sound.

The Kiwi sheep business even has a folk hero, a Robin Hoodish type named **James McKenzie**. A devious Scot, McKenzie and his sheepdog, Friday, stole sheep from the rich farmers around the Canterbury District and snuck them back into the mountains. When they finally caught him in 1855, he had more than 1000 purloined sheep. He was tried, convicted and sentenced to five years, but pardoned after one. Friday, his faithful dog, wasn't so lucky—he was tried as a witch and hanged.

If you want to see the sheep business up close, try one of the farm stay properties; nine out of 10 will likely be raising some sheep. And if you're on the North Island the first week in March, head for Masterson, a small farming community 100 kilometers northeast of Wellington, where you will find the annual Golden Shears contest, which decides the best shearer in the country. Contestants are each given 20 sheep, which they shear at the rate of about one a minute (which is light speed), but are also judged on the quality of their cutting. *New Zealand and the EEC continue to be the world's major dairy product producers.* New Zealand has almost 3 million cows on 16,000 dairy farms. The small country is responsible for about 25 percent of the entire world's dairy product production.

Oh, Give Me a Home

So there you are, driving along through the clean, green, nuclear-free farmlands of New Zealand, admiring the view, admiring the clean air, admiring the farm animals, sheep, of course, cows, hogs, horses, almost every one with a protective blanket, sheepdogs, **deer**. *Deer? Yes, indeed, one of the country's most lucrative farm animals, deer.* More than 5000 New Zealand farmers are now involved in raising deer in one form or another, and at the moment, there are in excess of 1.5 million deer behind fences in New Zealand.

The hope is that farm-raised deer meat—venison—will become a staple in the red meat markets of the world. Venison, they tell you, is designer red meat, with less fat than chicken breasts, fewer calories than broiled salmon and the same amount of cholesterol as broiled bass. Also, they will tell you, farm-raised venison does not have the gamy taste of deer killed in the wild. And because it's being raised in mostly pollution-free New Zealand on mostly grass and no chemicals, it's about as pure as meat can get. *The major market for New Zealand venison is Germany,* which imports several million pounds a year. (Germany usually imports a total of more than 10 million pounds of venison from various sources—they definitely like their jaegerschnitzel in the German Republic.) New Zealand meat is also shipped to Japan, Switzerland, Australia and Sweden. The total import of New Zealand deer meat to the United States runs around a million pounds. Industry estimates are that about *85 percent of all venison served in American restaurants comes from New Zealand.* Current estimates are that venison exports are running about $NZ80 million a year.

The deer business is particularly important to New Zealand these days because many deer operations were set up in hopes of adding supplemental income to farmers dependent on the usually volatile international wool and mutton/lamb markets. The country has had some hard economic times recently, and there's a lot riding on the success of the deer industry. One of the things that makes deer farming so attractive is that after capital costs (fence, barns, buying the stock), it costs something like $10 a year per animal to raise a deer. "Just stick them in a field and give 'em some grass," one farmer said. Growers say deer require less land per pound of meat than other animals, and are up to three times as profitable as raising cattle or sheep. Raising deer in New Zealand these days is fairly pastoral. But it wasn't always so. Ironically, the industry began as a conservation measure. Starting in the late 1850s, colonial settlers in New Zealand imported red deer from Australia and Europe for sporting purposes. Red deer—actually a species of elk—are hardy, adaptable animals. That, coupled with the fact that there are no natural predators in New Zealand, meant that by the 1930s, red deer were a plague all over the country, destroying their own environment and causing problems for farmers.

The government finally allowed hunting to begin in the early 1970s, and hunters soon discovered there was a market for deer meat, and more importantly, for deer velvet, the soft new antler growth produced every year by male deer. Hunters are now allowed to sell venison to restaurants. The Asian market for velvet (and other deer parts) as a medicinal aid—especially in South Korea—is enormous and highly profitable. Not too long ago, velvet was selling for as much as $US200 a kilogram (it's now down to around $US60 a kilo). To harvest the velvet, stags are tranquilized and the soft horn removed with a bone saw; a good stag can produce excellent velvet for 10 or 15 years.

The Helicopter Wars

The market for New Zealand deer—alive or dead—became so attractive that what came to be called "the Helicopter Wars" began. At first, there were few attempts to capture deer live; rather they were shot from helicopters. Then, some farsighted farmers figured it would be cheaper—and more profitable—to start their own herds and began capturing the animals. *The traditional capture method was for some crazy Kiwi to ride the skids outside a chopper, then jump onto the back of a deer. This was not only dangerous, but very*

THE LAND

inefficient. But many New Zealand farmers got started in the deer business that way. (Later, they started using nets, sometimes with success, sometimes not.) At times, the competition got very nasty—helicopters were sabotaged by putting sugar in gas tanks, pilots were shot at. Some years, 50 or so helicopters were involved in the killing/capturing business. It is estimated that some choppers made 12,000 kills a year, and that sometimes as many as 100,000 carcasses were sent through abattoirs annually. In the process, 130 helicopters crashed, and 25 pilots or crew were killed in accidents.

Today, the majority of venison exported from New Zealand is farm raised, although there are still a few hunters in business, and quite a few hunters from around the world come down to pursue red deer in the wild. *Most of the deer raised in New Zealand are red deer, but some farmers are raising wapiti— North American elk, virtually the same species as the red deer.* The vast wild red deer herds have been reduced to a manageable level. And in the process, the New Zealand deer industry has become very sophisticated and very successful, a far, far cry from the days of the helicopter wars.

Farmers are now also trying to cash in on a new animal market also enjoying a boom in the United States and Australia: ostriches. At the moment, there are fewer than 1000 of the birds in the country, but speculators are hoping the benefits of raising ostriches—meat, eggs, feathers—will rapidly increase the numbers and make them a money-making addition to the country's rural economy.

THE PERFECT VACATION

Queenstown's Shotover River is great for jet boating.

In New Zealand, it's not what to do, it's how to narrow down the choices. Given the size of the country (easy to get around), and the varied climate, New Zealand is Vacationland out of Central Casting—you want it, you can do it. Every taste, every pocketbook.

But the emphasis in Kiwi country is definitely on outdoor recreation, especially hiking (they call it tramping), skiing, fishing and hunting. Oh, yes, and that most insane of all New Zealand activities, bungy jumping. We'll try to explain.

55

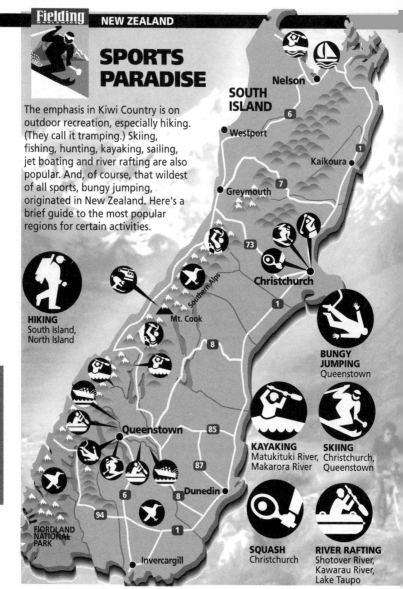

Fielding WORLDWIDE **NEW ZEALAND**

SPORTS PARADISE

The emphasis in Kiwi Country is on outdoor recreation, especially hiking. (They call it tramping.) Skiing, fishing, hunting, kayaking, sailing, jet boating and river rafting are also popular. And, of course, that wildest of all sports, bungy jumping, originated in New Zealand. Here's a brief guide to the most popular regions for certain activities.

SOUTH ISLAND

Nelson

Westport

Kaikoura

Greymouth

Christchurch

Southern Alps

Mt. Cook

HIKING
South Island,
North Island

BUNGY JUMPING
Queenstown

Queenstown

Dunedin

KAYAKING
Matukituki River,
Makarora River

SKIING
Christchurch,
Queenstown

FIORDLAND
NATIONAL
PARK

Invercargill

SQUASH
Christchurch

RIVER RAFTING
Shotover River,
Kawarau River,
Lake Taupo

THE PERFECT
VACATION

BICYCLING
Everywhere

DEEP SEA FISHING
Bay of Islands

BIRD WATCHING
Otago,
Southern Alps,
Fiordland
National Park

DIVING
Cavalli Islands,
South Island

SAILING
Bay of Islands,
Nelson

FISHING
Waikeromoana
Lake, Whakatane

MOUNTAIN CLIMBING
Southern Alps

GOLF
Rotorua,
Christchurch
Bay of Plenty

CANOEING
Whanganui
River,
Lake Taupo

SPELUNKING
Waitomo Caves,
Ruakuri Cave,
Aranui Cave

SEA KAYAKING
Coromandal, Bay
of Islands, Abel
Tasman Park

HELI-SKIING
Tasman Glacier,
Fox Glacier,
Mt. Cook

JET BOATING
Shotover,
Kawarau River

Whangarei

Auckland

NORTH ISLAND

Hamilton

Otorohanga

Tauranga

Rotorua

Whakatane

Taupo

Gisborne

New Plymouth

Lake Taupo

South Taranaki Bright

Napier

Wellington

THE PERFECT VACATION

Bungy Jumping

You find a highway bridge, or a trestle or a hot-air balloon or actually any place as long as it's high and dangerous. Then you get a big rubber band maybe 200 feet long (the bungy itself), and you attach it to the bridge. Then you wrap the other end around your ankles. Then you jump. Now, most observers of the passing scene would have you believe that New Zealanders are sedate and calm compared to their earthier, louder cousins, the Australians. But beneath that Kiwi calm, there must be a vein of total idiocy, and bungy jumping might just be the tip of the iceberg.

Two of the best bungy jumping spots are in Queenstown.

If you want to join the thousands of other crazed folks who have taken a dive, two of the best spots are near Queenstown on the South Island: the historic suspension bridge over the **Kawarau River gorge** on Highway 6 northeast of town, and the **Skipper's Canyon bridge** over the Shotover River north of town. The Kawarau jump is 143 feet; Shotover, 229 feet. It'll cost between $NZ90 and $NZ200 to do a jump or series of jumps. The best outfit in Queenstown that does bungy jumps is run by A. J. Hackett, who took a dive off the Eiffel Tower and is generally regarded as the daddy of the bungy jumping business. The motto of his company: "Jump with the professionals—you'd be crazy not to." Right. A.J. ain't crazy. His operations are now run at nine sites around the world, including France and Las Vegas, and his company has branched out into a line of sports clothing and white-water rafting. The trip to the Shotover Bridge is worth a try by itself—especially in the winter. The narrow dirt road hugs the side of a cliff and getting there can be downright hairy. The company also offers jumps from helicopters. Part of the services you can buy in addition to the basic price include a North American standard videotape of your jump and photographs. Find his place at the corner of Shotover and Camp streets in Queenstown; ☎ *(03) 442-7100; FAX 442-7121.*

Because we insist on being as accurate for you folks as possible, we decided we had to try it at least once. It fell to the male member of the team (cut of the cards, in fact) to do the deed, which he did from the Kawarau River bridge. It was pretty neat, and the Hackett company is very slick. You have to sign a release before you jump, then decide if you want a video tape and photos taken of the jump (We bought the whole package, figuring we might never try again.) The guys on the bridge ask you how far into the water you want to go, then adjust the bungy. They were accurate to the inch and it was a great trip.

Having said that, we should also point out that there were three bungy accidents in 1997 that proved the sport is not altogether safe. In fact, two of the accidents were A.J. Hackett jumps, one from Skipper's Canyon and one from the Kawarau River bridge. In both cases, the ankle attachments came loose and the jumpers ended up in the river; both were rescued and both were injured. Worse was the accident at a rehearsal for the 1997 Super Bowl in New Orleans when a professional bungy jumper was killed when she hit the floor of the Super Dome. Like anything else that involves a risk, bungy jumping is something you should really think about.

For the saner members of our audience, try these diversions:

Take a Hike

Kiwis like to walk so much that Parliament has passed legislation setting up a national system of trails intended to run from the north tip of the North Island to the south tip of the South Island. The system isn't completed yet, but there are hundreds of trails around the country, from gentle urban walkways to serious wilderness tracks that are only for the very fit. Many of the tracks are old Maori trails. You can go walkabout by yourself or on a guided tour; you can go for an hour or for a week. Many of the best hikes are in the country's system of national parks and nature preserves.

Some of the finest trails in the country are in the south, either in the Alpine country or amongst the fjords on the southwest coast. Indeed, *the most fa-*

mous of all New Zealand's trails is in the fjords, the world-renowned Milford Track. The track runs from Lake Te Anau to Milford Sound, a distance of about 30 miles.

(Note: many of the major treks, because of climatic conditions, are closed during the New Zealand winter; always check ahead.)

The Abel Tasman Coast Track is a pleasant hike along beaches and scenic bays.

Because the Kiwis are so keen about hiking, they have made it relatively easy—and comfortable—to keep your body dry and warm out in the boonies. *There are something like 1000 back-country huts, from the basics to some owned by private companies that have everything but a butler.* There are no fees to walk around national parks or reserves, but there is a charge for using most of the huts.

The government has designated a number of hiking areas as "Great Walks," which are the country's most popular trails and have the best-equipped huts. Great Walks include North Island: **Lake Waikaremoana** in the Te Urewera National Park southeast of Rotorua; **Tongariro Northern Circuit** in the national park, and **Wanganui Journey** on the southwest of the island. South Island: **Heaphy Track** in Nelson Forest Park; **Abel Tasman Coast Track**, Abel Tasman National Park; **Routeburn Track**, Mt. Aspiring and Fiordland national parks; **Milford Track,** Fiordland National Park; **Kepler Track**, Fiordland National Park, and **Rakiura Track**, Stewart Island.

The huts basically come in four categories, depending on level of services available. Great Walks huts are $NZ14 a night per person. All huts in Mt. Cook National Park are also $NZ14. Campsites in the Great Walks areas are $NZ6 a night. Note that you will need a date-specific pass for huts in the

Great Walks area; huts in the other parks are on a first-come basis. Basic huts run between $NZ4 and $NZ8 a night. Coupons for the huts are $NZ4 each; at some huts you'll need two coupons a night. They can be purchased at any Department of Conservation office in the country. (Mt. Cook passes must be purchased at the park's visitors center, and Milford Track passes must be obtained from the Fiordland National Park Visitors Centre in Te Anau. Milford Track passes, which include huts and water transport, are about $NZ130.) If you're planning a long stay or a series of treks, consider an annual hut pass, available from the DOC and visitors centers for about $NZ60; they are not good for Great Walks or Mt. Cook National Park trails.

Split Apple Rock, Abel Tasman National Park, is a natural wonder.

A word about guided hikes in general: Most include day packs, meals, rain gear, accommodations in lodges or hiking huts and the guides themselves. They can be booked from North America through travel agents. Or you can book them in New Zealand, realizing that if it's summer, many parties will already be filled, and if it's winter, some trails are closed. The guided tours can be for single tracks or a series of trails, and can be hard or soft. For example, one tour company, Alpine Recreation Canterbury Ltd. headquartered in Lake Tekapo (northwest of Timaru), offers a series of outings, using minibuses to get you to places to take day hikes throughout the South Island. The 13-day small-group tour, including meals, rental equipment, accommodations, guides and boat cruises, runs about $NZ2500 per person (discount for groups). The company also has shorter trips, including the Ball Pass and Mackenzie Basin trails. (See "Essentials" under "Mount Cook" later in the book.)

There are literally dozens of companies offering guided hiking tours all over New Zealand. *Generally, these guided tramps will start around $NZ100 a day per person.* Many are combined with other activities, such as river rafting, helicopter trips, jet boating or camping. *One of the most popular trekking areas is Abel Tasman National Park northwest of Nelson.* The best trail is probably the coastal track, with great views of Tasman Bay. The trek up the coast will take a couple of days; the stretch down the interior of the park a bit longer. Check with Tasman National Park Enterprises in Motueka, ☎ *(03) 528-7801. Be prepared for sand flies. It's usually crowded in the summer and the huts might be full; take a sleeping bag.*

The New Zealand government, realizing that some of us really do like to frolic in the snow, has licensed a company to take hardy hikers on treks during the Kiwi winter. The company, The Great Walk Way Ltd., runs what it calls the *Routeburn Winter Classic,* a two- or three-day package using a Department of Conservation cabin on the gorgeous Routeburn Track near Queenstown. (Yahoo, the sand flies are hibernating!) Daily treks follow trails in the Mount Aspiring and Fiordland national parks, returning each night to the heated cabin for candlelit dinners. The cost of an all-inclusive trip from Queenstown (meals, equipment, transportation) is $NZ420 per person for the two-day, $NZ590 for the three-day. The tours can be booked through the New Zealand Tourism Office in Santa Monica, California, or by calling the company in Queenstown at ☎ *(03) 442-6794.*

Milford Track has been rated one of the best hiking trails in the world.

While not as well known, there are several tracks on the North Island worth a visit, especially around Tongariro National Park, Lake Taupo and Urewera

National Park. The Tongariro trails get you right in among the volcanic activity; it's probably the most interesting of the North Island excursions.

A final note. *In addition to the most powerful bug dope you can find, be sure to take along some water purification equipment* (or boil the drinking water). The once-pristine rivers, lakes and streams of New Zealand are now subject to giardia, a very nasty little bug that can cause major internal distress.

A transplanted American living near Nelson, Alan Riegelman, has a company that offers two- and three-week tours for day hikers and backpackers. Day hikers are given modest accommodations in private homes, farm stays or an occasional motel; backpackers do the campground number. Riegelman and his staff do 90 percent of the cooking to save money. The three-week tours, which include airfare from Los Angeles to Christchurch, run about *$NZ5500* per person; two week tours are around *$NZ3100* for backpackers and *$NZ3300* for day-trippers. Information on the tours is available from his company, **New Zealand Travelers Inc.**, *P.O. Box 605, Shelburne, Vermont 05482*; ☎ *(802) 985-8865; FAX (802) 985-8501.* Or his New Zealand operation at Tealcot, *Teal Valley RD1, Nelson, New Zealand;* ☎ *(03) 545-1141; FAX (03) 545-1777.* Complete three-week tours from Los Angeles, including airfare, accommodations and most meals, will run about $US3500 per person, depending on season and itinerary.

Mount Cook line also offers trekking trips from Los Angeles. A 10-night stay, which includes the Milford Track, is about $US2800, including airfare, accommodations and transfers. U.S. information: ☎ *(800) 688-9716; FAX (310) 640-2823.* Other companies to check are **Kiwi Outback Bush Walks**, which has treks with overnight stays and an emphasis on endangered birds, glowworms and star-gazing. Depending on itinerary, look to pay between $NZ20 and $NZ100. The company is based in Rotorua, ☎ *(07) 332-3629.* Also try **Kauri Coast Motor Camp** near Dargaville on the west coast near Whangarei. Guided night walks through kauri forests, a chance to see giant weta insects, kiwis, kauri snails, owls and glowworms. Only $NZ6. ☎ *(09) 439-0621.*

Mountain Climbing

The next step up from serious hiking is, of course, mountain climbing. Does the name Edmond Hillary ring a bell? He's the man who, with sherpa Tensing Norkay, became the first human to climb Mt. Everest. The New Zealander did a lot of his pre-Himalayan training in the Darren and Humboldt mountains between Queenstown and Milford Sound. The series of 10,000-foot-plus peaks in the Southern Alps offer climbing challenges from easy to advanced, from rock-face to ice fields. The government has placed mountaineering huts at strategic spots, or you can put your tent where you decide to stop. In addition to specialized companies, there are also local climbing clubs, and information is available from national parks. Two good sources of information about mountain climbing possibilities are the **New Zealand Alpine Club**, *P.O. Box 1700, Christchurch,* ☎ *(03) 332-1222,* or the **Canterbury Mountaineering Club**, *P.O. Box 2415, Christchurch,* ☎ *(03) 332-2232.*

Fishing

Trout fishing on the Mohaka River

New Zealanders are justifiably proud of their streams, filled with salmon, steelhead and trout, as well they should be. They get a little carried away now and then, proclaiming it to be the best in the world, but they might be close to right. What New Zealand offers that you don't often find in other great fishing spots is solitude. A tour bus driver on the way to Milford Sound said some of the streams we were passing were full of rainbow trout. "You see maybe two fishermen a year along here," he said, whereupon some of us collapsed into a mumbling heap, remembering the elbow-to-elbow crowds on the Au Sable in Michigan and the San Joaquin up by Mammoth Lakes in California. What this lack of fishing pressure means is large average catches. Eight-pound browns are not uncommon, for example.

Hiking to a secluded fishing hole in the Wairinaki Forest

And the other beauty of fishing in New Zealand, aside from the silence, is the fact that there are great streams all over, some private, many public. *As we noted in the accommodations section, it's possible to spend a bundle and stay at one of the upscale fishing lodges on both islands. Or you can find a motel near a stream and have at it, as well.* Many lodges have their own private streams. The North Island, especially around the Bay of Islands, prides itself on great saltwater fishing, but the South Island isn't far behind, with some fine opportunities for marlin and shark. New Zealand is surrounded by water, remember, meaning that surf casting is everywhere. And, to cap everything off, the Kiwis make it fairly cheap to cast a line. They do like it when you catch and release, which is the only civilized way to fish, anyway. A one-day license goes for about $NZ11, or a month for about $NZ30. Guides are also inexpensive, compared to some other places (Alaska comes to mind). Look for stream and lake trout guides to run from around $NZ200 to $NZ500 a day. There is **trout fishing** all year. Some specialty outfits will put you on a helicopter and drop you right next to a virgin mountain stream—this is where old trouters go to die. You can fish any style you want, but *most Kiwi trout fishers stick to fly fishing.*

Salmon fishing is found along the east coast of the South Island where a series of glacier and snow melt rivers flow to the sea. The country is majestic, the salmon fishing quite literally some of the best in the world. If you haven't tried it, fly fishing for salmon is one of the great challenges in life, right up there with throwing a fly at a bonefish or tarpon. One of the more popular east coast rivers is the Rakaia River, only 35 miles southwest of Christchurch.

Deep-Sea Fishing

For serious deep-sea activity, the waters around New Zealand, especially the east coast of the North Island, have some of the most active and least known sport around. **Striped marlin** average 200 to 300 pounds off New Zealand, with larger fish weighing in at 400 pounds or so. But there are also **blue marlin** up to 500 pounds and even an occasional **Pacific black marlin** that can go over 600 pounds.

As a for instance, there are about two dozen charter boats in the Paihia/ Russell area of the Bay of Islands. The charter boats go from $US350 to $US600 per day and up. The fees normally include food, accommodations and tackle. Close in, for light tackle types, there are kingfish, cod, flounder and snapper, among others. No license is required for ocean fishing. **Frontiers** (see below) offers a number of deep-sea fishing packages on the North Island. One special option is to take your catch, smoke it, and drop you and a pal on a deserted island for the day.

One good bet for a fishing tour is through **The Best of New Zealand Fly Fishing**, an outfit located in Los Angeles. It represents a number of fishing lodges in New Zealand, and has a variety of packages available. For example, a two-week, three-lodge tour of the South Island runs about $US4600, which includes airfare from Los Angeles, a rental car, accommodations, meals, fishing guides and helicopter fly-ins. A week at one lodge, including all the goodies and guides, runs around $US3800. To get a free brochure with information on the lodges, tips on New Zealand fishing and a section on saltwater fishing, contact Mike McClelland at the company, *2817 Wilshire Boulevard, Santa Monica, CA 90403;* ☎ *(310) 998-5880 or (800) 528-6129; fax (310) 829-9221*.

Another very good outfit to contact is **Frontiers**, a Pennsylvania-based company that also organizes fishing/ hunting trips. As with the Best of New Zealand, Frontiers makes use of the many excellent Kiwi fishing lodges. At the Tongariro Lodge at Lake Taupo on the North Island, for example, the price is about $US400 per person double occupancy including a shared guide. Information: *P.O. Box 959, 100 Logan Road, P.O. Box 959, Wexford, PA 15090-0959;* ☎ *(800) 245-1950; FAX (412) 935-5388.* In Pennsylvania, ☎ *(412) 935-1577.* Another possible is **Pathways International**, *P.O. Box 3276, Spartanburg, SC 29304;* ☎ *(800) 628-5060 or* ☎ *(803) 583-7234.*

For more information, contact **New Zealand Professional Fishing Guides**, *P.O. Box 16, Motu, Gisborne, New Zealand;* ☎ *(06) 863-5822; FAX (06) 863-5844.*

As noted, many of the fishing lodges are also hunting lodges, with game ranging from rabbits to elk. In addition to open range hunting, there are a number of private herds of game animals that can be hunted for a per-trophy charge.

Diving

There are several good diving areas in New Zealand, several of which are protected in marine reserves. The **Poor Knights Marine Reserve**, for example, is situated in the islands of the same name near Whangarei north of Auckland. The volcanic islands are filled with caves and lava tubes, and home to a wide variety of tropical fish and other marine animals. In the **Cavalli Islands**, off the east coast of the North Island near Whangaroa Harbour, *lie the remains of the Rainbow Warrior, the Greenpeace ship bombed in Auckland by the French Secret Service.* The ship was scuttled here to make an artificial reef and is an excellent diving spot. In the south, fjord diving offers a look at some of *the only black coral in the world growing less than 20 feet underwater*—layers of silty freshwater close off light, allowing the coral to grow. Underneath the freshwater is salt water with good visibility. The fjords and inlets of the South Island are also home to schools of friendly porpoises. There are dive shops throughout the country; to get air, you have to have a card certifying that you're a qualified diver. The New Zealand Tourism Board has brochures highlighting dive areas off both islands.

Rafting

Equipment check on the Mohaka River

*The **Shotover River** near Queenstown is famous as a white-water challenge, with some rapids up to Grade 5 and long stretches of narrow canyons and walls of water six feet high.*

One of the rapids is called "Mother." It is. There is also a little beauty called "**The Toilet**." Not far behind is another Queenstown river, the Kawarau. The **Kawarau** has a one-quarter-mile stretch called the **Chinese Dogleg**, which is about as hairy as it gets. On the North Island, there are several rivers worth a try, including the **Rangiaiki**, the **Wairoa** and the **Tongariro**, all of which can be as nasty as the southern streams.

There are literally dozens of companies offering trips, many of which combine accommodations, meals and helicopter trips as part of the package. You can do the rivers in short legs or days-long trips. In Queenstown, check with **Danes Shotover Rafts Ltd.**, which does the Shotover, the Kawarau and the hard-to-get-to Landsborough River. It also does the **Wiatoto River**, which is almost all Grade 4–5 rapids. On the North Island, try **Huka Jets** in Taupo; ☎ *(07) 374-8572.*

Jet Boating

Jet boating is also a popular sport in New Zealand, and, no surprise, the major rafting rivers are also the main targets for the jet boats. In the Queenstown area, it's the **Shotover** and **Kawarau** again, and on the North Island, the **Rangitaiki** and the **Waikato** are popular. Many of the jet boats are run in combination with helicopter trips and rafting excursions. For a jet boat trip only, expect to pay around $NZ40 to $NZ50. Combination trips run between $NZ100 and $NZ500. A good bet in Queenstown is **Shotover Jet**, which can be booked through any of the many tourist offices or by calling ☎ *(03) 442-8570*. On the North Island, try **Huka Jets** in Taupo.

Kayaking

The Shotover River is a challenge for kayakers.

Also popular in New Zealand is **kayaking**, both in streams and in the ocean. Popular ocean areas include the Marlborough Sounds and also the fjords of the southwest coast. Rivers offer top kayaking with many chances at Grade 5 rapids. You can rent kayaks and canoes or take escorted tours. Kayak rentals run about $NZ30 a day, canoes $NZ20 a day or so. For example, in the Bay of Islands on the North Island, check out **Bay of Islands Sea kayakers**, based in Paihia. A four-hour guided trip from Waitanga Beach goes for about $NZ40 per person. For the adventurous, try the three- to five-day trips that combine sea kayaking with snorkeling and beach walks for about $NZ170 person, including half-day guides. Food, clothing and camping equipment not included. Or just rent a kayak for $NZ35 a day. *Information* ☎ *(09) 402-8105 or 402-8151 or 403-7951.* Canoe trips on the Whanganui River are available from **Canoe Safaris** in Oahkune. Rates for a guided, five-day tour, November–April, are $NZ450–550. (Trips available on request other times of the year.) ☎ *(06) 385-8758.* Sea kayaking in the Abel Tasman National Park area is available through the **Ocean River Adventure Co.**, based in Motueka near Nelson. Rates range from about $NZ90 for a one-day trip to $NZ540 for a five-day outing (four-person minimum); some tours include some accommodations and meals; rentals without guides also available, $NZ95 per person for two days, double occupancy. The company also has winter wildlife trips. *Information: Ocean River* ☎ *(03) 527-8266; fax 527-8006. For North American information, contact* **Down Under Answers**, ☎ *(800) 788-6685 or write to the company at 13501 100th Avenue, N.E., Suite 5010, Kirkland, WA 98034.*

Golf

We have some friends who would probably trade in their first-born for a chance to play a good 18 holes any Saturday, any place, so it was no surprise a few years ago when they spotted one of the periodic good deals for air/drive trips to New Zealand and took off for a 10-day golfing spree. Part of their package included an RV, and they hit the ground putting, stopping wherever they could find a course. *They didn't have much trouble finding a course, either, what with more than 400 scattered around the country.* They are still raving about it. The Kiwis would have us believe that you can't drive 30 miles in any direction without hitting a golf course, and we'll take their word for it, because the whole country looks like a golf course to begin with.

Our golfing friends were also blown away by the prices and the lack of crowds. Some of the courses they play around Northern California can charge as much as $US200 for 18 holes. Top courses in New Zealand might charge

$US25, and the courses are almost always in excellent condition. *Many courses do not have golf carts; some, in fact, don't even allow pull-carts* They have this silly idea that golf is supposed to be exercise. At the clubs that do offer electric carts, expect to pay about $NZ20 for a cart per round.

New Zealand has more than 400 golf courses.

Most clubs welcome visitors, but note that some courses will be crowded in the summer. *Most of the private courses offer reciprocal memberships to members of North American clubs—just bring a letter of introduction from the club secretary.* The New Zealanders, who mostly disregard reality when it comes to weather, claim you can play golf all year, and thus off-season is dandy for overseas visitors because nobody's on the course. But there's a down side, too. We saw the course at Greymouth one spring day when the wind was blowing a full gale, and the rain was so heavy, a golf ball wouldn't have rolled three inches on a green.

At any rate, you'll find special tour offers from time to time, such as one not long ago for a nine-day golfing tour for about $US1600 per person, which included airfare from Los Angeles, green fees, accommodations, all internal travel, two meals a day, sightseeing and other special activities.

You can do what our friends did—toss your clubs on the plane and just take pot luck—or book a full tour in advance. Your best bet for information or tour bookings is **New Zealand Golf Excursions Ltd.**, *2041 Rosecrans Avenue, No. 103, El Segundo, CA 90245;* ☎ *(800) 622-6606; FAX (310) 322-9900.* A 14-day escorted tour, including accommodations, most meals, greens fees and cart hires, transfers and some trout fishing, will run about $US3800 including airfare. Extensions to Australian courses are available. Tours are normally guided by John Lister, a New Zealand pro. In New Zealand, contact the company at *Strawberry Fields Golf Course, P.O. Box 65083, Mairangi Bay, Auckland;* ☎ *(09) 415-6804; FAX (09) 415-6805.* A couple of other companies to check for golf packages are **New Zealand Golf Excursions**, ☎ *(800) 622-6606,* and **Kiwi Golf Tours,** ☎ *(800) 873-6360.* General golf information in advance of your trip to New Zealand is available from Executive Director, **New Zealand Golf Association**, *P.O. Box 11-842, Wellington. N.Z.* If you're in Auckland between planes, try a round at the Aviation Country Club at the airport. The 18-hole course goes for $NZ20 a round weekdays, $NZ25 weekends. Club hire is around $NZ20; electric carts, $NZ25 for 18 holes. *Information* ☎ *275-4601.*

Sailing

Once upon a time, gazing out over the 30-below-zero snowbanks in our front yard in Minneapolis, we said, "This sucks," and decided, with some other demented friends, to build a boat and sail away from it all. Which, five years later, we did. It was a 38-footer, and we took it all the way down the Mississippi to the Bahamas. Paradise turned out to be a tad boring, so eventually we sold the boat and went back to work—in Minnesota. But the bug had definitely bitten.

Due to pecuniary problems and logistics, we haven't had a boat since, but that hasn't stopped the sailing. That first trip qualified us to the point that we can lease a bareboat yacht almost anywhere in the world, which, from time to time, we do. It is probably the most perfect of all vacations. It's not for everybody, of course, but if you are like us, or know somebody qualified to run a 30- to 40-foot boat, *New Zealand offers some of the finest—and safest—sailing waters in the South Pacific.*

And just to compound the problem, some of the deals available from time to time are downright criminal—for sailing vacations, that is. Like around $US4000 a couple, which includes round-trip international air, a one-week charter of a 32-foot Beneteau (sure, they're beamy, but they're also very safe), an additional week's rental of a car and all accommodations, plus transfers. If you're a little unsure of your sailing skills, for an additional $US210, a professional, licensed sailing instructor will spend the first three days aboard showing you the ropes. As these things go, this is a very nice deal.

A lot of the sailing packages base you in the Bay of Islands, which is relatively mild because of the many anchorages and the fact that you're almost never out of sight of land. It's very much like sailing in some of the smaller Greek island groups. If sailboats aren't your thing, there are also cruisers for rent—a group of six aboard a 36-footer runs about $US1500. There are a number of companies offering bareboat or crewed boats. One that seems to consistently have good deals is **Moorings Rainbow Yacht Charters**, which works with Air New Zealand and Mount Cook Line. A 32-footer will run between $US160 and $US290 per day depending on season. In Auckland, call Moorings Rainbow at ☎ *(09) 378-0719.* In North America, contact Rainbow at ☎ *(800) 227-5317.*

Skiing

Some folks, not content with just looking at those gorgeous mountains, just have to ski them. No doubt about it, the chance to ski down a glacier or through absolutely virgin snow accessible only by helicopter is highly tempting to gung-ho skiers. Most of the country's ski areas are in the South Island, within easy access of either Christchurch or Queenstown, the ski capital of New Zealand. In all there are about a dozen commercial ski areas and a dozen private club ski areas. Many of the private areas offer ski packages through tour agents. These areas tend to be a bit less sophisticated than the commercial ones, but many offer good skiing. There are also plenty of cross-country trails available. In addition, there are several companies that offer heli-skiing.

Packages are almost always available. Mount Cook Line and Air New Zealand usually offer winter packages (June–August) starting around $US1400 per person, which includes air travel to New Zealand from Los Angeles, interior flights, first-class accommodations and ski-lift tickets for **Coronet Peak** or the **Remarkables**, two of the best ski areas in the country. Check with **Mount Cook Line** in North America, *1960 E. Grand Avenue, Suite 910, El Segundo, CA 90245-5070;* ☎ *(800) 345-3504.*

Depending on location, the ski season can start as early as June and last through November. Generally it starts earlier on the South Island and lasts longer on the North Island. More than half of the commercial resorts have snowmaking equipment. Most commercial areas charge about $NZ30–50 a day for lift tickets. In addition, just to make you grind your teeth, many commercial areas also have a road toll. Private roads, you see, and maintenance costs...still, it's a bit cheeky.

As an example of what you might expect from private club areas that do allow nonmembers to come and play is the **Mount Olympus** area, about 130 kilometers from Christchurch. There are four rope tows, accommodations in heated dormitory-style huts ($NZ25 with three meals) and lift tickets for nonmembers going for $NZ22. *The North Island's two commercial ski areas are on either side of 9174-foot Mount Ruapehu, an active, often smoldering volcano and the tallest mountain on the North Island; N.B. The slopes have been closed now and then these past few years when the volcano started belching; expect anything.* Both areas are inside **Tongariro National Park**, about 350 kilometers equidistant from Wellington and Auckland. The two areas are:

Whakapapa

☎ *(07) 892-3738.*

It has 43 trails on 3322 acres of terrain, with a total vertical drop of 675 meters (2214 feet). Among the lifts available are two quad chairs, five doubles and six T-bars. It has about a dozen advanced trails, some very hairy. It has three cafés and a restaurant. No accommodations.

Turoa

☎ *(06) 385-8456.*

The drop here is 720 meters (2362 feet), with about 900 acres of skiable terrain. It has two quads, two triples and three T-bars, plus other lifts. Like Whakapapa, it's possible to ski down to the bubbling lake in the mountain's crater. It has three cafés and a restaurant; no accommodations.

South Island commercial slopes include the following:

Mount Lyford

☎ *(03) 315-6178.*

Lyford has a vertical drop of 1000 meters (3281 feet) and only four rope tows. The lift tickets are about half the cost of other developed areas, however. It's about 140 kilometers north of Christchurch. It has a café, chalets for rent. Close-on accommodations are available at Waiau, 23 kilometers from the mountain, or at Hanmer Springs, about 50 kilometers away.

Rainbow Valley

☎ *(03) 521-1861.*

The farthest north of the commercial areas on the South Island, with much better slopes than Lyford. *It has some short but nasty advanced slopes* (Dick's Drop comes to mind), but a lot of intermediate territory. It has a vertical drop of only 322 meters (1056 feet). It's about 140 kilometers southwest of Nelson. It has a café, no accommodations. Road toll. Accommodations are available at St. Arnaud, about 30 kilometers from the ski area.

Porter Heights

☎ *(03) 379-7087.*

This is the closest ski area to Christchurch (90 kilometers), and has what many Kiwi skiers rate as *two of the best advanced runs in the country:* Big Mama and Bluff Face (we're talking damned near vertical drops). The owners have installed a snow board run. The Heights also has the honor of being one of the few ski areas that has on-site accommodation—a 40-bed bunkhouse-style facility with meal service. The area has a vertical drop of 670 meters (about 2200 feet), three T-bars and other lifts. Road toll.

Mount Hutt

☎ *(03) 302-8811.*

This is the prestige ski area in New Zealand, host to the first-ever World Cup ski races held in New Zealand. It sits in a huge bowl at the top of the mountain, with virgin powder fields at the top accessible only by helicopter. In addition, it has about 900 acres of skiable terrain, with 10 lifts including a quad, a triple and three T-bars. It has an advanced snowmaking system, which means it opens in May, closes in November. It has a restaurant, café and snack shop. It's about 100 kilometers from Christchurch. Road toll. There are no accommodations, but the resort village of Methven, about 25 kilometers away, has almost 30 lodges and motels.

Mount Dobson

☎ *(03) 685-8039.*

As yet a small operation, Mount Dobson sits in a nice range of peaks near Lake Tekapo about 100 kilometers northwest of Timaru. With only a 415-meter drop (1360 feet), it's not the longest of areas, but *there are some short and tricky advanced runs* and huge areas of challenging intermediate stuff. It has only one T-bar and several other tows. It has a café.

Ohau

☎ *(03) 438-9885.*

This area claims the longest T-bar in New Zealand, 1033 meters (3390 feet) and has a very nice and very reasonable lodge on site (which is noted for some of the biggest ski parties in New Zealand). A double is about $NZ100-130, which includes breakfast; special rates on lift tickets. The area has a vertical drop of about 1300 feet, and overlooks Lake Ohau where the lodge is situated. It's about 150 kilometers from Oamaru.

The five Queenstown-area commercial regions:

The Remarkables

☎ *(03) 442-4615.*

Named after the mountains that overlook the city, this area is about 20 kilometers north of town on the Invercargill highway. If you go all the way up the Shadow Basin chairlift, you get an incredible view of Lake Wakatipu and Queenstown. *It has a 325-meter vertical drop (about 1070 feet), two quads and a double.* It has a self-service restaurant; road toll. Like all the Queenstown-area facilities, buses run from town to the ski area and back. Note: None of the buses is free; expect to pay around $NZ20 for a round-trip; the good news is that most of them will pick you up at your hotel. Combination lift tickets are available that let you also ski nearby Coronet Peak.

Coronet Peak

☎ *(03) 442-4620.*

This is the oldest area around Queenstown, and while quite popular and well admired for some of its runs, is *subject to chancy snow conditions because of its relatively low top altitude* (although snowmaking equipment has now been installed). It has a 428-meter drop (about 1400 feet), with a quad, one triple, a double and a T-bar. It has two cafés and a restaurant; no road fee.

Cardrona

☎ *(03) 443-7411.*

Fully 75 percent of this sprawling area is set aside for beginner and intermediate, and was the site of the 1991 national snowboard championships. *It has two quads and a double.* There are two cafés and a restaurant; road fee. It's about 60 kilometers from Queenstown, which is easily spotted on a clear day from the top of the Captain's Quad.

Treble Cone

☎ *(03) 443-7443.*

This is where the experts come to play, with 40 percent of the slopes devoted to advanced trails. The vertical drop is 660 meters (about 2165 feet). There are several nice beginners' slopes as well as some aggressive intermediate. *There is also an excellent snowboard run.* The best advanced run is named—what else—Top Gun. It has a six-seater express tow, one double and two T-bars. It's about 100 kilometers from Queenstown.

Ski-planes on the Tasman Glacier

Waioru Nordic area

☎ *(03) 443-7541.*

This is the South Island's premier cross-country facility, opened in 1989. *It is the only nordic-only area in the country*, offering about 25 kilometers of groomed

Whale-watching, Kaikoura

Pohutu Geyser, Rotorua, shoots water 100 ft. into the air.

Franz Josef Glacier is seven miles long and is a good place for helicopter trips and hikes.

Waterfall at Milford Sound

Mountain biking at Milford

Governor's Bay, Queen Charlotte

Punch Bowl Falls, Arthur's Pass

Clutha Riverjet, Wanaka

Snowboarding

Tawhai Falls, Ruapehu

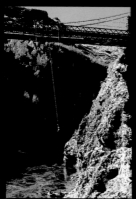
Bungy jumping at Kawarau Gorge

Pristine Beach, Coromandel

trails—about 10k of which are beginners' trails. There is a ski rental shop, cafeteria and huts for overnight ski treks. The area is near Cardrona, about 50 kilometers from Queenstown. Fees are $NZ20 for adults; equipment rental about $NZ10. The season is July–September.

Heli-Skiing

Heli-skiing is popular all over the Southern Alps, including what some folks think is the greatest experience of all, skiing down the Tasman Glacier. The company to talk to about getting off the beaten path is **Harris Mountains**, a heli-ski outfit based in Queenstown and Wanaka. A three-run day will cost about $NZ535–600 depending on season. ☎ *(03) 443-7930 in Wanaka.*

First, they recommend that in order to try heli-skiing, you should be able to ski at least intermediate level. Normally, they will take you in a group of five or six similarly experienced skiers. The company offers 280 runs on 140 peaks on six separate mountain ranges, with runs varying between *2000-* and *4000-*foot vertical drops. The company builds its trips around the total vertical feet you can ski. For instance, you could shoot for the 100,000-foot vertical drop total, taking 12 days and 13 nights, for around $NZ8000, including accommodations, meals, guides and the helicopter lifts.

One of the country's major chopper companies, The Helicopter Line, runs heli-skiing trips from the east side of the mountains. The trips, which normally take skiers into the range of peaks known as the Ben Ohaus Range, start from the helicopter base at Glentanner about 25 kilometers south of Mount Cook on the shores of Lake Pukaki. A day's trip will normally include three or four runs for about 3,000 vertical feet or so. The company also has trips onto the Tasman Glacier. Information is available from Southern Alps Guiding, Box 32, Mt. Cook National Park, New Zealand; ☎ *(03) 435-1890 fax and phone, or free* ☎ *(0800) 650-651;* Glentanner base is ☎ *435-1855,* or contact the Helicopter Line offices in Fox Glacier or Franz Josef.

On the other side of the mountains, **Alpine Guides** also runs heli-skiing trips, including the ride up to the Tasman and Fox glaciers, plus runs on Mount Cook for advanced skiers. These trips cost about $NZ450, which seems to be the normal fee charged by most heli-skiing companies. Further information is included in a free ski guide available from the New Zealand Tourism Board in Santa Monica. ☎ *(310) 395-7480 or* ☎ *(800) 388-5494; FAX (310) 395-5453.*

Cycling

Mountain bikers enjoy Otago's scenery.

The scenic views and lack of traffic along New Zealand's highways make for almost ideal cycling tours of the country. On the South Island, especially, there are challenges for the experienced biker or easy riding for novices—or lazy types. And New Zealanders, unlike folks in some parts of the world, don't go out of their way to force cyclists into ditches or off cliffs.

There are bike rental agencies in most major cities and tourist centers. Or, you can book them ahead from North America. One company worth a try is **Pedaltours of New Zealand**. Tours can be road cycling or mountain biking or a combination of both, lasting from a week to 20 days or so, with routes on both North and South Islands. Prices, depending on itineraries and duration, run from about $NZ1500 to $NZ4000, which includes accommodations, meals and transfers; airfares extra. The company also arranges hiking packages. Information and brochures are available by contacting **Down Under Answers**, *12115 100th Avenue, NE-Kirkland, WA 98034;* ☎ *(800) 788-6685; FAX (206) 820-5571.*

Another good bet is **Adventure South Limited**, a company based in Christchurch that offers bicycle trips all over the South Island. A 10-day trip in the Milford Sound area, including bike hire, meals and accommodations, will run about $NZ2100. Contact the company at *P.O. Box 33-153 in Christchurch;* ☎ *(03) 332-1222; FAX (03) 332-4030.*

Cyclers enjoy a picnic under Nikau palms at Punakaiki.

THE PERFECT
VACATION

If you're into budget group tours, try the trips offered by **Flying Kiwi**. The company's buses are designed for groups of 20 or so, and come equipped with kitchen, shower, share tents and equipment. In addition to cycling tours, the company also does hiking and other outdoor activities. A 24-day "Grand Traverse" trip on the South Island runs about $NZ1200. Information from **Flying Kiwi**, *Deer Park Road, Koromiko, R.D. 3, Blenheim, New Zealand;* ☎ *(03) 573-8126; fax same number.*

For those of you who like to stay up late and watch reruns of *Easy Rider*, and pretend you're some kind of depraved Hog pilot, we note that several companies are offering motorcycle rentals and tours in New Zealand and Australia. On the North Island, try **Liberty Motorcycle Tours**, based in Auckland, for trips to the Bay of Islands, the Coromandel Peninsula, Rotorua and other scenic spots. Rates run from one-day at about $NZ300 per person to $NZ1270 for a five-day trip. Information ☎ *(09) 812-8685.*

Beach's Motorcycle Adventures, a New York–based company, does two- or three-week tours on both islands using mostly BMW K75 cycles. A three-week tour will run $US3650 for rider, $US2750 for a passenger. Two-week tours are $US2600 rider, $US1900 passenger; single occupancy available. The price includes accommodations and some meals. **Beach's**, *2763 W. River Parkway, Grand Island, NY 14072;* ☎ *(716) 773-4960; free brochure.*

For equestrians, many riding areas and stables can be found on both islands. Information is available from the International League for the Protection of Horses New Zealand Ltd., which works through New Zealand tourism offices.

THE ESSENTIAL
NEW ZEALAND

A Clutha river jet speeds through Wanaka.

Helpful Hints and Insider Tips

When to Go

The weather in New Zealand, being Down Under, is upside down compared with North America. Seasons below the equator are reversed; thus summer in New Zealand is December–February; fall is March–May; winter is June–August and spring is September–November. Generally, the North Island is warmer than the South Island, although, as noted, it snows in parts of

the North Island, sometimes enough to block major highways and cause all sorts of horrid driving conditions. *And the hottest temperatures in the nation are likely to hit on the northeastern end of the South Island.* In the winter, you are almost guaranteed lousy traveling conditions on the west coast of the South Island as storms roar in across the Tasman and drop gallons of water or stiffer precipitation. Even in the shoulder seasons, spring and fall, it's not uncommon to run into weeklong periods of rain and fog. Many a visitor has been disappointed driving down the highway expecting to see grand views of the Alps, but because of low clouds and rain, never catching sight of towering Mount Cook or the glaciers. Aside from the west coast of the South Island, *the heaviest rainfall totals are found around the Bay of Plenty on the North Island, which gets something like 65 inches a year.*

Wellington—Windy Wellington, sitting on the Cook Strait—also rains at the drop of the hat, averaging about 50 inches a year. Sometimes down south, it seems the storms are definitely anti-Yank. They hit the west coast and start going counterclockwise, and if you're driving the same way, say from Greymouth to Invercargill and up to Christchurch, the deluges follow right along. After three days of seeing nothing but windshield wipers and wet sheep, you will wonder why you came. But another group of tourists, just a few days behind you, will have nothing but bright sunlight all the way. Note also that it's not unusual to have a nasty storm roar in during the summer, chilling the air and dampening the party. It can get plumb hot too, especially the Canterbury Plains where Christchurch sits. Christchurch has been known to get well above 100 degrees. Still, in spite of the sometimes iffy weather, we think the best times to see New Zealand are in the off-seasons. Airfares tend to be lower, all the Kiwi kids are in school, the hot tourist spots are nearly vacant and you can drive around for hours, particularly on the South Island, and see maybe two cars an hour. In the summertime, by contrast, especially during the Christmas holidays, it's almost impossible to get your RV aboard the Cook Strait ferries because they've been booked for sometimes a year ahead. And given a complete choice, *we'd opt for February–April, when things tend to be just a bit more settled.*

The only way to approach New Zealand weather is with a leery eye. It's no joke that some days, you get all four seasons in an hour, and the chance of rain is almost a universal given. It's a good idea to take an umbrella and rain gear. And a periscope. Wait till you get there to buy a sweater, however.

How to Get There

New Zealand is about 6500 miles southwest of San Francisco, 4600 miles from Honolulu, 1300 miles from Australia—in any direction, a long haul.

Mt. Tarawera can be seen by 4-WD or helicopter.

By Plane

While cruise ships do call in from time to time, flying is the obvious way to get there. The cheapest fares will be from the West Coast, and folks living back East will have to add the time—and the money— needed to get to Los Angeles, San Francisco or Honolulu onto their travel plans. In some instances, as we have noted, a trip to New Zealand is part of a package that includes Australia. Often these itineraries begin in Australia, then fly from Sydney to either Wellington or Auckland. The major international airport in New Zealand is in Auckland, where most West Coast- or Hawaii-originated flights will land. The airport, about 14 miles outside town, is new and modern and split into two parts, domestic and international, about a quarter-mile apart. A taxi from the airport to town costs about $NZ35; an airporter bus which hits the main hotels is about $NZ10. There are also international airports at Wellington and Christchurch.

The only U.S. company currently serving New Zealand is United Airlines. Canadian International and Air Pacific fly from Canada. Most of the Los Angeles–Auckland flights are nonstop; flights from San Francisco and Vancouver normally stop in Honolulu. Most West Coast flights leave between 8 and 10 p.m., arriving in Auckland early in the morning, but because of the International Dateline, you lose a day overnight. Some flights on Air New Zealand are routed through Wellington. Major foreign airlines are Air New Zealand (the national carrier), Qantas (the Australian national carrier) and UTA (part of Air France). Polynesian Airlines (Western Samoa) has service to Auckland from Los Angeles through Samoa. Fares from the West Coast depend on when you go. In the off-seasons, expect to pay about $US800–900 per person for a round-trip ticket. In high season (Kiwi summer), fares will run around $US900–1000. New Zealand needs tourist dollars, and it seems there are always some very attractive packages to lure us down, many offering free or reduced rates on cars or campers or accommodations. To check on what current deals are available, contact the airlines, the New Zealand Tourism Board, your local newspaper ads or your travel agent. We fancy Air New Zealand because of its service and relatively young fleet of aircraft. Also, the airline has the Coral Route, a ticketing scheme that lets you stop at a number of Pacific destinations going to or from New Zealand or Australia. Break up your trip with a few days in Fiji or the Cook Islands. Current airline policy is that you don't have to reconfirm international flights; we do anyway. The Coral Route ticket, depending on itinerary, will run about $US1300. We'd also like to take a minute here to lay a kudo or two on Air New Zealand: other airlines, please pay heed. The airline, realizing that sitting in a cramped seat for 10 hours or more makes tourists seriously unhappy, has expanded the legroom in all its 747s and 767s. The pitch (distance between seats) is now 34 inches, huzzah. It's a start, mates. Information on Air New Zealand packages: ☎ *(800) 438-2543* or ☎ *(800) 262-1234* For Qantas, ☎ *(800) 227-4500* and United ☎ *(800) 241-6522.*

NOTE: *New Zealand charges a $NZ20 airport international departure tax that must be paid at the airport in New Zealand currency. However, major credit cards may be used in lieu of Kiwi dollars. Some domestic airports are also pondering a departure tax—keep some cash handy. Also note that on some international tickets, the departure fee is prepaid; check with your travel agent before departure.*

Formalities

Passports are required for U.S. and Canadian citizens. They must be valid for at least three months after the passenger's arrival in New Zealand. Entry permits will be issued at the airport on arrival and are good for three months. New Zealand, like Australia, is free of many diseases prevalent in other parts of the world—such as rabies—and wants to keep it that way. You will have to fill out a declaration form listing what foods, plants or animal materials you are carrying. *Fishers note: You can bring rod, reel and lures, but no flies made from chicken feathers* (if in doubt, leave the flies at home). There is no limit on the amount of currency, foreign or New Zealand, that can be brought into the country. There are **currency exchange** offices at the Auckland airport and at most banks in towns and cities. Visitors can bring in these amounts of taxable goods: 200 cigarettes, or 250 grams of tobacco, or 50 cigars or a mixture of all three weighing not more than 250 grams (about 8 ounces);

4.5 liters of wine (six regular-sized bottles of wine, 750 milliliters) and a quart bottle of booze (not to exceed 1125 milliliters).

Medicine

New Zealand's liberal medical services are not extended free to visitors. The Kiwi government strongly recommends that you have health insurance that covers personal problems overseas. Some American HMOs and **health insurance** companies do have overseas coverage. Check with your company or insurance agent, before leaving. **Trip insurance**, which can cover everything from lost luggage to major medical emergencies, is available from travel agents. A policy we looked at, for example, offered a US$50,000 policy for about US$200. It included death and dismemberment coverage, as well as lost luggage and trip cancellation insurance. It also included enough money to ship your body home if you died overseas. We raise this because a couple from California was killed in New Zealand, and the family did not have enough money to ship the bodies home. The U.S. government will not pay for such services, nor will the governments of most foreign nations. *Visitors are covered, however, for accidents. Under New Zealand law, you are entitled to benefits as the result of an accident, regardless of blame.* Benefits normally include hospitalization and medical treatment. New Zealand, because of its isolation, has no dangerous reptiles or other nasties— except for one very rare, semi-dangerous spider; see "Animals." It's a good idea to bring a prescription for any drugs you might carry into New Zealand to avoid trouble with customs; also you'll need a prescription to get refills for some medicines.

Money, Weights and Measures

The Kiwis, like the Americans, Canadians, Australians and a bunch of others, call their currency the dollar. It always causes confusion in prices to have all those different dollars running around. *All prices in this book, unless otherwise noted, are in New Zealand dollars* because of the fluctuations in the exchange rates between our dollars and theirs. The mid-1990s exchange rate is somewhere around 60 to 70 cents U.S. to the New Zealand dollar. Kiwi banknotes come in 5-, 10-, 20-, 50- and 100-dollar denominations. Coins come in 5-, 10-, 20- and 50-cent pieces, plus $NZ1 and $NZ2 coins. Banks are normally open from 9:30 a.m.–4:30 p.m., Monday–Friday, but some also have currency exchange windows open on Saturdays and some holidays.

Major credit cards are accepted everywhere—especially MasterCard and Visa. Foreign currency traveler's checks are accepted by large hotels, banks and resorts. *Note that most places will not accept foreign currency traveler's checks.* Everybody seems to take New Zealand traveler's checks—you might think about changing your Yankee checks into Kiwi ones to save bank time. Gas stations and dairies (the corner market) are usually open seven days. We found that Westpac branches will not charge to cash American Express traveler's checks; there is, however, a NZ5-cent government tax per check. Westpac also sells Amex checks.

Weights and measures are officially metric, although you'll find many folks still hanging in with the old English measures. It wouldn't be uncommon to hear somebody measuring a board say it was "two meters and about a quarter-inch." And in some parts of the country, they still figure beer in ounces and vow to never give in to the metric system. Canadians, who have already gone metric, will supposedly have no problems. For Americans, all you need to know is that gasoline comes in liters, distances are posted in kilometers, temperatures are in Celsius and things are weighed in kilograms. It's not that tough. If you're in a rental car, the speedometer is in kilometers, so if the limit is 60, just drive 60 and forget miles. (If you absolutely have to know, multiply the number of kilometers by .62 and you'll get the miles.) For temperatures, just remember water freezes at 0, 20 is mild, 30 is hot and if it's 40, you're probably in the Canterbury Plain area in mid-summer and need a cold beer immediately. A kilogram is about 2.2 pounds. If you forget all this, don't worry, just ask somebody. After all, they've only been at this metric business a few years themselves.

Electricity

New Zealand current is 230 volts, 50 hertz. Just to be difficult, the usual European two-round-prong plug is not used. Instead, they use a three-pronged flat plug that looks like a smaller version of the plugs Americans use on electric clothes driers. Many international travel kits have a plug that will work in New Zealand and Australia (two, rather than three prongs, but they're okay) and converter plugs can be found in some department stores and camping outlets in New Zealand. The kits are a good idea, anyway, because most contain a 50-watt or 1600-watt transformer in case you're carrying appliances that won't convert to 220. If you're going upscale, forget all the electricity differences, because *most high-grade hotels in the country have 110-volt outlets and 200-volt irons and hair dryers in the bathrooms,* or if not, loaner transformers will do the job. (Many of the 110 outlets will not safely handle hair driers and other high-wattage appliances, however.)

Phones

Phone service is efficient and relatively expensive. Local calls are NZ20 cents a minute. Overseas calls from pay phones are high, in the neighborhood of $NZ3 a minute to North America. We find the easiest way to call home is by using AT&T's USA Direct service. Just dial 000-911 and you'll be connected to a Ma Bell line; you can then call collect or charge the call. Note: Some hotels will still bill you for access to the AT&T number, a practice we find really snotty. So we normally just go to a pay phone and do it for free. *Most pay phones will not accept coins. Instead, they take plastic cards with magnetized strips* that come in various denominations from $NZ5 to $NZ50. Just stick the card in the phone, dial your New Zealand number, and the fee is automatically deducted from the card. A display on the phone tells you how much money is left on the card. The cards, which can be bought in many local stores displaying a Telecom PhoneCard sign, are quite colorful, showing various scenes from New Zealand life. *The phone numbers we list in this book are subject to change.* Currently, New Zealand numbers, like those in Australia, are not standardized. Some places have seven digits, some five or six. The New Zealand government phone service, Telecom, is trying to standardize numbers. So if a number we listed turns out to be completely wrong, we apologize. *The emergency number in most localities to summon police or fire is 111—no coin or card required.* You get the operator by dialing 010; for directory information, 018. To reach an international operator, dial 0170. To call home, dial 00 and then the country code; in the case of the United States and Canada, the country code is 1, followed by the area code and phone number. If you do much calling in New Zealand, you'll soon run into the Kiwi habit of doubling and tripling numbers when they talk. For instance, an American would read this phone number—544-1117—as "five-four-four, one-one-one-seven." But the Kiwis would say "five-double four, triple one-seven," which, when spoken rapidly and with a New Zealand accent, can be most confusing. They also double and triple street addresses.

Time

New Zealand is just the other side of the International Date Line from North America, so it's always ahead of us. Like Tonga, it's close enough to the dateline for New Zealanders to claim that they live where time begins. (Auckland sits at about 175 degrees east latitude.) Anyway, New Zealand is 12 hours ahead of Greenwich Mean Time. That means from April-October, it's 20 hours ahead of Los Angeles. And that means when it's noon in Wellington, it's 4 p.m. the day before in Los Angeles. So you want to call home? One way to make it a little easier is just forget the 20-hour bit and figure that Wellington is four hours behind Los Angeles, but a day ahead. Make sense? If it's 10 a.m. Monday in Wellington, then it's four hours later in San Francisco, or 2 p.m., but a day earlier, or Sunday. The country goes on daylight savings time from October to March. The easy way around the whole thing is to buy a watch with room for two times zones, or not to call home.

Getting Around

Many of the special packages offered by New Zealand or North American agencies combine air travel with either a rental car or RV. There are also many fly/car-drive packages that include accommodations. We discuss motoring vacations in the "Driving Down Under" section later in this chapter. *For those who simply can't afford to drive, or because of one thing and another will not drive in New Zealand, there are still many options that will let you get out and around to see the country.* In fact, we know of no other country that makes it so easy to see it all, whether you're a backpacker or a stock broker.

Leave the Driving...

At the top of the list are dozens and dozens of bus tours, which is a very good way to see the country—New Zealand has an excellent group of tour operators who can tailor a guided vacation to your special needs or desires. You can stay in New Zealand private homes, farms, B&Bs, motels, top hotels, hostels. Or you can do your own bus tour on your own time at your own pace. A bus in New Zealand, by the way, is called a "coach." **Guided bus tours** come in all sizes, all shapes, all itineraries. Generally, a tour of sights and attractions on both islands is set on a 12-day schedule, although there are a number of tours that go longer. Prices also vary widely, depending on style of accommodation, destination, meal policy and tour length. We saw one trip advertised for 16 days around both islands for about $US2300 per person, not including international air and including two meals a day. But another company was offering a 14-day tour of both islands for $US2000 per person, including round-trip air from the U.S., accommodations and breakfasts. So you have to shop around. In addition to the grand tours, it is also possible to take short bus tours around interesting spots. For instance, one Kiwi company was offering a three-day tour from Auckland to Rotorua for about $NZ430 per person, double occupancy. The price included most meals, guided tours and superior accommodations. There is also an hour and a half tour of Auckland for $NZ20, or take a coach tour of the city followed by dinner on a sailing yacht for about $NZ80—endless possibilities. Many of these bus tours can be booked from North America; or if you choose, you can wait until you get to New Zealand.

Reservations are probably a good thought in the summer for some of the more popular tours, such as Queenstown or Te Anau to the Milford Sound. But, you say, you hate tour groups, wouldn't be caught dead on a tour bus, want to do it your way or no way at all. Not to worry. New Zealand has an extensive **public transportation** system. The major bus line is *InterCity*, which also operates the nation's passenger train service, both of which connect to the Interislander vehicle and passenger ferry service between the two islands.

Buses

The buses go to more than 1000 communities and all major tourist spots. This means *with a travel pass from InterCity, you can see the whole country without buying additional tickets.* The **InterCity Travel** line offers the Tiki Tours Coach Pass. The pass comes in three types: seven days of travel in a 14-day period for about $NZ395; 14 day's travel in a 30-day period, about $NZ495, and 21 days in a 42-day period, about $NZ595. The passes can be purchased in North America from travel agents, or in New Zealand.

InterCity also has two forms of what it calls the Travelpass, which combines coach, rail airline and inter-island ferries. The "Three-in-One" pass covers rail, bus and ferry service only and starts at about $NZ350 (five days of travel in a 10-day period) and goes up to $NZ700 (22 days travel in an eight-week period). The "Four-in-One" adds one flight sector on Air New Zealand to the package. This pass starts at about $NZ600 for five days of travel in a 10-day period, up to about $NZ950 for 22 days of travel in an eight-week period. The air/ground pass starts at about $NZ700 for the eight-day/three-week package. The company also has a special pass for backpackers, good for 30 days. It combines the InterCity buses, the Interislander ferries and most trains with a special backpacker's bus, the Kiwi Safari. The bus (actually several buses) runs from Auckland to Wellington and back, and from Picton to Queenstown to Christchurch to Picton. You can get on and off the buses at will as long as you confirm your seat. Using the Kiwi Experience and the other buses and trains, you can pretty much go where you want, when you want. Note: Most all public transport services offer senior citizen discounts. InterCity, for example, has a 30 percent discount, as does Mount Cook Line.

Presently, the backpacker passes are not available in North America, but can be purchased at InterCity offices or travel agencies in New Zealand. The passes are actually a packet of vouchers. Two vouchers are used for a train trip, for example, or one for each InterCity bus trip. The prices are 10 vouchers, about $NZ315; 15 vouchers, $NZ420, and 20 vouchers, about $NZ525. InterCity also has a **Youth Hostel Association** pass. The pass gives you 50 percent off on all InterCity services except sight-seeing buses. The 14-day card is about $NZ80 or 28-day for about $NZ110. Another choice in the South Island is Mount Cook Landline, which serves most of the major southern cities. The company offers the **Kiwi Coach Pass**, which is used in conjunction with other bus companies to provide service to the whole country. The pass, depending on what season you travel, starts at seven days during an 11-day period for about $NZ330 to 33 days in a 45-day period starting at about $NZ700. Passes are available both in New Zealand or from travel agents at home. A North Island alternative is **Newmans Coach Lines**, which also uses other bus lines for additional service. The Newmans passes are good either for one island or both. Two-island, seven-day passes are about $NZ400, 15-day about $NZ600. The one-island passes are about $NZ300 for seven days, about $NZ500 for a 15-day pass. The company also has a 14-day one-way Wellington-Auckland or Auckland-Wellington pass (many stops allowed) for $NZ99. The passes can be purchased before or after arrival in New Zealand. Newmans Coach Lines operates an express bus service between Wellington and Auckland called the Starlighter. The nightly service leaves Auckland at around 7:50 p.m., arrives in Wellington at 6:50 a.m; hours from Wellington to Auckland are the same. The service costs about $NZ65 one way.

Air Travel

There are three major domestic airlines in New Zealand: **Air New Zealand**, **Ansett New Zealand** and **Mount Cook Airlines**. All three have travel passes. Air New Zealand offers the Explorer Pass, which is good for three sectors (minimum) at $NZ495, up to eight sectors for $NZ1320 per person. Other discounts are also available. Ansett has the See New Zealand Fares, which represents a saving of about 30 percent on internal travel. The pass can be purchased either inside or outside New Zealand. Note, however, that tickets purchased before arrival are not subject to the current 12.5 percent goods and services tax. Mount Cook's reductions are covered by its **Kiwi Air Pass**, which also allows discounts on the airlines' flight-seeing trips to the glaciers and other destinations. The pass can be purchased before or after arrival. The cost is about $NZ900. The domestic airlines use a combination of modern short-haul aircraft, including 737s, BAE Whisperjets and Dash 8s. If you are not on an air pass, here are some samples of one-way fares: Auckland-Christchurch, $NZ320; Auckland-Queenstown, $NZ540; Wellington-Christchurch, $NZ200; Auckland-Wellington, $NZ240.

Train Travel

Modern, fairly fast, efficient, comfortable—if train trips are to your liking, several routes in New Zealand are right up your tracks. They're less expensive than air travel and a bit smoother than buses. The main cities are routinely served, as are several scenic routes. *As noted, the InterCity passes are also good for rail travel.* Most trains are nonsmoking. We have heard very few complaints about Kiwi trains. They do tend to keep them a bit overheated in the winter, the legroom and seats are a tad small and the overhead storage is undersized. **The Silver Fern** is the daytime commuter special between Auckland and Wellington. The trip, about 430 miles, takes about 10 hours, and leaves both ways Monday–Saturday at around 8:30 a.m. Morning and afternoon snacks, as well as lunch are served; bar service is available. The cost is about $NZ100 one way. Overnight, non-sleeper service between the two cities is available on the **Northerner**, which leaves both ways around 8 p.m. and arrives around 6:40 a.m. Light meals are for sale, as are tickets to a lounge where videos are screened. The cost is about $NZ75. **The Coastal Pacific** runs from Christchurch to Picton daily along the east coast of the South Island, often offering some very nice scenery. (Sit on the right side going north.) The daily service leaves Christchurch at 8:10 a.m. and arrives in time to catch the 2:20 p.m. ferry to Wellington—the ferry doesn't sail until the train arrives. Southbound, the train leaves at 2 p.m. and arrives in Christchurch at 7:25 p.m. It's a nonsmoking car and has food and beverage service. The cost is about $NZ50 one way. One of the more popular trips is on the daily **Tranz Alpine Express**, which runs from Christchurch up over Arthur's Pass to Greymouth. The trip over to Greymouth and back can be done in a long day. The express leaves Christchurch at 7 a.m., arriving in Greymouth at 12:25 p.m. You can take a bus tour of Greymouth during the hour or so you're there, which is no big deal. The return trip starts at 1:40 p.m. and you return to Christchurch around 6 p.m. The scenery is marvelous, and you'll marvel at the engineering, including about 20 tunnels, one of which is about five miles long. Food and bar service available. Round-trip cost for the trip is about $NZ235, including hotel transfers in Christchurch.

Information in Christchurch: ☎ *(03) 359-9133; FAX 359-9058.* **The South-erner** is the main South Island route, and runs from Christchurch down the east coast to Invercargill, Monday–Friday. It leaves Christchurch about 8:40 a.m., arrives in Dunedin around 2:30 p.m., then Invercargill around 6:10 p.m. The same service leaves Invercargill at 9:20 a.m., arriving in Christchurch around 7 p.m. Buffet car and bar service are available. One way is about $NZ70. In addition to these express trains, there is other service on slower, less-scheduled timetables between major cities, as well as service to smaller communities and resort areas.

Across the Strait

It was the last crossing of the day, leaving Picton about 7:45 p.m., and it was one of those nights—windy, spitting rain, cold. Behind the ticket agent in the Picton Interislander Ferry office is a big wheel with an arrow on it to tell passengers at a glance what the sea conditions are like. While we watched, he moved it from bad to worst: high seas, lousy visibility, a nightmare for anybody who gets even remotely seasick. It was an interesting crossing, seas running very high, big car ferry heeling over and over until the decks seemed to almost touch the water. They closed the bars and only a few people were wandering around. Three hours of either hell or fascination, depending on your inner ear. We raise this only to point out that *the Cook Strait separating the North and South Islands can be very wicked*—so bad that on rare occasions the crossings are cancelled.

By Ferry

It's the only break in a 900-mile stretch of mountains, and the roaring Forties are funneled through the strait with a vengeance. Winds of up to 150 miles an hour have been recorded at Wellington. But it's not always a tempest—on other trips we've taken, it's been almost like glass. *That's the way it goes in New Zealand—if you don't like the weather, wait a minute.* New Zealand is fairly rare, as countries go, because it is divided in two by water. Maybe some day in the distant future, they'll build a bridge over the strait (about 15 miles across at the narrowest point), but in the meantime, if you want to go north or south you either fly or take the ferry.

For North Americans, it's amazing to discover there are a number of New Zealanders who have never visited one island or the other. Take the trip in the daytime, at least one crossing. *The scenery is wonderful, particularly coming out of Picton, up Queen Charlotte Sound and into the strait.* It reminded us of the trip between Helsinki and Stockholm, fir trees and islands and fjordlike waters. Coming into Wellington, you are greeted by hundreds of seabirds, especially large Dominican and red-billed gulls. *The Interislander line makes the crossing quite comfortable on its two modern passenger/vehicle ferries, the Arahura and Aratika,* plus the freight ship, *Arahanga,* which has limited vehicle space. Both the passenger ships are equipped for handicapped travel (elevators, special toilets), and come with all the amenities you'd expect on a small cruise ship—cafeterias, restaurants, fast-food outlets, movie theaters, bars, observation lounges, souvenir shops, arcade games, kiddy play areas, television. The crossing, depending on the weather gods, takes about three hours. The food is good, not great. But the beer is cold.

The normal schedule calls for three or four sailings each way all week, with the first around 1:30 a.m. from Wellington or 5:30 a.m. from Picton, and the last crossing at 6:40 p.m. from Wellington, 7:40 p.m. from Picton. Service is restricted on Mondays. The fare schedule depends on the time of year, and is divided into standard and off-peak seasons. The fare periods are fairly complicated and subject to change, and should be checked before leaving for New Zealand. A number of discounted fares are available, including senior citizen rates. Some approximate sample fares: During off-peak periods, passengers on foot, one way, are about $NZ30 per person. But if all you want to do is ride the ferry as an outing, a one-day excursion fare for a round-trip is also $NZ30; the excursion tickets must be purchased a week in advance. During standard periods, add about $NZ10 to these fares. Kids under 4 travel free. Two passengers plus a small RV would be about $NZ120 in the bargain periods, and about $NZ150 in the standard periods. Good deals are available if you travel on any weekend, except the period between early December and mid-February. This is holiday time in New Zealand, and spaces are often reserved a year in advance, especially vehicle spaces. Under New Zealand law, the ships must undergo safety and maintenance surveys once a year, so there will be periods when only two of the three will be in service. It's important to make reservations during these times.

If you're making the crossing in fall or spring, you probably won't have a problem getting aboard without reservations, but calling ahead is always a smart idea. If you are hoofing it, note that the Picton dock is within walking distance of the train station, and free buses are provided in Wellington to get you from the dock to the trains—except for the ferries that arrive in Wellington after 10 p.m.

If you're in a mad rush, during the summer there's a high-speed multi-hull ferry that makes the crossing in an hour and 45 minutes. The boat, named the Lynx, has three sailing a day. From Wellington, it leaves at 7:30 a.m., 1 p.m. and 6 p.m., arriving at Picton at 9:15 a.m., 2:45 p.m. and 6 p.m. It leaves Picton at 10 a.m., 3:30 p.m. and 8:30 p.m. Passengers are about $NZ60 per person one way; standard cars are $NZ190. The schedule is subject to change and, of course, the weather.

Information

Your first look at New Zealand probably will be in **New Zealand Simply Remarkable,** a magazine-style publication available free from the country's tourism offices in North America. It's a bit lacking in basic information, but does have lots of photographs, suggested itineraries and advertisements from many of the major companies that offer services in New Zealand. The tourism offices also have a number of special interest publications available on such things as fishing, farm stays and adventure travel. The North American offices of the New Zealand Tourism Department are located at *501 Santa Monica Boulevard, No. 300, Santa Monica, CA 90401,* ☎ *(800) 388-5494;* and at the New Zealand consulate at *Suite 1200, 888 Dunsmuir Street, Vancouver, B.C.,* ☎ *(800) 888-5494.* Once in New Zealand, you'll find that every community of any size has a visitor information office where you can check on local attractions, as well as get information on accommodations and food. There are also a number of regional tourism offices.

For informational purposes, New Zealand is broken up into six regions by the New Zealand Tourism Department in Wellington, which are in turn divided into subregions.

Region I, also known as Northland, is all of the country north of Auckland.

Region II takes in Auckland, the Bay of Plenty, Coromandel Peninsula, East Cape, Hawkes Bay, Rotorua and the Lake Taupo area.

Region III is the south half of the North Island, including the area around lovely Mt. Egmont and south to Wellington.

Region IV is basically the west coast and north end of the South Island, including Franz Josef and the Fox glaciers.

Region V is the Canterbury area on the east coast of the South Island, including Christchurch, Mount Cook National Park, Akaroa and Lake Tekapo.

Region VI is the fjord country of the southwest coast, the Otago Peninsula and Dunedin, Stewart Island and the famous Milford Track. Among the many local tourist offices available are the following:

For **Region I**, *the Whangarei Visitors Bureau, Tarewa Park, Otaika Road,* ☎ *(09) 438-1079, FAX (09) 438-2943; open from 8:30 a.m.–5 p.m.* **For Region II**, *Auckland International Airport Visitor Centre, open 24 hours at the International Terminal,* ☎ *(09) 275-6467, FAX (09) 256-1742 or downtown Auckland at 299 Queen Street,* ☎ *(09) 366-6888, FAX (09) 358-4684.* **Region III**, *Wellington City Information Centre, Wakefield Street, Old Town Hall Building,* ☎ *(04) 801-4000, FAX (04) 801-3030; open 9 a.m.–5 p.m.* **Region IV**, *Nelson Visitor Centre, Trafalgar and Halifax streets,* ☎ *(03) 548-2304, FAX (03) 546-9008; open 8 a.m.–5 p.m.* **Region V**, *in Christchurch, the Can-*

terbury Information Centre, Worcester Street and Oxford Terrace, ☎ *(03) 379-9629, FAX (03) 377-2424.* **Region VI**, *Queenstown, New Zealand Travel and Visitors Centre, Shotover and Camp streets,* ☎ *(03) 442-4100, FAX (03) 442-8907.*

Holidays

The major national holiday, the equivalent of the Fourth of July, is **Waitangi Day** on the 6th of February, which commemorates the signing of the Treaty of Waitangi in 1840. Despite mixed feelings in the Maori community, Waitangi Day usually sees a fair share of traditional Maori festivals throughout the country, especially at the spot near Russell where the pact was signed. Other national holidays include **New Year's Day** (January 1), **Good Friday**, **Easter Monday** and **Anzac Day** (commemorating the landing of Australian and New Zealand troops at Gallipoli in 1915, April 25), as well as **Queen's Birthday** (first Monday in June), **Labour Day** (fourth Monday in October), **Christmas Day** (December 25) and **Boxing Day** (normally December 26).

In addition to the national holidays, there are many local observances throughout the year, which might find you facing closed banks and stores. Always check ahead with a local tourist office and with the New Zealand tourism offices in North America. **School holidays** usually mean families are out and about, meaning crowds. The actual dates vary from year to year, but generally expect these school holiday periods: **May holidays**, for both primary and secondary, second to fourth weeks in May; **Mid-term break**, primary and secondary, first two weeks in July; **August holidays**, primary, first two weeks of September; and secondary, last week of August, first two weeks of September; **Christmas holidays**, primary, last two weeks of December, all of January; secondary, last three weeks of December, all of January.

Hours

Normal shopping hours in New Zealand are Monday–Thursday, 9 a.m.–5:30 p.m., Fridays 9 a.m.–9:30 p.m. and Saturdays 10 a.m.–1 p.m. Some stores in tourist areas might be open on Sundays. Banks, as noted, are generally open from 9:30 a.m.–4:30 p.m. Monday–Friday. Post offices are open from 8:30 a.m.–5 p.m. Monday–Thursday and until 8 p.m. Fridays.

Embassies

In case of trouble, both the United States and Canada have embassies in Wellington. U.S. citizens should note that American embassies and their consular sections are limited in the amount and type of help they can offer. They are not travel agencies, they are not banks, they are not welfare agencies. They will not, for example, pay hospital costs or pay for airplane tickets to get you home if you become stranded or critically ill. They can help you by contacting relatives back home and are able to replace passports if they have been lost or stolen. The U.S. embassy is at *29 Fitzherbert Terrace, Thorndon;* ☎ *(04) 472-2068*. The Canadian High Commission is in the *ICI House, Molesworth Street;* ☎ *(04) 473-9577*.

Where to Stay

Fielding's Highest-Rated Hotels in New Zealand

★★★★★	Carlton Hotel, Auckland	$NZ320–1800	*page 299*
★★★★★	Stamford Plaza, Auckland	$NZ340–1500	*page 299*
★★★★★	Nugget Point, Queenstown	$NZ250–375	*page 202*
★★★★★	Parkroyal, Christchurch	$NZ300	*page 149*
★★★★★	Lake Brunner Lodge (near Greymouth)	$NZ400	*page 170*
★★★★	Gardens Parkroyal, Queenstown	$NZ265–360	*page 202*

Fielding's Most Exclusive Hotels in New Zealand

★★★★★	Huka Lodge, Taupo	$NZ1115-1294	*page 340*
★★★★★	Moose Lodge, Rotorua	$NZ441–702	*page 331*
★★★★★	Okaito Lodge, Russell	$NZ620–1180	*page 383*
★★★★★	Kimberley Lodge, Russell	$NZ400–550	*page 383*
★★★★	Puka Park Lodge, Coromandel Peninsula	$NZ290–1540	*page 313*
★★★★	Lilybank Lodge, Lake Tekapo	$NZ1120	*page 256*

Fielding's Best-Value Hotels in New Zealand

★★★	The Hermitage, Mt. Cook	$NZ170–280	*page 260*
★★★★	Stewart Island Lodge	$NZ350	*page 236*
★★★	Château Tongariro	$NZ110–160	*page 346*
★★★	Duke of Marlborough, Russell	$NZ75–200	*page 384*
★★★	Gerrard's Hotel, Invercargill	$$NZ80–95	*page 230*

**Fielding's Best-Value
Hotels in New Zealand**

| ★★ DeBrett's Thermal Hotel, Taupo | $NZ30–90 | *page 343* |
| ★★ Fox Glacier Hotel | $NZ115 | *page 180* |

One of the real joys of a visit to New Zealand is the huge variety of places to hang your hat, everything from farm stays to five-star hotels, trout-fishing lodges to thermal spas, youth hostels to motel chains. And, being New Zealanders, they go out of their way to make it easy to pick your choice. As we have mentioned, government travel agencies, national airlines and North America-based wholesalers and travel agencies are zealously trying to lure travelers Down Under, and there always seem to be some excellent package deals available, almost all of which include accommodations. And in most cases, the choice of accommodations is up to you. One of the very best ways to get up close to New Zealand and its friendly folks is to stay in their homes. There are literally hundreds of home stay places around the country, or if you want to get close to the national animal—the sheep—scads of farms ready to roll out the red carpet. These sorts of accommodations are available to independent travelers on their own way in bus, car or train and are also part of escorted tours.

Home and Farm Stays

There are several nationwide organizations that among them represent nearly all home and farm stay places in the country. Using North American wholesalers and travel agencies, you can book and prepay a whole series of stays allowing you to tour one or both islands. Some samples: **Rural Holidays New Zealand Limited** offers South Island farm stays, complete with three meals, for about $NZ80 per person a night; kids between $NZ30 and $NZ45 depending on age. These rates are without tax.

A typical farm might have sheep and deer, maybe some horses, often a private trout stream, perhaps a tennis court, swimming pool and lots of "tramping" trails. Some are large, most small, and all are willing to show you how the rural life is practiced in Kiwiland. They'll even let you milk the sheep, if you've a mind. If you like set itineraries, **New Zealand Farm Holidays** has self-drive or coach/rail packages covering both islands.

A farmer chats with a visitor to Raikaia Valley.

For instance, a weeklong tour of the South Island, including an unlimited kilometerage, manual rental car, accommodations, meals and insurance, will run about $NZ1800 for a couple. If you have your own rental car, you may purchase accommodations/meal vouchers for around $NZ80 per person per day. There is also a seven-day rail/coach tour for about $NZ1300 per person, which includes transfers from public transportation centers to the farms. Or a four-day, self-drive trip around the North Island goes for about

$NZ700 per couple. Another good bet is the **Farmhouse and Country Home Holidays** group, which also has self-drive or rail coach packages. Prices are comparable to the others; a week self-drive around the North Island will run about $NZ1400.

A farm stay in Hawkes Bay

Heritage Inns, a group of upscale, five-star-rated accommodations, is now operating B&B stays around the country. Rooms in these properties are in the $NZ100–200 a night double range. The 30 or so inns are in historic houses or cottages built before 1940. Examples are the Lisburn House in Dunedin (1865), the Hulbert House in Queenstown (1889), the Peace & Plenty Inn in Auckland, the Cashmere House in Christchurch and Mapledurham in Nelson. Note: Many of these properties indicate they are "not suitable" for small children. The inns at present can be booked at municipal visitors centers around the country. A list of the properties is also available at the centers. There is also a new group of B&Bs called **Hospitality Hosts**, which covers properties on both islands, and can be booked at visitors centers.

Overnight in a Pub?

One interesting group, which we tried several times with great success, is **Pub Beds**. Yes, indeed, they put you up in—or usually over—a friendly Kiwi pub in cities and towns all over the country. The pubs run from historic and quaint to new and modern. Some are hotels with pubs attached; some are pubs with rooms attached. And most are economy priced, and the rooms, while not fancy, are clean. One of our favorites is the **Law Courts in Dunedin**, complete with family restaurant and two very comfy bars for about $NZ75 for a double with private bath.

Another is McFees Warterfront Hotel in the heart of Queenstown, $NZ65 double with private bath. Note: Reservations to the member pubs must be made directly, not through a travel agent. Your host at a member pub will, however, make reservations ahead for you at no cost. For information, contact **Pub Beds**, *Box 32-332, Auckland;* ☎ *(09) 445-4400; FAX (09) 445-1010.*

If you're in Auckland, check with the folks at the **Esplanade Hotel** in Devonport for information about the group. The Esplanade, a Victorian modeled after the Esplanade Hotel in Brighton (England), was restored in 1994. In Rotorua, try the **Grand Hotel**, corner Hinemoa and Fenton streets near the Polynesian Thermal Pools. Members of the group have brochures that entitle you to discounts.

There are several **motel chains** in New Zealand, and in all, there are some 1400 motels and motor inns around the country. Most of the chains have discount passes for tourists. Prices for a good unit will run you between $NZ70 and $NZ100 or so. Many, such as the motels in the Golden Chain group, have kitchen facilities. Popular chains are Flag, Budget and Quality hotels. *Also, New Zealand, like Australia, has the very civilized practice of including an electric kettle and tea/coffee makings in motel rooms.* Most motels can be booked ahead from North America or at member motels in the country after arrival.

New Zealand has a new rating service for accommodations throughout the country called "Qualmark," which replaces the former automobile association ratings. Look for a big blue Q with a silver fern. The rating system, a joint effort of the New Zealand Tourism Board and the New Zealand Automobile Association, is voluntary and ranges from one to five stars. Basically, the more stars, the better—plus more stars also means more services offered.

RV Parks

Another cost-saving alternative is to stay at a caravan park—what we'd call an **RV park**. Many parks have permanent tourist units for rent, either in cabins, small motel-style units or in camper vans. Prices vary, but on-site camper vans will run about $NZ40 per unit, which usually includes cooking gear. Bedding is usually available for rent. Cabins without cooking facilities or hot and cold water will run around $NZ30 per couple; cabins with cooking facilities and water about $NZ40 per couple, and "en suite," or cabins with private bath but no cooking facilities, about $NZ40. The full shot—a tourist flat, complete with private bath and cooking facilities—will run around $NZ50 per couple. We suggest you stick whenever possible to RV parks which are part of either the Top 10 or Kiwi Camps groups.

Youth Hostels

The backpacker business in New Zealand is alive and well—it is, as a matter of fact, a major source of tourism income in the country. About 20 percent of all foreign visitors to the country are backpackers, something like 150,000 a year, and they spend around $NZ3500 each on their stays. The industry has noted that backpackers are no longer just the 18- to 30-year-old crowd. Industry sources say they have noticed a large increase in the number of backpackers using credit cards, an indication that backpacker and budget are no longer synonymous. There are around 300 hostels, ranging from huge (300 beds in Auckland) to tiny (eight beds on Stewart Island). Prices range from around $NZ15 (multiple share) to $NZ45 for doubles. Any tourist office in the country will have a bunch of brochures on local hostels, as well as hostel groups with units around the country. The hostels are generally first-class and are found in big cities, as well as in popular tourist areas. Remember that many will be fully booked during prime vacation times. Most hostels rent bedding, but it's a wise idea to carry a sleeping bag. Most also have laundries, cooking facilities and often amenities, such as a swimming pool. Many hostels are open to all, on a first come, first served basis. To stay at a facility that is associated with the International Youth Hostel Association, you must be a member.

Remember, however, that membership is open to all, regardless of age. You can join by contacting any **YHA hostel** in North America or at YHA centers in New Zealand. *Or just show up at a Kiwi hostel and join on the spot.* New Zealand adult memberships run about $NZ40 per person. Kids under 15 have free membership. A guide to all 5300 hostels around the world is available from YHA offices for a small cost.

Information: **YHA offices**—Christchurch, corner of Gloucester and Manchester streets, ☎ *(03) 379-9535;* Auckland, corner of Customs and Gore streets, ☎ *(09) 379-4224.* **Budget Backpackers**—*Taupo, Rainbow Lodge, 99 Titiraupenga Street,* ☎ *(07) 377-1568;* **New Zealand Backpackers Hostels Association,** *Kiwi Hilton Travel Desk, 430 Queen Street, Auckland,* ☎ *(09) 358-3999;* or **New Zealand VIP Backpackers**, *Box 991, Taupo,* ☎ *(07) 377-1157.* In addition, tourist information offices usually have several free newspapers printed especially for backpackers, full of tips, information, discounts and advertisements—invaluable stuff for the backpacking crowd.

Upscale Digs

You can spend as much as you want on a bed in New Zealand, which has a number of very upscale lodges and resorts scattered about. Such places as the **Huka Lodge** in Taupo, the **Puka Park Lodge** on the Coromandel Peninsula or the **Kimberley Lodge** in Russell offer refined stays with top cuisine, excellent service and lush surroundings. The **Moose Lodge** near Rotorua, for example, sits on a gorgeous lake and has its own private thermal pool. Many of the lodges and resorts are "sporting lodges," which specialize in hunting and fishing and have guide services. The rates for these places are in the $NZ400 to $NZ1500 a night per couple range. The rates almost always include meals. Travel agents have lists of some of the better lodges, or you can get information from New Zealand tourism offices in North America. By mail, contact the **New Zealand Lodge Association**, *Paxus House, P.O. Box 1697, Wellington, New Zealand.*

Driving Down Under

One of the best drives in New Zealand is on Arthur's Pass Highway from Christchurch to the west coast of South Island, and through the Southern Alps.

To our minds, the best way to see a place is to rent a car or RV and just take off. We're too lazy to take a bike, too proud to hitchhike, too independent most of the time to take tour buses. One of our favorite methods of getting around, especially when we're doing research, is to get a small camper. It's a trade-off, of course. You sacrifice the speed and ease of driving you get with a car, but on the other hand, you save bucks on accommodation costs.

A driving vacation in New Zealand is especially attractive because the country is small and easy to move around in, and also there are scads of very attractive fly/drive vacation packages available all the time. These trips are among the most popular ways to see New Zealand. We fully understand that driving in a strange country isn't for everyone, but still, if you can work it out, *it's probably the single best way to get a full taste of what's going on.*

We got our basic training for driving on the wrong side of the road in England and Australia. The English drive fast and recklessly on narrow roads, and the Aussies aren't much better. New Zealanders, we are happy to report, drive on the wrong side of the street, too, but at a much more intelligent pace. Aside from a few freeways around the major cities, Kiwi highways are two-lane and, in the off-seasons, particularly on the South Island, relatively deserted. There are a few things to ponder, however. We have driven all over New Zealand, from the twisty, foggy stretches over Arthur's Pass to the barren, mystic Desert Highway north of Wellington, to the straight stretches through the sheep-laden farms of the Canterbury Plains and the narrow precipitous lanes of the Banks Peninsula on the road to Akaroa. And seeing that we highly recommend that anybody serious about seeing New Zealand rent a car or camper, it's only fair that we try to fill you in on some of the subtler forms of fun and games you can run into tooling around Down Under.

The Right Way to Drive
on the Left Side of the Road

The basic problem is, of course, the fact that we drive on the right and the New Zealanders drive on the left. Depending on your coordination and reaction times and common sense, this can be a very large deal, indeed, or no big thing. The most common mistake North Americans and continental European drivers make is looking the wrong way at the wrong time, usually at cross streets. The basic rule is the same that you see painted at every pedestrian crosswalk in London (where they lose an American at least once a day): LOOK RIGHT. This tendency to look the wrong way cuts both ways, of course. No less a personage than Winston Churchill was hospitalized in 1931 after being knocked on his poopdeck by a New York City taxicab while he was trying to walk across Fifth Avenue. (He forgot to look left.)

A sense of direction is particularly important Down Under when approaching that devilish English invention, **the roundabout**. We'd call it a traffic circle. *Just remember to look right, because anybody coming that direction has the right of way.* Once on the roundabout, remember, clockwise, go clockwise. Once on the circle, you supposedly have the right of way, but we observe the California Freeway Right-of-Way Rule: If they want it, let 'em have it. When turning left onto a street, the traffic coming from the right has the right of way.

You'll also notice that if you've rented a camper or car with a manual transmission, you have to shift left handed (the foot controls are the same). This is no problem, and allows you to get a driver's tan on your right arm for once in your life. The bottom line is probably this: If you're a good driver in Fresno or Vancouver, with a little thought and concentration, you'll be a good driver in New Zealand. **Note**: New Zealand drunk driving laws are tough. The basic limit is 80 milligrams of alcohol per 100 milliliters of blood; this means that for an average-sized human (150-pound male, 120-pound female), more than a can of beer or so an hour will put you over the limit. Failure to wear a seat belt (anybody in the car) can mean a $NZ75 fine. Speeding fines can go as high as $NZ500.

North and South Island Time Chart

This Travel Time Chart shows times in hours and minutes for a driver traveling at 50 miles per hour on open stretches of road, plus a safety factor of 5 to 10 minutes per hour for traffic delays and short refreshment stops. All times are approximate. At the end and beginning of New Zealand vacation times, it would be necessary to allow extra time.

North Island

	Whangarei	Wellington	Wanganui	Taupo	Tauranga	Rotorua	Palmerston North	New Plymouth	National Park	Napier	Kaitaia	Hamilton	Gisborne
Auckland	2:15	8:10	6:10	3:50	3:00	3:30	7:00	5:00	4:15	5:30	4:00	1:50	6:20
Gisborne	8:40	7:00	6:20	4:20	4:05	3:50	5:30	8:20	5:45	3:10	10:30	4:20	
Hamilton	3:10	6:50	4:10	2:30	1:35	1:36	5:00	3:00	2:55	4:15	6:00		
Kaitaia	2:30	12:15	10:10	8:05	6:10	7:00	11:00	9:05	8:20	9:40			
Napier	7:45	4:40	3:12	2:20	4:30	3:25	2:20	5:15	3:10				
National Park	6:30	4:35	1:50	1:30	3:35	2:30	2:45	2:10					
New Plymouth	6:10	4:45	2:00	4:00	4:10	4:35	3:35						
Palmerston	9:15	2:15	0:50	3:15	5:35	4:15							
Rotorua	5:00	6:15	4:20	1:00	1:05								
Tauranga	5:15	7:20	5:15	2:10									
Taupo	6:00	5:12	3:20										
Wanganui	8:20	2:40											
Wellington	10:20												

South Island

	Wanaka	Tekapo	Te Anau	Queenstown	Picton	Nelson	Mt. Cook	Invercargill	Haast	Greymouth	Dunedin	Christchurch	Blenheim
Christchurch													4:00
Dunedin												4:50	8:55
Greymouth											7:35	3:20	4:15
Haast										4:20	5:30	7:35	8:35
Invercargill									5:35	9:15	3:15	7:25	11:25
Mt. Cook								6:00	4:50	7:00	4:10	4:15	8:15
Nelson							9:35	12:45	8:30	4:10	10:15	5:25	1:50
Picton						1:40	8:50	12:00	9:10	5:00	9:30	4:40	0:35
Queenstown					10:50	11:00	3:40	2:40	3:15	7:35	3:50	6:10	10:10
Te Anau				2:10	12:40	12:55	5:30	2:35	5:15	8:35	4:00	8:00	12:00
Tekapo			5:20	3:30	7:20	8:00	1:30	5:00	4:40	5:30	4:20	3:20	6:20
Wanaka		2:55	3:20	1:30	10:10	10:10	3:05	3:10	2:25	6:00	3:45	5:35	9:30
Westport	7:35	7:00	10:15	8:25	4:05	3:25	8:25	10:45	5:50	1:30	8:25	4:20	3:30

A Few More Tips on Driving Down Under

Kiwi highways are every bit as good as North American ones, perhaps just a tad narrower. They are well marked (make sure you're up on your international traffic signs) and well maintained. There are few unpaved roads in the country, and some of them are off-limits to RVs anyway.

Basic speed limits are about what you'd expect—50 kilometers an hour in built-up areas (or slower) and **100k** on open highways. Don't try to work that out in miles per hour—the speedometer is in kph, so just look at the gauge. One note: Americans and Canadians by now are used to turning right after stopping at a red light. This is a no-no in New Zealand—don't turn left at a red light after stopping. There's also one sign you'll come across that is a bit perplexing: **LSZ**. It stands for "limited speed zone" and means slow down and be careful.

One other little peculiarity you'll run into, especially on the South Island, is the **one-lane bridge**. They always seem to be situated just as you come around a curve. The New Zealanders have tried to make these equitable by placing right-of-way signs at both ends of the bridge. The signs will have two arrows, one large, one small, pointing different directions. If the large arrow is pointing toward the bridge, it means you have the right of way; if the small arrow is going your direction, you must yield. Often, you'll come to a bridge where you have the right of way but a car is already on the bridge heading your way—just wait until the other car passes. The bridges also have pull-over spots at either end so that cars can get out of the way to let traffic pass. Basically, it's just a matter of common sense and good manners.

A few words might throw you, as well. "Verge" is the shoulder of the road and a "shingle road" is gravel. "Give way" mean yield and "motorway" means freeway.

One further twist. In a few places, the one-way bridge is also a **railroad bridge**—yes, indeed, cars and trains both share the same road. There's only one rule here: The train wins. *If you meet a train on a one-way bridge, you may have to back off to let it pass.* If you want to see one of these beauties, turn north at Kumara Junction (intersection of the Arthur's Pass highway and Highway 6) and go a couple of miles toward Greymouth. It's an eye-opener. Another caution: If you're in New Zealand in the early spring or late fall, be aware that the weather can change quickly and dump snow on the major west-east passes. If the passes are closed to traffic—and this happens—you can be stuck on one side of the country or the other until things clear. Make sure if the weather is iffy to carry chains—and ask the rental agencies to supply them.

Rental and Insurance

New Zealand has an **Automobile Association** that is the same as the AAA and the CAA. If you're a North American member, you have reciprocal membership privileges in New Zealand, which gives you free maps and trip planning services, as well as towing and accommodations guides. There are AA offices in all major cities. *Make sure you take your card.* By mail, write to the *New Zealand Automobile Association, P.O. Box 5, Auckland, New Zealand.*

Most of the major international car rental companies are doing business in New Zealand—Hertz, Avis, Budget, etc., and you can get almost any size car you want. It's easy to rent a car or camper in New Zealand. Canadians and Americans just need their normal state or provincial driver's license. *Buying New Zealand vehicle insurance is usually mandatory.* As we mentioned earlier, visitors to New Zealand are entitled to medical care if they are involved in an accident, regardless of fault. There is usually a three-day minimum to get discount rental rates. We rented a small Hertz car in Wellington for the one-day drive to Auckland and it ran about $NZ200, including insurance. Average rental rates for a bottom-line car (small compact) will run around $NZ500–$NZ700 a week, unlimited kilometerage. But there's always a special going on. One we saw not long ago was through Avis, and offered a 10-day vacation for about $US1200, which included a car and round-trip airfare. Many of the farm-stay, B&B vacations or fishing and hunting packages also throw in a free car. From time to time the airlines serving New Zealand will also offer special fly/drive packages. In addition, Budget has a fleet of rental cars adapted for handicapped drivers. All cars, as well as camper vans, can be booked in advance from North America, either through the car companies themselves or through a travel agent. Or they can be hired in New Zealand.

Economy 4WD Rental Company in Christchurch will rent camping equipment to go with its four-wheel-drive rental vehicles. Camp kits, for two people or more, are $NZ15 per person a day, and include a tent, sleeping bags, cots, towels, gas stove, cooking equipment, dishes, table and chair and tools. The vehicles themselves, for a minimum of six days with unlimited kilometers, insurance and taxes, start at $NZ115 and go up to $NZ175. *North America Information: So/Pac Travel Marketing,* ☎ *(800) 551-2012.* Gasoline (they call it petrol) is expensive in New Zealand. Last time out, we were paying between 90 cents and $NZ1 a liter, which translates out to about $US2.30 a gallon. *Diesel, for those driving the larger RVs, is a tad cheaper.* One of the things you can do to keep the copilot occupied while you're driving is converting kilometers-per-liter to miles-per-gallon, then figuring out your cost per gallon. Or you can just forget it and drive.

The Camper Scene

RV travel is one of the favorite ways Kiwis get out and around their country on vacations, as the large number of RV parks will attest. In New Zealand, like Australia, these are often called **Caravan Parks, or more and more, camper or holiday parks**, and they range from one-lung mom-and-pop joints up to spiffy modern parks with swimming pools and tennis courts. Most RV parks will have an electric kitchen with sinks, a coin-operated laundry, TV/recreation room and what the Kiwis call "an amenities block," meaning showers and toilets. Many camps also have tent spaces, cabins and on-site RVs for rent. Many have bars and restaurants.

Lake Wanaka in Central Otago

In addition to independent parks, there are several groups that are dotted all over the country. Our favorite is the **Top 10 Group**, which has about 40 parks on the islands, almost all of which are well equipped and have a good standard of amenities and cleanliness. Top 10 parks, like most Kiwi RV camps, will run you somewhere between $NZ10 and $NZ20 a night for a powered site. Another group of parks worth a nod is **Kiwi Camps** of New Zealand, with about 50 parks. Many parks in both groups are also members of the Camp & Cabin Association of New Zealand. *Brochures and guides to caravan parks are usually found in tourist information offices, or will be given to you when you rent your RV.* One of the best guides is **Jason's Budget Accom-**

modation, which sells for about $NZ5, but is usually provided free. In addition to RV parks, it also lists hostels, B&Bs, farm stays, country pubs and other low-cost accommodations. And, as mentioned, AA offices also have RV and other accommodations guides.

It's simple to rent an RV from North America, and the deals are always coming, it seems. The first time we went to New Zealand, it was because Air New Zealand was offering round-trip air from the West Coast for under $US1000 per person—and threw in a free camper for 10 days. We bit like sharks. You'll find the New Zealanders especially anxious to deal in winter, when all their kids are in school and the fleets of RVs are just sitting there.

For instance, **Maui Campas**, the largest camper rental agency in the country, not too long ago was offering a two-berth RV for about $US350 a week and threw in free stays at any Top 10 park in the deal. The big boys—six-berth deluxe RVs—were going for under $US600 a week. Another deal, this one from Mount Cook Line, offered an Air New Zealand package for about $US1200 per person and threw in a week's RV rental for a dollar more per person. You can also check with Suntrek, which has rental RVs and cars. The campers are the high-tops (permanent pop-top) and run about $NZ155 a day during the high season, $NZ70 a day in the off periods. Discounts are available for rental periods longer than 22 days. Automatic or standard transmissions available. *Information:* ☎ *(09) 520-1404 in Auckland.*

RV Rental Costs

For normal, no-deal rentals, expect to pay between $US600 and $US1000 a week for a two-berth unit, between $US850 and $US1400 for a six-berth, the prices depending on the time of year. Most RV rentals, specials included, are for unlimited kilometerage; in some cases, minimum rental periods are required. *Insurance, which is mandatory, is usually offered two ways. The first method is a charge put on your credit card, usually around $NZ500,* which covers damage to the vehicle. At the end of the trip—providing you haven't had an accident—they tear up the credit card charge. The problem is, the insurance is $NZ500 deductible. Which means if you get a rock through the windshield (about $NZ350 to replace), it comes out of that $NZ500 deposit. This is the cheapest way to go, if you figure you either won't have an accident or can afford to part with the money.

The second method—and the one we always take—is a flat, daily charge of around $NZ20. No refund at the end of the trip—lost money. But no deductible and it covers everything: busted lights, cracked windshields, crushed bumpers. We've never had an accident in New Zealand but traveled more comfortably knowing everything was covered.

Well, almost everything. *No insurance covers damage to the top of the vehicle.* This rule makes you conscious of low bridges and the low roofs in some gas stations. Also, there are a few roads around the islands off limits to RVs—drive on them, have an accident, and the whole thing is your responsibility.

One of the major wholesale companies providing camper rentals to travel agents is Leisure Port, which has Maui Campas, Newman's Motorhomes, Budget Motorhomes, Mount Cook Motorhomes and Horizon Holidays. **Leisure Port** has large facilities at the airports in Auckland and Christchurch. After you clear customs, you wait for one of the company's free vans, which takes you to the rental office. Give them your voucher, sign this and that, and usually within an hour, you're in your RV heading for wherever—if you're smart, the nearest RV park to get over jet lag. Very fast, very efficient. Information: Auckland ☎ *(09) 275-3529*, Christchurch ☎ *(03) 358-4159*.

Tips on RV Travel

Don't expect super mileage from a camper. Depending on terrain and how fast you drive, you're looking at around 17 to 20 miles a gallon, less with larger vehicles. And it probably goes without saying that in the smaller, two-berth units, you'd better be on good terms with your bunkie. Space is tight, you're always misplacing stuff, and there is no way you'll ever keep the floor clean. All that aside, it's a great way to travel and a good opportunity to meet a lot of similarly minded New Zealanders. (Although, in the winter, the chances are the folks in the camper next door are probably from Cleveland.)

The fleets of RV vehicles available in New Zealand are new and modern, and come equipped with most of the necessities of life, including bedding, dishes and cooking equipment, interior lights, brooms, dishwashing stuff and—this is a necessity—heaters. Some are now being equipped with microwave ovens, the camper's best friend. Some even have TV sets, basically useless on the South Island where TV signals are few and far between. The only complaint we have is with the can openers—never met one yet that worked right. We take our heavy-duty opener from home. Saves primal screaming trying to open a can of beans. If you really get serious, you might also bring along a small cutting board, or buy it when you arrive.

Food and Drink

There's a lot more to New Zealand cuisine than mutton and lamb chops. New Zealand produces world-class wines, beers and cheeses, and, remember, it's an island nation, and that means the supply and variety of seafood and fish are su-

perb. Especially marinated mussels. Huge, maybe two inches across, sweet, saucy. You can buy them in almost any market, and they come in a variety of sauces, from plain marinade to honey or hot. They are highly addictive and one thing we will always miss when we're not in New Zealand.

As for lamb. Well, if you've never had **Kiwi lamb**, you've never had lamb. It's so good it's sinful, the best in the world, and the New Zealanders, not surprisingly, know how to prepare it properly. They also do good work with beef and venison.

The Good and the Bad

On the other side of the coin, you can also find some really vile stuff, particularly some of their fast foods. A packet of fish and chips from a mom-and-pop joint comes to mind, probably the greasiest and worst chunk of lunch we've ever had. The Kiwis, like the Australians, are also big fans of pies—meaning **meat pies**. Done correctly, these can be quite good. Done badly—and many times they are—it's instant heartburn. Fast-food coffee should be avoided at all costs—it's truly abominable. Like the Aussies, the Kiwis sometimes eat spaghetti for breakfast, sometimes on toast. A normal roadside café or restaurant breakfast will include steak, scrambled eggs with chips, sausage (bangers) or bacon (Canadian-style), baked beans and yes, spaghetti. Eggs benedict with spinach seems to be a national fave at the moment, often quite good. Pork and beans should be avoided in almost all cases. Actually, almost anything they put tomato sauce in—canned or fresh—is quite strange, many of the canned offerings tasting something like a stew made from vienna sausage and ketchup. Another Kiwi delicacy we can live without is **Muttonbird**, a Maori favorite. It's basically an oily, salty sooty shearwater (*titi* in Maori), preferably smoked. Yecch. But generally, you'll find that Kiwi cuisine is quite acceptable, and you'll never starve. Actually, in the better hotels and some of the more with-it wineries, the cuisine is far advanced and very sophisticated. Some of the best deals on food—and even on occasion really good eats—are found in pubs at noontime.

If you have a Yankee attack, rest easy—the major cities are full of American fast-food chains: McDonald's, the Colonel, Pizza Hut. There are also scads of ethnic places, especially for lunch. Chinese take-outs are popular and often will be the only thing open late at night. Many restaurants, even in major cities, operate on limited hours, so always check before venturing out. Vegan and vegetarian cafes and restaurants are also gaining popularity around the country.

Fruits are high on New Zealanders' lists, and the many orchards and groves around the country supply excellent fare. You'll find stalls near most orchards where the local crop is on sale in season. Californians already know about two of New Zealand's better exports, **Granny Smith apples** and **Kiwi fruit**.

Kiwi Fruit

Kiwi fruit, long associated with New Zealand, is actually the Chinese goose-berry, which originated in the Yangtze Valley. They were introduced into New Zealand around the turn of the century and went commercial in the 1930s on the North Island. *They were named kiwi fruit in the 1950s, partly because the brown fuzzy skins resemble the bird,* partly as a marketing gimmick. In addition to having a wonderful taste, kiwi fruit are also higher in Vitamin C than apples, and contain all sorts of good minerals, plus being low in so-dium. They are also rich in enzymes—the juice is used to marinate squid. A major center of the kiwi industry is at Kerikeri near the Bay of Islands on the North Island. During the harvest season—May to July—you can buy enough kiwi fruit to feed an army for a few dollars, more than you'll ever be able to eat.

Fresh from the Farm

In addition to the excellent Granny Smith apples, orchards also produce Red Delicious, Golden, Sturmer and Gala types. *The two major apple-grow-ing areas are Hawkes Bay on the North Island and the Marlborough and Nel-son areas of the South Island.* Picking season is March to November. The Nelson area also produces berries—**loganberries**, **elderberries**, **strawberries** and **blackberries**. Other fruits you'll run into are **pepino melons**, **passionfruit**, **kiwona melons** and **the nashi, a sort of apple-pear**. The Kiwis tell us that Queen Elizabeth's favorite honey comes from the *pohutukawa* (Christmas tree), which produces a white honey and can even be bought by us commoners.

New Zealand honey, coming as it does from some exotic New Zealand plants, has some remarkable flavors, and is widely used in candy and candles. It's also used to make *mead*, the Druidic potable that's sweet and will get you swacked at the same time. If you've a thirst, try Havill's Mazek Mead Company in Christchurch, which uses honey produced from Canterbury clover. And for more honey products than you thought existed, check out **Honey Village** outside Taupo.

Driving down a road near the Coromandel Peninsula, we were amused to see signs saying: "Swedes for sale." No, not the white slave trade, but the **New Zealand rutabaga**. Other farm produce you'll find are **courgettes** (zucchi-ni), **capsicum** (bell peppers), **aubergine** (eggplant), **silverbeet** (Swiss chard) and **witloof** (celery-like plant). Being a Polynesian culture as well, New Zealand also has taro (used in place of potatoes), yams and kumara. **Kumara**, which originated in South America, is a sweet potato, brought to New Zealand with the first Maori settlers 1000 years ago. The Kiwis also are fond of **beetroot** (red beets), but haven't gone nationally insane like the Austra-lians, who put it on everything, including, yuk, hamburgers; still, we've run into carrots and beets on burgers, so always ask. **Cheese** country is to the southwest of the North Island in the Mt. Egmont area. The city of Eltham, particularly, is a good place to explore Kiwi cheeses. Try the **Galaxy Cheese Factory** on High Street, which has a cheese bar and will mail cheese back home. For those who like excitement in their cheeses, we recommend **Ferndale's Blue de Bresse**, a superior blue-vein product. *The traditional cheese in New Zealand was a mix of Gouda and white cheddar,* but now the industry has branched out and produces gruyere, mozzarella, brie, camembert, feta, romano and many other varieties. The Kiwis pride themselves on the purest cheese on earth—the old "clean, green and nuclear-free" thing again.

Sheep and Other Animals

Lamb. Well, it gets tough after a while, driving around in the spring and seeing all those wee sheep being born or romping around the paddocks, to keep eating lamb, but there's no doubt it is superb.

A **lamb roast** is the usual Sunday dinner in many Kiwi homes—eaten, we might add, without that awful mint jelly. They also eat a lot of mutton, which is not strong and gamy. And rather than spring lamb, many New Zealanders prefer "**hogget**," a Scottish word for a year-old sheep, which they claim has more flavor. Lamb and mutton are cheap in local supermarkets, and come in a variety of cuts, often pre-breaded. Sometimes, however, the lamb on sale is from Australia, which floods the market from time to time. Many New Zealanders think Aussie lamb is inferior. It's not a battle we choose to get into.

Children adore feeding lambs at Rainbow Farms, Rotorua.

While not especially known for **beef**, New Zealand does raise excellent meat, tender, flavorful, fairly low-fat. *They have a tendency to overcook it, however, so make sure if you like it a bit rare, you tell the waiter exactly what you want.*

As for **venison**, raised in prodigious quantities, you'll probably have to go to an upscale restaurant to find it, although it's becoming more available at meat markets, where it's found under the marketing name of **cervena.** (See the section on deer.) If you do find some in a market, one thing to remember about Kiwi venison if you cook it without liquids (broiling, frying)—*it must be cooked quickly and never well done because of its low-fat content.* In restaurants, it often comes in a stew form or roasted with a marinade. It can be pretty bland, for all its low-calorie benefits. Breakfast meats offer a mixed bag. There are basically two kinds of **bacon**, middle and shoulder, both of which are quite lean like Canadian bacon. **Sausages** tend to be English-style bangers, made with a cereal/meat mix, very bland, virtually tasteless to somebody used to Jimmy Dean–style sausage. You can also find lamb sausage (also fairly bland) and venison sausage, which has a nice flavor—just don't overcook it. When you encounter a **moloo burger,** you'll discover it's a square-shaped beef patty. Many of the better restaurants around the country are also high on wild game: boar, quail pheasant.

On the South Island, we spotted what we thought were North American–style wild turkeys—which turned out to be just that. Farmers look on them as pests because they eat grains and grasses used to feed sheep and cattle. There are enough of them flying around, however, that come Christmas, they are hunted down, and served up with all the trimmings (the traditional Kiwi Yuletide feast). This method keeps the turkey population under control. The farmers, we were told, wouldn't touch a turkey with a three-meter pole, preferring, perhaps, a lamb roast at Christmas dinner.

Seafood

Seafood, seafood. No menu is without it, from **crayfish to cod**, **oysters to smoked marlin**. Fish by the ton, including **John Dory**, **sole**, **eels**, **albacore tuna**, **trevally**, **flounder**, **salmon**, **snapper**, **monkfish** and **shark** (also used in fish and chips). Bivalves, including the aforementioned green-lipped mussels (arguably the best in the world—marinated, steamed or broiled), scallops, paua **(abalone)**, toheroa **(a special clam)**, tuangi **(cockle)**, plus Rock lobster squid. But no trout. *It's against the law to sell trout commercially. If you catch one at a farm or lodge, they'll be glad to cook it up for you, however.*

And for Dessert...

Kiwis do like their desserts—rich and fattening. Like **"Lamingtons,"** pieces of sponge cake dipped in chocolate or fruit syrup, then sprinkled with shaved coconut. Or **Pavlovas**, a baked meringue with fruit and whipped cream. Or **trifle**, sponge cake soaked in brandy or sherry and topped with custard or canned fruit. Or **cream buns**, a jellyroll stuffed with sweet cream paste. In restaurants, they roll out the dessert trolley, stacked with an assortment of goodies to drive anybody on a diet to drink. They encourage you to try several selections, then send for a block and tackle to get you out of the chair.

No place in New Zealand is without a **teahouse**, where you get **Devonshire Tea**—tea and scones (pronounced skawns) served with whipped cream. And markets sell dairy custard, a sweetened milk and egg mix that comes in small milk cartons and is used to make a quick dessert with fruits.

Because of some language differences, you're likely to run into some things in markets and on menus that might seem strange. Like "unadulterated milk" which turns out to be whole milk. And one of the most confusing is "tea," which means either the drink, a mid-morning snack, mid-afternoon snack or the evening meal, very confusing and time-sensitive. Anyway, while not a complete dictionary, here are a few of the terms:

THE NEW ZEALAND FOOD DIRECTORY

Green ginger	Unpeeled, fresh ginger root
Punnet	A half pint dry measure; for example, the way berries are often packaged
Castor sugar	Confectioner's sugar
Gingernuts	Gingersnaps
Golden syrup	Honey-colored light molasses
Rice Bubbles	Snap, crackle and pop
Wheetbix	A sort of granola bar
Hokey pokey	Butterscotch ice cream
Bickies, or biscuits	Cookies
Chips	French fries
Chook	Chicken
Cuppa	Tea or coffee
Dairy	The neighborhood market, selling everything from newspapers to ice cream cones, usually open late
Junket	A dessert, sort of like a thin pudding
Marmite, or vegemite	A salty yeast product that we think tastes like piano polish but which is worshipped in New Zealand and Australia
Milk bar	A shop selling dairy foods and hot fast foods
Mince pie	Ground meat pies in a pastry shell, hot or cold
Pudding	Generic name for any dessert

THE NEW ZEALAND FOOD DIRECTORY

Take away	Fast food
Supper	A snack before going to bed; the evening meal is often referred to as tea
After	Dessert, as in after a meal
Griller	A broiler chicken
Tomato sauce	Ketchup
Trolley	Grocery cart
Hangi	The Maori luau, cooked in an underground pit
Scroggin	Gorp, or trail mix, designed for hikers
Tamarillo	The tree tomato, often used in preparing sauces; it's shiny and egg-shaped

We should mention in passing that at least one famous chef owes his inspiration to New Zealand—Graham Kerr, the Galloping Gourmet. Originally from the United Kingdom, Kerr spent seven years in New Zealand, a period that he says was "the most important stop in my life." He wrote his first cookbook in New Zealand, then went on to be a TV celeb in the United States in the late 1960s. The book, *Graham Kerr—the Galloping Gourmet,* uses recipes based on New Zealand foods, and is worth checking out of your local library before heading off to New Zealand.

What to Wear

Some rules. New Zealanders, while essentially laid back and pretty informal, do tend to dress for dinner. Jackets are a good idea, and, in fancy spots, you might need a tie. In the summer, men can wear sports coats, walking shorts and long socks (buy them there). For women, a skirt and blouse, perhaps a floral-print dress. Pants suits and slacks are proper in resort areas.

Tipping

Tipping is generally not done, but on special occasions or in very fancy places with very fancy service, it's not a total tabu. You'll also notice that most restaurants do not add service charges to the tab. Menu prices might or might not include the 12.5 percent goods and services tax, so check.

Drinking

Liquor licenses in New Zealand, like Australia, are hard to obtain, so many restaurants and cafés are BYO (Bring Your Own), usually beer or wine. You stop off at a bottle shop and pick up some wine, and the restaurant will de-cork and serve it for you. Often, there is a corking fee, sometimes not much, sometimes outrageous. (We paid $NZ5 to uncork an $NZ8 bottle of wine once.) Some BYOs have beer, wine and liqueurs, but not hard booze. The main beers in New Zealand are the Lion brews and Steinlager. But, like the United States, small independent breweries are catching on all over. Some of our favorites are **Shakespeare's** in Auckland, the **Loaded Hog** in Christchurch and Auckland, and the **Cork and Keg** in Renwick near Blenheim. For wines, see the WINE section later in this chapter.

On-Site Restaurants

Many motels and small hotels have a restaurant on site, which is often cafeteria-style. The usual procedure is to pick up your salads and cold foods, order your hot food, and find a place to sit. They'll either call you for the order or deliver it to the table. The food is often basic—stews, macaroni and cheese, curries. But note well, they tend to think everybody who eats is a farmhand, and the servings can be prodigious. In pubs that serve counter meals, you normally must order and pay for beer or wine separately from the food.

As a general guide when eating out, look for a place that has a yellow-and-white emblem with "KiwiHost" on it. This means the establishment has personnel specially trained in the gentle art of pleasing tourists. The program is administered by the New Zealand Tourism Department.

Finally, we have tried to rate the restaurants, not only from a quality standpoint, but from a monetary one, as well. To simplify things, we have three levels of cost: budget, moderate and expensive. These ratings apply to basic meals, and do not include wines or other meal extras. Budget means a meal for two persons in the $NZ15–40 range; moderate is $NZ40–90, and expensive is from $NZ90 up.

Wine Producing Regions

Californians, at least Californians from our neck of the woods, tend to be fairly sophisticated about wine. It's not that we go out and study enology from dawn to dusk, or that we take classes on how to be really snotty when it comes to picking wines. It's basically because, like France, California has a lot of wine-growing areas and a professional group of vintners producing world-class wines, and your level of expectations in this sort of situation is always bound to be high.

Hotel Du Vin, south of Auckland

Which is why it's such a delight finding that our southern cousins are producing wine every bit the equal of Europe or California.

Big-league wine growing and appreciation in New Zealand is a recent development, although the first wine was produced near the **Bay of Islands** around 1835. Prior to 1960, there was a small industry, with virtually no exports at all. But by 1980, things were beginning to expand rapidly, and by 1990, almost 400 growers were producing wine. The total vine area is estimated at around 15,000 acres or so, at the moment, with an annual production of more than 11 million gallons. By contrast, California's Napa Valley has more than 100 wineries—and one of the largest, St. Helena-based Sutter Home, produces something like 34 million liters (almost 9 million gallons) of wine a year by itself.

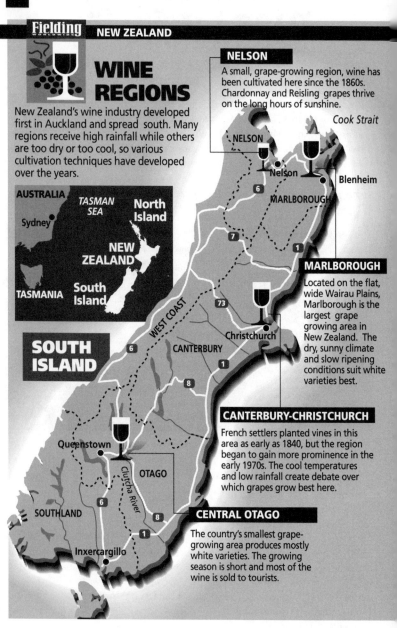

Fielding WORLDWIDE **NEW ZEALAND**

WINE REGIONS

New Zealand's wine industry developed first in Auckland and spread south. Many regions receive high rainfall while others are too dry or too cool, so various cultivation techniques have developed over the years.

AUSTRALIA

TASMAN SEA

North Island

Sydney

NEW ZEALAND

TASMANIA **South Island**

SOUTH ISLAND

WEST COAST

NELSON

A small, grape-growing region, wine has been cultivated here since the 1860s. Chardonnay and Reisling grapes thrive on the long hours of sunshine.

Cook Strait

NELSON

Nelson

Blenheim

MARLBOROUGH

MARLBOROUGH

Located on the flat, wide Wairau Plains, Marlborough is the largest grape growing area in New Zealand. The dry, sunny climate and slow ripening conditions suit white varieties best.

Christchurch

CANTERBURY

CANTERBURY-CHRISTCHURCH

French settlers planted vines in this area as early as 1840, but the region began to gain more prominence in the early 1970s. The cool temperatures and low rainfall create debate over which grapes grow best here.

Queenstown

Clutcha River

OTAGO

CENTRAL OTAGO

SOUTHLAND

Inxercargillo

The country's smallest grape-growing area produces mostly white varieties. The growing season is short and most of the wine is sold to tourists.

Major wine-producing areas

Other wine-producing areas

Regional boundary

TASMAN SEA

NORTHLAND

WAIKATO AND BAY OF PLENTY

The Waikato vineyards are near Hamilton and the Firth of Thames, while the Bay of Plenty is farther east. Most widely grown varieties include Muller-Thurgau, Chardonnay and Sauvignon Blanc.

GISBORNE

Gisborne is promoted as "the Chardonnay capital of New Zealand." It's mainly a white wine region with Muller-Thurgau the leader, followed by Chardonnay and Muscat.

AUCKLAND

Auckland is New Zealand's oldest wine region, but only 4% of the country's grapes are grown here. The area is primarily a red wine region concentrating mainly on Cabernet Sauvignon.

Auckland

Hamilton

Tauranga

BAY OF PLENTY

WAIKATO

BAY OF PLENTY

GISBORNE

Gisborne

NORTH ISLAND

New Plymouth

TARANAKI

HAWKE'S BAY

MANAWATU-WANGANUI

Hastings

WAIRARAPA

Known as New Zealand's "new" wine region, this area is internationally known for its red wines made from Pinot Noir. Some white varieties are also grown.

HAWKES BAY

This region produces some of New Zealand's finest wines. Chardonnay is the most widely planted grape, followed by Muller-Thurgau, Cabernet Sauvignon and Sauvignon Blanc.

WELLINGTON

Wellington

0 25 50 miles

Cook Strait

Wine Producing Regions

Although the bulk of New Zealand wines are white, the reputation of its cabernet sauvignons is gaining world status. Among the whites, New Zealand sauvignon blancs already are on a par with any in the world, and some critics put them at the top.

About 75 percent of the country's wine is produced along the east coast of the North Island between the Hastings/Napier area and Gisborne—basically the areas behind Hawkes Bay and Poverty Bay. Another important region is the Marlborough district on the northeast coast of the South Island near Blenheim and Nelson. But such is the growing popularity of interior consumption, as well as exports, that there are vineyards almost tip of coast to tip of coast on both islands. In addition, you'll find a number of places that produce ciders and dessert wines; if these are more to your taste than regular table wines, you might want to contact the **Fruit Winemakers of New Zealand**, *P.O. Box 10 050, Wellington;* ☎ *(04) 473-5387; FAX 471-2861.*

Like California, many wineries welcome tasters, and in many cases, with normal Kiwi hospitality, they offer local cheeses to go along with the samples. Also like California, many winery showrooms are also galleries and many wineries conduct tours to educate first-time sippers. Often there will be a tasting charge, refunded if you decide to buy a bottle or two. And it's not uncommon to find a good restaurant attached to the winery.

The success of the Kiwi wineries is such that almost every wine-growing region has at least one company that specializes in wine tours. Or, if you have wheels, you can do what we Californians do on a weekend—go winery hopping. This spoils us, of course, but makes us all the more eager to sample the pressings of other countries when we have the chance. We won't try to list all the New Zealand wineries. You can get a more complete listing when you visit major cities close to the vineyards.

Where to Sample New Zealand's Wines

Auckland region

Near Auckland is the wine-growing area of West Auckland. The vines are about a half-hour from downtown, in the Henderson area to the west of the city. The most common variety in the region is cabernet sauvignon, with substantial plantings of merlot and pinot noir. Among the 15 or so wineries around Auckland are the following:

Wine Producing
Regions

Babich

Babich Road, Henderson. ☎ *(09) 833-7859; FAX 833-9929.*
Chardonnay, fume vert, Muller-Thurgau, pinot noir, cabernet sauvignon. Sales and tasting 9 a.m.–5 p.m., Mon.–Fri.; 9 a.m.–6 p.m. Sat., and 11 a.m.–5 p.m. Sun. Picnic area. Tours by appointment.

Collard Bros.

303 Lincoln Road, Henderson. ☎ *(09) 836-8341; FAX 837-5840.*
Chardonnay, chenin blanc, Rhine riesling and Merlot. Sales and tasting 9 a.m.–5 p.m., Mon.–Sat.; 11 a.m.–5 p.m. Sun. Picnic and barbecue area. Tours by appointment in the summer only.

Coopers Creek

State Highway 16, Huapai (northwest of the city). ☎ *(09) 412-8560; FAX 412-8375.*
The winery features some well-made vintages from several wine regions, including Hawkes Bay merlots, which are exceeding tasty. It's probably better known for its whites—Riesling and chardonnay. One of its most famous efforts was a 1994 limited issue of Riesling bottled under a label called Tutaekuri, named after a small stream on the property. The name means "dog poo" in Maori, but the winery decided to stick with it despite the chuckles. The wine, by the way, was excellent. Sales and tasting 9 a.m.–5:30 p.m. Mon.–Fri.; 10:30 a.m.–5:30 p.m. Sat.–Sun. Tours by appointment.

Corban's

426 Great North Road, Henderson. ☎ *(09) 837-3390; FAX 836-0005.*
One of the country's oldest and largest wine companies. Also distributes under the Cooks, Stoneleigh and Longridge labels. Grapes from all over New Zealand are used. Chardonnay, fume blanc and sauvignon/merlot. Sales and tasting 9 a.m.–6 p.m., Mon.–Sat. Picnic area. Daily tours.

Delegat's

Hepburn Road, Henderson. ☎ *(09) 836-0129; 836-3282.*
Here you will find, as far as we know, the only brother and sister act in the New Zealand wine biz: Jim and Rose Delegat. Primarily Hawkes Bay grapes. Chardonnay, cabernet sauvignon, fume blanc. Sales and tasting 10 a.m.–5 p.m., Mon.–Fri, 10 a.m.–6 p.m., Sat.–Sun. Tours by appointment.

Matua Valley Wines

Waikoukou Valley Road, Waimauku. ☎ *(09) 411-8301; FAX 411-7982..*
Given credit for introducing sauvignon blanc to New Zealand. Sales and tasting 9 a.m.–5 p.m., Mon.–Fri.; 9 a.m.–6 p.m. Sat., and 11 a.m.-4:30 p.m. Sun. This is home to the famous Hunting Lodge restaurant, a four-star establishment open on weekends. (**See Auckland restaurants for a review.**) It also has a croquet ground and a picnic area. Tours by appointment.

Selaks

Old North Road and Highway 16, Kumeu. ☎ *(09) 412-8609; FAX 412-7524.*
Award-winning sauvignon blanc, as well as Methode Champenoise wines. Sales and tasting 9 a.m.–5 p.m., Mon.–Fri.; 10 a.m.–5:30 p.m. Sat. and 11 a.m.–4 p.m. Sun.

On the premises is the always popular and normally good restaurant, **Allely House** ★★★, open for dinner Wed-Sun. and lunch Thurs-Sun. Tours by appointment.

For tours of Auckland-area wineries, contact a visitors center or try **Robbie's "Double-Decker Fun Bus"** ☎ *(09) 413-8222.*

The Gisborne Area

Some observers feel that the Gisborne area has declined as a major wine area because it generally produces sweeter, flusher wines in an era when the direction seems to be going toward drys. Several of the major wine companies still have vast vineyards growing in the area, shipping the grapes to Auckland facilities for processing and bottling. Gisborne also has a number of so-called "bio-grow" wineries, meaning no chemical sprays. Some wineries:

Matawhero Wines

Riverpoint Road, Matawhero, Gisborne. ☎ *(06) 868-8366; FAX 867-9856.*
Gewurztraminer, chenin blanc, cabernet merlot, chardonnay. Sales and tasting 10 a.m.–4:30 p.m., Mon.–Sat.

Milton Vineyard

Papatu Road, Manutuke, Gisborne. ☎ *(06) 862-8680; FAX 862-8869.*
One of the bio-grow companies. Muller-Thurgau, riesling, sauvignon blanc/semillion, chenin blanc. Sales and tasting 9 a.m.–6 p.m., Mon.–Sat., Oct.–June.

Tai-Ara-Rau Wines

Stout Street, Gisborne. ☎ *(06) 867-2010; FAX 867-2024.*
This is the only training facility in the country with public sales, a part of Tairawhiti Polytechnic. The students, all aiming at careers in the wine biz, produce merlot and chardonnays. Tours, sales and tastings are by appointment only.

Hawkes Bay

It's pretty hot around the bay, and the result is some truly world-class red wines, especially cabernet sauvignon, merlot and pinot noir. Hawkes Bay wines are noted for their fullness, aging well with deep flavor. But the area is also producing some very good chardonnays. Some wineries:

Brookfields Vineyards

Brookfields Road, Meeanee. ☎ *(06) 834-4615; FAX 834-4622.*
Try a cabernet sauvignon, cabernet merlot, pinot gris. Sales and tastings 9 a.m.–5 p.m., Mon.–Sun. Lunches available in the summer, or on weekends and holidays.

C.J. Pask

Omahu Road, Hastings. ☎ *(06) 879-7906; 879-6428.*
Cabernet sauvignon, sauvignon blanc, chardonnay, pinot noir. Sales and tastings, 9 a.m.–5 p.m., Mon.–Sat.; 11 a.m.–4 p.m. Sun.

Crab Farm

54 Main Road North, three kilometers north of the Hawkes Bay airport. Phone and FAX ☎ *(06) 836-6678.*

A small winery with a good location (right on the highway). Muller-Thurgau, sauvignon blanc, cabernet sauvignon. Sales and tasting 9 a.m.–5 p.m., Mon.–Sat.; 11 a.m.–4 p.m. Sun. Tours by appointment in the summer. Light lunches available.

Esk Valley Estate

745 Main Road, Bayview. ☎ *(06) 836-6411; 836-6413.*
Chenin blanc, cabernet merlot, sauvignon blanc, cabernet sauvignon. Try the merlot cabernet Franc 1992. Sales and tasting 9:45 a.m.–6 p.m., Mon.–Sat. in the summer; to 5 p.m. in the winter. Tours by appointment.

Mission Vineyards

Corner Avenue and Church streets, Taradale (near Napier) ☎ *(06) 844-2259; FAX 844-6023.*
The oldest (1851) winery in the country, and one of the most popular, especially for Big Name concerts. The winery, run by the brothers of the Society of Mary, has been home to concerts by Ray Charles and Dame Kiri Te Kanawa, among others. The winery specializes in champagne, chardonnay and Riesling. Sales and tastings 8 a.m.–5 p.m., Mon.–Sat.; 1–4 p.m. Sun. **Brother Marty's Most Magnificent Moment Tours** are at 10:30 a.m. and 2 p.m. Mon-Sat. Lunch available; call ahead.

Ngatarawa

Ngatarawa Road, Hastings. ☎ *(06) 879-7603; FAX 879-6675.*
Housed in elegant old stables, specializing in dry wines. Sauvignon blanc, chardonnay, Stables red. Sales and tasting 10 a.m.–5 p.m., Mon.–Sun. Tours by appointment. Picnic area.

Te Mata Estate Winery

Te Mata Road, Havelock North. ☎ *(06) 877-4399; FAX 877-4397.*
One of the area's more prestigious companies, noted for its cabernet-merlots and chardonnays. It also now produces some wines using syrah grapes. Very stylish (i.e. Mediterranean) winery buildings. Sales and tasting 9 a.m.–5 p.m., Mon.–Sat.; 11 a.m.–4 p.m. Sun. Tours at 10:30 a.m. Mon.–Sat. in January; by appointment the rest of the year.

Bay Tours in Napier offers a winery tour, which includes visits to several wineries, tastings, tours, talks with winegrowers and a number of tourist stops. *Information: phone and FAX* ☎ *(06) 843-6953.* Also offering tours are the **Hawkes Bay Wine Trail Co**. ☎ *(06) 835-6788*, and **Eastland Tours,** ☎ *(06) 844-8806.*

The **InterCity** network also offers some tours to the Hawkes Bay wine country, with a train trip from Wellington to Napier, plus added attractions (earthquake tour, kiwi house) and wine tours. The packages include some meals, accommodations and tastings. Two-day packages run around $NZ200 per person; one-day trips are about $NZ100 per person.

Marlborough

This section of the South Island is Montana Country. When the company decided to plant here, it increased the national vineyard supply by 30 per-

Wine Producing Regions

cent. This is mainly a sauvignon blanc area, but chardonnay and rieslings are also coming of age. The wineries (almost three dozen) are mostly tightly grouped around Blenheim. A few:

Allan Scott Wines & Estates

Jacksons Road, Blenheim. ☎ *(03) 572-9054; FAX 572-9053.*
What wine tasting and all its various delights should be, one of the better places in the area. Chardonnays, sauvignon blanc and rieslings are the specialties. The moderately priced on-site restaurant, the **Twelve-Trees Vineyard Restaurant ★ ★ ★**, is very good. Try the smoked salmon quiche or the chicken and mushroom pie; open noonish–3 p.m. daily. Sales and tasting 9 a.m.–4:30 p.m., Mon.–Sun. all year.

Cairnbrae Wines

Jacksons Road, Blenheim. FAX and phone ☎ *(03) 572-8048.*
Along with Allan Scott, Corbans and Cloudy Bay plus others in the vicinity, Cairnbrae is becoming ground zero for the connoisseurs visiting the area. The winery produces a limited supply, concentrating on sauvignon blanc, semillion, chardonnay and riesling. The on-site restaurant has great vittels for wine tasters, things like bacon and avocado foccacia, olive bread salmon sandwiches and various cheese and seafood platters. It's open 9 a.m.–5 p.m. seven days. Sales and tasting 9 a.m.–5 p.m. daily.

Cellier Le Brun

Terrace Road, Renwick. ☎ *(03) 572-8859 or 572-9001; FAX 572-8814.*
Sparkling wines à la champagne are the specialty here. Bruts, rosés, blanc de blancs and nonsparkling chardonnay. The blanc de blancs, especially, have won numerous awards and have an international reputation; not surprising because the vintner is a 12th-generation champagne maker. The winery specializes in—what else—champagne breakfasts but also has lunch from 10 a.m.–3 p.m. Sales, tours and tasting 9 a.m.–5 p.m., daily.

Cloudy Bay

Jacksons Road, Blenheim. ☎ *(03) 572-8914; FAX 572-8065.*
Here is where we ran into one of our favorite Kiwi sauvignon blancs, and the winery's chardonnays seem to be coming along, as well. The sauvignon blanc is almost its own worst enemy—it's so popular and well-known, it's hard to keep in supply. Sales and tasting 10 a.m.–4:30 p.m. daily. Tours by appointment.

Corbans Marlborough Cellars

Jacksons Road, Blenheim. ☎ *(03) 572-8198; FAX 572-8199.*
This is a joint venture with Australia's giant wine company, Wolf Blass. Riesling and sauvignon blanc plus chardonnay. Recently, it has started to produce very good boutique wines under the Cottage Block label. Sales and tasting 10 a.m.–4 p.m., daily. Tours by appointment.

Highfield Estate

Brookby Road, Omake Valley. ☎ *(03) 572-8592; FAX 572-9257.*
Spectacular view, Italian-style tasting room, award-winning wines. Sauvignon blanc and chardonnays are the specialities, along with decent *methode champenoise* and promising merlot. Sales and tasting 10 a.m.–5 p.m., daily. Lunch available. Tours by appointment.

Hunter's

Rapaura Road, Blenheim. ☎ *(03) 572-8489; FAX 572-8457.*

Jane Hunter has made her mark as the queen of the Marlborough wine area, and her efforts as both general manager and viticulturist at Hunter's have resulted in a huge reputation for her wines. Late-harvest chardonnay is a speciality, and the Poms went mad for the sauvignon blanc at a recent show in London. It's one of the few wineries we've seen anywhere with a swimming pool. The winery restaurant, **Vintner's ★ ★ ★**, is very popular, and open for lunch from noon–3 p.m. and dinner 7–9 p.m. daily. Outrageously good seafood. There is outdoor dining if you wish. ☎ *572-8803.* Winery sales and tasting 9:30 a.m.–4:30 p.m., Mon.–Sat.; 11 a.m.–3:30 p.m. Sun. Tours by appointment.

Montana Marlborough Winery

State Highway 1, Blenheim. ☎ *(03) 578-2099; FAX 578-0463.*

This is the largest winery in the country, plus the New Zealand base for a French champagne company working with Montana. Sauvignon blanc and Rhine riesling are some of the best in the country. The company produces so many different labels it's hard to keep up. Sales and tasting 9 a.m.–5 p.m. Mon.–Sat., 11 a.m.–4 p.m. Sunday. Tours on the hour 10 a.m.–3 p.m. Mon.–Sat; by appointment Sun.

A good bet for a coach tour of the Marlborough area is the **DeLuxe Travel Line** in Blenheim. The all-day tours normally hit at least three major wineries, usually ones with restaurants (food is not included in the tour price). The tours also do some sight-seeing: Except in the winter, the buses travel around Queen Charlotte Sound and stop at other spots of local history. The normal price for these and other such tours is about $NZ35-40 per person. If you're on the North Island and just want to a day trip to the wineries, that can also be arranged through DeLuxe, which has packages for about $NZ65-70 per person that connect with either the InterIslander or the Lynx ferries. Information: *DeLuxe Travel Line, P.O. Box 147, Blenheim, New Zealand.* ☎ *(03) 578-5467; FAX 578-2416.*

Another good choice, for tours in small vans, is **Highlight Tours** in Blenheim, which specializes in tailored-to-your-taste tours, with stops at wineries and good area restaurants. Basic prices start around $NZ45 not counting food, and you can do either full-day or half-day trips. Information: ☎ *(03) 578-9904; FAX 577-8070.*

Or if you want your wine—and some skiing at the same time—**Back Country Safaris** in Blenheim can arrange a two-day package that includes ferry service to and from Wellington, a tour of about a half-dozen area wineries, transportation to the Rainbow ski area, a day's skiing (including equipment and lift tickets) and overnight accommodation, all for about $NZ300 per person; other packages can be arranged. Information ☎ *(03) 575-7525 or 578-9259.*

Wine Producing Regions

Nelson

This is probably the most French-like grape area in the country, a beautiful stretch of forests and low mountains, with loamy soils and cool nights. The climate is often compared to Burgundy. The Nelson area is often bypassed by travelers in a hurry to get to the Alps or Queenstown, which is a very, very big mistake. It's close to the northern fjords, several wonderful national parks, and some great wines. The main wines are sauvignon blanc, chardonnay and Rhine riesling. A few wineries:

Glover's Vineyard

Gardner Valley Road, Upper Moutere. ☎ *(03) 543-2698.*
Super scenery looking toward the Alps, specializing in cabernet sauvignon, pinot noir and sauvignon blanc. Very limited production of very good wines. Sales and tasting. 10 a.m.–6 p.m., Mon.–Sat.

Neudorf

Neudorf Road, Upper Moutere. ☎ *(03) 543-2643; FAX 543-2955.*
Dry chardonnays, pinot noir, riesling and sauvignon blanc. Really good chardonnays. Sales and tasting 10 a.m.–5 p.m. in summer.

Pelorus Vineyard

Patons Road, Nelson. ☎ *(03) 542-3868.*
Chardonnay, of course, plus pinot noir and riesling; the company also bottles area plantings of sauvignon blanc. The riesling is particularly good. Sales and tasting 10 a.m.–5 p.m. daily Nov.–Mar.

Seifried Estate

Main Road, Upper Moutere. ☎ *(03) 543-2795; FAX 543-2809.*
This is the largest winery in the area, accounting for something like 75 percent of the production. It specializes in sauvignon blanc, chardonnay and riesling, but also produces some decent pinot noirs and cabs. The winery operates a very nice tasting room and **Seifrieds Restaurant ★ ★ ★** on the main drag (SH60 along the bay) which has lunch seven days and dinner seven days during the summer and weekends in winter. It's a stylish place for a meal; dinner reservations necessary. ☎ *(03) 544-1555.* Sales and tasting 9 a.m.–6 p.m., Mon.–Sat.

For winery tours in the Nelson area, try **Agriland Explorer Tours** ☎ *(03) 528-9480;* **Nelson Day Tours** ☎ *(03) 545-1055* or **Sunshine Tours,** ☎ *(03) 548-7304.* All of these tours and others can be booked through the *Nelson Visitor Information Centre,* corner of Trafalgar and Halifax streets, ☎ *(03) 548-2304.* If you'd like to sample some area wines but not do any tours, check out the wide selection of locally produced goodies at **The Cellar On Robinsons**, a wine shop with an excellent range of products including malt beers and ciders. It's on the Main Road Stoke in Nelson. ☎ *(03) 547-5060.*

Canterbury

The wine area to the north and south of Christchurch along the coast started developing in the 1970s, but wine has been produced here since the

French settled Akaroa in the early 1800s. (There is still a winery at French Farm.) The normally dry climate of the area in and around Waipara, about 35 miles north of Christchurch, produces reds of good quality. A few wineries:

Amberley Estates

Reserve Road, Amberley. ☎ *(03) 314-8409.*
Dry riesling, chardonnay, gewurztraminer, pinot noir, chardonnay, sauvignon blanc. This is a very small winery with limited production. Tasting and sales 11 a.m.–5 p.m., Tues.–Sat.

Glenmark Wines

Weka Plains, Mackenzies Road, Waipara. ☎ *(03) 314-6828.*
Here's a success story: the winery has been winning awards since it first opened in 1986 and the wines are getting better every year. Combined with the **Winegarden Restaurant ★ ★ ★**, Glenmark is a great place to sample some very good reds and equally stunning chardonnays and dry rieslings. The restaurant is open Fri.–Sun. from 10 a.m.–6 p.m. Oct.–March. Tasting and sales 10 a.m.–6 p.m. daily.

Pegasus Bay

Stockgrove Road, Amberley. ☎ *(03) 314-6869; FAX 355-5937.*
Think it's too mild around here to grow merlot? Nope, and it's a fetching concoction as well. The winery's cabernet merlot is quite good, as is the pinot noir. And the chardonnay is not too shabby, either. Sales and tasting 10 a.m.–5 p.m. daily.

St. Helena

Coutts Island Road, Belfast. Fax and phone ☎ *(03) 323-8202.*
The first commercial vineyard in Canterbury, planted in 1978. Several of the company's pinot noirs have been international award-winners. Sales and tasting 10 a.m.–5 p.m., Mon.–Sat. Tours by appointment.

For a Waipara-area wine tour, contact **Quality Wine Tour Trail** at ☎ *(03) 342-9528.*

Queenstown

Some of the finest scenery for wineries you'll see anywhere is in the Queenstown area, which given the climate make wine-growing a somewhat iffy proposition, but somehow they have managed to outwit not only the weather, but skeptics. In truth, we'd have to say the better vintages offered in the area are from other grape-growing areas, especially Marlborough, but local vineyards are starting to produce some promising wines. These two wineries are close enough to bungy jumping sites you can either drink up some courage or decompress after throwing your body off a bridge above a roaring river:

Gibbston Valley Wines

Main Queenstown-Cromwell Highway. ☎ *(03) 442-6910; FAX 442-6909.*
This is our favorite, located not far from the bungy jumping bridge at the Kawarau Gorge about 25 kilometers from town. The winemaker here is an example of the often close contacts between the wine business in Australia, New Zealand and the

United States—he learned his trade in California. The owners claim it's the south-ernmost winery in the world, and there are vineyards on the property. Included in the offerings are pinot noir, pinot gris, gewurztraminer and Muller-Thurgau. Do try the Marlborough chardonnays, and especially try to have lunch here. The restaurant is open from 10 a.m.–5:30 p.m. Mon.–Sat. and noon–5:30 p.m. Sun. Winery sales and tastings are 10 a.m.–5:30 p.m., Mon.–Sat.; noon–5:30 p.m., Sun.

Chard Farm

Chard Road, near the Kawarau Bridge about 25 kilometers from Queenstown. Phone and FAX ☎ *(03) 442-6110.*

Here's another stunning location, perched above the river gorge, not far from the bungy site. In addition to pinot noir, chardonnays and riesling, the winery has taken a page from the German winemakers book and capitalized on the cold climate to produce some late-season ice wines—very sweet, very special. Winery sales and tast-ings are 11 a.m.–5 p.m. daily; tours by appointment.

THE SOUTH ISLAND

The South Island offers myriad scenic views.

We admit it, we're biased—if forced to pick only one locale in New Zealand to visit, it would just have to be the mountains, fjords and rugged country of the South Island. Hopefully, you'll have enough time to do both islands, but if not, we strongly suggest you concentrate on the south. Most tour groups do both, and in some cases, the delights of New Zealand flash by in a blur. We realize that, for some, this will be the only chance to see the country, and after spending all that time and money, you'll want to see it all. But there's just something about going slowly, seeing Mount Cook, hiking one of the alpine tracks or driving over a pass through the Southern Alps that makes the delights of the North Island pale a bit. If you are doing both islands, it's probably better to start in the north; going north after being on the South Island is a bit of an anticlimax.

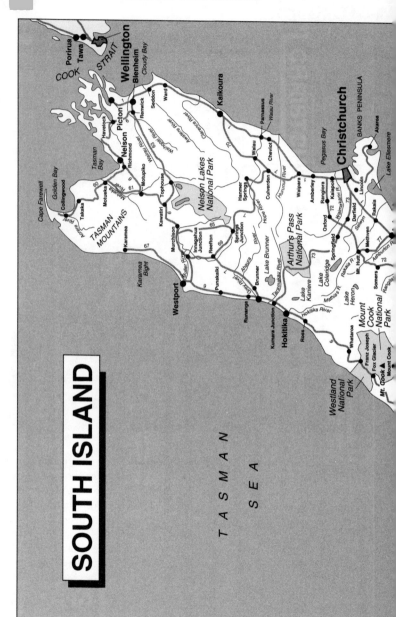

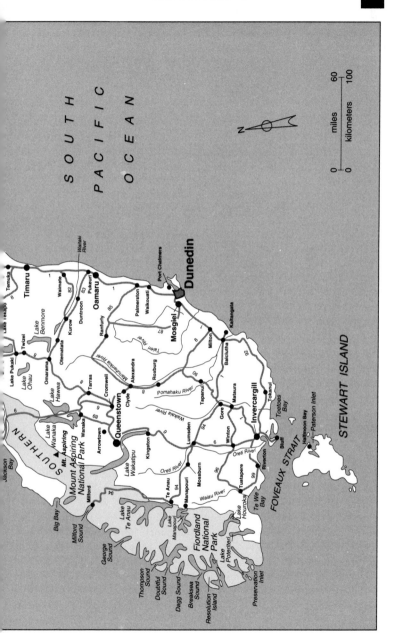

The major draw for the South Island, in addition to its diverse and wonderful scenery, is the lack of population. Christchurch, the biggest city in the south, is tidy and manageable with only about 320,000 people, and traffic on the southland's highways tends to be light. The male member of this party, being a Coloradoan by birth, is drawn to mountains like a moth to a bug zapper, and standing on top of a mile-high glacier in the Southern Alps is an experience right up there with marinated mussels and beer.

The road system in the south is good, and you can go all the way around the island with little difficulty. Most people make their way from the Picton ferry dock to Christchurch, either driving themselves or taking the coast train. From Christchurch, you can either go south or west to reach the mountains and fjords.

The Fastest Way to the Alps

Our suggested route, and the fastest way to the Alps and the glaciers from Christchurch, is to take Highway 73 west over Arthur's Pass, then south on Highway 6 to Fox Glacier and Franz Josef. From Fox Glacier, you go over the lovely Haast Pass highway to Queenstown, the center of activity in the mountain country. From Queenstown, you can go to the fjords, south to Invercargill and Stewart Island, or east to Dunedin and the coast. Christchurch to Franz Josef is about 400 kilometers (240 miles or so), and Franz Josef to Queenstown is about 215 miles. The highways in the south are mostly well-paved, a bit narrow and filled with one-lane bridges. Some highways are subject to closure in the winter.

In the beginnings of Maori colonization—and later in the European era—the South Island was the population and economic center of the country. This century, however, the North Island began to dominate. Until now, only about a third of the total population lived in the south. The Maoris probably got their name for New Zealand—Aotearoa, the Land of the Long White Cloud—from the clouds that often obscure the Southern Alps. The mountains split the island into two distinct climatic areas. On the west is a narrow belt of heavy precipitation and lush rain forests. To the east, the land is drier and has been built up into huge plains by deposits washed down from the mountains. Because of the divide, the climate in the south is at once the coldest and the hottest of both islands, as well as the wettest and driest. Most of the country's national parks are on the South Island, including Fiordland, the largest. The plants of the south are both subtropical and subantarctic, and there are large populations of seals and the only on-land rookery for the royal albatross.

Christchurch

Antarctic Centre, Christchurch

Christchurch is often described as a very English city, what with the River Avon and Anglican cathedrals and large expanses of lawn, a statue of Good Queen Vickie in the central park.

Perhaps. But to our minds, the comparison is a bit stretched. Christchurch is a very pretty, very green city, but it's too Down Under to really be English. It's like saying downtown Boston is English, which it is, sort of. Christchurch is a city that's easy to get around, a city with lots of arts and theater going on, a city with some very nice restaurants and some exceedingly fine hotels. The pace is much closer to town than city. Green? It's estimated that more than 10 percent of the city is parks or preserves. Whatever, it's our favorite city in New Zealand.

The Canterbury Region

Christchurch is the focal point of what is called the Canterbury Region, which is that portion of the South Island that generally lies east of the Southern Alps, and from just south of Kaikoura to just north of Oamaru along the coast. The city is the third largest in the country and dates from around 1850. It sits just to the north of the Banks Peninsula, with Pegasus Bay and the city's harbor, Lyttelton, to the east. It began life as a Church of England settlement (hence the name) and was supposed to be a haven for landed gentry and good Christian souls of lesser caste. Utopia in the Antipodes, perhaps. But economic reality reared its ugly head, and soon, to make ends meet, the fledgling community was forced to let in riff and raff, including—and here's where the downfall truly started—Australians fed up with conditions across the Tasman. As a church community, it was probably doomed from the start—there were so many clerics in town in the early years, there were church wars with bishops of all sorts stumbling around cheek by jowl trying to take control of minds and souls. Critics also suggested that the caliber of clergy being sent to the community was not the highest—mostly parsons who couldn't make it in the real world and had to settle for an island in the middle of the South Pacific.

The city was laid out in grids with the Avon meandering through the heart of town. (The river was named after a Scottish brook, by the way, not Will Shakespeare's famous creek.) Because of its wanderings, there are many bridges in the city, one of the most poignant being the Bridge of Remembrance, built in 1923 to commemorate the casualties of World War I—plaques to honor other war dead were added later. It's on Cashel Street.

On to Antarctica

Christchurch has a special connection to Antarctica. It was from here that the Englishman Robert Falcon Scott first set out to explore the frozen continent, and from here in 1910 he left on his misguided and doomed attempt to beat Roald Amundsen to the South Pole. There is a statue of Scott, standing in winter gear, on Oxford Terrace next to the Avon. At Victoria Square, there's also a statue of Captain Cook, another explorer who sailed from New Zealand to explore the polar regions. The city is also headquarters for the U.S. Antarctic mission, which, given the New Zealand attitude toward the environment and the abysmal record the United States has had of fouling its own nest in Antarctica, might not last. Some years back, the United States used explosives to blow up a toxic waste dump at McMurdo Sound, not an act designed to amuse the Kiwis, who have a very protective attitude about the frozen continent. Maybe it wasn't us—blame it on the French. The

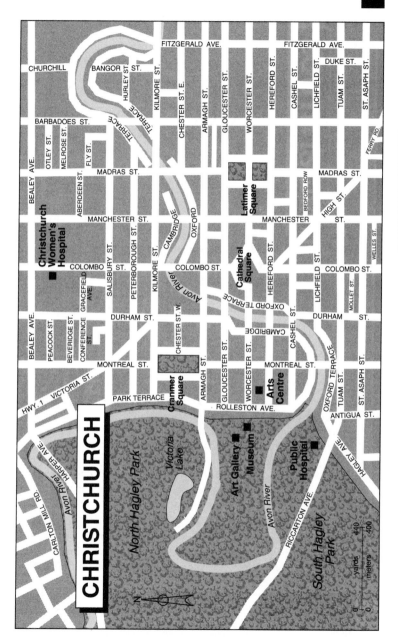

Americans, meanwhile, have been threatening to pull their polar operations out of New Zealand because of the country's anti-nuke policies.

The International Antarctic Centre near the airport has a splendid display of icy exhibits about the Frozen Continent: ice caves, a polar aquarium, photos and an audiovisual show. It was built to resemble large ice formations and is part of a complex that provides services for the Antarctic research programs run by the United States, Italy and New Zealand. It also includes a bar, gift shop and café. It's located on Orchard Road about five minutes' walk from the airport. (We think **Kelly Tarlton's Antarctic Encounter** in Auckland is better, but the Christchurch offering is pretty good.) Handicapped access. *Open 9:30 a.m.–8:30 p.m. daily Oct.1–Mar. 31; 9:30 a.m.–5:30 p.m. Apr. 1–Sept.30. Adults $NZ10, kids $NZ6.* ☎ *(03) 358-9896; FAX 353-7799.*

The Gothic Heaps

One of the striking things about Christchurch, in addition to its feeling of genteel comfort, is the stash of lovely old Gothic heaps left over from the Victorian era. The wallahs in charge of publicity for the city say right up front that Christchurch has the finest collection of such edifices in Australasia—a statement which might be taken amiss by Australians looking down Macquarie Street in Sydney. Still, there are some dandies in Christchurch, and many of the best examples are churches, just what you'd expect given the city's genealogy.

The premier building is probably the **Anglican Cathedral**, begun in the 1860s and finished in 1881. The church tower is 215 feet above the square, and gives a commanding view of the central downtown area. Of interest inside is a panel with the Lord's Prayer in Maori. Outside is a statue of Robert Godley, the father of Christchurch. Tuesdays and Wednesdays at 5:15 p.m. the cathedral choir does evensong. You can climb the 133 steps up to the tower 8:30 a.m.–4 p.m., weekdays and Saturdays, 11:30 a.m.–4 p.m., Sundays. Admission is about $NZ2 for adults; many choral performances. *Information* ☎ *(03) 366-0046.* The Cathedral is the centerpiece of Cathedral Square, a pedestrian area flanked by the church and several other old lovelies, including the **Press Building** (1909), housing the city's oldest newspaper; the **Regent Theatre** (1905), and the former **Central Post Office** building (1879).

The square (public toilets available) is the Hyde Park of Christchurch, with speakers odd, sincere or both taking voice during the lunch hour. For the past two decades, the most famous of these has been **the Wizard**, who wears a wizard suit, stands on a ladder and is generally given credit for establishing the right to have a Speaker's Corner in the square to begin with. The real name is Ian Brackenbury Channell, an Englishman who arrived in Christchurch in 1974. Prior to that, Channell, with a degree in sociology and psychology, had been a teacher. He started his Wizard ways at the University of

New South Wales in Australia, and arrived in New Zealand with credentials indicating he was, in fact, a genuine Aussie wizard. The Christchurch city dads were less than amused by his presence, and it took several very public battles to establish his right of free speech in Cathedral Square. He's also a former Royal Air Force navigator, collects hundreds of videos of old movies, and is now in his mid-60s. Of late, the Wizard has decided he'd rather travel than orate and has cut back on his public appearances. You'll only see him in the square in the summer and only when the mood hits him. When he does travel, by the way, his passport identifies him as "The Wizard of New Zealand." Like Bigfoot, you'll be very lucky if you actually get to see him, but he does have a special place now in the hearts of the Christchurchians. According to the free local tourist paper, the Wiz has been classified as a "living work of art." Some people think he's a sexist and a bit of a racist. You judge.

Many architectural judges think the best Victorian Gothic structures in the country are the **Provincial Council Buildings**, a gaggle of structures of both wood and stone built between the 1850s and 1860s. Particularly impressive is the 1865 Council Chamber with its high tower, vaulted ceilings and stained-glass windows. The complex is located near the corner of Armagh and Durham streets, southwest of Victoria Square. It's open weekdays from 10:30 a.m.–5 p.m. and guided tours are offered. ☎ *(03) 366-1100.*

Some other buildings worth a look are the **Theatre Royal** (1908) on Gloucester Street; the **Roman Catholic Cathedral of the Blessed Sacrament** (1905) on Barbadoes Street, classed as the finest neo-Renaissance church in the country; the **McKenzie and Willis** buildings (1878) on Tuam Street; and the **Canterbury Club** (1874) on Cambridge Terrace.

Canterbury University

While Cathedral Square has its allures, we prefer to go walkabout near the city's **Botanic Gardens**, which lie west of the river—from Cathedral Square, just walk down Worcester Street and keep going. *Information:* ☎ *(03) 366-1701.* Just before arriving at the Botanic Gardens, you'll come to the impressive former campus of **Canterbury University**, with a series of Gothic stone buildings begun in 1876. In one of the buildings is the den used by New Zealand's most famous scientist, Ernest Rutherford, who received the Nobel Prize for chemistry in 1908 for work involving the atomic nucleus. It's open for visits. The campus and its buildings are now the home of the **Christchurch Arts Centre**, which houses a ballet troupe, a theatre company, a school of music, several small galleries and artisans and a couple of movie theaters. Musical performances are given in what is probably the most impressive of the old buildings, the Great Hall, built in 1882. In addition to the 40 or so crafts shops (which include hand spinning and weaving, stringed instrument manufacture and Maori arts), there are a couple of restaurants and offices of the

Nuclear Free Society and an animal rights group. The Centre is open daily, and on weekends is home to arts fairs where local artisans display their wares. *For information,* ☎ *(03) 366-0989.*

Christchurch Arts Centre offers pleasant outdoor dining as well as arts fairs and cultural attractions.

A bit further on, where Worcester meets Rolleston Avenue, you'll find the **Canterbury Museum**, housed in some 1870 buildings. The highlight of the museum, which has displays of Maori culture and early colonial life, is the **Hall of Antarctic Discovery**, a first-rate presentation about the men who explored the last continent. The museum also has a snack bar, bird hall and the new Maori gallery, *Iwi Tawhito-Whenua Hou* (Ancient People-New Land). The museum complex is open daily, 9 a.m.–5 p.m. Admission is free, but donations are welcomed. There is a gift shop and four free guided tours daily. ☎ *(03) 366-8379.*

Behind the museum is the **McDougall Art Gallery**, which has some fine Maori portraits and a couple of Rodin statues. It also houses a striking display of paintings and other objects relating to the two world wars. Basically the same hours as the museum; admission free. ☎ *(03) 365-0915.*

Also behind the museum is the main entrance to the **Botanic Gardens**. The gardens (1863) are actually part of 450-acre **Hagley Park**, situated on a loop of the Avon. The oldest sports building in the country is here—the Hagley Oval, home to Kiwi cricket—and the gardens themselves are full of native and imported trees and flower beds. You can walk or, in the summertime, catch the electric-powered "Toast Rack," a trolley that takes visitors around (no service June and July). Look for the 30-foot-high totem pole at the north end of the park. It was donated by the state of Oregon as a tribute to New Zealand support for U.S. service personnel stationed in Antarctica. Hours for the gardens are 7 a.m.–dusk daily. In the center of things is **Victoria Lake**, a favorite for radio-control boat fans. You can pick up lunch at the **Gardens Restaurant**, not far from the lake, which has a daily noontime smorgasbord. ☎ *(03) 366-5076*.

Another favorite stroll is to start at Victoria Square, itself a nice urban park with a statue of Queen Victoria herself, Capt. James Cook and a carved Maori statue, and walk down the Avon to the Montreal Street bridge. Here you'll find the **Antigua Boatsheds**, built in 1882 for the all-male Christchurch Boating Club but now willing to rent paddle boats and canoes to all comers for around $NZ10 an hour. ☎ *(03) 366-5885*. Or if you feel like being pampered, you can be punted down the Avon for about $NZ15 per person for a 45-minute trip. Punts in this case are not what you do on fourth down, but rather the English gentry's equivalent of the Venetian gondola. Punts leave from the Canterbury Information Centre, the Town Hall restaurant and the Thomas Edmonds restaurant. Bookings can be made at the information center: ☎ *(03) 379-9629*. Punts operate from 9 a.m. until dusk.

The folks who live in Christchurch have always loved their flowers, and for the past 10 years or so, the Christchurch Beautifying Association has planted something in excess of 20,000 daffodil bulbs along Park Terrace on the banks of the Avon next to North Hagley Park. Unfortunately, the project might not continue because thieves keep stealing the bulbs. At one point, it was estimated that almost 90 percent of the plants had been taken.

Around Christchurch

Some other spots in and around Christchurch worthy of a visit:

Air Force World

☎ *(03) 343-9532*.

For war and/or airplane freaks, a great place, full of displays, flight simulators, aircraft and memorabilia about the Royal New Zealand Air Force from World War I on. If you've never seen a Spitfire or P-51 up close, here's your chance. *It's open from 10 a.m.–4 p.m. seven days. Admission is about $NZ10. The museum is located at Wigram Aerodrome, a few miles west of town on Highway 1 (the Main South Road). If you're afoot, take a No. 8 or No. 25 bus from Cathedral Square.*

Mona Vale

☎ *(03) 348-9660*.

This turn-of-the-century mansion shows you how the swells used to live in Christchurch. The huge house was built in 1900 and bought in 1905 by Annie Townend, the millionaire daughter of a wealthy sheep rancher. It's located on the Avon, a couple of kilometers from town. There are morning and afternoon teas and smorgasbord lunches daily except Saturdays. *The grounds themselves are open from 8 a.m. to 7:30 p.m in the summer.* Punting at Mona Vale is also available for about $NZ10 a half-hour per person. Tickets are available at Mona Vale or at the Christchurch information center. *The mansion is entered from Fendalton Road.*

Orana Park Wildlife Trust

Information (including feeding times): ☎ *(03) 359-7109.*

Okay, animal fans, here's your chance to see two of the biggies in the New Zealand fauna world in one shot—the kiwi and the tuatara (see "Animals" in "The Land" chapter). In addition to native New Zealand animals, the reserve also has 400 species of exotics, including kangaroos, lions, zebra, rhinos and giraffes. The park is located on McLean's Island Road, northwest of the international airport. Admission is about $NZ10 for adults. It's open daily from 10 a.m.–4:30 p.m.

Another interesting animal scene is the night-time exhibits at the **Willowbank Wildlife Reserve** north of the central city. The park, open from 10 a.m.–10 p.m., features an evening tour of kiwis and other nocturnal animals. The tour is free if you eat at the Colonial Kiwi restaurant on the premises. Otherwise, the entry fee is $NZ8 for adults. The park is on Hussey Road, which is reached by going north on Highway 1 (Main North Road) to Styx Mill Road and then to Hussey. *Fax and phone* ☎ *(03) 359-6226.* **(You can also hit Willowbank on a dinner/sight-seeing tour; details in TOURS section below.)**

Ferrymead Historic Park

☎ *(03) 384-1970.*

This is sort of a 20th-century Down Under Williamsburg. The theme is a busy little town from the turn of the century, with a working printer's shop, bakery and artisans shops. It's a self-contained village with the emphasis on vintage technology—cars, railroad engines, airplanes and agricultural equipment. Included in the displays are a working railroad and a tram line. It's located off Ferry Road on the Heathcote River, southeast of the city. *It's open daily 10 a.m.–4:30 p.m. Adult tickets are about $NZ7; $NZ5 for kids.*

Nga Hau E Wha National Marae

☎ *(03) 388-7685.*

In Maori life, the tribal meeting area was the center of village life. These places, called *marae* in Maori, can be found all over New Zealand, and this new one in Christchurch is the biggest in the country. The intent here is to offer tourists who come to Christchurch, especially international visitors, a chance to see Maori cultural events. The program will vary, but you can always expect to be greeted with a *haka* and pig out at a *hangi* or two. About the only other place with a Maori exhibit as authentic are the various performances in and around Rotorua on the North Island. The marae is located on Pages Road, which is northeast of the central city heading for New Brighton Beach, and also features a selection of Maori art. There are tours as well as welcoming ceremonies, usually four times a day except on weekends. Information is available at the downtown visitors information center or by calling the marae itself. There are admission charges for the tours and other ceremonies.

Christchurch Casino

☎ *(03) 365-9999; FAX (03) 365-2920.*

As in the United States, it seems the gambling bug has hit big time in Australasia; every major city in Australia has a casino, and the Kiwis aren't far behind. The new casino in Christchurch is located on Victoria Street just off Kilmore Street. It has the usual casino offerings, including table games and "pokies," poker machines. There are a couple of bars and restaurants. To make it easy to lose your dollars, the casino operates a courtesy bus service on three routes around town, picking up players from large hotels and other locations. *The service operates from 6 p.m.–2 a.m. seven days.* There is no fixed schedule; simply call and they'll come and get you. ☎ *(03) 372-8887. Casino hours are 11 a.m.–3 a.m. Mon.–Wed., and 24 hours from 11 a.m. Thurs.–3 a.m. Mon.* There is a dress code: no jeans, shorts without long socks, thongs, T-shirts or workboots. Minimum age is 20.

Christchurch Gondola

☎ *(03) 384-4914; fax 384-4923.*

Here's a chance to view the ChCh area, look over at the Banks Peninsula, Lyttleton Harbour, Mt. Hutt and on a clear day, the sweep of the Southern Alps. The gondola starts from the base on Bridle Path Road, goes about three-fifths of a mile and rises to more than 1600 feet on the top of an extinct volcano rim called the Port Hills. The four-passenger gondolas run from noon to late and cost $NZ12 per person. Once on top, there are shops and the Ridge Restaurant and for snacks, the Red Rock Cafe. If you wish, you can get back to town by renting a bike or by tandem paragliding. A weekend brunch at the Ridge Restaurant plus gondola rides is $NZ22 per person and runs from 10 a.m.–2:30 p.m. Getting to the gondola is easy: Take the free shuttle from the visitors center across from Noah's Hotel (or from most major hotels); take the No. 28 Lyttelton bus; or catch the City Circuit Bus (take the Port Circuit.).

Queen Elizabeth II Park and Leisure Centre

☎ *(03) 383-4313.*

If you want to go for a swim—or relieve a teenager who's climbing the walls, this is the place for you. The centerpieces of the complex, built for the 1974 Commonwealth Games, are its four indoor heated pools, squash courts and running track. It also has bumper cars, miniature golf, two water slides, a maze, a poolside café and an outdoor snack stand. *The amusements are open daily from 10 a.m. to 6 p.m. daily; pool hours vary.* The facility is located in New Brighton, on the coast north of Christchurch. There's a good beach nearby, as well.

The Essential Christchurch

Climate

The city sits next to the ocean on the Canterbury Plains, so it gets climatic influences from mountains, plains and sea—meaning the weather is changeable. Look for summer highs to be around 20–25 degrees Celsius (70 to 80 degrees Fahrenheit, 50s at night) and winter lows in the 4–6 range (40s) with highs in the 50s. Rainfall is heaviest in the summer. It might snow once in a while.

Information

Your best source of city and regional information is the **Christchurch/Canterbury Visitor Centre** at the corner of Worcester Street and Oxford Terrace opposite Noah's Hotel. In addition to written information, maps and brochures, the center is also where a number of local services, such as city tours, rental cars and accommodations, can be booked. During the week, it's open from 8:30 a.m.–5 p.m.; weekends and holidays from 8:30 a.m.–4 p.m., extended hours in the summer; ☎ *(03) 379-9629; FAX (03) 377-2424.* Information is also available at the airport. The **Department of Conservation** office at *133 Victoria Street* has all manner of information about national parks, camping permits and general information about the South Island's outdoor areas. ☎ *(03) 379-9758.*

The city also has a special information service for handicapped travelers. *Located at 314 Worcester Street,* the office has information about equipment, facilities and access. Hours are Monday–Friday 9 a.m.–5 p.m. ☎ *(03) 366-6189.*

Banks

Normal banking hours are weekdays from 9 a.m.–4:30 p.m. (Tuesdays, open from 9:30 a.m.) Hours for bureaux de change at the airport and at downtown locations vary; some are open Saturday mornings. We found most of the banks clustered near Victoria Square; some did not charge for changing traveler's checks, but Thomas Cook did.

Phones

The area code for Christchurch is *(03). The emergency number (police, fire, ambulance) is 111.* For police nonemergency: ☎ *(03) 379-3999.* The number for the U.S. consulate is ☎ *(04) 379-0040 (it's in Wellington.)* There is a free general information service called **Infophone**, a 24-hour phone line with information about almost every service and attraction in the city. ☎ *(03) 363-5000.*

Getting There

By Air

The Christchurch airport is being greatly expanded in a $US60 million project due to be completed in 1998. The pressure on the Auckland International Airport is getting so severe, it's likely that a lot of international travel will be routed to Christchurch sometime in the near future. Existing facilities are being upgraded and expanded; the new terminal will be 2.5 times bigger than the present facility. Included in new features will be several large shopping areas, a café/bar inside the international departures area and new parking and aircraft handling areas. The airport handled almost 800,000 passengers in 1994-95, and by 2004, this is expected to rise to almost 2 million.

Christchurch is served internally by **Ansett** and **Air New Zealand** from the North Island and other cities on the South Island, and by **Mount Cook** from the resort areas on the South Island. Daily service from Auckland to Christchurch is about $NZ320 per person, one way. Daily service from Wellington is about $NZ200. South Island fares to Christchurch from various cities include Dunedin, $NZ190; Invercargill, $NZ230; Nelson, $NZ170; Queenstown, $NZ260; and Mount Cook,

$NZ220. These fares include the goods and services tax but are lower using one of the many air passes available. United has offices in Christchurch; ☎ *(03) 366-1736.*

By Bus

The fare from the ferry dock at Picton to Christchurch is about $NZ60 per person, one way. Other fares into the city include the following: from Fox Glacier, $NZ70; Mount Cook, $NZ60; Queenstown, $NZ90; Invercargill, $NZ90; and Dunedin, $NZ50. These fares include tax but are lower with passes. There is also a coast-to-coast service from Christchurch to Greymouth and back with stops at Arthur's Pass. The service, called **Coast to Coast Shuttle**, picks up passengers at any YHA, or back-packers hotel. The buses will take bikes, luggage or skis at no extra charge—and no, you don't have to be a backpacker to ride the bus. Christchurch to Arthur's Pass is $NZ25; Christchurch to Greymouth, $NZ35; round-trip Christchurch–Greymouth–Christchurch, $NZ60 (must be used within three days). Buses leave the city around 7:30 a.m., and return around 5:30 p.m. The company recommends reservations; *for information, call* ☎ *(0800) 800-847.*

By Rail

From Picton, the daily **Coastal Express** fare, one way, is about $NZ60. Other rail fares on the South Island to Christchurch (which may mean some bus segments) include Nelson, $NZ85; Te Anau, $NZ120; Greymouth, $NZ75; Dunedin, $NZ60; Fox Glacier, $NZ90;, and Franz Josef, $NZ90. The train terminal in Christchurch is on Clarence Street just west of Hagley Park in the suburb of Addington. ☎ *(0800) 802.*

How to Get Around

By Taxi

They don't cruise in Christchurch, so find a cab stand (or a hotel) or call them. Try **Blue Star Taxis**, which has vans and also wheelchair taxis available, ☎ *(03) 379-9799.*

By Bus

There's an extensive bus system around the Christchurch metro area. Fares are per zone; the normal fare around town and to close-by environs is about $NZ1.60. The city also runs hourly buses from the airport to Cathedral Square for about $NZ3; takes about a half-hour. **Carrington's** also runs a shuttle for about double the price and will pick you up at your hotel; ☎ *(03) 352-6369.* Or try **Super Shuttle**, ☎ *(03) 365-5655.* For information about city bus service, check with the Canterbury Information Centre, the bus kiosk in Cathedral Square, or call **Businfo** at ☎ *(03) 366-8855.*

By Tram

A quickie way to see the edges of the downtown, plus a classy building or two along the way, is to hop aboard the new (1995) **Christchurch Tramway**, which makes a 2.5-kilometer circuit every half-hour. One stretch goes down New Regent Street, the first and probably still the classiest shopping mall in the city. There is a running commentary and the lovingly restored trams do stop at several key locations, including the visitors information center and Cathedral Square. Tickets are $NZ4 for one hour; $NZ6 for four hours, or $NZ10 for a full day; you can buy them on the trams. *Information:* ☎ *(03) 366-7830; FAX (03) 366-6943.*

By Bike

Christchurch is a flat city, ideal for bikers who can remember to stay on the proper side of the road. There are several bike rental shops in town. Try **Cyclone Cycles** at *245 Colombo Street,* ☎ *(03) 332-9573*; both mountain bikes and touring bikes available. Or try **Christchurch Leisure Sports**, *94 Gloucester Street,* ☎ *(03) 377-2827*; it has bikes, mopeds (no special license needed), mountain bikes, twin bikes—almost any kind of sports equipment is available for rent. Or try **Christchurch Rent-a-Bike**, *82 Worcester Street.* Depending on type of bike, insurance rates and the individual outlet, expect to pay around $NZ10 to $NZ15 a day, or around $NZ60 to $NZ100 a week. The Canterbury Information Centre has biking maps for the city and nearby countryside; it also has maps of city walks and hikes in the area.

Rental Cars/RVs

All the major multinationals have offices in Christchurch: Budget, Hertz, National, Thrifty, Avis—plus a bunch of locals. For rental costs for automobiles and camper vans, see "Driving Down Under" in "The Essential New Zealand" chapter. Among the locals worth checking with are **Newmans** and **Maui**, both national companies. Maui is especially recommended for RVs. There are also some cut-rate local agencies that we haven't used which offer pretty good deals. Hey, it's New Zealand—they have to be honest, right? The **Automobile Association** office downtown is at *210 Hereford Street*, next to the Occidental Hotel, ☎ *(03) 379-1280.*

Tours

The major attractions downtown are within fairly easy walking distance—remember the city is flat—but for those who choose to ride, there are a number of tour companies that offer scenic drives around the city, the environs or day trips, and longer, to attractions in the Canterbury district. Most of the tours can be booked through your hotel, through the tourist offices, travel agents or by calling direct. Among the best:

CTL Coachlines

☎ *(03) 379-4268; after hours,* ☎ *(03) 366-1999. The Queenstown office is at 37 Shotover Street,* ☎ *(03) 442-7028.*
The historic three-hour Christchurch tour does all the necessary spots, and runs about $NZ20 for adults. The company also has tours to Akaroa (one-day) about $NZ30; a trip to Orana Park and a salmon farm (half-day), about $NZ25; a trip to Milford Sound and Queenstown (one long day), about $NZ120. Local tours leave from the CTB kiosk at Cathedral Square. Local and tour passengers will be picked up at hotels prior to departure if requested in advance; the tour prices do not include meals.

City Circuit Bus

☎ *(03) 385-5386; FAX (03) 385-5389.*
This company operates a fleet of small vans that run two circuits around the city stopping at most of the major sites. Tickets are good for an eight-hour period and

can be used over two days. The rate is $NZ25 per person. The vans leave from the visitors center on Worcester every day from 9 a.m.–6 p.m.

Christchurch DoubleDecker Bus Company

☎ *(03) 377-1644; FAX the same.*
The green-and-white double-deckers run from the Worcester visitors center at 10 a.m., noon, 2 p.m. and 4 p.m., and at 6 p.m. Nov.–Mar. The 90-minute tours of the city hit dozens of sites. Tickets are $NZ22 adults, $NZ10 children.

Eco Safaris

☎ *(03) 374-5857; FAX 349-3038.*
This is a great one for kids or folks interested in history, nature and conservation. A series of trips is offered, many combining jet boats, harbor cruises, caves, hikes, museums and nature watching. Some tours visit old Maori rock art, others do whale watching, still others visit *pas*. One of the better trips is a full-day jaunt to the Banks Peninsula, with a winery tour, a ride on the catamaran at Akaroa Harbour, forest walks and a penguin tour. Including morning/afternoon tea and lunch, it lasts about 9 hours and costs about $NZ185 per person. There are also half-day trips available. All tours depart Christchurch at 8 am. Tours can be booked by calling ahead or by writing to *Exclusive Wilderness Safaris Ltd., P.O. Box 16414, Christchurch, New Zealand.*

Ecotourism Australasia

55 Highstead Road, Christchurch, ☎ *(03) 379-9904; FAX: (03) 379-9939*
Ecotourism and adventure travel are the specialties of this Christchurch-based outfit. Activities range from hiking and bush walking to bungy jumping, rafting and ballooning. Nature tours include flora and fauna, marine mammals, wildlife parks, farm visits and private gardens. Special interest cultural and shopping tours are also available.

The Hanmer Experience

☎ *(03) 359-9133; FAX 359-9058.*
The Hanmer Springs area north of Christchurch is one of our favorite parts of the South Island (see more detail in the "Around Canterbury" section later on), and here's a chance to take a day trip up to see why. The all-day tour run by **Pacific Tourways Ltd**. stops at the Balmoral Homestead south of Hanmer Springs for morning tea, then goes on to the Waiau River for a jetboat trip. After lunch, you have a choice of activities, including bungy jumping, a dip in the famous local thermal pools, nine holes of golf or a shopping excursion. The tours leave Christchurch at 7 a.m., return around 6 p.m. The cost is $NZ235 person. City tour (half-day), about $NZ25, which includes snacks and hotel/motel pickup; leaves at 9 a.m. and 1:30 p.m. The Pacific Tours office is at 502a Wairakei Road in Christchurch.

Kiwis by Night

☎ *(03) 355-4458; FAX 377-2991.*
Here's the night tour to the Willowbank Reserve we mentioned. The tour includes a trip around the city to several noted spots (Mona Vale, the university, etc.), plus a five-course dinner and that rendezvous with the creatures of the night. The tours ends with a trip out to the Sign of the Takahe to see the lights of the city. The four-hour tour departs at 6:30 p.m. at the downtown visitors center (or hotel pickup by

prior arrangement) and costs about $NZ90 per person. It can be booked at the visitors center.

Christchurch Sightseeing Tours

☎ *(03) 366-9660.*

City tour (half-day), about $NZ25, which includes snacks and hotel/motel pickup; leaves at 9 a.m. and 1:30 p.m.

Gray Line New Zealand

☎ *(03) 343-3874.*

Always a good bet, the Gray Line operation in New Zealand is no exception. There are two city tours, one in the morning, one in the afternoon, for about $NZ25 for adults. The price includes free motel/hotel pickup and snacks (there is an optional airport drop-off on request). Tours depart from the Canterbury Information Centre.

Gray Line, in cooperation with Mount Cook Lines, also runs a tour to Kaikoura, about 2.5 hours north of the city on the coast where you can pick up a boat to go searching for whales, dolphins, seals and seabirds—or you can take a glass-bottom boat trip. The round-trip to Kaikoura is about $NZ45. The best time to see the 70-foot sperm whales along the coast is in the winter. The whale-watching trips leave about two hours after arrival, and return just before the bus heads back. The cost is about $NZ80 per person. The glass-bottom boat trips run about four hours and include lunch; price is about $NZ50 per person. You can stay over in Kaikoura and catch another return bus. For current whale-watching prices (or to book without a bus tour), call ☎ *(0800) 655-121.*

There is also a tour from Christchurch to Queenstown with a stop at Mount Cook—you can return from Mount Cook or stay over in Queenstown. The Christchurch–Mount Cook–Christchurch fare is about $NZ80, no meals; the trip to Queenstown is about $NZ60, no meals. City tours depart from the Canterbury Information Centre; regional tours depart from the Mount Cook Lines depot at *40 Lichfield Street.* Hotel/motel pickups available on request. *Information in Christchurch,* ☎ *(03) 379-0690*; throughout the country, ☎ *(0800) 800-904.* **Newmans Coaches** also has service to Kaikoura; ☎ *(03) 379-5641.* Or if you want to splurge, **Whalewatch Air** will whip you to the whales for $NZ165 per person round trip. The company also does short whale flights from Kaikoura itself for about $NZ80 per person. In Christchurch, contact the company at ☎ *(03) 358-8334.*

Sports

Skiing

Christchurch is within a few hours of a bunch of ski areas, including **Mt. Hutt** and **Mt. Dobson**, and many people actually base in the city to bus or drive down to ski near Queenstown. Thus, the town has a number of companies offering ski packages from Christchurch to almost any ski resort of your choice. For further information, see the "Skiing" section in "The Perfect Vacation" chapter.

The Rakaia River and Mount Hutt, Canterbury

Golf

There are four courses in Christchurch. Serious golfers will want the 18-hole **Waitikari** championship course at Burwood; ☎ *(03) 383-1400*. Or another 18-holer, the **Coringa Country Club** course, ☎ *(03) 359-7172*. Green fees will be in the $NZ20-30 range, and club rentals are available. Or try the Russley Gold Club about eight kilometers northwest of the city ☎ *(03) 358-4748*.

Tennis

You might get invited to a private club, or else try **Tourist Tennis**, which has 10 lighted courts and equipment rentals. ☎ *(03) 351-6826*.

Squash

There are a number of public squash courts, including those at the Queen Elizabeth II Park. ☎ *(03) 383-4313*.

Beaches

The Christchurch beaches are on the coast, east and northeast of the city, most within 10 kilometers or so. Local word is that sharks are few and far between but that there are often nasty undercurrents. Many areas of the beaches are patrolled. There are also swimming areas in Lyttelton Harbour and on the Banks Peninsula southeast of the city. Two of the more popular beaches are Pegasus Bay and New Brighton.

There are many other activities available—bowling, horseback riding, go-carts, fishing, dancing—you name it. Check with the Canterbury Information Centre.

Shopping

Normal weekday shopping hours in the central city are from 9 a.m. to 5:30 p.m. Monday–Friday; Friday night to 9 p.m.; Saturday 9 a.m.–1 p.m. Most tourist-type shops stay open weekends. Many of the stores in the malls and in the suburbs also stay open weekends; hours vary. Credit cards are widely accepted.

There are several shopping complexes in the city, including the dozens of stores that sit around the pedestrian-only **Triangle Centre** mall running along Cashel Street, then down High Street to Hereford (they say Haira-furd). Also worth a try downtown are the first shopping mall in the city (1931) and the Spanish-motif shops along **New Regent Street** (designed by a California architect, hence the decor). It's now a designated historic district. Many of the stores and cafés in Christchurch, by the way, are totally smoke-free. Two new suburban shopping centers:

Riccarton Mall

Located on the road of the same name, a bit over a kilometer west of Hagley Park. ☎ *(03) 348-4119*.
You'll find everything from a Kmart to Canterbury stores, plus a food court and 90-odd shops. Open Thur. and Fri. nights.

Linwood City Shopping Centre

At the corner of Linwood Avenue and Buckleys Road, which is a couple of miles east of the city center. Open Thurs. and Fri. nights.
City Arts Centre in the old Canterbury University campus has a number of crafts shops and galleries, normally open seven days a week. One we recommend taking a peek at is **Riki Rangi**, a Maori arts studio that specializes in carvings of native wood,

bone, stone and shells. Adjacent to the workshop is a gallery where the finished products are on sale. It has some of the best greenstone jewelry around. *Hours are 9 a.m.–5 p.m., weekdays and 10 a.m.–4 p.m. weekends.* ☎ *(03) 366-4943.* The outdoor **Arts Centre Market** on Worcester Street, next to the campus, is open weekends, 10 a.m.–4 p.m.

Sheep stores are everywhere you turn, one of which is the **Sheep Station** at the corner of Colombo and Gloucester streets. Lots of lambskin clothing, suedes, leathers and rugs. Another good store is the **Skin Pool** at *76 Moorhouse Avenue.* Also try **Woolpak** at *30 Battersea Street,* which has a large assortment of rugs and car seat covers. Or the **Rusa Leather Co.** factory at *174 St. Asaph Street.* **The Tannery**, on Worcester Street next to Noah's Hotel, has deerskin and mohair goods. For some flashy knitwares and designer scarves, try **Nature's Choice** at *755 Colombo Street.* Most stores will ship stuff home if it's too bulky to pack or carry on the plane. If you'd like to see jewelry made from greenstone, as well as paua shell works, try the **New Zealand Greenstone Gallery** downtown at *37 Cathedral Square;* it's open Saturdays.

Canterbury clothing is found all over New Zealand. The Canterbury line of jerseys is world famous and is worn by many of the world's soccer and rugby teams. You can pick up a version of the All-Blacks rig almost anywhere. Canterbury stuff ain't cheap, but it's exceptional quality and well worth the money. Sir Edmund Hillary, conqueror of Everest, is now a spokesman and designer for some Canterbury lines. Ed Hillary, as he signs the ads, is flogging 17 types of outdoor wear from shoes to extreme-weather gear. One place with a large assortment is the **Canterbury of New Zealand** store in the Riccarton Mall.

Where to Stay

Parkroyal   **$NZ300**   ★★★★★

Situated at the corner of Kilmore and Durham streets next to the new Town Hall and overlooking Victoria Square. ☎ *(03) 365-7799; FAX (03) 365-0082.*
This is our favorite of the biggies downtown. The centerpiece of the eight-floor building is a glass atrium, a nice place to be on a sunny day. The 300-room hotel, built in the shape of a truncated pyramid, has a laundry room plus 24-hour laundry service, a business center, a gym, a sauna, TV and coffee/tea. Traditional Japanese food is served in the **Yamagen Restaurant** ★★★, expensive, and the **Victoria Street Café** ★★ in the atrium has a good salad bar and light lunches, moderate. The **Canterbury Tales** ★★★ restaurant serves upscale meals; look for the wall tapestries depicting scenes from Chaucer's classic, expensive. **Rumpole's Bar** is popular with the local barristers, not because of the PBS-familiar name but because of the hotel's proximity to the Town Hall courts. The **First Edition Bar** has live music and meals until late. It offers casino packages (the casino is across the street). Standard singles and doubles are about $NZ300 plus GST; there are also luxury suites.

Noah's   **$NZ205–875**   ★★★★

Corner of Worcester and Oxford Terrace. ☎ *(03) 379-4700; FAX (03) 379-5357.*
Another popular hotel, it looks sort of like a giant, bowed computer chip, but lots of business types use it for their Christchurch base. It has 208 rooms, with main din-

ing in the **Waitangi Restaurant** ★★★, expensive, and the **Brogues Brasserie** ★★ for meals at all hours, budget to moderate. There are three bars, including the very nice **Worcester Bar.** Standard single/double rooms are about $NZ205; deluxe are $NZ230; suites start at $NZ515, and the royal suite is $NZ875.

Centra $NZ285   ★★★

Corner of High and Cashel streets. ☎ *(03) 365-8888; FAX (03) 365-8822.*
Excellent location downtown near the Cashel Street Triangle Mall complex. The newest major hotel in the city, it is designed for business people but also caters to tourists. Rooms come with all sorts of amenities, including minibars, ironing boards, writing desks and satellite TV. There are a bar/brasserie, free airport shuttle, gym, secretarial service and indoor parking. Doubles start at about $NZ285.

Quality Hotel Central $NZ145   ★★★

776 Colombo Street, another hotel overlooking Victoria Square. ☎ *(03) 379-5880; FAX (03) 365-4806.*
The hotel (formerly the Hyatt Kingsgate) was remodeled in 1995 and has about 90 rooms, with a nice second-floor restaurant, the **Terrace** ★★, overlooking the square, moderate. There is a ground-floor coffee shop. Doubles are about $NZ145.

Commodore Airport Hotel $NZ150   ★★★

447 Memorial Avenue, about a kilometer from the airport. ☎ *(03) 358-8129; FAX (03) 358-2231.*
This is our favorite close-to-the-airport lodge, especially nice if you have a rental car to return. In addition to free 24-hour shuttle service, it has a great pool/hot tub, nice restaurant/bar and good rooms. Standard doubles are about $NZ150.

Airport Plaza $NZ115   ★★

On Memorial Avenue and Orchard Street in Harewood, close to the airport. ☎ *(03) 358-3139; FAX (03) 358-3029.*
Motelish. Pool, courtesy van to the airport, restaurant/bar. Standard doubles are about $NZ115; suites available.

Château on the Park $NZ150–300   ★★

On Dean's Avenue near the west side of Hagley Park. ☎ *(03) 348-8999; FAX (03) 348-8990.*
It has handicapped access, TV, coffee/tea and the **Camelot Restaurant** ★★★, all darkly medieval with an excellent wine list (Tues.–Sat.), expensive, and the **Lamplighter Restaurant** ★★, open seven days, moderate. Standard doubles are $NZ150; suites $NZ170–300.

Cotswold Hotel $NZ175   ★★★

88-96 Papanui Road, Edgeware (15 minutes from the airport, five minutes from downtown). ☎ *(03) 355-3535; FAX (03) 355-6695.*
If you don't mind being away from central downtown, this is a dandy. About 70 rooms including one- and two-bedroom suites. The exterior is Norman half-timbered, all bunched around a central courtyard. It has a pool, spa, gym and an airport courtesy van. Doubles start around $NZ175.

George, The $NZ225   ★★★

50 Park Terrace. ☎ *(03) 379-4560; FAX (03) 366-6747.*

One of those pastel and earth-tones places, lots of glass, lots of marble. It has a very nice location, right on the Avon, across from Hagley Park. The **Pescatore** ★ ★ ★ offers upscale Kiwi food, specializing in seafood and venison; live entertainment, Fri.–Mon., expensive. The **Piano Bar**, with fireplace, is a cozy spot in the winter; there's a brasserie for casual dining. Standard doubles start at about $NZ 225; suites $NZ 300 and up.

| **Quality Inn Durham Street** | **$NZ160** | ★ ★ |

Corner of Durham and Kilmore streets, northeast of Cathedral Square. ☎ *(03) 365-4699; FAX (03) 366-6302.*

About what you'd expect: boxy, centrally located, quite serviceable. Spa, tea/coffee, sauna, handicapped access, fridge, minibar, gym; bar and **Sarah's Brasserie** ★ ★, with light snacks or five-course meals, moderate. Standard doubles are about $NZ160.

If all else fails in Christchurch, just drive down **Papanui Street**—it's lined with small motels and bed-and-breakfasts. Three of the better B&Bs are:

| **Worcester** | **$NZ155–210** |

15 Worcester Blvd. ☎ *(03) 365-0936; FAX (03) 364-6299.*

A very elegant old Victorian located in a perfect spot across from the Arts Centre and close to the Botanic Gardens and downtown. The B&B has three guest rooms, including one with king bed and two with queens. All rooms have bathrooms. Either Continental or cooked breakfast. It's a real find.

| **Hambledon** | **$NZ90–145** |

103 Bealey Ave. ☎ *(03) 379-0723; FAX (03) 379-0758.*

This seven-bedroom classic (dating from 1856) is situated near the north edge of Hagley Park, well within walking distance of Cathedral Square. All rooms have bathrooms, coffee and tea equipment, TVs and phones. It's all very woody and antique laden. Continental breakfast. Some suites have two bedrooms.

| **Windsor Hotel** | **$NZ60–128** | ★ ★ |

52 Armagh Street. ☎ *(03) 366-1503; FAX (03) 366-9796.*

A real jewel; we like it a lot. Overlooks Cranmera Square and within walking distance of downtown. Classy colonial-style, real English-style breakfasts. It prefers nonsmokers. Coffee/tea, laundry. Doubles $NZ85.

Actually, the town is full of places to stay. Always check major hotels and motels for weekend reductions. A few of the two- or three-star motels:

| **Abel Tasman Motor Lodge** | **$NZ70–135** |

110 Sherborne Street, 15 minutes from the airport. ☎ *(03) 366-9085; FAX the same.*

All kitchen units, some family, some suites, studios. Spa available, laundry room, breakfast available. Rates $NZ70–135, depending on unit.

| **Airport Gateway** | **$NZ90–125** |

45 Roydvale Avenue. ☎ *(03) 358-3654; FAX (03) 358-3654.*

Our choice for the last night in Christchurch before flying out—or perhaps the first place to crash after you land. Whatever, it's close to the airport and the Antarctic

Centre, has a laundry, an airport courtesy van, kitchen facilities and some spas. Very handy, very friendly.

Akron Hotel $NZ80

87 Bealey Avenue. ☎ *(03) 366-1633; FAX (03) 379-1332.*
A Golden Chain motel, all kitchen units, studios and two-bedrooms. Laundry, tea/coffee, microwaves, bike available, bus stop at the gate. Doubles about $NZ80.

Russley Hotel and Villas $NZ80

75 Roydvale, not far from the airport. ☎ *(03) 358-6500; FAX (03) 358-6501.*
Sits on eight acres of grounds, with nice pool, very decent restaurant, courtesy coach; situated next to a golf course..

Carlton Mill Lodge $NZ80

19 Bealey Avenue, opposite north Hagley Park. ☎ *(03) 366-1068; FAX (03) 365-2331.*
Some with kitchens, some suites; laundry room, minibars, courtesy coach, bar and restaurant. Golf and tennis close by. Standard doubles start around $NZ80.

Latimer Motor Lodge $NZ110

30 Latimer Street. ☎ *(03) 379-6760; FAX (03) 366-0133.*
Tudor-style buildings in the heart of downtown off Worcester Street. Some with kitchens; tea/coffee, fridge, minibars, laundry, handicapped facilities, restaurant, bar. Doubles, around $NZ110.

Pacific Park $NZ105

263 Bealey Street, 15 minutes from the beach areas. ☎ *(03) 379-8660; FAX (03) 366-9973.*
Fridge, minibar, tea/coffee, laundry room, bar and **Aggie's Restaurant** ★ ★ ★, a New Zealand Lamb Board gold-medal winner; moderate. Rooms are about $NZ105.

These next three are for backpackers or budget-minded travelers planning on catching a bus or train at the Moorhouse Avenue station. Both are within several blocks of the station.

Ambassador's Hotel $NZ60

19 Manchester Street. ☎ *(03) 366-7808; FAX the same.*
Pretty basic, with shared and private facilities and backpackers rooms. TV lounge, laundry room. Courtesy van to the station. $NZ60, double, B&B.

Coker's Backpackers $NZ70–80

Century-old hulk farther down, at 52 Manchester. ☎ *(03) 379-8580; FAX (03) 379-8585.*
Three bars, a restaurant, live music. Private and shared facilities, most rooms refurbished. Doubles, $NZ70–80.

Bush Inn, The $NZ60

364 Riccarton Road, Upper Riccarton. ☎ *(03) 348-7175; FAX (03) 343-3312.*
Restored coach house built in 1852. Member of the Pub Beds group. **Cobb & Co.** restaurant, two bars, garden bar, next to a shopping mall. Free continental breakfast. Double with shower $NZ60.

Others

Colombo Travelodge   **$NZ60**

965 Colombo Street. ☎ *(03) 366-3029; FAX (03) 366-3433.*
Discount for AA members, coffee/tea, fridge, electric fry pans, breakfast available.
Doubles $NZ60.

Meadow Park Holiday Park   **$NZ35–60**

39 Meadow Street. ☎ *(03) 352-9176; FAX (03) 352-1272.*
A Top 10 RV facility, with pool, spa, laundry, TV lounge, BBQ facilities. Supermarket and dairy a few blocks away; bus stop. Cottages, $NZ60 double; cabins, $NZ50; smaller cabins, $NZ35.

Hostels

YMCA   **$NZ16–100**

12 Hereford Street. ☎ *(03) 365-0502; FAX (03) 365-1386.*
New, 100 rooms, bunks, apartments, motel units; game room, 24-hour check-in,
TV lounge, laundry, gym, coffee/tea. The Y claims to have the biggest climbing
wall in New Zealand. The basic price is $NZ16 per person; motel units $NZ50–75
double; two-bedroom apartment $NZ100.

Christchurch Central YHA   **$NZ20**

273 Manchester Street. ☎ *(03) 379-9535; FAX (03) 379-9537.*
Centrally located downtown with rooftop views. Rooms are mostly twins, with a
few four-bed units. Doubles around $NZ20.

YHA Rolleston House

5 Worcester Street. ☎ *(03) 366-6564; FAX (03) 365-5589.*
Opposite the museum and arts center, a short walk to Cathedral Square. Free car
parking.

Where to Eat

More than a dozen restaurants in Christchurch, including many of the top spots, do
not allow smoking. Many more have no-smoking sections. It's a growing trend in
Christchurch to have smoke-free environments in stores and restaurants.

Some of the best lamb we ever had in New Zealand was in an unlikely place, the **Lone
Star ★ ★ ★**. We must report that despite the decor (drugstore cowboy) and some of the
main courses (Tex-Mex stuff named after John Wayne and other stars, Redneck Ribs,
Sunofabitch Tulsa Black-Eyed Beans and Lasso of Hog), the Lone Star manages to put
out excellent food in a very lively atmosphere. The service is fast and efficient and it's so
popular that if you're not in the place by 5 p.m., you might have an hour's wait. What a
lot of folks do is sign up for a table, then go spend the hour waiting at the nearby **Loaded
Hog** brew pub, which serves up some very tasty beer. The Lone Star serves a grilled lamb
with mint salsa that'll knock your socks off. It's at *26 Manchester Street*, down from the
train station, across from the Ambassadors Hotel. *Open for dinner from 5:30 p.m to late.*
Yes, it does have Lone Star beer. Moderate. ☎ *(03) 365-7086.*

Annie's Wine Bar and Restaurant   **$$–$$$**   ★ ★ ★

At the old university Arts Centre, corner Hereford and Rolleston. ☎ *(03) 365-0566.*

One of the city's best wine lists, housed in a rustic, bare-brick walled building, stained glass. Mediterranean-style cuisine plus hideously good desserts. *It's open 11 a.m.–11 p.m. seven days.* A good bet.

Dux De Lux $–$$

Located at the corner of Hereford and Montreal streets. ☎ *(03) 366-6919.*
In the area of the old university Arts Centre, this restaurant proves that vegetarian and seafood dishes can be prepared so even dedicated carnivores won't scream. It's set in a Tudor building with garden seating in warmer months. There's live local music, and a brew pub is next door with tapas. Mushrooms stuffed with capers are a specialty at the Dux. *It's open from 11 a.m. to midnight, dinner starting at 5:30 p.m.* Very popular.

Thomas Edmonds Restaurant $$ ★★★

Corner Cambridge Terrace and Manchester Street. ☎ *(03) 365-2888; FAX (03) 365-2888.*
Maybe the best location in town, as far as great scenery is concerned. Sits on the banks of the Avon and can be reached by punt. Devonshire teas, venison, local wines and cheeses. *Open 11:30 a.m.–2 p.m. Sun.–Fri.; dinner from 5:30 p.m. Mon.–Sat.*

Michael's of Canterbury $$$ ★★★★★

178 High Street. ☎ *(03) 366-0822.*
A continual award winner. Fairly romantic setting with white china, candlelight and long drapes. Very eclectic stuff, with all sorts of combos such as pastry-baked mushrooms with herb walnuts, chicken breasts in Grand Marnier. The local gourmet society meets here—nuff said? *Dinner from 6 p.m. Mon.–Sat.*

Pedro's $$ ★★★★

143 Worcester Street. ☎ *(03) 379-7668.*
An award-winning eatery run by an Iberian who takes Las Ostras and grills them, then puts them inside a corn shell with ham, celery and cheese. Or mussels with garlic and lemon, any seafood with a zap of Spanish flavor. Pedro's, located near Cathedral Square, is very popular and his portions are huge. It claims to be the only Spanish restaurant in the entire country. (Bullfight posters, Franco stamps, the works.) *Open Tues.–Sat., 6–10 p.m.*

Camelot, The $$$ ★★★★

In the Château on the Park, 189 Deans Avenue. ☎ *(03) 348-8999.*
Medieval decor, vaulted ceiling, fireplaces. Award-winner with fine dining. Expensive but excellent cuisine: baby quail with orange sauce, Canterbury duck, sevruga caviar, salmon. Great desserts. *Dinner from 6 p.m. seven days.*

Grimsby's $$ ★★★

Kilmore and Montreal streets. ☎ *(03) 379-9040.*
Overlooking Cranmer Square. Housed in an old-stone former schoolhouse with a 30-foot-high ceiling. Nifty kauri-wood beams, stained-glass windows. When the place was renovated, a time capsule was discovered (1874), and the contents are on display in the foyer. Good seafood, lamb and game. *Open seven nights for dinner.*

Clarendon Restaurant   **$$**   ★★★

Level One, Clarendon Tower, corner of Worcester and Oxford Terrace. ☎ *(03) 366-2400.*
Across from Noah's Hotel and the visitors center. Overlooking the Avon, popular as a lunch stop for the downtown white-collar crowd. Nouvelle fare with a South Pacific bent. *Open for lunch and dinner seven days.*

Botanic Gardens Restaurant, The   **$–$$**   ★

In the Botanic Gardens. ☎ *(03) 366-5076.*
The place to haul into if you're doing the tour of the Botanic Gardens and Hagley Park. It serves a decent smorgasbord lunch for around $NZ15 per person, and also morning and afternoon teas. *The smorgasbord, which fills up rapidly, is open from noon to 2 p.m.; teas are at 10 a.m. and 4 p.m.* It's fully licensed.

Leinster House   **$$–$$$**   ★★★

158 Leinster Road, Merivale. ☎ *(03) 355-8866.*
French fine-dining establishment, candlelight, silver, the works. Seafood, saddle of hare, pheasant, wonderful desserts. *Dinner from 7 p.m. Mon.–Sat.*

Oxford on Avon Restaurant   **$–$$**   ★★★

794 Colombo Street. ☎ *(03) 379-7148.*
At the corner of Colombo Street and Oxford Terrace. Salad bar, blackboard menu, traditional Kiwi meat dishes. *Open 11 a.m.–9 p.m., Sun.–Thurs.; 11 a.m.–10 p.m., Fri. and Sat.*

Six Chairs Missing   **$$–$$$**   ★★★

New Regent Street. ☎ *(03) 366-4197.*
Always a local favorite, now housed in the yuppified New Regent area on the tram line. This is a great place to try venison or lamb and maybe some home-made ice cream. The name? Well, the word is one of the city trams came roaring around the corner and crushed six chairs the restaurant had set out on the sidewalk. Whatever, the food's good. *Open for lunch from 10 a.m.–5 p.m.; dinner 6–10 p.m. Wed.–Sun.*

Mainstreet Cafe   **$–$$**   ★★

840 Colombo St. ☎ *(03) 365-0421.*
If you're into a vegetarian diet, this is the spot, rated by some critics as one of the best in the country. In addition to good food and a good bar, the Mainstreet also has jazz several nights a week. It's smoke-free but not, thank God, garlic-free. Inhale some of the cafe's garlic pancakes and go chase vampires. The cafe is located near Victoria Square. It's open daily from around 5–11 p.m. Located in the old Apostolic Church.

Chung Wah   **$–$$**   ★★

63 Worchester Street. ☎ *(03) 379-3894.*
Located in the old Apostolic Church. Barnlike but very popular Cantonese eatery. *Open for lunch and dinner daily.*

Sign of the Takahe, The   **$$$**   ★★★★★

☎ *(03) 332-4052.*
Located out of town but among Christchurch's best, in Cashmere Hills on the Summit Road over the Banks Peninsula. The Takahe is one of several "Sign" road-

houses built along the highway (Sign of the Kiwi, Sign of the Bellbird) but is definitely the most ornate and best preserved. It's a baronial-style castle with views of the city and, on a clear day, the Southern Alps. The emphasis here is on silver service and candlelight. The specialties are crayfish, wild venison, game birds, caviar and lamb. Or go for a Devonshire tea if the purse is a little strained. *Lunch and teas from noon to 2 p.m.; dinner from 6 p.m, Mon.–Sat.*

We throw in the unpretentious **Café Bleu** ★ as a representative of the small specialty cafés you'll find scattered around the city. This one, in the Cashell Street mall, serves up huge portions of pub-style food. Try their potato hunks with salsa and cheese—a meal by themselves. Lunch and a couple of beers, for under $NZ20. While you're around town and need a caffeine hit, look for any of the **Robt. Harris** outlets, the Starbuck's of New Zealand. Among locations are the Riccarton Mall and the Triangle Centre.

Clubs and Entertainment

Great Hall and Court Theatre

☎ *(03) 366-6992.*

At the Arts Centre is one of the better venues in Christchurch for a wide variety of music, from madrigals to jazz, flamenco guitar to African dancing. Hours of concerts vary. *Luncheon concerts every Fri. at 1 p.m. Box office hours and information: 9 a.m.–8 p.m. Mon.–Fri.; 10 a.m.–8 p.m. Sat.*

Palladium

Gloucester Street, opposite the public library. ☎ *(03) 379-0572.*

The music is live Thurs. through Sat. Disco and laser show. *Open seven days 9 p.m. till late.* Bar, snacks.

Caeser's Night Spot

☎ *(03) 379-4317.*

Located at the corner of Gloucester Street and Chancery Lane. The Spot is part of the Chancery Tavern and Restaurant. Jazz and rock bands. *Open seven days, 7 p.m.–3 a.m.*

Excalibur's Theatre Restaurant

144 Gloucester Street. ☎ *(03) 366-6366.*

Located on the ground floor of the Coachman Hotel. Raunchy, often sexist, mostly hilarious and bawdy. It says, up front, it's "all in the worst taste, of course." Four-course meals, lots of wine. Dancing following the shows. *Call for performance times.*

Around Canterbury

Jet boating is a favorite activity on the Waiau River, Canterbury.

Lyttelton

Lyttelton Harbour, Christchurch's port, is the collapsed and flooded crater of an ancient volcano, one of two that formed the Banks Peninsula and blew apart, creating the harbors at **Lyttelton** and **Akaroa**. Modern Lyttelton still shows signs of the colonial past, despite the intrusion of heavy ship traffic moving in and out of the container and bulk terminals.

A number of Victorian buildings still stand, including several from the 1860s, such as the remains of a jail and the **Most Holy Trinity Anglican church**.

You can tour the harbor by boat, and there is regular service to two historic islands in the harbor, **Ripapa** and **Quail**; rates about $NZ15. It was at this harbor that the original settlers of Christchurch landed in 1850. The Banks Peninsula District Council is currently spending money to beef up London Street in the city center with a central square and other improvements. Take the No. 28 bus from Cathedral Square. Two other attractions of note are the **Lyttelton Museum** and the **Timeball Station**. The museum houses maritime displays as well as a colonial museum and an Antarctic gallery. *Hours are 2–4 p.m. Tuesday and Saturday and weekends.* ☎ *(03) 328-8972.* The Timeball Station is a castlelike structure that was used to signal the time to ships in the harbor by dropping a ball each day; supposedly it is only one of five in the world that is still running. Admission is $NZ3. *Hours are 10 a.m.–4 p.m. Monday–Thursday, and 10 a.m.–5 p.m. weekends.* ☎ *(03) 328-7311.*

Akaroa

Around Canterbury

The choicest piece of land near Christchurch, to our minds, is the almost-but-not-quite-Irish country of the Banks Peninsula with its chief tourist attraction, Akaroa. It's some of the most attractive real estate in the whole country, well worth a drive or a tour. The highway—Summit Road—gets narrow and twisty here and there, but *the scenery is great with valleys and meadows covered with sheep and deer.* It's about 90 kilometers from Christchurch to Akaroa, much shorter as the crow flies. Akaroa was founded by the French in the 1840s and was one of the reasons Her Majesty's Government was so anxious to take control of New Zealand. The village is, well, quaint and a popular tourist spot. There are remnants of the French settlers—one house dates to the original colonists—and there are French names here and there. The main drag is Rue Lavaud (aka Beach Street), and a sign down the street advertises, we are sad to report, "Le Mini Golf." The **Bank of New Zealand** is worth a photo stop. How many lavender and violet banks have you seen? Intercity runs a day tour to the peninsula with stops in Akaroa for about $NZ60 per person. ☎ *(03) 304-7641*

There's a **harbor tour** available from **Akaroa Harbour Cruises** (dolphins, penguins, a volcanic sea cave). *The two-hour tour on the Canterbury Cat begins at 1:30 p.m. daily; November to March there is also a sailing at 11 a.m.* Cost is about $NZ27. ☎ *(03) 304-7641; FAX (03) 304-7643.* There are several hotels or **B&Bs** around the Akaroa harbor area, one of which is the **Grand Hotel** ★★, an old queen of a place, a tad seedy but still popular with the locals. It serves a good lunch and has a pair of resident cockatoos (name of Crackers and James) to watch while you sip a brew. **The Grand**, at *6 Rue Lavaud*, charges $NZ50 double with breakfast. ☎ *(03) 304-7011; FAX (03) 304-7304.* More modern and more expensive is the **Akaroa Village Inn** ★★★

with doubles starting around $NZ90, suites for about $NZ180. It's on Beach Road. ☎ *(03) 304-7421; FAX (03) 304-7423.* There are also places to stay at other spots along the Summit Road, such as the **Des Pecheurs Hotel** ★ ★ in Duvauchelle with rooms for about $NZ80. ☎ *(03) 304-5803.* Check out the excellent **Relais Rochefort** ★ ★ ★ ★ restaurant in Duvauchelle, fairly expensive but very good; *closed Tuesday in winter, Wednesday all year. Open 11 a.m. and closes late.* ☎ *(03) 304-5832.*

Included among restaurants worth a try in Akaroa are the moderately priced **LaRue Restaurant** ★ ★ ★, specializing in French cuisine and lobster, on the *Rue Lavaud;* ☎ *(03) 304-7658.* The best place in town for breakfast and fresh pastries is the **Akaroa Bakery**, ☎ *(03) 304-7663.* For budget fast food or sit-downs, try the cafe located on the pier where the *Canterbury Cat* ties up. Information on dining, accommodations and activities in Akaroa and the Banks Peninsula is available from the **Canterbury Information Centre** *in Christchurch;* from the **Akaroa County Council** *in Duvauchelle* or from the information center at the **Akaroa Museum**, *corner of Rue Lavaud and Rue Balguerie;* ☎ *(03) 304-7614.* Information on the peninsula is available from the **Information Centre** *on Rue Balguerie in Akaroa.* ☎ *(03) 304-8600.* There are two daily buses from Christchurch to Akaroa, the **Akaroa Shuttle**, ☎ *(03) 379-9629,* or the **French Connection**, ☎ *(03) 377-0951.*

On the southwest corner of the peninsula (named, by the way, after Joseph Banks, the famous botanist on Cook's first voyage) is **Little River**, home to a large bird sanctuary, plus gemstone collecting and fishing. The bird area is wheelchair-accessible. At Barrys Bay on Akaroa Harbour is the **Cheese Factory**, where you can watch cheese being made as well as try a taste. The three cheeses involved are gouda, cheddar and Maasdam. *Hours are 8 a.m.–5 p.m. weekdays, 9:30 a.m.–5 p.m. weekends.* ☎ *(03) 304-5809.* Near Le Bons Bay toward the tip of the peninsula is the **French Farm Winery**, which has wine tasting and light lunches seven days; late on Saturday night. (The wine is not produced locally.) Try the Waypara sauvignon blanc. ☎ *(03) 304-5784.*

Hikers note: There's a great privately owned track that circles the peninsula in about four days with some often interesting cliffs and spectacular coastline. Accommodation is in huts. In peak season, Dec.15–Feb. 15, the tour costs $NZ100; otherwise, $NZ90. There are also stand-by rates. The track is closed May 12–Oct.15. Registration is necessary because the route passes private land and the number of hikers per day is restricted. Hikers are picked up in Akaroa and hauled to the first hut. Huts have running hot water, showers, cooking equipment and toilet facilities—one even has a wood-fired hot tub. For information, call the **Outdoor Recreation Information Centre**; transportation from Christchurch to the track start can be arranged. ☎ *(03) 304-7612.*

Seals are a frequent sight along the coast.

Kaikoura

This is whale-watching central, a bit of irony because this was a major whaling area in the 1840s and into the middle of this century. Indeed, the last sperm whale was harpooned off the coast here in 1964. Fittingly, whales are important to the economy here once again, but now it's tourists and not whale oil that are bringing in the bucks. There are a number of companies taking tourists out to the whales, a business that sees about 20,000 people a year come for a look, and that generates something in excess of $NZ1 million. Whale watching seems so lucrative, in fact, that several additional companies have put in bids to start boat tours. The end result will probably be limits on the number of boats allowed to operate in the whaling waters, much the same as the controls on whale-watching excursions off the coast of California. It's also possible to see the whales from the air, which seems to be cutting down on the number of waterborne trips. There are air charters from either Christchurch or Kaikoura itself. Try **Whalewatch Air**, which will fly you from Christchurch for $NZ275. The company also has boat trips in conjunction with flights. Short flights from Kaikoura are about $NZ80 per person. *In Kaikoura, ☎ (03) 319-6580, FAX (03) 319-6663; in Christchurch ☎ (03) 358-8334, FAX (03) 358-9444.*

Many whale-watching tours originate in Christchurch (see prices in the "Tours" section under "Christchurch"). But there's more to see than whales—including rare **Hector's dolphins**, **blue penguins**, **fur seals** *and flocks of seabirds, including* **albatross** *and* **petrels**.

Whale Watch Kaikoura is one of the major seagoing whale-watching companies in Kaikoura, owned by the local Maoris. *The office is located in the old train station; ☎ (03) 319-5045.* If you're lucky, you will spot giant sperm whales and humpbacks as well as right whales. Reservations are a must during the June–July whale season, usually two to three weeks in advance. Weather permitting, there are usually four trips a day. The cost is about $NZ95 per person for a 2.5-hour trip. A trip aboard a glass-bottom boat will run about four hours and includes lunch; price is about $NZ50 per person. For current whale-watching prices (or to book), call ☎ *(0800) 655-121.* A good bet for general sealife activities is the **Kaikoura Wildlife Centre**, also in the old train station, which offers whale watching as well as snorkeling and scuba, helicopter flights and guided nature walks. A swim with the seals will run you about $NZ90, including snorkeling equipment. Scenic helicopter flights are about $NZ90 for a half-hour. ☎ *(03) 319-6622; FAX (03) 319-6868.* Or you can try a snorkel with dusky dolphins with **Dolphin Mary Charters**. The 3.5-hour tours run from October through April. Snorkel equipment, including wet suits, is supplied. Adults are $NZ80. ☎ *(03) 319-6777; FAX (03) 319-6534.*

The presence of whales also means scientists hang around Kaikoura, as well. Recently, the focus of one expedition was giant squid, a favorite meal for sperm whales. Several of the giant squids have been caught in commercial fishing nets, and scientists, using deep-diving robots equipped with cameras, explored the trenches offshore—in some places more than 1500 feet deep.

Another local attraction is the **Maori Leap Cave**, a 2-million-year-old sea-created limestone cavern only discovered in 1958. The cave is located three kilometers south of town. **Cave Tours** operates a 40-minute trek. Wear good walking shoes, photos are permitted. *Tours are 10:30 a.m., 12:30 and 2:20 p.m.* Be at the cave about 15 minutes before the tour. Prices are $NZ7.50 for adults; $NZ2.50 for kids. There is a café at the cave open seven days from 7 a.m.–8 p.m. ☎ *(03) 319-5023.*

The town sits about halfway between Christchurch and Picton on the main road (Highway 1) and is also on the Coastal Pacific train route (it's about 200 kilometers northeast of Christchurch). The population of the town is about 3000, and it is situated along a curved harbor with the main road, the

Esplanade, running along the ocean to the tip of the peninsula where the town was built.

There is a very nice hike from the end of the paved road southeast of the town road along the tip of the peninsula. The **Kaikoura Peninsula Walkway** starts at Point Kean and runs back to town, about five kilometers. Part of the trail is the so-called "**Shoreline Walk**," which goes over tidal platforms and passes some spectacular sea stacks and sea caves near Atia Point. There is also a cliff-top walk that parallels the sea trail. A good half-day itinerary is to take the clifftop trail to Whaler's Bay, descend to the shoreline trail, then return to Point Kean. If the seas are high, do check with the visitors center in town or the *Department of Conservation office on Ludstone Road,* ☎ *(03) 319-5714.*

There is a nice little museum in town, full of Maori information (evidence suggests Maori presence here a millennium ago). It also has displays from the early whaling days. The museum, just up from the town center, is usually open on weekends. The town's *information center* is in the Westend business complex across from the post office on the Esplanade; ☎ *(03) 319-5641; FAX (03) 319-5308.*

Because of its growth as a tourism center, Kaikoura has a number of motels and a couple of old hotels. The best lodge in town is probably the **White Morph Motor Inn** ★★, named after the giant southern petrel. It's at *92-94 the Esplanade.* Rates are from $NZ95 for studios to $NZ160 for luxury units. Some have two bedrooms, some have kitchens. ☎ *(03) 319-5014; FAX (03) 319-5015.*

Two-star motels, all of which have prices in the $NZ70 double range, include the **Alpine View**, *146 Beach Road,* ☎ *(03) 319-5429, FAX (03) 319-6679;* **Blue Seas**, *222 the Esplanade,* ☎ *(03) 319-5441, FAX the same;* **Sierra Beachfront**, *160 the Esplanade,* ☎ *(03) 319-5622, FAX the same;* and the *Willow Bank, 183 Beach Road,* ☎ *(03) 319-5566.* All these facilities have great deals in the off-season, sometimes as low as $NZ30 a night.

A good B&B is the **Bevron House**, *196 the Esplanade,* ☎ *(03) 319-5432.* It has a swimming beach, courtesy car to the bus and train stations, a tour desk; nonsmoking. Excellent fully cooked brekkies. Rates are $NZ60 double.

The place to park your RV is at the **Searidge Holiday Park**, a Top 10 facility. It's at *34 Beach Road (Highway 1),* ☎ *(03) 319-5362.*

Hostels include the **Maui YHA**, *270 the Esplanade,* ☎ *(03) 319-5931,* and **Moby Dix's**, *65 Beach Road,* ☎ *(03) 319-6699.*

For food, not high on the list of things to attract you to Kaikoura, try the **White Morph** ★★, located in an old bank building on the Esplanade. Eclectic, though somewhat undistinguished cuisine; seafood is a specialty. Fixed price three-course meals, moderate. ☎ *(03) 319-5676.* A hair more upscale is **Act One** ★★★, north of town on the main highway. Pizza ovens, chili, chicken salads, very laid-back. The pizzas are excellent. Moderate. ☎ *(03) 319-6760*. A third choice is the restaurant/wine bar at the **Adelphi Hotel** ★ ★ ★ at Westend on the Esplanade; moderate. The **Lobster Room** specializes in scallops, crayfish, baby salmon; moderate. ☎ *(03) 319-5141*. **Note**: You'll probably see a giant crayfish on the right side of town coming in from the north. The place is called the **Suntrack**. Despite a promising menu, it has lousy food and crappy service.

Things have to improve, however. The town is famous for its crayfish—Kaikoura in Maori means "to eat crayfish," and now every year in October, the city is host to **Seafest**, a three-day festival of eats, drinks and nonsense, including cray races, music, arts and crafts and New Zealand wines and beers. It's worth the drive up.

Hanmer Springs

There are several ways to get to the West Coast from either the Picton area, Blenheim or Christchurch, all weather dependent and subject to snowy conditions in the winter. Most visitors will go from Picton to Christchurch, then either go south to Mount Cook or take the Arthur's Pass route to the glaciers. A really nice drive, one not often used, is the Lewis Pass route that starts at Waipara north of Christchurch and runs over the pass to Greymouth. It's officially Highway 7 and it's a gorgeous trip. But the reason most of the locals in the area head up Highway 7 is to get to the small town of Hanmer Springs, the best and just about only thermal area on the South Island. The mineral springs, combined with nearby outdoor activities, makes the area a popular year-round weekend getaway for Christchurch residents as well as folks from the Marlborough area.

The first European to see the pools of hot water came by in 1859, and the first bathhouse on the site was built in 1885. The facilities here served as a rehabilitation center for New Zealand veterans after both world wars. A major redevelopment ($NZ1.6 million) took place in the early 1990s, and today, the springs are one of the most popular destinations on the South Island, attracting more tourists than Milford Sound or the Waitomo Caves. The whole setup is first class, in much better shape than the going-to-seed facilities in Rotorua and much less touristy. This should definitely be a stop on your South Island visit.

The springs are about 90 minutes north of Christchurch, and the drive gets really special from the small town of Culverden up Highway 7 to the turnoff to Hanmer Springs, Highway 7A. At one point, you pass the Waiau ferry bridge where you can take a bungy jump; this is also good white-water country and there are several companies that run trips. Highway 7A runs about 10 kilometers from the main highway into Hanmer Springs.

Around Canterbury

Hanmer Springs Thermal Reserve

Once in Hanmer Springs, it's impossible to miss the pools. The settlement is small and the main entrance to the springs is right next to the main drag, Amuri Road. There are seven thermal pools, a toddler's area and a freshwater swimming pool on the site. Water temperatures range from 32-40 degrees Celsius (roughly 90-105 Fahrenheit). In addition to the public areas, there are several private pools with their own shower and change facilities, and you can also get a massage, use the gym or try some food at the **Garden House Cafe** located on the site (see below under "Where to Eat.") *It has a bar and is open daily from 10 a.m.–midnight. The pools are open 10 a.m.–9 p.m.* Adult entry fee is $NZ6. Suit hire is $NZ3, towels are $NZ2. Private pools are $NZ10 per person per 30 minutes. The sauna and steam room are also available by the half-hour. Information: *fax and phone* ☎ *(03) 315-7511.*

Activities

As befits its role in life as a recreation center, Hanmer offers all sorts of close-by outdoor activities. These include bungy jumping off the Waiau Bridge, skiing at the nearby Amuri ski area, golf at the 18-hole country club near the springs, mountain biking, jet boating, squash, helicopter tours and heli-skiing, farm tours, whale watching air trips or lawn bowling. All of these activities can be booked in Christchurch, and further information is available from the Hurunui Visitor Information Centre, ☎ *(03) 315-7128; fax 315-7264.* (This is also the Department of Conservation information center.)

Where to Stay

Braemar Lodge   **$NZ400**   ★★★★

South of the city off Highway 7A. ☎ *(03) 315-7049; FAX (03) 315-7104.*
The most upscale digs in the area, and one of the New Zealand Lodge Association properties. It's situated on the Hanmer River about 10 kilometers south of the town, and is set in a very bucolic area. The lodge has an enormous rock fireplace, cozy bar, floor-to-ceiling windows, and offers a range of activities including tennis, a spa room, swimming pool, croquet and skeet shooting. The lodge is also a popular conference center. And it often has weekend specials. The house restaurant is very good, and room rates include breakfast and dinner.

Alpine Spa Lodge   **$NZ70–180**   ★★★

Corner of Amuri Drive and Harrogate St.reet. ☎ *and FAX (03) 315-7311.*
This is where we hang out hat when we come to take the waters in Hanmer Springs. It's within walking distance of the pools, very clean, all knotty pine and glass, and the tower rooms with spa tubs and nine-foot-diameter circular beds and kitchens. The smaller rooms are just fine, as well, and there's ample off-street parking.

Hanmer Inn Motel   **$NZ80–125**   ★★★

16 Jacks Pass Road. ☎ *(03) 315-7516; FAX 315-7471.*
Very decent new motel complex close to the town center, a short walk to the pools and the golf course. There are three studio units, a couple with spa baths and several with handicapped access. Basic units are $NZ85; the spa units are $NZ125.

Glenalvon Lodge B&B   **$NZ70–135**   ★★

20 Amuri Avenue. ☎ *(03) 315-7475; FAX 315-7361.*

Here's a mix of choices, from shared facility units to a honeymoon suite. Some of the units are located in cottage-style suites behind the main building. The suites have fridges and small kitchens, and the honeymoon suite has a spa bath. Breakfast can be brought to your unit on request; dinners available by request.

Mountain View Holiday Park   **$NZ17–65**

Bath Street, south edge of town. ☎ *and FAX (03) 315-7113.*

A Top 10 RV park just down the street from the thermal pools. Tent sites are $NZ17; powered sites $NZ19, and on-site cabins range from $NZ33-65.

What might eventually become the classiest joint in town used to be the Hanmer Lodge Motel, a rambling, white old heap that was once the queen of the spa. Now seriously in need of paint, plumbing, modernization—especially the heating—and a lot of TLC, the lodge still has its devotees. It has a pool, bar, guest lounge water-beds. It's a tad musty but could be up there with the Hermitage and other classic Kiwi lodges. It's on Conical Road centrally located. Rooms range from $NZ50-115. ☎ *(03) 315-7021; FAX 315-7071.*

Where to Eat

Jaywalk Cafe and Wine Bar   **$$–$$$**   ★★★★

Conical Hill Road near the Hanmer Lodge Hotel. ☎ *(03) 315-7214.*

Here is where you take a Saint Clair sauvignon blanc from the Marlborough area, lap up some fettucini with mushrooms, bacon and white wine sauce, and finish it off with iced orange pralines with whipped cream. Good? It's outrageous, almost worth the drive all the way from Christchurch. Mushroom and cheese ravioli in pesto sauce, chicken breasts in a cashew nut crust. To die for. It's open at various hours depending on season; check ahead.

Old Post Office   **$$–$$$**   ★★★★

Jacks Pass Road near the Hanmer Lodge Hotel. ☎ *(03) 315-7461.*

Toss-up as to which is the better, because the Post Office is very good, as well. Housed in an old post office—hence the name—it has an extensive wine list and specializes in venison, seafood and other Kiwi goodies. Reservations are always a good bet, and the hours are sometimes strange, so call ahead.

Alpine Village Inn   **$–$$**   ★★

Jacks Pass Road near the Hanmer Lodge Hotel. ☎ *(03) 315-7005.*

Pub/bistro scene, popular with the locals, complete with a bottle shop. Between 5:30 and 8:30 p.m., it serves a good country dinner—stick-to-your-ribs stuff at good prices.

Garden House Cafe   **$–$$**   ★★

Located in the thermal pool reserve. ☎ *(03) 315-7115.*

The spa cafe has light snacks and meals all day, with an expanded dinner menu. If the weather's decent, you can sit on the terrace and watch people broil in the pools. It's open seven days, 10 a.m.-midnight.

Arthur's Pass

One of the best drives in New Zealand is the trip on Highway 73 from Christchurch to the west coast of the South Island, up and through the Southern Alps. You get to see most of the ecosystems prevalent in the south, from the wide, grassy Canterbury Plains, to the subalpine and alpine country around **Arthur's Pass National Park**, to the windswept, damp rainforests of the coast. And about two-thirds of the way along is the hamlet of **Arthur's Pass**, a most excellent place to haul in for a day or so to eat, hike or just enjoy the scenery. It's also a stop (or a stay-over) for passengers on the Tranz-Alpine Express, which runs from Christchurch to Greymouth.

In the winter, it's a handy place for skiers (**Temple Basin**, **Porter Heights** and several other areas are close by), and, in the summer, it's popular with hikers and campers. The road can be a true test in foul weather with gale-force winds, fog and snow, all on top of some very curvy stretches. But when it's clear, the scenery is great, particularly going through the **Otira Gorge** on the Greymouth side of the pass. The South Island's continental divide is nearby, and the top of the pass itself is about 3000 feet above sea level, not high by North American standards but still exposed to the full force of the Roaring Forties. The pass was originally used by the Maoris from the west coast to trade greenstone with their neighbors on the east side. The road was pushed through by Christchurch merchants wanting to cash in on the 1860s gold rush and was built mostly by pick and shovel. The road was opened in 1866; the railroad followed in 1923. The national park is about 390 square miles of 7500-foot peaks, gorges, rivers and glaciers—the most northerly glaciers on the South Island. Note that the highway is subject to snow closure even in late spring or early fall. In an effort to relieve some of the sometimes-dangerous driving through the Otira Gorge, plans are now under way to build a 400-meter-long viaduct where the worst zigzags at the top of the pass are located. The span will sit atop 180-foot-high pylons and is expected to be completed in 1999.

The park is a hiker's paradise with a number of serious tramps plus some leisurely strolls. There are also some excellent mountaineering opportunities. The park is full of huts—about 90 huts and shelters are scattered about. Information about the park, the trails, the huts and park wildlife (red deer and chamois abound) is available from the information center and national park headquarters in Arthur's Pass, *open daily 8 a.m.–5 p.m. Information: Park Headquarters, Box 8, Arthur's Pass;* ☎ *(03) 318-9211, FAX (03) 318-9271.* Just behind the park headquarters is the beginning of a trail that goes almost straight up along a series of waterfalls to the top of the low mountains in back of the village. Not technically difficult, great scenery. Note the **keas** wandering around—don't feed them or the rangers will get rancorous.

Punch Bowl Falls at Arthur's Pass in Canterbury is definitely worth the trek.

The range of accommodations is not extensive, on purpose. Growth of the village, indeed the whole area, is rigorously restricted; most of the permanent population of fewer than 100 are railway workers. The village has a school, post office, tearooms, one licensed restaurant and a chapel.

Where to Stay

Chalet, The $NZ75–85   ★★★

☎ *(03) 318-9236; FAX the same.*

This cozy place has eight rooms, some with in-room facilities, with TV and continental breakfasts. The decor (as with many things in the village) is Alpine, in this case, Swiss. There is a coin laundry. This place is a favorite with us. Doubles are $NZ75, shared facilities, $NZ85, private bath.

Alpine Motels $NZ45–70   ★

☎ *(03) 318-9233.*

A standard motel with kitchen facilities and TV. Doubles run about $NZ70; backpackers' rooms, about $NZ45.

The store down the road from the Chalet has groceries and potables and serves light lunches and snacks. The Chalet has a snack bar that serves light budget lunches (although the proportions are generous) from 9 a.m. to 5 p.m. There's a gift shop as well. The licensed restaurant is very good, especially for dinner. Now it can be told—here is where we had our first bottle of Montana cabernet and munched on our first stewed Bambi. Lamb and venison are great, and the service is rural-Kansas friendly. Dinner hours are tight: 6 p.m.–7:45 p.m. (Non-guests are welcome.) Moderate.

The only spot we know in Arthur's to plug in an RV is at **Oscar's Haus Alpine Crafts and RV** site Located down the street from the Chalet. There are also tent sites; powered RV sites are about $NZ15. There is also the **Sir Arthur Dudley Dobson Memorial YHA** in the village, with spots for about $NZ20 a night; ☎ *(03) 318-9230.* The crafts part of Oscar's Haus has some very good hand-spun yarns and knitwares for sale, as good as any we saw in Christchurch or Wellington. For budget accommodation:

Mountain House, The

☎ *(03) 318-9258; FAX (03) 318-9201.*

Across the street from the YHA, has bunk-style beds. During the winter (May–Sept.), there are package prices for two- and three-night stays.

Bealey Hotel $NZ75

☎ *(03) 318-9277; FAX the same.*

Located in Bealey, about 15 kilometers toward Christchurch from Arthur's. It has motel-style units with doubles going for about $NZ75; kitchen units.

Otira Hotel $NZ50   ★

☎ *(03) 738-2802.*

West of Arthur's Pass in the hamlet of Otira. Passengers aboard the Tranz-Alpine will remember Otira as the beginning of a five-mile tunnel through the Alps. In 1908, teams started from both sides of Mt. Barron and met in 1918—according to the park service, there was a bit more than an inch difference in the alignment. Because of widening work and installation of electricity and concrete, the first train went through in 1923. The Otira Hotel, on the main highway, is a bit run-down but has double and single rooms. Doubles go for about $NZ50.

The West Coast

A nature walk on the West Coast offers sea views.

The Kiwis call the narrow strip on the West Coast between the mountains and the sea **"Westland,"** and its history has mostly evolved around minerals, starting with Maori greenstone and going through the Gold Rushes to modern-day coal mines. The area is definitely laid-back and rife with individualists. *It is also one of the most photogenic spots on both islands.* Along that narrow strip are grand vistas of ocean and mountain, glaciers and rainforest. The towns, such as they are, are small, many the remnants of once-booming Gold Rush settlements. The main road down the coast is Highway 6, which you pick up at the western end of the Arthur's Pass highway.

Greymouth

So named because it's at the mouth of the Grey River, this city of about 12,000 is another spot that got its start as a Gold Rush settlement. *It's the largest city on the West Coast, and, as the saying goes, it's close to a lot of nice places.* There's not a lot to do aside from wander the beaches and shop. *Most of the tours offered by local operators are Gold Rush-oriented,* although you can also find fishing guides and jet boating trips. Greymouth is the gateway to the largest lake on the West Coast, **Lake Brunner**. There are some nice walks around the lake, including a trail through **Moana Reserve**, a 150-acre park with many typical South Island West Coast rainforest plants, including several species of orchids. At **Moana Township**, there is a golf course, hotel and restaurant, as well as boat rentals, helicopter tours and fishing trips. Also in the area is the **Moana Kiwi House and Conservation Park**, which has a nocturnal kiwi viewing area and meals. ☎ *(03) 738-0009.* For a look around, try **Lakeside Jet Boating Tours**, ☎ *(03) 738-0036,* in Greymouth. Moana Township is a stop on the Tranz Alpine Express. There is a very good inn available, the **Lake Brunner Lodge ★ ★ ★ ★**, a trout-fishing lodge with excellent food, established in 1872. Rooms, breakfast and dinner a day go for about $NZ400 double, ☎ *and FAX (03) 738-0163.* Dry-fly fishing guides are available for about $NZ410 a day (two anglers maximum); reduced rate for longer stays. The lodge also has eco-tours to nearby podocarp forests and duck shooting. Most of the trout found on the West Coast are browns; the only place with rainbows is Lake Brunner.

Information on the Greymouth area is available from the *information center* at the corner of Mackay and Herbert streets, ☎ *(03) 768-5101; FAX (03) 768-0317.* The AA office is at *84 Tainui Street,* ☎ *(03) 768-4300.*

Where to Stay

Greymouth is fairly popular with seaside tourists in the summer, so there are a number of two- and three-star motels available in the city.

Highpark Motor Inn $NZ75–85 ★ ★

90 High Street. ☎ *(03) 768-4846; FAX (03) 768-9746.*
One of the newer facilities in town. It has ground-floor handicapped units, studios, and one- and two-bedroom units. Breakfast is available; laundry service. Standard doubles are $NZ75–85.

Quality Hotel Kings $NZ100–130 ★ ★ ★

Mawhera Quay on the Grey River. ☎ *(03) 768-5085; FAX (03) 768-5844.*
Restaurant with bar, sauna, spa; some kitchenettes, some apartments. Guest laundry, handicapped access. Standard doubles are $NZ100–130.

Willowbank Pacifica Motor Lodge $NZ100 ★ ★

Three kilometers north of town. ☎ *(03) 768-5339; FAX (03) 768-6022.*

Full kitchens, laundry, courtesy car, spa, pool, breakfast and evening meals available. Doubles are $NZ100.

Ashley Motel and Motor Inn $NZ90–140   ★★
70-74 Tasman Street. ☎ *(03) 768-5135; FAX (03) 768-0319.*
Heated pool, spa and gym, restaurant, bar, some kitchen units, laundry, tea/coffee. Doubles around $NZ90–140.

Charles Court Motel $NZ80–110   ★★
350 Main South Road. ☎ *(03) 762-6619; FAX (03) 762-6594.*
Kitchenettes, beachfront, pool, spa, BBQ. Doubles from about $NZ80–110.

Oak Lodge B&B $NZ130   ★★★
Coal Creek north of town. ☎ *(03) 768-6832; FAX (03) 768-4362.*
Private facilities, antique decor, large garden, local foods and wine. Laundry, spa, pool, tennis. Doubles from about $NZ130.

Greymouth Seaside Holiday Park $NZ15–60
Chesterfield Street, south of city center on the beach. ☎ *(03) 768-6618; FAX (03) 768-5873.*
Communal kitchens, car wash, laundry, spa. *Not one of the better Top 10 facilities, but serviceable.* Powered sites $NZ18. Tourist flats, double: $NZ60; cabins, doubles, $NZ40; bunkhouse, $NZ15 per person.

There are two hostel facilities:

Kainga-Ra YHA, The $NZ15
15 Alexander Street. ☎ *(03) 768-4951; FAX the same.*
About 8 kilometers north of Shantytown in the bush. Members, $NZ15.

Noah's Ark Backpackers $NZ15
16 Chapel Street, off Tainui Street. ☎ *(03) 768-4868; FAX the same.*
In a former monastery near the train and bus station. Laundry, kitchen, double rooms, tent sites. Courtesy shuttle, shop and barbecue facilities. $NZ15 per person a night.

Where to Eat

We suggest you keep going to **Hokitika** to eat, because it has a better selection of restaurants than Greymouth, including one of the best on the West Coast. While in Greymouth, however, there are a few good possibilities:

Café Collage $$ ★★★
115 Mackay Street, upstairs. ☎ *(03) 768-5497.*
This café offers everything from in-season shellfish to great lamb and venison. The scallops are especially tasty; whitebait in season. *Hours 6 p.m. until late for dinner.* BYO and licensed, closed Sun. and Mon.

Red Wagon Wheels Restaurant, The $–$$ ★★
☎ *(03) 768-7055.*
This restaurant and pub in Revingtons Hotel is popular and has good-quality family fare. *It's open all three meals, closed Sun.*

Railway Hotel, The $ ★
Mawhera Quay, across from the bus and train depots. ☎ *(03) 768-7023.*

Open for lunch and dinner, entertainment Friday and Saturday nights, basic pub food fare.

Activities

Like Hokitika, Greymouth is a *greenstone center*. It's the home of one of the more famous jade carvers in the country, **Ian Boustridge**. Boustridge's works are on display at the National Museum in Wellington. His house/studio is at *25 Coates Street*. Ask anybody in town for directions, but call first: ☎ *(03) 768-6048*.

Greymouth is on the Picton-Fox Glacier train route, and is served by bus from various cities. Air service is out of Hokitika (shuttle available). There are major car rental agencies, as well as bike and moped agencies.

About eight kilometers south of Greymouth is a Gold Rush attraction called **Shantytown**. It offers gold panning, steam-train rides, horse-drawn vehicles, a working sawmill and about 30 old buildings depicting a "typical" West Coast gold mining town in the 1890s. It costs about $NZ10 to get in; another $NZ5 to pan for gold. There's a licensed restaurant for lunch and morning/afternoon teas. *Open daily from 8:30 a.m.* ☎ *(03) 762-6634*.

Hokitika

This was apparently the first place in New Zealand spotted by European explorers—the Dutchman Abel Tasman arrived here in December 1642. In Maori times, it was an important greenstone trading center, and in the 1860s, exploded during the Gold Rush. It was largely because of the gold madness around Hokitika that the Arthur's Pass road was developed.

It's now a peaceful town of around 4000, just south of the intersection of Highway 73 (Arthur's Pass Road) and Highway 6. If you're interested in the history of the area, stop at the **West Coast Historical Museum** on Tancred Street, *open weekdays, 9:30 a.m.–5 p.m., closed weekends during the winter.* It has several good **Gold Rush displays** and a 20-minute historical audiovisual program. Admission is about $NZ3. ☎ *(03) 755-6898; FAX the same.* There are several **greenstone factories** in town open for tours and sales. **Visitor information:** *Westland Visitors Information Centre, Weld Street,* ☎ *(03) 755-8322, FAX (03) 755-8026.*

There are a number of greenstone and gold crafts shops in the city. Try the **Hokitika Craft Gallery Cooperative**, *25 Tancred Street,* which has works by about 20 local artisans. In addition to greenstone, it has works in wool, bone, wood and pottery. Hours are 8:30 a.m.–8:30 p.m. seven days. ☎ *(03) 755-8802.* Note: Hokitika also has one of the few **public laundromats** in the area, located at *137 Revell Street.* It also has hot showers. Two bucks to wash clothes, two bucks to dry. *Hours are 9 a.m.–10 p.m. seven days.*

Skyline view of Queenstown

Helicopters, jet boats and rafts converge on the Shotover.

New Zealand is the largest wool, lamb and mutton exporting nation in the world.

McKinnon Pass (1073m) on Milford Track offers impressive views.

Sailboat regatta, Whitebread Village, Auckland

Maori concerts take place regularly in Rotorua

Also in Hokitika is a glowworm grotto near the hospital and the Goldsborough Motel, worth a shot at night if you haven't seen the little beauties. It's called the **Glowworm Dell**.

Where to Stay

If you want to spend the night before going south to the glaciers or north to the Westport and Nelson areas, there are several two- and three-star motels:

Jade Court Motor Lodge   **$NZ75**

85 Fitzherbert Street. ☎ *(03) 755-8855; FAX (03) 755-8133.*
Units sleep two to six persons; all have kitchen facilities. Guest laundry, cooked breakfast available, barbecue area. Doubles are about $NZ75.

Hokitika Motel, The   **$NZ75**

221 Fitzherbert Street. ☎ *(03) 755-8292; FAX (03) 755-8485.*
Some two-bedroom units, kitchenettes, laundry, a mini-store, tea/coffee, spa and a courtesy van. AA discount. Doubles are about $NZ75.

Goldsborough, The   **$NZ80**

252 Revell Street. ☎ *(03) 755-8773; FAX the same.*
Offers all the amenities offered by the Hokitika Motel, plus breakfast is available. It's close to the beach. Spa and pool. Doubles are about $NZ80.

Southland Hotel, The   **$NZ45–90**

111 Revell Street. ☎ *(03) 755-8344; FAX (03) 755-8258.*
A Flag group facility, family owned for more than 100 years. Handicapped facilities, laundry, rooms with spa baths, on the shore of the Tasman. Some budget rooms available. Good restaurant (see below). Regular doubles $NZ90.

Teichelmann's Central B&B   **$NZ65–85**

20 Hamilton Street. ☎ *(03) 755-8232; FAX the same.*
Housed in a historic house once occupied by Ebenezer Teichelmann, a physician and famous mountaineer who lived in the area in the late 1890s. The six guest rooms are either private or shared facilities; no kids under 10 allowed. Good location in the city center. It has a TV lounge, coffee/tea, laundry and courtesy van. Dinner available. Doubles start at about $NZ65.

Hokitika Holiday Park, The   **$NZ10–50**

242 Stafford Street. ☎ *(03) 755-8172; FAX the same.*
A Kiwi Camp facility. Has on-site units, plus a laundry, communal kitchen and TV lounge. Powered sites are $NZ10. Tourist flats, equipped with cooking equipment, are $NZ50; bedding extra. Cabins are $NZ40, and a bunkhouse that sleeps 12 is $NZ10 per person.

Where to Eat

The moderately priced **Café de Paris** ★ ★ ★ ★, *19 Tancred Street*, has a well-deserved reputation as one of the best restaurants on the West Coast. As the name suggests, the fare is French-influence, but leans heavily on local produce, including excellent whitebait in season, scallops and wild venison. The decor is black and white, airy, blackboard

The West Coast

menu with a decadent array of desserts. *Open for lunch and dinner seven days 10 a.m. until late.* Moderate to expensive. ☎ *(03) 755-8933.*

Another good choice is the moderately priced **Tasman View Restaurant ★ ★** , *111 Revell Street at the Southland Hotel.* Again seafood, especially whitebait, and regional dishes. *Open 7:30–9 a.m. breakfast; dinner from 6 p.m.* Moderate. ☎ *(03) 755-8344.* For casual budget to moderate dining—cappuccino, sandwiches, New Zealand wines— stop at **Trapper's** or the **Filling Station**, both on Revell Street. Also try **Millie's Tearoom** on Weld Street, the **Preston Bakery and Tearoom** on Revell Street, or pub food at the **Westland Hotel** at the corner of Weld and Revell streets.

Getting There

There is rail and bus service to the town, as well as regular air service from Christchurch and Nelson. From Christchurch, the fares are about $NZ135; from Nelson, about $NZ165. There is also service from Auckland, Wellington, Dunedin and Invercargill.

Activities

A couple of spots near Hokitika are worth a stop. About 25 kilometers southeast of town on the Kokatahi-Kowhitirangi road is the **Hokitika River Gorge**, a very pleasant spot for a walk. There's a suspension bridge over the river.

About 30 kilometers south of Hokitika is the hamlet of **Ross**, another relic of the gold madness, notable for being the location where the largest nugget in New Zealand history was found. It weighed in at more than six pounds and was immediately made a celebrity. It was named "the Honourable Roddy," after a government official, then paraded all over the country. Eventually, being good little colonials, they shipped the chunk off to George V as a coronation gift. He, having no sense of style, promptly had it melted down to embellish tableware at Buckingham Palace, the twit. If you've a mind, there are several walks around the village that take you past the diggings; stay on the paths because there are mine shafts all over. There's also some gold panning to be done. There's a little museum where you can see a replica of Roddy.

Modern-day miners, using 20th-century technology, have determined that the Gold Rush diggers left big deposits of gold around Ross and they would very much like to get at it. Only problem, to do so would result in a big hole—right underneath the present town. Debate continues. Check out the old **Empire Hotel**, dating from 1906, where you can sup, drink or stay in budget accommodation ($NZ50 for two with private bath.)

About 60 kilometers south is a spot called **The Forks**, where you can catch a dirt road that goes to the coast at a place called Okarito. Along the beach, you'll see plenty of white heron, and a kilometer or so north on the coast is **Okarito Lagoon**, a tidal marsh where a white heron sanctuary is located. There's a YHA hostel and beach campground at the end of the road. Tours of the sanctuary by jet boat are available through **White Heron Sanctuary Tours**, located in Whataroa. ☎ *(03) 753-4120; FAX (03) 753-4087.* There is also an office in Franz Josef.

The Forks also marks the northern edge of **Westland National Park**, a 222,000-acre (348 square miles) park that has *the most elevation extremes of all the country's national parks.* It goes from sea level on the West Coast to the top of 11,500-foot Mt. Tasman.

The result is a wide series of ecosystems, from rainforest to subalpine to glaciers. Although technically **Mount Cook** is on the other side of the mountains (and inaccessible by road from the West Coast), New Zealand's highest mountain is still the center of attraction in the Westland National Park area. Included in the park are the South Island's two other great tourist attractions, the **Fox** and **Franz Josef** glaciers. Mount Cook is actually in its own national park, which abuts Westland.

What makes the Southern Alps and the glaciers so striking is that, compared with the glaciers of Alaska and Canada, they are framed by lush rainforests. Within a few miles inland from the ocean, you're at the glaciers' faces, and your first sight of them will be through the dense canopy of the coastal vegetation. They are, simply, startlingly beautiful and worth a visit to New Zealand by themselves.

Franz Josef and Fox Glacier

The farthest north of the pair, Franz Josef was named after the head of the Austro-Hungarian Empire in 1865 by Julius von Haast, an Austrian explorer. The glacier is about seven miles long. **Fox Glacier** was named after Sir William Fox, the premier of New Zealand in the early 1870s. Fox is a bit longer and wider than Franz Josef. They rise in the mountains at a height of about 8500 feet and end at about 980 feet above sea level. The glaciers gave rise to small communities with the same names, both of which now have Westland National Park visitor centers. The centers have information not only about the glaciers, but hiking, camping, accommodations and activities in the park. *Of the two communities, Fox Glacier is the best equipped, as far as eateries and accommodations are concerned*. Both settlements, however, offer a variety of glacier-oriented activities, from flight-seeing to hikes over—and onto—the glaciers themselves. Both have medical clinics.

Getting to the Glaciers

There is no airline service to either Fox Glacier or Franz Josef, but both can be reached by train/bus or just bus connections. From Christchurch, the Tranz-Alpine train connects with a bus to both villages. There is also bus service from Queenstown, Greymouth, Nelson and Wanaka. Fares from Christchurch to the glaciers are about NZ$80; from Queenstown, about $NZ80.

Franz Josef

Coming from the north, Franz Josef is the first glacier village you come to. It has a permanent population of fewer than 600, and, like Fox Glacier, *it can be almost impossible to find a place to spend the night in the peak holiday season*. At last count, there were about a half-dozen places to stay in the village, including hostels. The village also has a grocery store, a gas station and a small church—**Our Lady of the Alps**. And there are at least two companies offering either airplane or helicopter rides over and onto the glaciers. The visitor center is located in the Department of Conservation office on the right side of the road coming from Hokitika, and is open 8 a.m.–5 p.m. In the summer, it will often have evening programs on the ecology and geology of the glacier area. There are also accommodation information, souvenirs, booklets and maps available. ☎ *(03) 752-0796; FAX (03) 752-0797.*

Franz Josef Glacier is seven miles long and offers a variety of activities, from helicopter trips to hikes.

A good way to get a first look at the glacier country is at the semi-Omnimax theater performances in the **Alpine Adventure Centre** on the main drag in Franz Josef. The film, called *Flowing West,* is a helicopter and ground view of the area from the top of Mount Cook down a river to the sea; at $NZ10 per person, well worth a stop. The center also serves as a booking office for various area activities, including helicopter flights, white heron sanctuary tours, and fishing services; there is a small café and shop; also mountain bikes for hire.

Where to Stay

Westland Motor Inn   **$NZ150–200**   ★ ★ ★

☎ *(03) 752-0729; FAX (03) 752-0709.*

Just on the north edge of town about six kilometers from the glacier. Our choice for Franz Josef; a Flag property. Around 100 rooms, including suites, spa, handicapped access, bar and two restaurants, open-fire lounge, laundry, game room and tea/coffee. Rooms range between $NZ150 and $NZ200; off-season discounts.

Franz Josef Glacier Hotel   **$NZ160–200**   ★ ★

☎ *(03) 752-0719; FAX (03) 752-0709.*

A complex of lodge, motel and backpackers rooms located a few kilometers north of the village. Open Oct.–April. On 2.5 acres with glowworms. There is a bar, two restaurants and a bottle shop. The bottle shop and backpacker units are open year around. Motel rates are about $NZ160–200 double.

Glacier View Motel $NZ80   ★★

☎ *(03) 752-0705; FAX (03) 752-0761.*
Also a bit north of the village. The glacier view is great. Rooms range from studios to family style. Coffee/tea, courtesy van, spa, breakfast available. Doubles are around $NZ80.

Westwood Lodge $NZ95–130   ★★

☎ *(03) 752-0111; FAX the same.*
Just north of town. A B&B facility with a large guest lounge, woody interior, hand-icapped access, laundry, nonsmoking areas. Especially friendly and helpful owners. Doubles are between $NZ95–130, depending on season.

Alpine Glacier Motor Lodge $NZ65–90   ★★

Cron Street, a block from the city center. ☎ *(03) 752-0757; FAX the same.*
Studio, family and two-bedroom units. Some kitchens. Laundry, nonsmoking rooms, tour desk. Doubles are between $NZ65–90, depending on season.

Franz Josef Holiday Park $NZ8–50

☎ *(03) 752-0766; FAX the same.*
Across the Waiho River bridge south of town near the glacier access road. More than seven acres, including RV and tent sites, cabins, bunkhouses, tourist cottages and a lodge. Kitchen, laundry, game room, barbecues, pool, bus stop. Motel-style units are $NZ50 double. Tent sites are about $NZ8; bunkhouses are $NZ10 per person; cabins are $NZ25 for two persons; lodge rates are about $NZ15 per person.

Franz Josef Hostel $NZ16

2-4 Cron Street. ☎ *(03) 752-0754; FAX the same.*
Modern and close to town, doubles and family rooms. Shop, low-cost meals available. TV lounge, laundry. Rates are $NZ16 per person a night.

Where to Eat

Franz Josef is not an epicurean's delight, but you won't starve. Probably the best place in town is the **Blue Ice Café** ★★ in the village, which has very good pizzas plus some interesting pasta and Asian offerings. Open noon to late. Budget to moderate. ☎ *(03) 752-0707.* Others include the **Fern Grove**, a deli, grocery and wine shop; the **Glacier Store and Tearoom**; **D.A.'s Restaurant and Tearoom**; and **Batson's Tavern**, which has pub food and a bottle shop.

Activities

Glacier Landings

The highlight of your New Zealand tour, if you're not afraid of flying, is a flight to the glaciers, especially the flights where you actually land high in the mountains. Like everything else in Westland, glacier flights are weather-dependent. Even on clear, sunny days, it's not uncommon to have so much cloud cover around the peak of Mount Cook that it can't be seen.

These flights can be short or long, depending on the pocketbook, and you can either take a **ski-plane** or a **helicopter**. *We prefer the choppers because you can hover over the glaciers and take magnificent photos.* On the other hand, when's the last time you landed on snow in a ski plane?

There are a number of companies offering helicopter trips from both Franz Josef and Fox Glacier. As examples, **Glacier Helicopters** has a 10-minute overview flight for $NZ80 per person; a one-glacier, 20-minute landing is $NZ100; landing on both glaciers for $NZ150, or a 40-minute trip that lands on both glaciers and circles Mount Cook for $NZ230. The company's offices are located in the center of both villages: Franz Josef ☎ *(03) 752-0755 or 752-0726*; Fox Glacier ☎ *(03) 751-0803; FAX for both (03) 751-0738*. Other companies include **The Helicopter Line**, Franz Josef ☎ *(03) 752-0767, FAX (03) 752-0769*, and Fox Glacier ☎ *(03) 751-0767, FAX (03) 751-0722*; and **Heli Services**, Franz Josef ☎ *(03) 752-0793, FAX (03) 752-0764*, and Fox Glacier ☎ *(03) 751-0866, FAX (03) 751-0857*. Prices are about the same for both companies. *If you save up for no other trip on your New Zealand vacation, try to do this one. It's tremendous.* Trips can be booked from almost any tourist office or travel agency in New Zealand. It's wise to book several days in advance—and hope the weather's okay. Ski-plane rides are about the same price and offer the same itineraries. They are offered through Mount Cook Lines, ☎ *(03) 752-0714*. The company flies from both villages.

Hiking and Climbing

You can hike in the Franz Josef area by yourself or with a guided group; note, however, *you're not allowed on the glacier itself without a guide*. Some hikes:

Glacier walk

Go south just over the Waiho River bridge, and turn left onto the Glacier Road. Drive to the end where there is a parking lot and information kiosk. From the parking lot, it's about an hour to a viewing platform near the foot of the glacier. The valley walk shows you a classic glaciated valley, from the pockets of glacial debris to the gravel-bedded river to the river itself, a milky greenish-white from the deposits of ground-up rocks it carries. The fine rock particles, ground by the ice, are called glacial flour. The path is fairly level.

Alex Knob

A bit more for the serious hiker. It's listed as an eight-hour walk, but you can do it in five. It goes from about halfway down the glacier road up to an elevation of around 4200 feet, passing through some excellent rainforest and into alpine grasslands. If the weather's clear, you'll get a great view of the glacier.

Lake Wombat

On the Alex Knob track, but branches off to what is called a glacier "lakelet." An easy stroll through the rainforest.

Guided walks are offered by **Franz Josef Glacier Guides**, ☎ *(03) 752-0763*, and by **Alpine Guides Fox Glacier**, ☎ *(03) 751-0825, FAX (03) 751-0857*. Both companies supply boots and other equipment. You can take a three-hour hike onto the glaciers to look at ice caves, crevasses and other attractions, or do a helicopter fly-in, hike out trip as well as overnight trips to mountain huts. The three-hour treks go for about $NZ35, heli-hikes about $NZ145. The overnight stay (fly in, fly out) is about $NZ500 a couple, including equipment and food. Serious ice climbers and mountaineering types can also book trips through these companies. Another company with ice field trips is **Alpine Recreation of Canterbury Ltd.**, *Box 74, Lake Tekapo;* ☎ *(03) 680-6736; FAX (03) 680-6765.*

Fox Glacier

Here's where we suggest you base yourself in Glacier Country. There's more to do, and the same opportunity for flights, hiking and glacier trips are available, but there's more going on here and the accommodations are better. You're only 12 miles from Franz Josef if you want to go back and do the trails and activities there.

The Fox Glacier Visitor Centre will be on your right coming into town from the north and, as noted, will have pertinent information about trails, trips and accommodations. ☎ *(03) 751-0807; FAX (03) 751-0858.* Helicopter and ski plane trips can be booked here, as can short or extensive glacier treks with Alpine Guides.

Activities

Cone Rock Track

Of the many trails around both glaciers, we found the trip up to Cone Rock/Chalet Lookout to be unsurpassed for scenery and variety of ecosystems. Some of the overlooks down into the Fox River Valley are awesome, definitely not for folks with a fear of heights, and not recommended for small children. The Chalet Lookout portion of the trail is fairly even, but the Cone section is steep and fairly rigorous. Figure maybe three hours to the top of Cone Rock and back if you also do the Chalet. To get to the trails, take the Glacier Road just past the Fox River, south of town. *As noted previously, you can't go onto the glacier without a guide.*

The Beach

There are several trails along the beach, which is reached by driving down the Cook Flat Road about 10 kilometers off the main highway. One trail goes to a seal colony, passing some old mining ruins; it's about a three-hour round-trip.

Worms

Right in the village, near the Golden Glacier Motor Inn, is a **glowworm grotto**—in case you haven't had a chance yet on the trip to see the little creatures. In the summer, the information center often runs tours down to the grotto at night. The cave here is not as elaborate as some of the larger insect spots, but it does in fact have glowworms. It's called the Minnehaha Forest Glowworm Dell.

A couple enjoys the spectacle of a waterfall near Milford.

Where to Stay

Fox Glacier Hotel   **$NZ115**   ★★

☎ *(03) 751-0839; FAX (03) 751-0868.*

You can't miss it, a big, rambling white wooden building in the center of town. It is a bit seedy around the edges, but the rooms are good, the food is okay, and the owner is tops. The hotel is now a third-generation operation and is where many tour bus groups spend the night when they come to the glaciers. The hotel has old rooms and new rooms. We prefer the older ones, which have balconies and great views; the new ones are more motel-style and are, incidentally, where the tour groups are. There is a public bar where the locals hang out, or if you prefer privacy, a guests-only bar in the hotel wing. Also available are tea/coffee, laundry and a licensed restaurant. Standard rooms go for about $NZ115.

Glacier Country Hotel   **$NZ110**   ★★

☎ *(03) 751-0847; FAX (03) 751-0822.*

More modern and a bit more upscale, this Flag facility has an open-fire lounge, restaurant, bar, color TVs and a guest laundry. Handicapped access, bar meals. *Located adjacent to the glowworm grotto.* Doubles start around $NZ110.

A1 Motel $NZ80

☎ *(03) 751-0804; FAX (03) 751-0706.*
Of the several motel-style units, this is probably the best. *It's on the beach road, just past the Catholic Church.* Laundry, spa, courtesy van, squash court, kitchens. Doubles are about $NZ80. You could also try the **Lake Matheson Motel**, *(03) 751-00830,* or the **Mount Cook View Motel**, ☎ *(03) 751-0814.*

Fox Glacier Motor Park $NZ40–70

☎ *(03) 751-0821; FAX (03) 751-0813.*
A Top 10 RV park, also *on the beach road.* Large range of units from motel-style to tent sites. The motel units have kitchens; the tourist flats have rangettes. Motel units (listed as the "Alpine View Motels") run about $NZ70 double. Four-person tourist flats are about $NZ55 double. Cabins are about NZ$40 for two.

Glowworm Forest Lodge and RV Park $NZ70–90

☎ *Fax and phone (03) 751-0821.*
This is a comfy wood lodge with shared facilities—guests share bathrooms, kitchens and laundry, but the rooms are quite nice and the lodge is *centrally located not far from the local glowworm grotto.* The lodge also has RV facilities with 24 powered sites; about $NZ20 a night. Shared rooms start at about $NZ70.

Ivory Towers Hostel $NZ25–35

☎ *(03) 751-0838.*
Sullivan Road, on a hill above the village. All rooms heated, kitchens, lounge, recreation discounts, TV and video room, bike hires. Rates in the $NZ25–35 range.

Where to Eat

Cook Saddle Café & Saloon $–$$ ★★★

☎ *(03) 751-0700; FAX (03) 751-0809.*
These Down Under folks really like the Old American West, and this saloon is a prime example. You must ignore the more flagrant excesses of decor (boots, saddles, horns, guns) as well as the menu names: Howdy Doody Burger, Butch Cassidy's Sundance Salad, Billy the Kid's Fave, Pony Express Pork. The food, with a heavy emphasis on Tex-Mex, also features very good Kiwi stuff. There is an excellent wine list, great service and big portions. Really quite good, and the swinginest joint in town, yahoo. Moderate prices. It's in a complex with the **Fox Glacier Restaurant and Tearoom** and the **Cone Rock Café and Tavern** (which are pretty good, as well, for light meals).

Fox Glacier Hotel $–$$ ★★

☎ *(03) 751–0825.*
The only problem eating here is the herds of tour bus passengers who swarm in to dine. But good fare and service; moderate. There is also good budget pub food service at the bar. For sandwiches and budget light fare, try the **Hobnail Coffee Shop** in the Alpine Guides building back of the hotel.

The West Coast

Toward Queenstown

Makarora bush trail is a worthwhile hike.

The 300-odd kilometer drive from the glaciers to Wanaka over Haast Pass is a jewel among jewels and is probably *the single-best stretch of scenic rainforest highway on the South Island*. The road basically stays inland from Fox Glacier to Lake Moeraki, and the last stretch before the village of Haast parallels the **beaches** for a good 20 kilometers. The total effect is continuous green. Twists and curves, canopies of **rainforest** plants, occasional glimpses of the mountains and the sea. There are some small settlements here and there along the road with a motel or café. On the way, you will pass two lakes, Paringa and Moeraki, which have rest stops with picnic tables and views of the lakes, which are home to flocks of **black swans**.

For a good meal at Lake Paringa, try the **Lake Paringa Hotel** (great meat pies and soups). *It's open seven days, closed June and July;* budget prices. There is also a place to stay, the **Lake Paringa Heritage Lodge**, with lodge units for $NZ70 and cabins for $NZ40. ☎ *(03) 751-0894.*

About 30 kilometers north of Haast is the delightful and award-winning **Lake Moeraki Wilderness Lodge** ★★★★, one of the best places to haul in on the West Coast, especially if you're a nature buff. The lodge rooms are not pretentious, but the location is superb, nestled at the west end of the lake, a long canoe ride from the ocean, surrounded by World Heritage rainforests. There are trails into the forests, where you can see penguins, seals, tidal pools, birds and plants. The emphasis is on outdoor activities, from canoe trips to brown trout fishing to bird watching. The staff, led by Gerry Mc-Sweeney, a noted biologist, provides guided tours. A canoe trip from the lodge to the sea and back, lunch included, is about $NZ45 per person. Full-day hikes into the forests and waterfalls of the area are $NZ50–100, depending on route. Fishing guides are $NZ415 for a full day, two persons. The restaurant has good food, a fine wine list and a great view; moderate prices. Doubles are $NZ350-$480 a night, depending on season, and include breakfast and dinner and some equipment supplies. Very friendly, very relaxed. **One highlight**: a chance to see New Zealand long-finned eels, four feet long and weighing up to 55 pounds. ☎ *(03) 750-0881; FAX (03) 750-0882.*

Haast

Haast is about halfway between the glaciers and Wanaka, an easy half-day dawdle. Should you choose to call a pit stop, there are a few places to sleep and one restaurant. In the settlement is the **South Westland World Heritage Visitor Centre**, with information about the Haast Pass area. There is a 20-minute audiovisual program and displays. The center is open 8:30 a.m.–4 p.m. daily. ☎ *(03) 750-0809; FAX (03) 750-0832.*

Where to Stay

Erewhon Motels   **$NZ65**   ★★

☎ *(03) 750-0825; FAX (03) 750-0817.*
Located on Jackson Bay Road at Haast Beach, reached by turning right off the main highway and heading toward the ocean. Kitchens and a herd of pedigreed ponies. Doubles are about $NZ65.

World Heritage Hotel Haast   **$NZ90**   ★★

In Haast, near the Haast River bridge. ☎ *(03) 750-0828; FAX (03) 750-0827.*
Bar, licensed restaurant, suites, tearooms, jet boat hire available, laundry. A major pit stop for tour groups at lunchtime. Budget to moderate prices. The bar/bistro opens at 4 p.m. for light meals. About $NZ90 double. Activities such as helicopter flights and rookery visits can be booked here.

Heritage Park Lodge   **$NZ85**   ★★

Marks Road, Haast. ☎ *(03) 750-0868; FAX (03) 750-0869.*
Licensed restaurant and tearoom open 7:30 a.m.–8 p.m. Minibars, laundry, handicapped access, video library, TVs. About $NZ85 double.

Haast Highway Accommodation   **$NZ50–75**   ★★

Marks Road, Haast. ☎ *(03) 750-0703; FAX (03) 750-0718.*
Motel units, cabins and powered and tent sites. General store, laundry, handicapped access, kitchens. $NZ50–75 double.

Haast Motor Camp   **$NZ16–45**

☎ *(03) 750-0860; FAX the same.*
Take the Haast Beach road south about 15 kilometers along Jackson Bay Road to a wide spot called Okuru. Right on the beach, communal kitchen, laundry, store, some units with cooking facilities; tent and powered sites. Cabins are about $NZ45 double. Backpackers, bunkrooms are $NZ16 a night.

Haast Pass Road

Past Haast, the road turns due east and begins a 150-kilometer run through the Alps to Lake Wanaka and the Queenstown area. It is one of the more picturesque treks *on the South Island, rivaling the Arthur's Pass route.* As the road climbs slowly along the Haast River, you'll see dozens of waterfalls, including one fat and active one called **Roaring Billy**. Starting in the rainforests of the coast, the road gradually takes you up into subalpine and alpine vegetation. Toward the top of the pass, you'll run into a few small stretches of unpaved but well-maintained road. The road started as a make-work project during the Depression, was delayed by World War II, and finally completed in the mid-1960s.

Along the road on both sides of the pass are more than a dozen hiking trails, most of them short forays to waterfalls or scenic vistas. (These are subject to weather; if the Haast River is full, the eastern bank trails might be inaccessible.) Among the trails to watch for are the half-hour round-trip to **Roaring Billy**; a five-minute excursion to **Fantail Falls**; the **Blue Pools trail** (watch for humongous trout in the Blue River); **Makarora Bush trail**, with examples of podocarps and silver beech forests (there's a visitors center here), and **Kidds Bush**, an easy nature walk loop. Many of the trails have toilet facilities and picnicking areas. The visitors centers at Haast and Makarora have trail information. At Makarora, there are a gas station, café and small motel, the **Makarora Tourist Centre**, with A-frames and cabins in the $NZ35–60 range. ☎ *(03) 443-8372; FAX (03) 443-1082.* The visitors center is ☎ *(03) 443-8365.*

Near the small settlement of Makarora at the head of Lake Wanaka, you enter the Wilkins River Valley, which has what seems like billions of sheep. The road then goes along the eastern shore of the lake. The road then abruptly turns east and goes through a gap to Lake Hawea. At the top of the gap, called **The Neck**, it's possible to see both lakes at once, a pretty photo op. There is also a picnic area overlooking Lake Hawea. This is open range country, so don't be surprised to come upon flocks of sheep wandering down the highway.

Wanaka

Lake Wanaka is a watersports and ski area popular winter and summer.

Activities

Like Queenstown, Wanaka is a watersports and ski area, popular in both winter and summer. Smaller, less frantic and a tad less touristy, Wanaka is favored by many Kiwis who find the pace at Queenstown too much. It's a toss-up as to which has the best scenery—both sit on lovely South Island lakes with snowcapped mountains in the background. Wanaka is ground zero for **Mount Aspiring National Park**, which sits between Haast Pass and Fiordland National Park to the south. The centerpiece of the 710,000-acre park is **Mt. Aspiring**, 9900 feet high and a classic jagged peak in the style of the European Alps. *One of the best views of Mt. Aspiring is from Glendhu Bay* on a paved local road west of Wanaka. Park information is available from the DOC office on Highway 89.

There are a number of fairly strenuous but scenic hiking trails in the park, which is *considered to be one of the wildest parks on the South Island.* **Mountain Recreation** in Wanaka has a series of guided treks in the park, some of which include mountain climbing or river rafting. A good bet is the three-day trip that goes around the base of the mountain and takes in the gorgeous country around Shovel Flat, a remote ice-covered valley. This trip, unlike the high-country treks, runs all year. It's about $NZ500 per person, including accommodations, meals, equipment—even hot showers. A perfect quickie Alpine trip. Private guiding into the mountains will run about $NZ400 per person a day. ☎ *Phone and FAX (03) 443-7330.* Similar services, plus heli-hiking and ski touring, are offered by **Mt. Aspiring Guides** in Wanaka, ☎ *(03) 443-9422 or 443-7930, FAX (03) 443-8876.*

The Wanaka area is noted for **trout fishing** as well as **white-water trips** on rivers feeding into the lake. Fishing information is available from the **Otago Fish and Game Council** at the DOC office on Highway 89. ☎ *(03) 443-7660; FAX the same.* We like the attitude of **Wanaka Lake Services**, which does lake trolling trips: "No Fish, No Pay." Charter rates for the lake will be around NZ$90–100 an hour, including guide, plus $NZ10 for a license. The company is on the Wanaka wharf. ☎ *(03) 443-7495; FAX (03) 443-1323.*

The Wanaka area is noted for trout fishing as well as white-water river trips.

Toward Queenstown

The region is also close to three major ski areas, **Cardrona**, **Treble Cone** and **Waiorau Nordic**. Cardrona is located in three basins with lift capacity for about 6000 skiers an hour. There are **heli-skiing** trips available through the Helicopter Line at Cardrona, as well as trips to Treble Cone and slopes in the nearby Harris Mountains. The nordic area has about 25 kilometers of **cross-country trails**. Lift passes at Cardrona and Treble Cone are about $NZ50; access charges at Waioru are about $NZ30. *Information:* Treble Cone ☎ *(03) 443-7443, FAX (03) 443-8401;* Cardrona ☎ *(03) 443-7411, FAX (03) 443-8818,* and Waiorau ☎ *(03) 443-7930, FAX (03) 443-8876.* Heli-skiing costs, depending on the number of runs, are between $NZ450 and $NZ650; glacier trips are also available. For information, contact **Harris Mountain Heli-Skiing** at ☎ *(03) 443-7943, FAX (03) 443-8876;* or **Backcountry Helicopters** at ☎ *(03) 443-1054, FAX (03) 443-1051.*

Wanaka is also a base for flights to Milford Sound, Mt. Aspiring and Mt. Cook, or the Fox and Franz Josef glaciers. Flights, through **Aspiring Air**, run between $NZ50 and $NZ200, depending on itinerary and duration. Aspiring Air is located at the Wanaka airport on the Wanaka-Queenstown highway; ☎ *(03) 443-7943, FAX (03) 443-8949.* The **Wanaka Visitors Centre** is on Highway 89 (across from the jetty downtown on Ardmore Street); it's open seven days, ☎ *(03) 443-1233, FAX (03) 443-9238.* The **Department of Conservation** office is at the same address, and has information on regional activities. ☎ *(03) 443-7660, FAX (03) 443-8776.*

A few other local points of interest:

New Zealand Fighter Pilots Museum

☎ *(03) 443-7010.*

With what is claimed to be one of the largest collections of still-flyable famous World War I and II planes on view (Spitfire, P-51, Corsair), plus displays, films and vintage photographs. At the airport north of town; small admission charge.

Rippon Vineyard

☎ *(03) 443-7010; FAX the same.*

Undoubtedly one of the most scenic locations in the world to try a little wine tasting. Pinot noirs a speciality. Open daily for tastings and cellar door sales; closed in June and July, except by appointment. On Mt. Aspiring Road on the shore of the lake.

Puzzling World

☎ *(03) 443-7489; FAX the same.*

The place to take the kids, or as they are affectionately known in these parts, "curtain climbers." It's a series of jumbled-by-design buildings, a 1.5-kilometer-long maze, hologram hall and 18-hole miniature golf facility about two kilometers east of town. There's also a great collection and demonstrations of puzzles of all kinds. Entry fee, depending on what you do, ranges from $NZ3–6 adults, $NZ2–3.50 for kids. East of downtown a ways.

Where to Stay

Edgewater Resort, The   **$NZ185**   ★★★

On Sargood Drive. ☎ *(03) 443-8311; FAX (03) 443-8323.*
One of the best in town, with great views of the lake. Hotel and motel accommodations; kitchens, spa, sauna, tea/coffee, bar and restaurant (see below), courtesy van. Hotel doubles around $NZ185.

Wanaka Motor Inn   **$NZ110–140**   ★★★

Mt. Aspiring Road, about 2 kilometers from town. ☎ *(03) 443-8216; FAX (03) 443-9108.*
Some suites with hot tubs, private balconies, laundry, ski-drying room, tea/coffee, bar and restaurant, courtesy van, excellent scenery. Nice view from the stone-and-wood bar/restaurant, the Rafters (see below.) Doubles around $NZ110; suites $NZ140.

Aspiring Lodge, The   **$NZ70–110**   ★★

Corner Dunmore and Dungarvon streets. ☎ *(03) 443-7816; FAX (03) 443-8914.*
A block off the jetty downtown. Studio units, suites, handicapped facilities. Kitchenettes with microwaves, cooked breakfasts available.

Fairway Lodge Motel   **$NZ65–85**   ★★

Corner MacPherson and Highway 89 near downtown. ☎ *(03) 443-7285; FAX (03) 443-9178.*
Studios, one- and two-bedroom units, adjacent to the Wanaka golf course. Pool, video movies, cooked breakfasts available. $NZ65–85 double.

Pembroke Inn, The   **$NZ60**   ★★

94 Brownston Street. ☎ *(03) 443-7296; FAX (03) 443-7620.*
One of the Pub Beds group, situated downtown a block off the jetty. Nice views, tea/coffee, sauna, kitchens, laundry, restaurant open seven days, fireside bar. Ski area transport; satellite dish for sports.

Te Wanaka Lodge   **$NZ70–90**   ★★

23 Brownston Street, one block from the jetty. ☎ *(03) 443-9224; FAX (03) 443-9246.*
A modern B&B in A-frame buildings, with two guest lounges and cooking facilities. All rooms with private bath. Nonsmoking. Hot tub.

Harpers B&B   **$NZ80**   ★

Stone Street, overlooking the lake. ☎ *(03) 443-8894 or 443-8844; FAX 443-8841.*
Up the hill from the town center, with great balcony views looking over the lake to the mountains. Two twin rooms with private bath; laundry facilities.

Clifford's Hotel   **$NZ75**   ★

Downtown at 71 Ardmore Street. ☎ *(03) 443-7826; FAX (03) 443-9069.*
Restaurant, bar, family lounge, spa, coffee/tea, some suites with hot tubs. Doubles around $NZ75.

Bay View Motel   **$NZ80–95**   ★★★

Mount Aspiring Road, 3 kilometers from town. ☎ *(03) 443-7766; FAX (03) 443-9194.*
Kitchens, some units with fireplaces, guest laundry, breakfast available. Doubles around $NZ80–95. Great views of Lake Wanaka and the surrounding mountains, family-sized pool/spa, huge children's play area, plus numerous amenities for skiers.

Toward Queenstown

Wanaka YHA Hostel   **$NZ16**

181 Upton Street, close to the lake. ☎ *(03) 443-7405.*
Ski rental and transport. $NZ16 a night.

Pleasant Lodge Holiday Park   **$NZ30–70**

On Glendhu Bay, a Top 10 RV park. ☎ *(03) 443-7360; FAX (03) 443-7360.*
Pool, spa, laundry, barbecues, store. Tourist flats with rangettes and fridges, $NZ55
double. Cabins $NZ30 double. Motel units, $NZ70 double.

Wanaka Motor Park   **$NZ13–50**

Brownston Street, near downtown. ☎ *(03) 443-7883; FAX the same.*
Laundry, community kitchen, spa, boat park, ski room. Tourist flats, $NZ50 dou-
ble. Cabins $NZ35. Bunkrooms $NZ13 per person.

Where to Eat

Relishes Café   **$$**   ★★★

On Ardmore Street in Central Wanaka. ☎ *(03) 443-9018.*
Licensed and BYO, café-style. Great for afternoon teas, the best coffee in town,
tasty chocolate concoctions. Excellent steaks and sinful desserts, and do try the sea-
food. Open fire, warm atmosphere. *Open 9:30 a.m.–3 p.m. and 6:30 p.m. until
late. Sometimes closed Tues.*

Cardrona Restaurant   **$$**   ★★★

Near the ski fields on Highway 89, due south of town. ☎ *(03) 443-8153.*
Restored Gold Rush building with interiors in kauri wood, scenery, great food—
sometimes German, sometimes Kiwi, sometimes seafood. When the weather coop-
erates, there's a "country" beer garden outside. Restaurant open seven days for dinner only. If you call, Cardona will send a courtesy bus.

Ripples   **$–$$**   ★★

Pembroke Village Mall (right downtown near the lake). ☎ *(03) 443-7413.*
BYO, Kiwi cuisine, outside dining in good weather. *Lunch noon–2 p.m.; dinner
from 6 p.m. until late.*

Nathaniel's   **$–$$**   ★★

Sargood Drive, in the Edgewater Resort Hotel. ☎ *(03) 443-8311.*
Licensed and BYO. Brasserie style, lake views, colonial furnishings, seafood a specialty. *Open for dinner from 6:30–10 p.m.*

Rafters   **$$**   ★★

At the Wanaka Motor Inn, on the Mt. Aspiring Road. ☎ *(03) 443-8216.*
Wonderful views. Open stone fireplace, casual, lamb, steaks and New Zealand blue
cod. Licensed. *Open for dinner 6–9 p.m.*

Capriccio   **$$**   ★★

123 Ardmore Street. ☎ *(03) 443-8579.*
Italian and New Zealand fare, on the lakefront with great views. Life cray tank,
homemade pasta, BYO and licensed. *Dinner from 6 p.m. until late.*

Clifford's Hotel   **$**   ★

On Ardmore Street. ☎ *(03) 443-7826.*

Pub-style meals, good wine list, open for lunch and dinner. Often has entertainment on the weekends.

Te Kano   **$–$$**   ★★
Brownston Street. ☎ *(03) 443-7028.*
Nationally famous vegetarian place housed in a small cottage. BYO. Excellent pizzas. Great for mulled wine in the winter. Large portions. *Open seven days 8 a.m.–10 p.m.*

Arrowtown

If you're in a car and the weather is decent, *the most scenic—and most direct route—from Wanaka to Queenstown is down Highway 89*, an unpaved road running through the Cardrona Valley. At 45 miles, the trip through the valley is shorter by about 10 miles, but probably slower due to the ruts and washboards in the road. But the scenery is great. *Note: The road is unsealed beyond the Cardrona Restaurant, and thus is verboten for rental RVs.*

The fast way is on Highway 6, which circles to the east and then drops into Queenstown and Lake Wakatipu from the north. Either way, you'll come within a short distance of Arrowtown, a gaggle of Gold Rush cottages and old buildings built in the 1860s, quite popular with tourists. Lots of photographs are taken along Bedford Street—**the Avenue of Oak Trees**. The village has the very good **Lake District Gold Mining Museum**, located on Buckingham Street, with displays on the town's history. *The museum is open from 9 a.m.–5 p.m. seven days.* It also serves as the community information center. ☎ *and FAX (03) 442-1824.* Arrowtown's main drag is lined with boutiques, galleries and souvenir shops. Excellent adult and children's clothing shops feature less expensive prices than some tourist areas. In summer, a red double-decker bus runs from Queenstown to Arrowtown for about $NZ20. One of the charming coffee shops doubles as a bookstore.

If you're interested in wool and sheep products, there's a **Sheep Station** outlet at the Arrowtown mall on Buckingham Street with a wide range of leather and knitwares. Open seven days, accepts all currencies and travelers checks.

Where to Stay

The bed scene in Arrowtown is mostly B&Bs and motels in the two-star category.

Golden View Motel   **$NZ70**   ★★
48 Adamson Road. ☎ *(03) 442-1833; FAX the same.*
Kitchens, laundry, car wash, store, pool.

Viking Lodge Motel   **$NZ75–80**   ★★
21 Inverness Crescent. ☎ *(03) 442-1765; FAX the same.*
A-frame chalets, laundry, pool, bikes for hire.

New Orleans Hotel   **$NZ13–55**   ★

27 Buckingham Street. ☎ *(03) 442-1745.*

A Pub Beds facility. Restaurant, bar, private lounge, bottle shop, tea/coffee. Doubles are $NZ55, including continental breakfast. Bunkrooms, $NZ13 per person.

Postmasters Guest House   **$NZ70–80**   ★ ★

150 Buckingham Street. ☎ *(03) 442-0272.*

As the name suggests, this B&B is housed in the old postmaster's residence, built in 1907. There is an adjoining art gallery. Doubles with private bath are $NZ80; breakfast prices not included. Shared doubles are $NZ70.

Cynthia Balfour Homestay   **$NZ90**   ★ ★

20 Wiltshire Street. ☎ *(03) 442-1326.*

A very comfy and friendly B&B housed in a rambling garden-surrounded cottage, complete with two house cats. It's nonsmoking, and guests share the bathroom.

Mace Motel   **$NZ75**   ★ ★

13 Cardigan Street. ☎ *(03) 442-1825; FAX (03) 442-1855.*

Two- and three-bedroom units, kitchens, fridge, laundry, spa, store.

Arrowtown Caravan Park   **$NZ8–30**   ★

47 Devon Street. ☎ *(03) 442-1838; FAX the same.*

Kitchen, laundry, dining room. On-site caravans are $NZ30 double. Closed Apr.–Oct. Powered site $NZ8 per person.

Where to Eat

There are a few fine dining places in the village, but what you'll find mostly are tea-rooms, pubs and small cafés all along Buckingham Street. Among the choices available are the **Wind in the Willows Bookstore/Café, Grannys Kitchen**, the **Stone Cottage Restaurant and Tearooms**, and the **Royal Oak Bistro and Bottle Shop**.

Between Arrowtown and Queenstown lies the large new conference center/retirement resort/country club/entertainment venue called **Millbrook**. It looks a lot like the places you see in Palm Springs or Scottsdale. There is an 18-hole course, two driving ranges and a pro shop. One of the major reasons to stop there is the **Clubhouse Restaurant** ★ ★ ★ ★, which is developing a national reputation as one of the country's finer eateries. The offerings are very French, using rabbit, wild game, excellent sauces and imaginative vegetable dishes. It's open for all three meals seven days. Moderate to expensive. ☎ *(03) 442-1563.* Accommodation ★ ★ ★ choices at Millbrook are in one-bedroom suites or two-bedroom villas. Doubles in the one-bedroom units start at about $NZ200. ☎ *(03) 441-7000; FAX 441-1145.*

Queenstown

Queenstown

Queenstown Mall is a fun place for lunch and shopping.

We have met some New Zealanders who refuse to go anywhere near Queenstown, it being, they say, too bloody frantic, touristy and tawdry. And by Kiwi standards, it just might be. But compared to the flashy-toothed, beautiful-people-laden ski spas around North America (Aspen comes to mind at once), Queenstown is pretty mild. *It's in a beautiful location, sitting beneath some sawtooth ridges called "the Remarkables," next to one of the South Island's incredible deep lakes, Wakatipu.* As for that, we think it's a toss-up which community has the best setting, Queenstown or Wanaka.

Whatever, Queenstown is the fun capital of the South Island, close to skiing, close to fishing, close to mountain hiking, close to Milford Sound. If you care, it's also the **bungy-jumping** capital of the world and world-famous for **white-water rafting**. For the last several decades, the city has held a winter festival in late June to kick off the start of the ski season. It runs for about 10 days, and includes fancy dress parades, celebrity sightings, mountain biking on the slopes, tubing, a "drag race" wherein local businessmen dress up in women's clothes, boozing, partying and general silliness. The festival has gone a long way toward convincing the more sedate portions of Kiwi society to avoid Queenstown like the plague—especially in late June. But if partying is your bag...

Detractors will tell you that Queenstown's comportment began at its birth in the 1860s as a wild mining town. It is close to the Shotover River, claimed to be one of the richest gold-bearing streams in the world. Some of the tales that came from those days would suggest it's probably true—cooks pulling huge nuggets of gold out of the gravel with a butcher knife, two guys rescuing a dog from the river and winding up with 25 pounds of gold by nightfall—you get the idea. But gold booms are usually followed by gold busts, and, by 1900, there were only 190 brave souls left in town. The Shotover is still reputed to be full of gold, but mostly it's used for sport now.

Lake Wakatipu is the third-largest lake in New Zealand.

Lake Wakatipu has always been the center of attention in the city, which sits wrapped around its edges. It's typical of the large southern lakes, carved deep by ancient glaciers—in this case, about **1240** feet deep, going well below sea level. It's the third-largest lake in New Zealand, S-shaped and stretching for more than 50 miles. It's a very popular sailing and fishing area, by North American standards very **underused**. In the Gold Rush days, there were four lake steamers bringing prospectors and supplies into the town, as

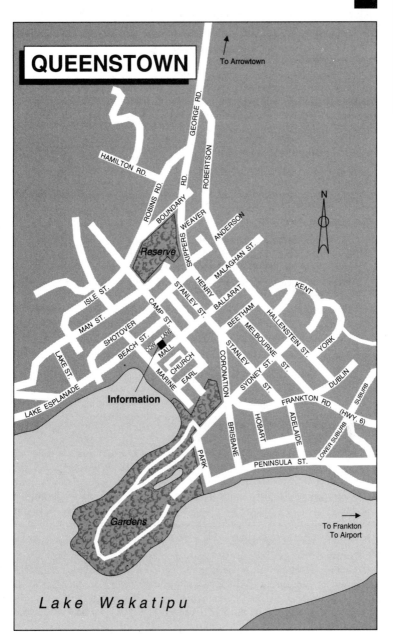

QUEENSTOWN

To Arrowtown

N

GEORGE RD.

HAMILTON RD.

ROBINS RD.

ROBERTSON RD.

BOUNDARY RD.

SKIPPERS

WEAVER

ANDERSON

Reserve

MALAGHAN ST.

ISLE ST.

STANLEY ST.

HENRY

BALLARAT

KENT

MAN ST.

CAMP ST.

BEETHAM

HALLENSTEIN ST.

YORK

SHOTOVER

MELBOURNE ST.

STANLEY

BEACH ST.

COW LANE

MALL

CHURCH

CORONATION

DUBLIN

LAKE ST.

MARINE

EARL

SYDNEY ST.

ST.

FRANKTON RD.

SUBURB

LAKE ESPLANADE

Information

HOBART

ADELAIDE

(HWY. 6)

BRISBANE

LOWER SUBURB

PARK

PENINSULA ST.

Gardens

To Frankton
To Airport

Lake   Wakatipu

well as taking supplies to the sheep and cattle stations that had been established here and there on the shores.

Activities

Views

Queenstown is a fairly compact town, easily walkable, with some very steep hills, particularly near the Parkroyal Hotel. The downtown area is compact, with lots of stores and the requisite number of sporting goods stores, boutiques, sheep shops, singles clubs, jewelry stores, hotels and more tourist information offices per square yard than almost any place we've been. It also has one of the prettiest golf courses in New Zealand. But Queenstown's main charm, really, is as a place to use as a base for some special trips around the Southern Alps and the fjords.

First, get your bearings, and the best way to do that is to walk up Brecon Street and catch the **Skyline Gondola** that goes up to the top of Bob's Peak.

Bob's Peak

☎ *(03) 442-7860; FAX (03) 442-6391.*

Located in back of town. It rises 1500 feet at a steep angle (37.1 degrees, we are told), and, from the top, you can see most of the city and big chunks of lake and mountains. There's a restaurant at the top that offers a special deal in connection with a bus tour to Milford Sound. (See "Where to Eat" section.) There is also a lounge bar and souvenir shop. It's possible to walk to the top of the peak if you're feeling strong. The ride up and down by gondola will cost about $NZ12 adults, $NZ25 family. It runs from 9 a.m. until late.

Mt. Coronet

Sits a few miles behind the city, facing the Remarkables. It also offers a great view of the area. A ski lift takes you up the 5400-foot peak, renowned for its fine winter powder, and a great place to scope out the countryside. The lift runs all year and costs about $NZ15. Buses run to the ski area in the winter.

Cruising

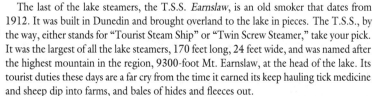

The last of the lake steamers, the T.S.S. *Earnslaw*, is an old smoker that dates from 1912. It was built in Dunedin and brought overland to the lake in pieces. The T.S.S., by the way, either stands for "Tourist Steam Ship" or "Twin Screw Steamer," take your pick. It was the largest of all the lake steamers, 170 feet long, 24 feet wide, and was named after the highest mountain in the region, 9300-foot Mt. Earnslaw, at the head of the lake. Its tourist duties these days are a far cry from the time it earned its keep hauling tick medicine and sheep dip into farms, and bales of hides and fleeces out.

The first lake cruise of the day is at 12:30 p.m., July–May, and takes an hour to make a fast trip around the lake, passing near the town; snacks available. There is a well-stocked bar aboard the *Earnslaw* as well. The cruises run about $NZ25 per person. There are also evening cruises aboard the boat, leaving at 5:30 p.m., 7:30 p.m. and a 9:30 p.m. excursion in the summer. These are also $NZ25 per person, and there is a buffet available for about $NZ25.

The T.S.S. Earnslaw steams past Mt. Earnslaw and the Remarkables.

In addition, there are three daily cruises to the *Walter Peak* homestead across the lake, a famous old sheep and cattle station founded in the 1860s. At its height, there were 40,000 sheep and 50 full-time employees on the 170,000-acre ranch. The morning cruise leaves at 9 a.m. Included is a tour of the station, where you get a shearing demo, spinning lessons and a look at some sheep dogs at work (they're worth the price of admission). Also included is morning tea at the **Colonel's Homestead Restaurant**. The afternoon cruise, which includes all activities above, leaves at 2 p.m. These cruises cost about $NZ40. The dinner cruise to Walter Peak leaves at 5:30 p.m. (7:30 p.m. in the summer), and costs about $NZ60. It's also possible to book horseback rides at the ranch.

Reservations can be booked at any Fiordland Travel office downtown or at the wharf across from the Park Royal, ☎ *(03) 442-7500; FAX (03) 442-7504.*

Animals

The female member of this team will always hold a special spot in her heart for Queenstown, for it was here, on a sunny fall afternoon, that she spotted her first—and as it turned out, last—kiwi. Perhaps here we should warn you about kiwi spotting as practiced in the darkened zoolets of New Zealand. The beasts are nocturnal, and the light levels in their displays are almost nonexistent. For the first 10 minutes, you're blind, then rapidly disappointed because, as much as you look, you can't see the bloody bird. Here's where old hands will win out—patience, people, patience. Eventually the beast will suddenly appear from the bushes, nine parts beak, and you can go home and die in peace. But if you've seen one kiwi—it's probably not worth going more than once unless you have something about big noses.

Kiwi and Birdlife Park

☎ *(03) 442-8059.*

Just down from the entrance to the gondola station. The place in Queenstown to spot *Archie Apteryx*. In addition to the kiwi house, there are a bunch of native and introduced birds wandering around, including Canada geese, shellback ducks and keas. *Hours are 9 a.m.–10 p.m. summer, 9 a.m.–5 p.m. daily winter*. Admission is about $NZ8 per person.

Tours

Because of its location, Queenstown is a logical location for flight-seeing trips into the Alps and over the fjords, especially Milford Sound. Several companies offer either fixed-wing or helicopter flights in the area. Among helicopter companies is the very dependable **Helicopter Line**. A flight around the city will run in the $NZ60 per person range for a half-hour or so; flights to Milford Sound and back will run $NZ100 and above. ☎ *(03) 442-3034; FAX (03) 442-3529*.

Flights from Queenstown to Milford Sound and back are quite popular, weather permitting, and most folks either do a round-trip or combine a bus trip to Milford, a boat tour of the sound and a return flight. The fly-boat-bus packages will run about $NZ265, and take about eight hours. A fly-boat-fly trip will also cost about $NZ250 and take about four hours. There are seasonal evening trips as well.

When it's operating, you can also take a biplane trip on a restored Tiger Moth. *The Moth, vintage 1938, will fly over the lake and peel around Coronet Peak for some great views for about $NZ150*. Book it by calling **Vintage Flights**, ☎ *(03) 442-3016*. Local flight-seeing trips on a conventional aircraft will run about $NZ50 for a quickie 15-minute buzz over town or about $NZ150 for a one-hour flight over the whole area.

There are also flights to Mount Cook, where you can hop a helicopter for a landing on a glacier near the mountain. That'll set you back about $NZ625. All sorts of combinations for flights around Queenstown and the southern South Island are available; basically tell them where you want to go, and they'll fly you there. The best bet is probably **Mount Cook Airline** in Queenstown, ☎ *(03) 442-4600, FAX (03) 442-4605*, or in Te Anau, ☎ *(03) 249-7516*. Another choice would be **Milford Sound Scenic Flights** with prices and itineraries in the same range, ☎ *(03) 442-3065, FAX (03) 442-3050*. A third is the family-run *Glenorchy Air*, which flies from Queenstown or from the small town of Glenorchy northwest of Queenstown. ☎ *(03) 442-2207*. Flights for any air service can be booked through any travel agent or the information center in town.

There are several companies running bus tours to and from Milford Sound. We recommend **Gray Line**, which has tours starting from Queenstown and Te Anau. (See "The Milford Experience" chapter.)

Shows

Maori Concert and Feast

☎ *(03) 442-8878; FAX (03) 442-7063*.

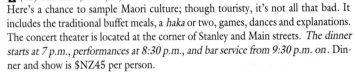

Here's a chance to sample Maori culture; though touristy, it's not all that bad. It includes the traditional buffet meals, a *haka* or two, games, dances and explanations. The concert theater is located at the corner of Stanley and Main streets. *The dinner starts at 7 p.m., performances at 8:30 p.m., and bar service from 9:30 p.m. on*. Dinner and show is $NZ45 per person.

Queenstown

Sports

Golf

☎ *(03) 442-9169.*

The Kiwis rate the links at 18-hole **Kelvin Heights** as one of the most beautiful in the country and "the sixth in the world for scenery." We're not sure what the first five were, and the PR folks aren't talking, but there's no denying it's a lovely stroll, especially the fifth hole from tee to green. The course is on an arm of land across from town, five minutes by water taxi from the Esplanade or 10.5 miles by car. Call the taxi at ☎ *(03) 442-8665.* The club has everything you need, from rental clubs to golf carts to shoes. It opens at 7:30 a.m.

Biking

☎ *(03) 442-8665.*

There are several bicycle hire offices in the city. We recommend **Queenstown Bike Hire** on Beach Street. A number of good routes are available from easy two-hour trips along the lake to all-day jaunts, including one that takes the Skippers Canyon road (very hairy, indeed) to the Shotover Bridge. The company will supply helmets, trouser clips and maps; guides available for groups. A 10- or 12-speed mountain bike goes for about $NZ25 a day; a 21-speed for $NZ28.

The thrill of bungy jumping can be experienced in Queenstown.

Bungy

☎ *(03) 442-7318; FAX (03) 442-6749.*

Earlier (see "The Perfect Vacation" chapter), we said a few words about bungy jumping, which has taken on an almost mythical life in Queenstown. In addition to **A.J. Hackett**, which we strongly recommend, there are other companies on the loose, as well. Among these are **Danes**, at the corner of Shotover and Camp streets. The company has one offering called the "Awesome Foursome," which combines aerobatic helicopter rides, white-water rafting, jet boating and a 230-foot bungy jump—all in one day. Similar trips are offered by **Kawarau Rafts**, Camp and Shotover streets. Prices vary depending on season, but expect to pay around $NZ200–300 per person.

Whitewater

☎ *(03) 442-8570; FAX (03) 442-7467.*

Danes, Kawarau Rafts and others also make much use of the city's nearby wild and scenic rivers for rafting and jet boating. For a half-day trip on the Shotover River, expect to pay about $NZ90; for a half-day on the Kawarau, about $NZ70. Prices for jet boating will be comparable. **Shotover Jet** is probably the best. The company is based at Arthurs Point on the Shotover River outside of town

Other madness

☎ *(03) 532-5961; FAX (03) 442-8869.*

For around $NZ275, the **Ultimate Jump** will take you up to 9000 feet, let you free-fall 4000 feet, then pop a chute and gently float you to the ground. It's a tandem affair, so you don't go down alone. You can also try tandem parasailing (parapente) for about $NZ100; call **Max Air** ☎ *(03) 442-7770.*

White-water rafting is popular on the Shotover River.

The Essential Queenstown

How to Get There

By Bus

Buses from Christchurch run to Queenstown daily on both the InterCity and Mount Cook Line. The trip takes about eight hours and costs between $NZ90 and $NZ95 one way. The buses from Dunedin to Queenstown run weekdays on Inter-City, weekends on Mount Cook Line. One-way costs are between $NZ50 and

$NZ60. There is a daily bus from Fox Glacier to Queenstown on InterCity for about $NZ80, and also from Franz Josef for about $NZ85. The trip from Inver-cargill is on InterCity weekdays and Mount Cook Line on weekends, and costs about $NZ40. Both bus companies have a daily route from Milford Sound, usually in the afternoon, for about $NZ70. They also make the run from Mount Cook, also in the afternoon, for about $NZ60. Daily Te Anau-Queenstown service on both lines runs about $NZ40. From Wanaka, daily on both is about $NZ30.

There is no train service to Queenstown.

By Air

There is daily service to Queenstown from Christchurch on both Mount Cook and Ansett. Most of the flights are morning and early afternoon. The price is about $NZ260 one way. Mount Cook has three daily flights from Mount Cook, costing about NZ205 one way. From Nelson, Air Nelson has daily service and Ansett has Mon.–Sat. service. The fare is about $NZ410.

From the North Island, Air New Zealand, Ansett and Mount Cook have regular ser-vice from Auckland to Queenstown for about $NZ540 one way. There are also daily flights on Mount Cook and Ansett from Rotorua for about $NZ530. Flights from Well-ington are on Air New Zealand and Ansett for about $NZ410. From way up north (Kerikeri on the Bay of Islands), you can fly on a Mount Cook puddle-jumper for $NZ720—the flight takes seven hours.

How to Get Around

Queenstown is so compact we can't think of why you'd want a taxi, but if you do, ☎ *(03) 442-7788; FAX (03) 442-7719*. Taxi service is available to Milford Sound ($NZ450 round-trip) or to the ski fields. A ride in from the airport is about $NZ15; there is also shuttle service. Better to rent a bike or a moped. There are several moped places around downtown. Basically all you need is a valid driver's license. You get gas and un-limited kilometerage for about $NZ50 a day.

Information

The **Queenstown Travel and Visitors Centre** is located in the Clocktower Centre at the corner of Shotover and Camp streets, ☎ *(03) 442-4100, FAX (03) 442-8907*.

The biggest tour company in the area is **Fiordland Travel**; if Fiordland can't arrange it, it probably can't be done. The company has offices in Queenstown, Te Anau and Ma-napouri. In Queenstown, *the office is at the Steamer Wharf (next to the Earnslaw);* ☎ *(03) 442-7500, FAX (03) 442-7504*. The **Automobile Association** office is located at *37 Stanley Street,* ☎ *(03) 442-5155*.

Where to Stay

Queenstown Parkroyal $NZ250–275 ★ ★ ★ ★
☎ *(03) 442-7800; FAX (03) 442-8895.*
On Beach Street across from the Steamers Wharf shopping center. About 140 rooms, **Steamers Lounge** ★ ★ (moderate) and **Bentley** ★ ★ ★ restaurant (expen-sive.) Pool, sauna, TV, fridge, coffee/tea makers. Good location but a bit sterile. Great lake views. During Oct.–Apr. high season, about $NZ250–275 a night double.

Nugget Point $NZ250–375 ★★★★★

Arthurs Point Road on the Shotover River north of town. ☎ *(03) 442-7273; FAX (03) 442-7308.*

This stunning lodge sits 400 feet above the river and is, we think, the best upscale lodge in this part of the country. The only drawback, if you can call it that, is its location a fair distance from the central city area, about six miles. The public areas are open and airy with wonderful views, and the rooms—actually small apartments—are excellent. The pool is heated indoor/outdoor with a bar, and other amenities include two tennis courts, two squash courts, a gym with sauna, spa pools, ski gear and a private helipad. The restaurant seats only 50 and the cuisine is top-notch. Expensive. Rooms have kitchenettes or full kitchens; the two-bedroom units and the suites have laundry facilities One-bedroom units start at $NZ250 for a garden view, executive suites are $NZ375.

Remarkables Lodge $NZ380 ★★★★★

South of town off Highway 6, near the ski area. ☎ *(03) 442-2720; FAX the same.*

Another upscale lodge, this one in the bungy-jumping, wine-tasting area south of town. The accommodations include three suites in the main lodge building and a garden cottage with spa bath. The cottage is wheelchair accessible. There's a swimming pool, billiards table and petanque (boule) court. Game is a speciality of the dinners, included in the price. Very close to the ski area. Very spiffy.

Gardens Parkroyal $NZ265–360 ★★★★

Corner of Earl and Marina Parade. ☎ *(03) 442-7750; FAX (03) 442-7469.*

An old favorite, done in lattices painted red, purple and yellow. Good location right next to the lake; inner courtyard and the Rose Garden, where barbecues are held. About 150 rooms and 20 apartments. **Buckham's Bar, Promenade Restaurant ★★** with lake view, moderate. Rooms have TV, minibars, laundry service, tea/coffee things. High season, about $NZ265 for a standard room, up to $NZ360 for suites.

Holiday Inn $NZ215 ★★★

Sainsbury Road, off The Esplanade and Fernhill roads. ☎ *(03) 442-6600; FAX (03) 442-7354.*

About 150 rooms. Two restaurants, including a good Italian café, **Reflections ★★** (moderate); bar, pool, tennis, gym, sauna, courtesy van, ski-drying area. All the facilities, but still Holiday Inn–ish.

Quality Hotel $NZ150 ★★★

Corner of Frankton and Adelaide streets. ☎ *(03) 442-8123; FAX (03) 442-7472.*

On a hill above downtown. About 100 rooms, bar, the very good **Pepper's Restaurant ★★★** (super views, moderate), spa, hair salon, TV, tea/coffee, laundry, fridge, courtesy van. Caters to the business crowd. Doubles start about $NZ150.

Quality Resort Terraces $NZ200+ ★★★

On the way to the airport at 48-64 Frankton Road. ☎ *(03) 442-7950; FAX (03) 442-8066.*

All rooms have private terraces looking out over Lake Wakatipu. **Hillary's ★★** licensed restaurant; moderate. Doubles start at about $NZ200.

St. James Executive Suites   **$NZ170–215**   ★★★

Coronation Drive. ☎ *(03) 442-5333; FAX (03) 442-5334.*
Located in a woodsy area on a hill overlooking downtown, next to the Queenstown
Gardens. The units, woody and modern, range from studios to executive suites. The
park has trails and a fitness path. The units offer microwaves and kitchen areas. Very
peaceful locale. Studios are $NZ170; one-bedroom suites are $NZ215.

Lodges, The   **$NZ170–190**   ★★★

6 The Esplanade. ☎ *(03) 442-7552; FAX (03) 442-6493.*
A condominium complex. Units have laundry and dishwashers, some spa baths, and
two bathrooms. Good location, nice view of the Remarkables. $NZ170–190; daily
service available. $NZ25 per person in addition. Good for groups or skiers.

Lakeland Resort Hotel   **$NZ150**   ★★★

14-18 Lake Esplanade. ☎ *(03) 442-7600; FAX (03) 442-9653.*
About as European-looking as you'll find in Kiwiland, popular with skiers. Next to
the lake on the Esplanade. About 180 rooms, TVs, pool, spa bar, **Clancy's Restaurant** ★★ (moderate), plus the **Ben Lomond Restaurant** ★★, great views, open
from 6 p.m. seven nights. Moderate. Also a ski-drying room, hair salon, sauna, tea/
coffee, off-season rates available. Doubles start at about $NZ150.

Queenstown is full of small motels, lodges and backpacker facilities in the two- to
three-star range. Among the best are the following:

Sherwood Manor Inn   **$NZ100–150**   ★★

Goldfield Heights Frankton Road, outside town, close to airport. ☎ *(03) 442-8032;
FAX (03) 442-7915.*
About 60 units, most with kitchen; spa, sauna, pool, gym, laundry, TV, tea/coffee,
ski-drying room, bar, restaurant, courtesy van. Very nice, actually.

Mountain View Lodge   **$NZ75–100**   ★

Frankton Road on the way to the airport. ☎ *(03) 442-8246; FAX (03) 442-7414.*
A multipurpose facility that combines kitchenette rooms with RV spaces and tent
sites. It has a restaurant, guest laundry, kiddie play area, barbecue.

A-Line   **$NZ185–215**   ★★

27 Stanley Street, up the hill a bit from the city center. ☎ *(03) 442-7700; FAX (03) 442-
7755.*
Alpine motif, overlooking the city. About 80 rooms, bar, good restaurant, spa,
laundry, gym, fridges. Some units up to five persons.

Alpine Village Motor Inn   **$NZ125**   ★

325 Frankton Road, toward the airport. ☎ *(03) 442-7795; FAX (03) 442-7738.*
Spa, pool, guest laundry, restaurant/bar, tennis; chalets or lakeside suites. On the lake.

Blue Peaks Lodge   **$NZ85–100**   ★

Corner of Stanley and Sydney streets, close to downtown. ☎ *(03) 442-9224; FAX (03)
442-6847.*
About 60 units, most with kitchens; handicapped facilities, laundry, TV, breakfasts
available.

Ambassador Motor Lodge   **$NZ110**

2 Man Street, on the hill near the city center. ☎ *(03) 442-8593; FAX (03) 442-8797.*

Close to the gondola and kiwi park. Units sleep two to six, with kitchens, balconies, laundry, spa, executive suite, courtesy rides.

Hotel Esplanade $NZ60–75

32 Peninsula Street. ☎ *(03) 442-8611; FAX (03) 442-9635.*
On a hill overlooking the lake. About 20 units, double/triple, TV, laundry, bar, ski-drying area, courtesy coach, breakfast available.

Goldfields Motel and Breakfast Inn $NZ80

41 Frankton Road. ☎ *(03) 442-7211; FAX (03) 442-6179.*
Motel kitchen units, chalets, laundry, TV lounge, tea/coffee, breakfast available. B&B double about $NZ80.

Queenstown Motor Park $NZ45–80

Man Street, steep walk to the top of the hill above town. ☎ *(03) 442-7252; FAX (03) 442-7253.*

A Top 10 RV park with other accommodations; dairy. Motel units, $NZ80 double; tourist flats $NZ60 double; cabins $NZ33; lodges $NZ45.

Economy accommodations

Thomas's Hotel on the Waterfront $NZ15–75

50 Beach Street. ☎ *(03) 442-7180; fax 441-8417.*
It's named after a cat named Tom, and you can't miss it because it's painted a bright violet. Central location downtown. All rooms have private baths; communal kitchen and lounge, café bar with outside dining. Handicapped facilities, laundry. Standard doubles $NZ75; budget doubles $NZ45; backpacker bunks $NZ17 per person. Double, triple or quad rooms, $NZ15 per person.

McFees Waterfront Hotel $NZ75

48A Shotover Street. ☎ *(03) 442-7400; FAX 442-7403.*
This place has more lives than a cat, and changes names and faces about every 10 minutes. Whatever, the location is always good in the heart of town, and the prices are budget. It has 30 rooms with private baths. It's a very good deal and quite pleasant.

Deco Backpackers $NZ18

52 Man Street, near the motor park. ☎ *(03) 442-7384; FAX (03) 442-7403.*
Housed in a restored Art Deco building. Paragliding center. Open fire, great views. Double, triple or quad rooms, $NZ18 per person.

Bumbles Hostel $NZ14–20

2 Brunswick Street, above the lake, near town. ☎ *(03) 442-6298.*
Big self-cooking kitchen, lounge, laundry, very popular place. Dorm beds $NZ14; doubles NZ$16–20 per person.

Wakatipu Lodge YHA $NZ18–22

80 Esplanade. ☎ *(03) 442-8413; FAX (03) 442-6561.*
Next to the lake, near the wharf. About 100 beds, modern, some family and doubles. Laundry, meals at night or on-site kitchen, late-night closing (3 a.m.), courtesy van, TV, storage, popular with skiers. $NZ18 a night, nonmembers, $NZ22.

Where to Eat

Queenstown is a tourist mecca, especially during the ski season, and like most tourist towns, the place is full of oases to feed your body and slake your thirst after a hard day's tramping or sitzmarking—or bungy jumping if you still have the urge to eat. In addition to the hotel restaurants we've listed, there are numerous other eateries worth a stop.

First things first. No day starts without coffee, and we found only one place open at 6:30 a.m., waiting for our bus to Milford Sound. It's the **Gourmet Express** ★★, which serves brekkie from 6:30–noon and stays open until 9 p.m. Budget prices, bottomless cup, good service. BYO and licensed, senior discounts. *Bay Center on Shotover Street.* (It's in sort of a shopping arcade.) ☎ *(03) 442-9619.*

There's a **Pizza Hut** and a **McDonald's** if you're feeling homesick, but the place to rub shoulders with the locals is at **Roaring Meg's Restaurant** ★★, situated in an old gold miner's cabin. Here's your chance to try some mutton bird, yahoo. Basic Kiwi food; BYO dinners Monday–Saturday from 6:30 p.m. Moderate to expensive; *57 Shotover Street,* ☎ *(03) 442-9676.*

Good Chinese food is available at the popular **Lai Sing Restaurant** ★★ upstairs in the O'Connell Pavilion. There are often all-you-can-eat specials, *the wine list is good and the drums tell us the martinis are the best in town.* (Gin is evil, thanks.) The main dishes (Szechwan and Cantonese) will run you around $NZ15–18. There's also take-away. *Open seven days, serves lunch noon–2:30 p.m., dinner 5:30–11 p.m.* Moderate. ☎ *(03) 442-7131.*

The town is popular with Japanese tourists, who tend to spend more per capita than most visitors, so it's a bit surprising there's only one sushi bar. Then, checking with the local press, we found it's the only sushi place on the South Island. Surely not. Anyway, it's called the **Minami Jujisei** ★★★★, and it's very popular. (Movie stars and opera divas have been known to stop in.) It's licensed and also serves lamb and beef Japanese-style dishes; live seafood tank, set menu. *Lunch Monday–Friday, dinner seven nights, reservations required.* Expensive. *It's at 45 Beech Street.* ☎ *(03) 442-9854; FAX (03) 442-7008.*

A comfy spot in the middle of downtown is **Chico's** ★★, a second-floor restaurant with fireside dining in the winter, stone walls, **à la carte** menu, live entertainment most nights. It's licensed. *Dinner weekly starting at 6:30 p.m.* Located on the Mall. Budget to moderate. ☎ *(03) 442-8439.*

The only Mexican restaurant in town is **Saguaro's** ★★, located in the Trust Bank arcade. It has live music at nights. Luncheon specials. Fully licensed, but you can **BYO** wine for dinner. *Open noon–2 p.m. for lunch, 5:30 p.m. until late for dinner.* Sometimes closed for lunch in the off-season. Moderate. ☎ *(03) 442-8240.*

More stone walls, more fireplaces, tight spaces, cramped quarters: the ever-popular **Cow** ★★★, an Italian restaurant. It's located on Cow Lane off Camp Street, hence the name. The building itself is a century old, and the Cow has been serving pizza here for more than 20 years. Tap beer, wine list. Take-away pizza. Open noon–10:30 p.m. Budget to moderate. ☎ *(03) 442-8588.*

Boardwalk Seafood Restaurant   **$$$**   ★★★
   Upstairs in the Steamer Wharf building on the lake. ☎ *(03) 442-5630.*

The best seafood places in town, but also has vegan offerings. Seafood dishes include such goodies as Westland crayfish, Nelson Bay scallops and Bluff oysters. Dinner reservations required. *Open for lunch 11:30 a.m.-2:30 p.m. and dinner 6 p.m.-late seven days.*

Pasta Pasta Cucina   **$$**   ★★

6 Brecon Street. ☎ *(03) 442-6762.*

As the name suggests, a pizza haven. Wood-fired ovens, fresh pastas, Northern Italian dishes, terra-cotta tiles, dark woods, very comfortable tables. Try the flat peasant breads and the fresh-made gelates. Definitely worth a try for that pizza fix. Also has take-aways. New Zealand and Italian wines, tap beer. Open for lunch and dinner seven days.

Skyline Gondola Restaurant   **$$**   ★★

☎ *(03) 442-7860.*

The place to eat above it all. It's atop Bob's Peak high above the lake, reachable by the gondola. For $NZ40 each, you get a carvery dinner featuring Kiwi meats, live entertainment, good wine list, popular buffets, nifty views of the harbor and the ride up and down. The dinner service starts at 6 p.m. There is also a cafeteria at the top that opens at 10 a.m. Reservations for dinner necessary.

A few choices, out of town:

Gantley's   **$$$**   ★★★★

Malaghan's Road, Arthurs Point. ☎ *(03) 442-8999.*

Up Gorge Road on the Shotover River not far from Nugget Point. Here's your basic 1860s trading post and hotel from the Gold Rush days, now on the National Trust of historic buildings. It's very popular with Queenstownites for dinner or garden lunches. *Venison on the menu, worthy wine list, altogether excellent.* Gantley's will send a complimentary shuttle to pick you up. *Open seven days from 11 a.m. until late.* Reservations for dinner necessary. Expensive but worth it.

Arthurs Point Pub   **$**   ★★

☎ *(03) 442-8007.*

Another Gold Rush relic, overlooking the Shotover River. Popular for Kiwi food (rump steaks, chook and chips). Very nice, budget prices. *Gorge Road toward Arrowtown. Open Mon.-Sat. from 6:30 p.m. for dinner; noon-8 p.m. Sun.*

Gibbston Valley Vineyard and Restaurant   **$$**   ★★★★

Just past the Kawarau Bridge bungy-jumping area on the main highway east of town. ☎ *(03) 442-6910; FAX (03) 442-6909.*

Probably the best and most scenic place in the area for lunch. Always crowded, great blackboard menu and exceptional wines (served here, but bottled and grown in the Marlborough area). A tasting tray of four wines while you wait to get in is $NZ4 per person. Look for the great cheese plates, the seafood cassolets, smoked salmon fritatas or a sinful dessert. *Open for lunch only 9:30 a.m.-5:30 p.m.*

Pubs and Nightspots

Swiss Iglu Fondue Factory   ★★

27 Shotover. ☎ *(03) 442-6878.*

Basically the place to have really good fondues, pastas and divine coffee. But every second Sunday night, it showcases local talent, including comedy, dance, cabaret shows and audience participation. Local musicians try out new stuff here. It can get very wild. Licensed bar.

Eichardts Tavern ★★

☎ *(03) 442-8369.*
Vintage 1862 building, white and proud, *sitting on the Mall at the waterfront. Tends to be very rockish and loud with faint overtones of heavy metal and a touch of rap.* Anyway, it's open from noonish to latish. If you don't like raucous, beer-drinking rugby fans, stay away. On the second floor is a nightclub. *Closed Sun.*

Lone Star Café ★★★

14 Brecon Street. ☎ *(03) 442-9995.*
Well, you just can't have a ski town without a cowboy bar, and this one has all the trimmings, including a TV set in the upstairs bar that shows old horse operas. Downstairs is a Tex-Mex restaurant (actually very good) full of boots and saddles and such. Après-skiers hang here big time and the ambiance is familiar to a real Son (or Daughter) of the Golden West. Yahoo. *It's open for dinner seven days; hours vary according to season.*

Café Station Red Rock ★★

48 Camp Street. ☎ *(03) 442-6850.*
The Red Rock is one of the most popular après-ski places in town. It's basically a dance club, and also is a hangout for the bungy crowd (there might be an A. J. Hackett sighting, but probably not). Also serves food. *It's open from 11 a.m.–3 a.m.*

McNeill's Brewery Café ★★

14 Church Street. ☎ *(03) 442-9688.*
Brewpubs make it Down Under, yessir. And this one's great, with the expected savory mini-brews and tasty cuisine plus, of course, some local wines. It's in an historic cottage with outdoor dining in season. *It's open seven days from 11:30 a.m. to late.*

Solera Vino ★★

25 Beach Street. ☎ *(03) 442-6082.*
A lively wine bar carrying about 35 South Island vintages; one upstairs bar, one down. Spanish influence; they serve tapas. *Open 4 p.m. until late.*

Shopping

The newest shopping area is the **Steamers Wharf** complex on the lake where the **Earnslaw** is docked. In addition to Fiordland Travel, some of the upscale stores in the complex include **Hermes, Tiffany's, United Colors of Benetton, Cartier**, a wine shop and a huge duty-free shop. Good sports and leisure clothing is available at **Mackenzie New Zealand Country**. The major sheep store in town is the **Sheep Station** on the Mall, which, like its counterpart in Christchurch, has very nice, fairly expensive leather and wool goods. Another good sheep store is the **Mountaineer Shop**, corner of Beach and Rees streets. *Oven seven days 9 a.m.–11 p.m.*

A group of stores is located in **O'Connell's Pavilion** at the corner of Beach and Camp streets. *Stores are generally open seven days from 7 a.m. until late.* Try **McKnight's for**

Mohair, which has home-spun wool and mohair, carded or already woven. **Action Down-under** carries pure wool knitwear and pure cotton goods, as well as deer-leather garments. **The Beer Essentials** has T-shirts, sweatshirts, rugby jerseys, shorts and hats with the logo of your favorite Kiwi beer. There is also a large **Canterbury of New Zealand** store in the center.

DF Souvenirs, *28-30 The Mall*, has a good selection of New Zealand souvenirs. There are a bunch of ski shops in town, but we suggest **Brown's Ski Shop**, *39 Shotover Street*. Or try **Kiwi Discovery** *on Camp Street*. Both places also rent ski equipment. If you fancy Australian opals, try the **Opal Centre** *at the corner of Beach and Rees streets*. There's a workshop. Or the **Aotea Opal and Gold Bar**, *across from the Parkroyal Hotel*, carries 18- and 14-carat gold jewelry, as well as opals.

And the **Duty Free Shop** on the Mall says it has same-day mailing service to some parts of the United States.

The Milford Experience

Milford Sound is the most accessible and picturesque of the Fiordland fjords.

The Kiwis have long noted the interest in the country's fjords in general and the Milford Sound in particular, issuing such modest assessments as "hiking capital of the world" and "the eighth wonder of the world."

So it's no surprise they stand ready any time of year to cart your old carcass to the Sound by bus, boat or plane. Milford Sound is on the southwestern coast of the South Island, a territory gouged and sharpened by huge glaciers—a land that in many ways is the spitting image of the southern Norwegian coast combined with the Canadian Rockies.

The sound is an actual fjord—an arm of the sea that has filled up a deep glaciated valley—and is one of several long fjords along the coast that are the center of **Fiordland National Park**, the country's largest and probably most beautiful preserve. It ranges for 200 kilometers or so along the southwestern coast from Milford Sound to the tip of the South Island, containing something like **4700** square miles with more than a dozen fjords. The park has been awarded World Heritage status—meaning, supposedly, that exploitation of the area's resources will never be allowed.

When to Go

Because of the weather around the sound, there really is no best time to go. There are some times to avoid, however: Kiwi winter and summer. In the summer, you can't move because of crowds, and, in the winter, you might not be able to move because of the weather.

In the winter (June–August), it snows in the Kiwi Alps, and avalanches sometimes close the road into the sound. It's not rare for busloads of passengers to be stranded at Milford because the road is closed. And sometimes there are such fierce storms blowing up the sound from the Tasman Sea, tour boats can't leave port. There are perfectly fine days in the winter, to be sure, but the South Island does freeze and it does snow. This leaves you with the shoulder seasons, September–November and March–May. The weather is sometimes chancy, as you'd expect for fall and spring, but it is offset by the lack of tourists. Going to the sound in the shoulders also has advantages because of usually lower airfares and seasonal specials.

How to Go

The easiest and least expensive way to see the sound (unless you're driving yourself) is by bus, either from Queenstown or the small village of Te Anau, the jumping-off point for most Milford Track hikers and also a base for many Milford bus trips. By bus, it takes about three hours to reach Te Anau, which is about 170 kilometers southwest of Lake Wakatipu. After morning tea at a local Te Anau hotel, the bus goes on through the mountains and rainforests to the sound. Most trips include a boat tour, which takes you from the end of the highway out to the open ocean and back again. The return trip gets you back to Queenstown around 7:30 p.m. or so.

The prospect of spending a full day with a pack of strangers on a bus is normally less than dazzling—but hold on a bit; here we have one trek that even us dedicated tour-group haters can actually enjoy.

Transportation Alternatives

What's more, the price—depending on what combination you want—is reasonable. Through Gray Line New Zealand, a round-trip bus trip, combined with a cruise on the sound, will run around $NZ75 per person, including morning tea (basically a continental breakfast); about $NZ50 from Te Anau. Should you choose, you can return to Queenstown or Te Anau in a hurry by plane. There are several companies offering fly-coach or fly-fly trips to the sound. One common example is taking a coach to the sound, doing the boat tour and flying back. A Gray Line coach-boat-fly package is about $NZ150 from Queenstown; a fly-boat-fly from Queenstown is about the same price. Some flights also go to Doubtful Sound, generally conceded to be the most beautiful of the fjords. These packages are available from travel agencies in Queenstown and Te Anau. In the shoulder season, your best bet is Queenstown; try **Fiordland Travel**, which has several offices in Queenstown; the main office is at the Steamer Wharf complex, ☎ *(03) 442-7500, FAX (03) 442-7504.* Gray Line information is available in the United States by calling ☎ *(800) 468-2665.*

The daylong bus trip will show you many slices of New Zealand, from the sheep-infested paddocks of flat farmland areas to the avalanche-packed mountains of the New Zealand Alps. You pass several of the country's largest lakes, and—if it's not raining—marvel at the clear, pollution-free air.

Te Anau

You can, as we noted, start the Milford Sound tour from here. There is regular daily bus service to Milford Sound (about NZ$35 one way), plus there are offices for most of the major tour groups (especially Fiordland Travel) and transportation organizations. The best part of the trip to the Milford Sound area, unless you're madly in love with sheep (thousands of sheep), starts in the mountains north of Te Anau. Te Anau is on the South Island's largest lake, **Lake Te Anau**, which is 1150 feet deep and surrounded by a vast Antarctic beech forest. Te Anau is a Maori word meaning "caves of rushing water." At the north end of the lake is Glade House, where the Milford Track begins. (See the "Great Walks" map for the course of the Milford Track.)

Te Anau is the headquarters of the Fiordland National Park, and the visitor center has lots of information about hiking, camping and other activities. Here is where you can book a Milford Track trek. Fiordland National Park, at 1.2 million hectares, is one of the largest in the world. The visitors center is open daily; ☎ *(03) 249-7921; FAX 249-7613.*

Te Anau itself is not much, but sits in a nice spot next to the lake and has the basics for hanging around a few days, including some comparatively expensive lodging and some good restaurants. The Te Anau visitors center is at the Fiordland Travel office on Te Anau Terrace. ☎ *249-8900; FAX 249-7022.*

Where to Stay

Te Anau Travelodge   **$NZ130–340**   ★★★
Lake Front Drive. ☎ *(03) 249-7411; FAX (03) 249-7947.*
Booking office for track treks, tours, boat cruises, etc. Laundry, pool, storage room, bar, two restaurants. Doubles around $NZ130; villas from $NZ300.

Village Inn, The   **$NZ80–180**   ★★
Mokoroa Street downtown. ☎ *(03) 249-7911; FAX (03) 249-7003.*

Family units, handicapped units, honeymoon suite, penthouse suites, kitchens, tea/coffee, minibars, laundry, baby-sitting. Bar and restaurant open for dinner 6–9 p.m. Doubles $NZ120–170.

Explorer Motor Lodge $NZ100   ★★

6 Cleddau, off Mokoroa Street, downtown. ☎ *(03) 249-7156; FAX (03) 249-7149.*
Trip bookings, laundry, golf clubs hire, breakfast available, kitchen units, nice garden setting. Off-season rate reductions. Doubles about $NZ100.

Fiordland Motor Lodge $NZ50–100   ★★

Luxmore Drive, main highway. ☎ *(03) 249-7511; FAX (03) 249-8944.*
Pool, spa, sauna, barbecue, restaurant, bar, laundry.

Black Diamond Motel $NZ65–80   ★★

15 Quintin Drive, off Mokoroa Street, downtown. ☎ *(03) 249-7459; FAX the same.*
Kitchens, laundry, putting green. Doubles $NZ65–80. Off-season rates.

Shakespeare House $NZ80   ★★

10 Dusky Street. ☎ *(03) 249-7349; FAX (03) 249-7629.*
B&B rooms with showers, some with baths. Cooked breakfasts, dinner available. Courtesy car. Doubles around $NZ80, off-season rates.

Te Anau YHA Hostel $NZ18–22

Milford Road, about 1.5 kilometers out of town. ☎ *(03) 249-7847.*
Farm setting, laundry, kitchen, store, booking facilities, storage, tent sites. NZ$18 per person, NZ$22 nonmembers.

Te Anau Backpackers $NZ18–40

48 Lake Front Drive. ☎ *(03) 249-7713; FAX (03) 249-8319.*
Laundry, barbecues, storage. Shared rooms, about $NZ18, double rooms about $NZ40.

Te Anau Motor Park $NZ20–75

Manapouri Road, about 1 kilometer from town. ☎ *(03) 249-7457; FAX (03) 249-7536.*
Laundry, sauna, tennis, bar and café, store, sewage disposal site. Cabins, $NZ20–55; motel unit, doubles $NZ75.

Te Anau Mountain View Holiday Park $NZ20–75

128 Te Anau Terrace. ☎ *(03) 249-7462; FAX the same.*
A Top 10 member. Laundry, sewage disposal site, boat park. Tourist flats and cabins from $NZ35–75; on-site caravans around $NZ30–40; powered sites $NZ10 per person.

Te Anau Downs Motor Inn $NZ85–115   ★★

At Te Anau Downs, about 30 kilometers north of town on the lake. ☎ *(03) 249-7811; FAX (03) 249-7753.*
Restaurant/bar, laundry, kitchen units, breakfast available. Doubles $NZ100–115. Also available are B&B units (private baths) with doubles from $NZ85.

Where to Eat

The best food is probably in the hotel restaurants. In addition:

La Toscana $$ ★★★

Town Centre shopping center, main road. ☎ *(03) 249-7756.*

Italian restaurant downtown. Just great tucker. BYO. Pizza, pasta, good coffees, home delivery and take-away. Moderate prices. *Open for dinner from 6 p.m. Mon.–Sat.*

Bailey's Restaurant   **$–$$**   ★★
Corner of Milford and Mokonui streets.
A popular bus tour stop. Breakfast available all day; morning and afternoon teas. *The place to buy take-away lunch for the Milford Sound boat trip.*

Henry's   **$**   ★★
In the Te Anau Travelodge. ☎ *(03) 249-7411.*
Family-style dining. Fiordland crayfish, Stewart Island salmon, lamb and venison, all at budget prices. *Lunch, noon–2 p.m.; dinner, 5:30–9 p.m. Open seven days.*

Bluestone Restaurant, The   **$$$**   ★★★
Lakefront Drive. ☎ *(03) 249-7421.*
Fine dining, all three meals. The dining room fireplace is made of river stone; good view of Lake Te Anau. Fresh fjord crayfish, smoked eel, South Island venison and lamb. *Hours are breakfast, 6:30–9:30 a.m.; lunch, noon–2 p.m. in summer, and dinner, 6–9:30 p.m. Open seven days.*

Toward Milford

MacKinnon Pass (3520 feet) on Milford Track offers impressive views.

Once past Te Anau, the road parallels Lake Te Anau for about 30 kilometers, then cuts inland to start its climb over the Alps to the sea. Once to the mountains—the Earl and Darren ranges—you begin to see why this stretch of highway can be so dangerous at times. There are avalanche warnings all over, and in late spring don't be surprised to drive through the remains of an avalanche that roared into the basins during the thaw.

It is against the law to stop in some danger spots. Tour bus drivers are under orders to report the license plates of offenders, so the police will be waiting to give you a pricey souvenir as you drive out of the park. The weather up in the heights is chancy, with rain a very definite possibility at any time. To throw a positive shaft of light into the negative tunnel, however, some fanciers insist the only time to do the trip is when it has been raining heavily. This, of course, flushes out the hundreds of waterfalls along the route—nice if you like overcast waterfalls.

The highway eventually arrives at a dead-end basin, which stopped further progress until 1935 when work began on the **Homer Tunnel**, a truly prodigious project dug through solid granite, at first by hand tools. The tunnel enters the mountain at 3000 feet above sea level and exits at 2000 feet. It's 354 feet wide, three-quarters of a mile long and has a 10 percent grade. Not too long after leaving the tunnel, you get a glimpse of **Mitre Peak**, a pyramid-shaped mountain that is probably the most photographed object in the Milford Sound area. Milford Sound—the community—sits at the southeastern end of the sound and is currently being redone. After years of relative disinterest, the New Zealand government finally decided that the number of tourists coming in and out of the area —not just hikers but also bus and airplane travelers—required some upgrading of services. About NZ$4 million was authorized to upgrade roads and water-sewer facilities. Something like 300,000 visitors a year come to Milford, and it's not uncommon to see 40 or 50 tour buses a day. It's probably going to get worse.

Helicopter tour of dramatic scenery near Milford Sound

Sailing on the Sound

The sound has a relatively small entrance on the ocean, but widens out enough to let cruise ships the size of the *Queen Elizabeth II* go up-fjord several miles—and turn around in one great circle. The mouth is so small, in fact, that England's Captain James Cook managed to miss the entrance to the sound while he was doing extensive charting around New Zealand in the 1700s. The trip on the sound is normally aboard one of the so-called "Red Boats" that run daily tours and take about two hours to run from the dock out to the Tasman Sea and back. The fjord (usually) is flat calm, flanked by steeply rising peaks and towering waterfalls. About a third of the way down the 14-mile-long sound is a wide spot where cruise ships turn around. The big ships don't stay long because there's no place to anchor—the fjord is 1000 feet deep at this point.

Weather permitting and waterfalls cooperating, the Red Boats usually ease their bows under a waterfall, where brave souls can get a drink of icy waterfall water. If they succeed (getting soaked in the process), they are given a shot of their favorite booze. Most people are content to just take photographs of the soakees. Food and drink are available aboard the boats, although food tends to be a bit pricey. A better suggestion is to buy a sandwich or two at Te Anau when the bus stops for morning tea. There are two trips a day; fares are about $NZ40 per person.

For the more pampered, we urge an overnight cruise aboard the **Lady of the South Pacific ★ ★ ★ ★**, a double-decker multi-hull that sails July–April. The staterooms are spacious and comfortable, and the fare includes a welcome drink, a four-course meal and a cooked breakfast. The boat leaves at 4:30 p.m., returns at 10 a.m., and, if the weather is fair, the trip is probably the most scenic way to do the sound. Deluxe A-Deck cabins go for about $NZ400 double; the almost-as-nice B-Deck rooms are about $NZ240 double. (Single berths available.) The Lady is also operated by Red Boat Cruises, part of Southern Pacific Hotels, and can be booked in Queenstown or Te Anau.

Finally, for the best below-water look at the sound, take a trip to the new Milford Sound Underwater Observatory, another project of Southern Pacific Hotels. By taking a spiral staircase down into the observatory, visitors can see the unique double-water biospheres of the sound, including black coral, just about the only way most people will ever see it in New Zealand. You might also get a chance to see sponges, anemones, cod, seahorses, crayfish, dolphins, seals and penguins. The observatory is reached by either taking a water taxi or a Red Boat cruise. The water taxi is about $NZ35 per person, which includes the entry fee; or there are Red Boar fjord cruises that also stop at the observatory. These are $NZ55 per person.

Tourists collect spray from a waterfall at Milford Sound.

If you make arrangements ahead, you can stay at Milford a day or two before going back. Accommodations at Milford—and indeed, at all the facilities in the sound area—are owned by the Southern Pacific Hotel Corp., which purchased the Milford assets from the Tourist Hotels Corp., a government agency. The main accommodations are at the **Milford Sound Hotel**, which has 33 rooms ranging from around $NZ60 to about $NZ200 for a suite. Standard rooms are about $NZ130. The hotel has a moderately priced restaurant and a pub, plus a cafeteria—it's about the only thing in town. Reservations are essential, especially after the hiking track opens in early November. ☎ *(03) 249-7926; FAX (03) 249-8094.* From North America, the Milford Sound Hotel can be booked by calling ☎ *(800) 835-7742.* Backpacker accommodations are available at the **Milford Sound Lodge** near the hotel, which has a shop, laundry, restaurant/bar, booking office and also caravan sites. The bus stop is out front. Room rates are about $NZ16–20 per person. ☎ *phone and fax (03) 249-8071.*

The Milford Experience

The Milford Track

Lake Quill, Milford Track, is a relaxing and glorious stop.

The Track—meaning, of course, New Zealand's Milford Track—is rated by some connoisseurs as the best hiking trail in the world. When enthusiasts laud its greatness, they most likely are thinking of the spectacular scenery you get along the track, the relative isolation and the camaraderie of the trail. However, when detractors list its faults, they consider the whole thing to be a 33-mile, weeklong stretch of overpriced, bug-infested, rain-sodden trail through the New Zealand countryside—gorgeous, indeed, but not always worth the sacrifice. *There is a saying around the Milford area: It's either rain-*

Fielding NEW ZEALAND

GREAT WALKS

Several of New Zealand's many tracks have been designated Great Walks. Of various length and difficulty, most require three to four days and take trampers past some of the country's most spectacular scenic vistas. Rudyard Kipling described Milford Sound, on the immensely popular Milford Track, as the "Eighth wonder of the world."

The Milford Experience

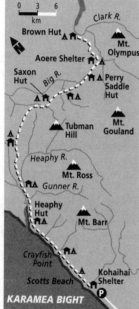

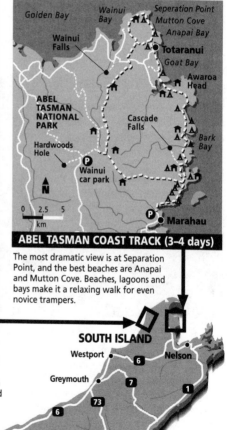

ABEL TASMAN COAST TRACK (3–4 days)

The most dramatic view is at Separation Point, and the best beaches are Anapai and Mutton Cove. Beaches, lagoons and bays make it a relaxing walk for even novice trampers.

HEAPHY TRACK (4 days)

Offers a wide range of scenery, from native forest, isolated river valleys and red tussock downs to palm-lined beaches. The track includes several bridges. The views of the Tasman Sea and Gunner Downs are excellent, and sunsets are spectacular.

SOUTH ISLAND

Westport

Nelson

Coo Stra

Greymouth

6

7

73

1

6

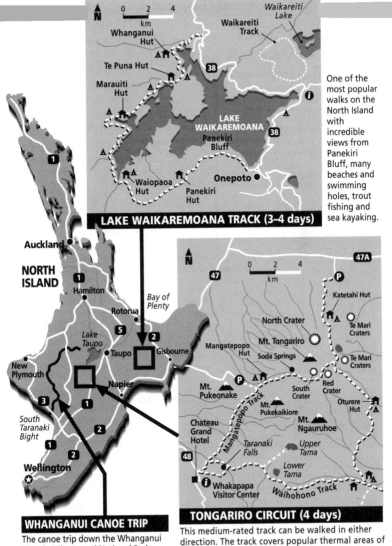

One of the most popular walks on the North Island with incredible views from Panekiri Bluff, many beaches and swimming holes, trout fishing and sea kayaking.

LAKE WAIKAREMOANA TRACK (3–4 days)

N

0 2 4 km

Whanganui Hut

Waikareiti Lake

Waikareiti Track

Te Puna Hut

38

Marauiti Hut

LAKE WAIKAREMOANA

Panekiri Bluff

38

O

Waiopaoa Hut

Panekiri Hut

Onepoto

NORTH ISLAND

Auckland

Hamilton

Bay of Plenty

Rotorua

Lake Taupo

Taupo

Gisbourne

New Plymouth

Napier

South Taranaki Bight

Wellington

WHANGANUI CANOE TRIP

The canoe trip down the Whanganui River in Whanganui National Park, (the second longest river in New Zealand) on the North Island is part of the Great Walks itinerary.

TONGARIRO CIRCUIT (4 days)

N

0 2 4 km

47

47A

P

Katetahi Hut

North Crater

Te Mari Craters

Mangatepopo Hut

Mt. Tongariro

Soda Springs

Te Mari Craters

P

Mt. Pukeonake

South Crater

Red Crater

Oturere Hut

Mt Pukekaikiore

Mt. Ngauruhoe

Chateau Grand Hotel

Taranaki Falls

Upper Tama

48

Lower Tama

O Whakapapa Visitor Center

Waihohono Track

This medium-rated track can be walked in either direction. The track covers popular thermal areas of the park and involves some climbing. Impressive views include Mt. Ngauruhoe, Mt. Pukeonake, Lake Rotoaira and Taranaki Falls.

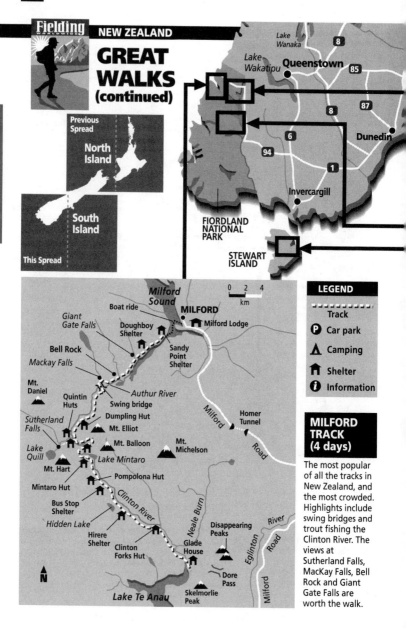

Fielding WORLDWIDE

NEW ZEALAND

GREAT WALKS
(continued)

Previous Spread

North Island

South Island

This Spread

Lake Wanaka

Queenstown

8

85

Lake Wakatipu

87

8

Dunedin

6

94

1

Invercargill

FIORDLAND NATIONAL PARK

STEWART ISLAND

LEGEND

- - - - - - - - **Track**
- **P** Car park
- **A** Camping
- **⛫** Shelter
- **ⓘ** Information

Milford Sound

Boat ride

MILFORD

Milford Lodge

Giant Gate Falls

Doughboy Shelter

Sandy Point Shelter

Bell Rock

Mackay Falls

Mt. Daniel

Quintin Huts

Authur River

Swing bridge

Dumpling Hut

Mt. Elliot

Sutherland Falls

Mt. Balloon

Mt. Michelson

Homer Tunnel

Milford Road

Lake Quill

Mt. Hart

Lake Mintaro

Pompolona Hut

Mintaro Hut

Clinton River

Neale Burn

Eglinton River

Bus Stop Shelter

Hidden Lake

Hirere Shelter

Clinton Forks Hut

Disappearing Peaks

Glade House

Dore Pass

Milford Road

N

Lake Te Anau

Skelmorlie Peak

0 2 4 km

MILFORD TRACK (4 days)

The most popular of all the tracks in New Zealand, and the most crowded. Highlights include swing bridges and trout fishing the Clinton River. The views at Sutherland Falls, MacKay Falls, Bell Rock and Giant Gate Falls are worth the walk.

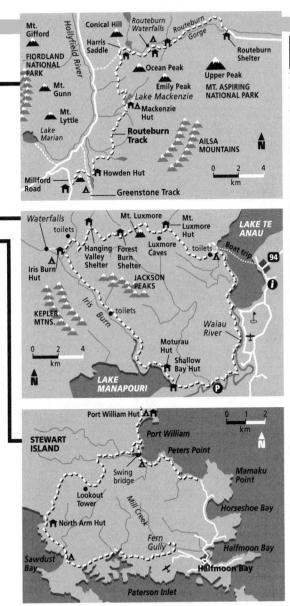

ROUTEBURN TRACK (3 days)

This famous alpine crossing includes breathtaking Mt. Aspiring and Fiordland National Parks. Expect to see rainforest and impressive views from ridges, peaks and saddles. Routeburn Falls and Lake Mackenzie are popular for overnight stays.

KEPLER TRACK (4 days)

This track makes a loop from the Waiau River to the south end of Lake Te Anau. The alpine crossing includes great views of Lake Te Anau, the South Fjord Arm, the Kepler Mountains and the Jackson Peaks.

RAKIURA TRACK (3 days)

The most popular track on Stewart Island is short, circular and of medium difficulty. The walk includes swing bridges, a number of hills, beaches, bays, historical sawmill sites, forest and a profusion of ferns.

ing, or it's about to. It's not unusual to get 400 inches of rain a year, and it rains an average of one out of three days—which, for some hikers, is about one day too much.

Sutherland Falls is one of the awesome sights along Milford Track.

Bugs? The track is infamous in summer for sand flies—nasty little varmints that are first cousins to the dreaded Canadian black fly. One guy in the know says the key is not wearing navy blue—they see blue, he says, they go crazy and start a feeding frenzy. An even better suggestion from us professional arthropod haters is to stay away from the flies in the first place. But this is mere piffle, of no moment to serious trampers. The track is, after all, the Track, and a badge most hikers would kill to wear. A small but grumbling group of democrats have always protested about government control of the track and the privately operated facilities at Milford Sound—and the fees charged to hike the Track to begin with. Because of its obvious popularity, and in an effort to keep human damage along the Track to a minimum, the number of hikers per day is limited (at present only 80 a day: 40 in groups, 40 independent).

As earlier noted, the Milford Track has been designated as one of the nation's "Great Walks," and hikers must stay in approved government huts along the track (one set of huts for groups, one for independent trampers). The track is not an easy stroll. It's a four-day, three-night hike, with often strenuous grades, rocks and the constant chance of snow, heavy rain, high winds, rapid temperature drops and flooding. You have to take everything you wear or eat with you, and rain gear is high on the list. No camping is allowed, and the trail-side shelters placed along the route cannot be used as overnight accommodation. Independent hut fees for the trail are about $NZ90 per person. Hikers must stay in huts, and all travel is one-way. The basic route for independent trampers (shown in the "Great Walks" map) looks like this:

First Day—*Te Anau to Clinton Forks Hut*. You must get from Te Anau to Te Anau Downs to catch the launch across Lake Te Anau to to Glade Wharf. The bus from Te Anau to the Downs is about $NZ11 per person. The launch is $NZ40 per person and departs daily at 2 p.m. From Glade Wharf, at the end of the lake, it's another two hours or so to the hut site. Clinton Forks hut has gas rings, wood-fired heating stoves, basins, tables and a communal bunkhouse with mattresses and a drying room. Cooking utensils are not provided.

Day Two—*Clinton Forks Hut to Mintaro Hut.* It's a 13-kilometer trek along the Clinton River to Lake Mintaro. The trail is cut by many small streams, some of which might have to be waded if there's been heavy rain. The Mintaro hut is equipped like the Clinton Forks facility.

Day Three—*Mintaro Hut to Dumpling Hut.* This stage of the trail is about 14 kilometers and goes up a fairly gentle slope to the top of Mackinnon Pass, where there is a toilet, gas cooker and lunch shelter. There is also a toilet and shelter farther along at Quintin Huts (a group camp.) It's another hour from the shelter to the Dumpling Hut, which is equipped like Clinton Forks and Mintaro.

Milford offers scenic views and physical challenges for experienced bikers.

Day Four—*Dumpling Hut to Sandfly Point (end of trail).* The last haul is the longest, about 18 kilometers. Some of the better scenery is on this stretch, including Mackay Falls, Giant Gate Falls and Lake Ada. When you finish, you must take a boat; there is no other way to get from the end of the trail to Milford. The boats taking you from the point to Milford leave at 2 and 3 p.m. The boat to Milford is about $NZ20. There is bus service back to Te Anau; the cost is about $NZ35. (It's the transport costs that have many Kiwi hikers enraged, especially the mandatory boat charges.) You must have confirmed transportation on and off the track before permits will be issued.

The whole trek, including transportation costs, can be booked by contacting the **Great Walks Booking Desk**, *Department of Conservation, P.O. Box 29, Te Anau, New Zealand;* ☎ *(03) 249-7921; FAX (03) 249-7613.*

The recommended minimum age on the Track is 10 years; children under 14 must be accompanied by an adult. **A special note**: The track is normally open from late October through the middle of April. Occasionally, bad weather closes the track; in that event, permits are cancelled and full refunds are made. If there are vacancies at a later date, you can re-book; otherwise, you're out of luck. Also, there are severe penalties if you cancel, starting at 25 percent and going to 100 percent for not showing up at all. Also note that Milford Track payments are not commissionable, so some travel agencies might not book the trip for you. If you're smart, you'll reserve the trip at least a year ahead.

A package that includes a night at Te Anau, a guided trip on the Milford Track, a stay at Milford, a cruise on the sound and return transportation to Te Anau can be booked for about $NZ1400 through Milford Track Guided Walk in Te Anau. The guides are radio equipped, and the price includes all meals, equipment, transportation and accommodations. It's a 6-day/5-night affair; arrangements for non-hikers are also available. ☎ *(03) 249-7411; FAX (03) 249-7590.*

Guided Walks

Many hikers choose to take one of the guided walks, which have been operated for the government by Southern Pacific Hotels for some time. SPH offers a six-day trip that includes a visit to the Fiordland National Park headquarters in Te Anau, a trip up Lake Te Anau, use of camping huts along the track, meals, some equipment and a cruise on Milford Sound. The price per person is around $NZ1255 plus GST for adults, $NZ750 for kids from 10 to 15 years old; prices do not include transportation to Te Anau, where the tours begin. Te Anau is served daily by air from Christchurch and Queenstown and by bus from those two cities plus Invercargill.

The age requirement on the tours is 10 to 70. Guides are equipped with radios for emergencies. Tour participants are supposed to be in good enough condition to do around 10 miles a day. The tours begin at the end of October and run through the first week of April. Reservations are necessary, and some periods, such as Christmas–New Year's, sell out early. In the United States, Mount Cook Lines is the booking agent for Southern Pacific Hotels; ☎ *(800) 262-0248.*

Other Tracks

The costs of doing the Milford Track, plus the tourist congestion at Milford itself, have driven many trampers onto the other equally lovely but less famous tracks in the Milford Sound area. These include the **Greenstone**, the **Routeburn** and the **Hollyford**. All tracks in the area are lined with a series of overnight huts. The huts basically come in four categories, depending on level of services available.

Routeburn

The views along Routeburn Track entice 10,000 people to walk it every year.

Alas, the same crowding and popularity that makes the Milford Track unpopular with the purists is overtaking the Routeburn. It has now been classed as a Great Walks trail, meaning during the prime hiking season, late October through mid-May, hut permits must be pre-purchased and dates reserved. Camping is allowed at specified areas along the track, but Great Walks camping permits are required. Huts are $NZ25 a night per adult; $NZ12.50 for children. Tent sites are $NZ6 a night for adults, $NZ3 for kids. In the off-season, only regular hut tickets are required.

Unlike the Milford Track, the Routeburn (also shown in the "Great Walks" map) can be done in both directions. Going east, the track begins at the Divide Shelter, on the road between Te Anau and Milford Sound, a spot about 80 kilometers from Te Anau. Going west, it starts at the Routeburn Shelter, northeast of Glenorchy about 75 kilometers from Queenstown. Bus service to both trailheads is available from Queenstown or Te Anau.

The Routeburn is a high-level track about 25 miles long, designed to be done in two moderately strenuous days or three easy days. It links Mount Aspiring and Fiordland national parks over a pass called the Harris Saddle, about 4100 feet. It follows a major fault zone, and provides stunning views of residual glaciers and craggy mountains. A number of alpine and subalpine ecosystems are involved, and the area is rife with birds, huge trout and deer. Huts are equipped with gas for cooking, mattresses, running water and flush toilets. There are several backpackers' and motel facilities available at Glenorchy, plus cafés, hiking gear rentals and bus companies. Great Walks permits can be obtained from the Department of Conservation office in Queenstown. Or write ahead to **Great Walks Booking Desk**, *Department of Conservation, P.O. Box 811, Queenstown, New Zealand;* ☎ *(03) 442-8916; FAX (03) 442-7932.* As with the Milford Track, there are penalties for cancellations.

Greenstone

The Greenstone is an ancient Maori trail through alpine valleys, past lakes, rivers and gorges. Its name comes from the fact that the Maori used it to reach the rich deposits of greenstone near Lake Wakatipu. The 21-mile, all-season track usually takes about three days. It's the easiest of the Milford area tracks. To reach the track, you take the Routeburn Track from the Divide Shelter, then turn south into the Greenstone Valley. It can be combined with the Caples Track, which takes another three days and will loop you back to the Routeburn. Or, if you wish, there is boat transport from the end of the Greenstone across Lake Wakatipu to Glenorchy. There are four huts provided on the two tracks.

Kepler

The Kepler Track (whose course is charted in the "Great Walks" map) is another tramp designated as a Great Walks trail (with the same permit and reservations requirements). It is a fairly strenuous trek, climbing from the shore of Lake Te Anau into the alpine ridges, but has splendid scenery and is one of the most accessible of all the area trails, being quite close to Te Anau. A round-trip on the loop trail will take about four days. There are two huts along the trail and camping areas. Bus service is available from Te Anau. Permits, as noted, are available in Queenstown.

Hollyford

The Hollyford is a gentle, 56-kilometer trail that runs from the end of the Lower Hollyford Road north of Te Anau to the ocean. It has the advantage of being an all-season track. It passes several beautiful lakes as well as meandering between the **Darran Range** and **Mount Tutoko**. You'll find ferns, orchids, mosses, then along Lake McKerrow (a fjord), seals, penguins and dolphins. Some ardent hikers then go around Big Bay, pick up the Pyke Track and return to the divide. Note: The Pyke Track is subject to flooding, and hiking parties have been stuck for several days until the waters receded. Guided trips are available from **Hollyford Valley Walk Limited** in Wakatipu; ☎ *(03) 442-3760* or in Te Anau, ☎ *(03) 249-8012*. There is private air service from the end of the trail to regional airstrips.

Dusky

The Dusky Track is remote and designed for well-equipped, experienced parties. Access is by boat from either Lake Manapouri or Lake Hauroko; private airplane service is also available. The trail takes about eight days and passes some of the most spectacular scenery in the area. The reward is, of course, at the end of the trail when you reach Dusky Sound, one of the most beautiful of the country's fjords, first visited by Captain Cook in 1773.

Other tracks in the area include the **Waitutu Tracks**, which run along the shore of Lake Hauroko, then along the seacoast west of Invercargill, with gorgeous scenery but strenuous tramping; the **Manapouri Tracks**, which are gentle trails near the shores of the lake; and the **George Sound Track**, which runs from Lake Te Anau, up over the mountains to **George Sound**, another beautiful fjord, a serious tramp that will take six days round-trip.

Going South

From the Queenstown area, you can wend your way south to Invercargill, the country's southernmost city; then east to Otago, that portion of the eastern South Island from Invercargill to Dunedin; north to Oamaru; wander back up north to Mount Cook and the east side of the Alps, or head back through the farmland and pastures to Christchurch. In any direction, the land flattens out as you leave the mountains and fjords, and the feeling becomes less scenic and a lot more pastoral.

Invercargill

Invercargill lives on sheep—the city is surrounded by meat processing plants that handle nearly 10 million animals a year, mostly lamb. Like Dunedin (as you can tell from the names), Invercargill was originally a Scottish settlement. If you've been to Scotland, you can appreciate why the Scots would feel comfortable here. The weather can be truly lousy, and there's nothing much between you and Antarctica. But the sheep folks admire the weather, especially the year-round rains, because there's always grass for the beasts. In New Zealand, especially around Wellington, you often hear jokes about the south end of the South Island, a lot like the jokes Canadians have for people who live in Newfoundland and Americans have for the residents of North Dakota. But if life is slow in the South, that seems to be the way they like it. In truth, many tourists don't even blink passing through Invercargill, which they see as simply a base for trips to the much more exotic sights of Stewart Island across the Foveaux Strait.

Most of the streets in Invercargill are named after Scottish rivers, the main drag being Dee. *There's nothing either very pretentious or very exciting about the city—it's basically just a nice, quiet agricultural center.* It has a couple of things going for it, however, including a museum where you can see the extremely rare New Zealand **tuatara**. It also has several **excellent restaurants**, some of the best on the South Island.

The tuatarium is housed in the **Southland Museum** in Queens Park, which has a pretty good **Maori gallery** as well. The main museum is free, although it appreciates donations. The chances of spotting the reptiles are usually pretty good, although babies are very hard to see. Also of note is the Roaring 40s Gallery and Exhibit, featuring audio-visual displays of life in the sub-Antarctic; $NZ2 entry. The museum also has an **observatory**, open Wednesday nights, April through October. *Museum hours are 10 a.m.–4:30 p.m., weekdays, 1–5 p.m., weekends.* ☎ *(03) 218-9753.* Weather permitting, **Queens Park** is worth a stroll. It contains about 200 acres of lawns, gardens and an 18-hole golf course. The city has two downtown-area heated swimming pools, four golf courses, tennis courts and rental facilities for bikes or horses. About 10 miles southwest of town is **Oreti Beach**, with a long stretch of good beach and sand dunes. Information about the city and the area is available at the Visitors Centre, located in the Southland Museum ☎ *(03) 214-6243; FAX (03) 218-9753.*

Where to Stay

Gerrard's Hotel $NZ80–95   ★★★

Corner of Esk and Leven streets. ☎ *(03) 218-3406; FAX (03) 218-3003.*
For our taste, the best place in town to eat and stay. Small, intimate, red-brick 1890s National Trust building across from the train station. Wonderful restaurant/bar. Many rooms newly redecorated. The restaurant ★★★★ is Victorian decor, with great seafood. *It's open for lunch Mon.–Fri.; dinner seven nights a week; reservations necessary.* Moderate to expensive.

Ascot Park Motor Hotel $NZ100–160   ★★

Corner of Tay Street and Racecourse Road. ☎ *(03) 217-6195; FAX (03) 217-7002.*
Four kilometers from the city on a 17-acre site. Indoor pool, spa, saunas, restaurant, bar, kitchens, some motel units, some suites. Hotel doubles are about $NZ160; motel units around $NZ100.

Kelvin Hotel $NZ110   ★★

18 Kelvin Street, city center. ☎ *(03) 218-2829; FAX (03) 218-2287.*
Molly O'Grady's Restaurant, bar, coffee/tea, laundry, handicapped facilities. Some suites.

Grand Hotel $NZ70   ★★

76 Dee Street. ☎ *(03) 218-8059; FAX (03) 218-8053.*
A Pub Beds facility in an old three-story landmark building, now refurbished. All rooms with private baths. Somerset's Restaurant, bar, some suites.

Monticello Travel Lodge $NZ75–95   ★★

240 Spey Street, downtown. ☎ *(03) 218-2503; FAX (03) 218-2506.*
Restaurant, kitchens, B&B, courtesy van.

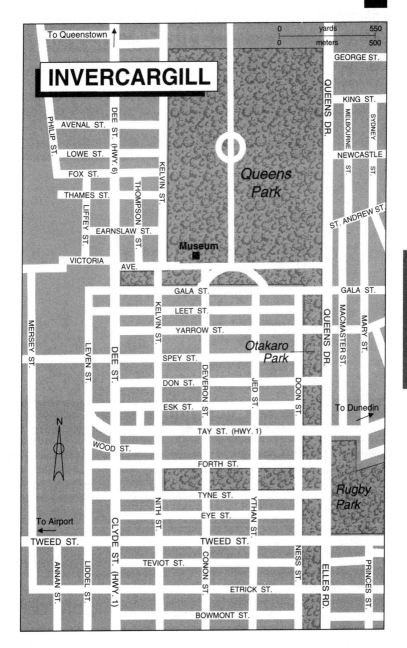

Don Lodge Motor Hotel   **$NZ60**   ★★

77 Don Street, center of city. ☎ *(03) 218-6125; FAX (03) 214-0222.*
Private baths, restaurant/bar, laundry, weekend rates. Doubles about $NZ60.

Townsman Motor Lodge   **$NZ95**   ★★

195 Tay Street, about a kilometer from the city center. ☎ *(03) 218-8027; FAX (03)*
218-8420.
Kitchens, spa baths, courtesy van, breakfast available, tea/coffee, adjacent to a grocery store. Some deluxe units.

Invercargill YHA Hostel   **$NZ18**

122 North Road, Waikiwi, about 3 kilometers from city center. ☎ *(03) 215-9007.*
Barbecue. Twin and family units, shuttle service to town. $NZ18 a night per person.

Southern Comfort Hostel   **$NZ18**

30 Thomson Street. ☎ *(03) 218-3838.*
Well-kept older house with gardens, modern kitchen, free use of bikes. Downtown
location. $NZ18 a night per person.

Beach Road Motor Camp   **$NZ8–40**

Near Oreti Beach. ☎ *(03) 213-0400.*
Laundry, TV lounge, store open seven days, kitchen. Cabins and tourist flats
$NZ25-40 double; powered sites $NZ8 per person.

Where to Eat

Donovan's   **$$–$$$**   ★★★

220 Bainfield Road. ☎ *(03) 218-8156.*
Popular, honored restaurant housed in a restored farmhouse. *Famous for game*
dishes and also for the house specialty, "Whiskey Lamb Deep Creek" (lamb sautéed
in booze). Good wine list. *Dinner from 6 p.m. Tues.–Sat.; lunches Nov. and Dec.*
Reservations.

Strathern Inn   **$$–$$$**   ★★★

200 Innes Road, off the Bluff Road. ☎ *(03) 216-0400.*
Another award winner, also in a cottage. Six dining rooms show history of the area.
Specialties include Stewart Island salmon, venison, smoked eel. *Lunch noon–2 p.m.*
(closed Sat.); dinner from 5 p.m. nightly. Reservations.

Birchwoods Brasserie Room, The   **$$**   ★★

In the Ascot Park Hotel, corner of Tay Street and Racecourse Road. ☎ *(03) 217-6195.*
New Zealand à la carte menu. *Open daily: breakfast 6–9 a.m.; lunch noon–2 p.m.;*
dinner 6–10 p.m.

Zookeepers   **$**   ★★

50 Tay Street. ☎ *(03) 218-3373.*
Basically just a café/bar with a zoo motif, but very casual and friendly. Good breakfast and lunches, late-night snacks. *Open seven days,* licensed.

Homestead Restaurant   ★★

Corner of Avenal and Dee streets. ☎ *(03) 218-3125.*
Family restaurant, family prices. Many seafood dishes. *Lunch 11:45 a.m.–2:15 p.m.;*
dinner 4:30–10:30 p.m. Open seven days.

H.M.S. Kings   **$$**   ★★
83 Tay Street. ☎ *(03) 218-3443.*
Done up like a sailing ship; *the food makes up for the decor.* Seafood and steaks a specialty. BYO. Closed Sun.

Ainos Steakhouse   **$$**   ★★★
Ruru Street, off North Road in the Waikiwi Shopping Centre. ☎ *(03) 215-9563.*
Open fire, steak and seafood. Licensed and BYO. It's the oldest restaurant in town and the owner still does most of the cooking; many awards. *Open for dinner 5–10 p.m.; closed Sun.*

Essentials

Getting There

Invercargill has daily air service from Auckland and Christchurch and weekday service from Wellington (one Saturday flight), Dunedin, Hokitika, Nelson and Rotorua. Service is offered either on **Air New Zealand** or **Ansett**. From Christchurch, the one-way fare is about $NZ230; from Auckland, about $NZ430; from Wellington, about $NZ320, and from Rotorua, about $NZ410.

The city is also the southern terminus of **The Southerner**, a nonsmoking train with a buffet car that starts in Christchurch with stops at Timaru and Dunedin. Daily service starts at 8:40 a.m., arriving in Invercargill around 5:30 p.m.; the return leaves at 9:20 a.m., arriving in Christchurch at 7 p.m. The one-way fare without a pass is about $NZ100. The city also has regular bus service to all parts of the South Island.

Information

The Invercargill Visitor Information Centre is located at Queens Park; ☎ *phone and FAX (03) 214-6243; FAX (03) 218-9753.* For information about national parks and other government facilities, including Stewart Island, contact the Department of Conservation office on Don Street; ☎ *(03) 214-4589.* The AA office is at *47-51 Gala Street*; ☎ *(03) 218-9033.*

The Other Island

New Zealand is actually considered to be three major islands—the third being Stewart Island, south of Invercargill. Virtually unpopulated (maybe 500 people, if that), the island is lush with plants, as well as animal and bird life. There are **brown kiwis**, **feral cats**, **red deer**, **possums**, **rats** and flocks of **bush birds**. Sections of the island are covered with **ferns** and **podocarps**, with the odd **orchid** thrown in here and there. It gets pretty dense. Stewart Island is the permanent home of the folks who drag **lobster** and the world-famous **Bluff oysters** from the waters of the Foveaux Strait. *But the island is also a national park, one of the most popular in the country.* It's 1700 square miles in area, has 450 miles of coastline and 130 miles of **hiking trails**. James Cook sighted it but thought it was part of the South Island. It was originally settled for timber, whaling and gold and other mineral mining, but now tourism and fishing are about all that's left. Judging from the look of things, fishing is still number one.

In a nation of changeable weather, Stewart Island is even more changeable than most, with tons of rain annually but, surprisingly enough considering how far south it is, very little frost. It's not a place for folks who like their action hot and heavy, there being only one settlement of any size, but *it's a bush-walker's paradise.* The trails come in all sizes and various degrees of difficulty, and the government has placed hiking huts all over the island.

The main settlement is called **Oban**, which sits in a little inlet called Halfmoon Bay. *It usually reminds people of the sort of seafaring village you see along the coasts of New Brunswick or Nova Scotia, weathered and wooden and 50 years behind the times.* But it's too green and not rocky enough to be anywhere in the Maritimes. It looks—well—very New Zealandish. Information about the island is available either at the information center in Invercargill or at the **Stewart Island Visitor Centre** on the island (right downtown, you can't miss it). ☎ *(03) 219-1218; FAX (03) 219-1555.* The island Department of Conservation office is *on Argyle Street;* ☎ *(03) 219-1130.* The island has a total of about 25 miles of paved roads, but give a Kiwi a road and he'll put a bus tour on it, in this case less than an hour but good for island backgrounding. Or you can rent mopeds or mountain bikes.

Native Tree Fern, Urewera National Park

It gets busy in the summer, and reservations are a must. There are only a couple of restaurants, and accommodations are limited. There is a food store, but the prices are about what you'd expect on an island.

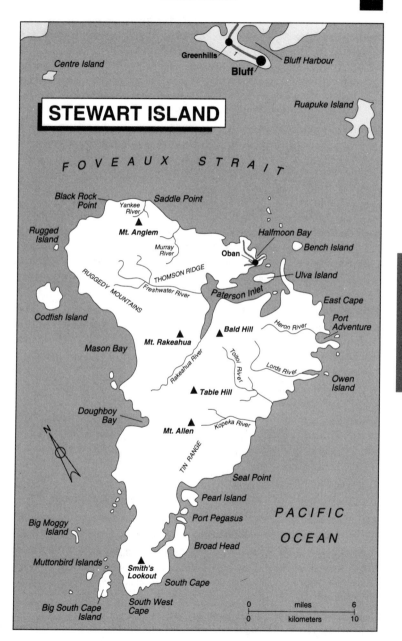

Centre Island

STEWART ISLAND

Greenhills
Bluff — Bluff Harbour

Ruapuke Island

F O V E A U X   S T R A I T

Black Rock
Point — Saddle Point
Yankee
River
▲ Mt. Anglem

Rugged
Island

Murray
River

Halfmoon Bay
Oban — Bench Island

RUGGEDY MOUNTAINS
THOMSON RIDGE
Freshwater River
Paterson Inlet
Ulva Island

Codfish Island

East Cape
Port
Adventure

▲ Bald Hill
Heron River

▲ Mt. Rakeahua

Mason Bay

Rakeahua River
Toitoi River
Lords River

Owen
Island

▲ Table Hill

Doughboy
Bay

▲ Mt. Allen
Kopeka River

TIN RANGE

Seal Point

Big Moggy
Island

Pearl Island
Port Pegasus

PACIFIC

OCEAN

Broad Head

Muttonbird Islands

▲ Smith's
Lookout
South Cape

Big South Cape
Island

South West
Cape

0   miles   6

0   kilometers   10

Where to Stay

Stewart Island Lodge   **$NZ350**   ★★★★

At Halfmoon Bay. ☎ *(03) 219-1085; FAX (03) 219-1085.*

These are the best—and most expensive—digs on the island. The lodge has five suites, and rates include all meals and alcohol. Stunning views; the lodge is set into a hillside overlooking the bay. Simply put, elegance and gourmet excesses. Courtesy pickup at the dock or airport; fishing/diving boat available.

Stewart Island Holiday Homes   **$NZ75**   ★★★

Elgin Terrace, Halfmoon Bay. ☎ *(03) 219-1057, or in Invercargill contact Peter and Jeanette Goomes, 131 Chelmsford Street.* ☎ *(03) 217-6585.*

An interesting alternative. The two homes sleep up to 10 persons, but you have to supply your own linens and food; linens can be rented. The homes are a few blocks from the wharf with a view of Halfmoon Bay. Rates for two persons are about $NZ75 a night; extra folks, $NZ15 each.

South Sea Hotel   **$NZ75–85**   ★★

Downtown on the waterfront. ☎ *(03) 219-1059; FAX (03) 219-1120.*

Annie Hansen's Dining Room (see "Where to Eat"), TV lounge, public and private bar. All rooms with shared baths; laundry, breakfast available, handicapped facilities. Room rates do not include meals..

Rakiura Motel   **$NZ70**   ★★

About a mile from town on Horseshoe Bay Road overlooking Bragg's Bay. ☎ *(03) 219-1096.*

Kitchens, laundry.

Shearwater Inn   **$NZ50**   ★★

Halfmoon Bay, near the post office. ☎ *(03) 219-1114; FAX (03) 219-1120.*

Complex has rooms with shared baths, but in-house dining room.

Jo and Andy's B&B   **$NZ15**

Corner of Main Road and Morris Street on the airport road. ☎ *(03) 219-1230.*

One double, one triple. Cooking facilities and laundry available. $NZ15 per person shared with linen supplied.

In addition, a number of private homes have rooms to rent. These can be arranged through the island information center or by contacting **Stewart Island Travel**, *P.O. Box 26, Stewart Island,* ☎ *(03) 219-1269, FAX (03) 219-1355.*

Where to Eat

The best restaurant in town is probably **Annie Hansen's Dining Room** in the South Sea Hotel. Seafoods are tasty, or you can try venison or a muttonbird, the island specialty. Reservations necessary. *Lunch from noon to 1 p.m.; dinner from 6–7 p.m.* Budget to moderate. ☎ *(03) 219-1059.*

For lighter budget fare, try the **Travel Inn Tearooms** down the street (run by the same folks who own Stewart Island Travel).

Going South

Milford Track is the most popular trekking area in New Zealand.

Whitewater rafting on the Shotover

Postcard view of Lake Waikaremoana

Breathtaking Milford Sound and Mitre Peak are at the end of Milford Track.

Arthur's Pass highway is one of New Zealand's most scenic drives.

Rimu Forest, South Westland

Activities

In addition to hiking or just lolling about, you can book helicopter trips in advance, look in on a **fish processing factory**, shoot deer (including some American whitetail) or, better, **take a cruise** around the area to look at the seals and other local residents. There are several boats for charter at Oban with rates around $NZ50 per person for a full day. Overnight trips, meals included, are around $NZ500 per day for a party of four. These can be booked in Invercargill or on the island itself. Check with Stewart Island Travel (listed above) or with the **Stewart Island Adventure Centre** located on the main wharf at Halfmoon Bay. It handles tours, diving, local transport, accommodations and other activities. ☎ *(03) 219-1134.*

Getting There

By boat or by plane. Like its big brother up north between Picton and Wellington, the Foveaux Strait is open to the westerlies and can get very rough. The small catamaran ferry that makes the trip runs at odd times during the off-season but daily during the height of the tourist season; the crossing takes about an hour. Check times with the Stewart Island Marine offices in Bluff, ☎ *(03) 212-7660, FAX (03) 212-8377,* or with the Invercargill information center. The one-way fare is about $NZ40. If you just want to go over and come back, you'll have about three hours on the island before the return trip.

The fastest (and usually the smoothest) way over is the 20-minute flight aboard one of Southern Air Ltd.'s small planes. During the winter, there are three flights a day going and coming; more in summer. The round-trip fare is about $NZ240 double; singles are $NZ140, kids, about $NZ70. The airline office can also book accommodations, charter a boat, set up bus tours or reserve whatever you want on the island. The office is at the Invercargill airport, ☎ *(03) 218-9129, FAX (03) 214-4681* or toll-free, ☎ *(0800) 658-876.*

Tours

The Almost-Antarctic Experience

From Bluff, the seacoast city south of Invercargill, Southern Heritage Tours runs cruises to some of the isolated near-Antarctic islands south of Stewart Island. The company, a New Zealand natural history travel company, has 11- to 15-day cruises that hit about six island groups. The cruises are aboard the 140-foot *Pacific Ruby*, which has a crew of 15, including a professional chef and a medical officer. The cruises run between December and February and cost about $NZ2400 per person, including meals—airfares extra. Information is available through the New Zealand Tourism Board in Santa Monica, California.

Going South

Heading North

Penguins at Sandfly Bay

From Invercargill toward Dunedin, you have a choice of fast and farmy or slow and scenic. Two highways branch from Invercargill to the settlement of **Balclutha**. The coast road, Highway 92, is worth the drive. At **Fortrose**, the land is grass-covered dunes as far as you can see, and, at low tide, the whole country is out digging for shellfish. The locals are slowly claiming the ocean verge as new farmland, what they call down here "winning the land," but much of it remains rugged and pristine. The drive takes you along cliffs and rainforest, and, if you have time, it might be worth stopping along the way at any of the several reserves and nature walks available. One good one is the trail up to **Purakaunui Falls**, about 15 kilometers east of **Owaka**. This is also the area of the **Catlins Forest Park**, just about midway between Dunedin and

Invercargill. *The park, about 144,000 acres, is mostly virgin coastal forest, with hiking trails to secluded bays, where you can see Hector's dolphins, seals and penguins.* Information and maps for the park are available at the Department of Conservation office in Owaka; ☎ *(03) 415-8341.* There's a very nice beach along the coast highway between the **Tautuku Peninsula** and **Papatowai**, which also has a good beach and a nice RV park.

At **Balclutha**, the roads converge to become Highway 1, which runs north through Dunedin to the tip of the South Island. Balclutha is of note because it sits on the Clutha River, the largest river in New Zealand in terms of discharge. *Clutha* is the Celtic form of the Clyde, a river back in Scotland. Balcluthans are inordinately proud of the historic arched bridge that spans the river. The **Clutha Information Centre** is at *63 Clyde Street.* ☎ *(03) 418-0388; FAX (03) 418-1877.*

Dunedin

The Royal Albatross Colony is at the tip of Otago Peninsula.

Dunedin proclaims itself the "Wildlife Capital of New Zealand," a bit of a boast, but allowable. The two most famous members of the wildlife set live out at the end of the **Otago Peninsula**, which juts north of the city—**the royal albatross** and the endangered **yellow-eyed penguin**. The city, population about 120,000, also calls itself the "Edinburgh of New Zealand," and, indeed, *Dunedin* is the Celtic form of Edinburgh. It started life aptly enough as a Presbyterian colony (no doubt as far away as possible from the leftist Angli-

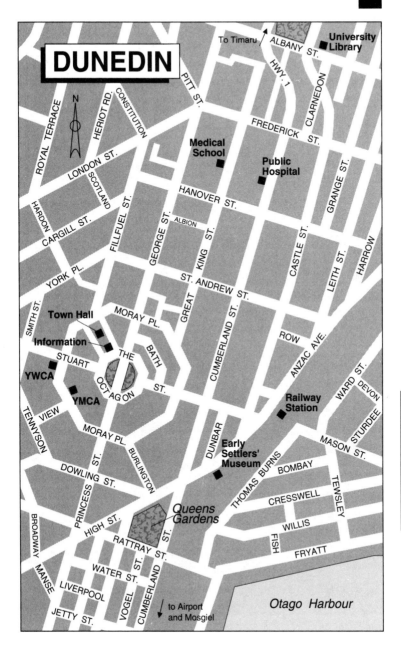

DUNEDIN

To Timaru

University Library

ALBANY ST.

PITT ST.

HWY. 1

CLARNEDON ST.

FREDERICK ST.

HERIOT RD.

CONSTITUTION

ROYAL TERRACE

Medical School

Public Hospital

GRANGE ST.

LONDON ST.

SCOTLAND

HANOVER ST.

HARDON

FILLFUEL ST.

GEORGE ST.

ALBION

KING ST.

CASTLE ST.

HARROW

CARGILL ST.

LEITH ST.

YORK PL.

ST. ANDREW ST.

GREAT

ST. ANDREW ST.

SMITH ST.

Town Hall

MORAY PL.

CUMBERLAND ST.

ROW

ANZAC AVE.

Information

THE

BATH

Town Hall

STUART

OCTAGON

ST.

WARD ST.

DEVON

YWCA

YMCA

Railway Station

STURDEE

TENNYSON

VIEW

MORAY PL.

DUNBAR

MASON ST.

DOWLING ST.

BURLINGTON

Early Settlers' Museum

THOMAS BURNS

BOMBAY

TEWSLEY

PRINCESS

HIGH ST.

Queens Gardens

CRESSWELL

BROADWAY

RATTRAY ST.

WILLIS

MANSE

WATER ST.

VOGEL ST.

CUMBERLAND ST.

FISH

FRYATT

LIVERPOOL

JETTY ST.

to Airport and Mosgiel

Otago Harbour

Heading North

cans up in Christchurch). The city is also home to the oldest university in New Zealand.

The First Church of Otago is an impressive architectural sight.

The harbor, formed by the peninsula and the east shore, was a favorite of early whalers because it's about the only decent anchorage on this stretch of the South Island. It had a fairly unsavory reputation as a place where whalers got eaten by Maoris and Maoris got slaughtered by whalers, but all was basically placid by the middle 1840s. The hills rise steeply from the harbor, giving Dunedin a sort of San Francisco look. And, like San Francisco, Dunedin got its start as a base for gold-mad miners, in this case part of the mobs who rushed to Queenstown and Arrowtown in the 1860s. A lot of gold fortunes were spent building gaudy Victorians all over town, and the city also became a banking center.

The heart of the city is the **Octagon**, a garden area flanked by several city landmarks, including an almost compulsory statue of **Bobbie Burns**. Also nearby is **St. Paul's Cathedral**, the signature church in the city, which, amusingly, is Anglican. Near it is **First Church**, the Presbyterian seat. Both are worth a look; First Church (1875) is Gothic Revival structure, currently being refurbished. Its bell tower has a dozen bangers. St. Paul's, built in 1915 of native stone, is probably the more dramatic of the two, with fine roseate windows and a huge organ. Evensong performances, open to the public, are held Tuesday, Wednesday, Thursday and Sunday. Tours are also available. Information is available at the cathedral office, *open 9:30 a.m.– 12:30 p.m., Monday–Friday.*

Another Dunedin landmark is the **railway station** on Anzac Street, an old Edwardian hulk now a bit chipped around the edges. It was built in 1904, and of some note is the mosaic tile floor with railroad motifs, plus gilt-edged mirrors and genuine Thomas Crappers in the loos. The guy who designed it was knighted. *De gustibus et coloribus non est disputandum.*

Some other relics, many built of native stone, are the **Municipal Chambers**, opened in 1880; the **Law Courts**, 1902; the **Otago Boys High School**, 1884; **St. Joseph's Catholic Cathedral**, 1886; a **Dominican priory**, 1877; **Knox Church**, 1876; **Southern Cross Hotel**, 1883, and the **Otago Star building**, built in the 1870s and still housing the newspaper it was named after.

Three of the major tourist targets in town are the many **rhododendron gardens**, the **Olveston mansion** and the **Cadbury Chocolate Factory**. The gardens are scattered all over town, so much so that the third week in October is celebrated as Rhododendron Week. One of the better gardens is the **Rhododendron Dell** at the Botanic Gardens, started in 1914. The gardens are off Great King Street (northbound Highway 1). Look for the statue of Peter Pan and Wendy. Information is available at ☎ *(03) 474-3309.* The Dunedin Rhododendron Group maintains a private garden, which you can tour for $NZ2.

Heading North

Rhododendrons are a major tourist attraction in Dunedin.

Olveston is a time capsule of how the posh got along around the turn of the century. It's a Jacobean mansion, filled to the gunwales with antiques, period paintings and collectibles. It was built between 1904 and 1906 and was left to the city by the family in 1966. The billiard room looks like an aircraft carrier, and the Great Hall, all oak and darkness, oozes money. Hourlong guided tours are available six times a day all week. Reservations are suggested; the tours, about $NZ10 for adults, can be booked at the visitor's center. The building is at 42 Royal Terrace. Information is available by calling the mansion at ☎ *(03) 477-3320.*

The Cadbury factory might be the most popular attraction on the South Island. It is almost impossible to get a tour because it's booked months in advance, especially during the school holidays. One-hour tours run twice a day Monday–Thursday, and can be booked at the visitor's center; free samples. The factory was opened in 1865 as a biscuit bake house. It became the Cadbury plant in 1930. (Scott took Cadbury products with him to the Antarctic; he still froze to death.) Or try a $NZ5 visit to **Speights Brewery**. More free samples on one-hour tours. Information: ☎ *(03) 477-9480.* Or take a tour of Wilson Distillers, the only whiskey distillery in New Zealand. Samples, $NZ5 tour fee ☎ *(03) 474-3300.* The city also has an excellent museum, with a really fine display of Maori art and architecture. The **Otago Museum** is on Great King Street, adjacent to the university. One of its major attractions is a Maori meeting house, carved in 1872. It's a classic—remember to take your shoes off before going in. There are also displays of canoes, greenstone carvings, and relics from other Pacific cultures. The museum, built in 1877, is also noted for a remarkable collection of classic works from Greece and Rome. Admission is free. *Hours are 10 a.m.–5 p.m., Monday–Friday; 1–5 p.m., weekends. Information* ☎ *(03) 477-2372.*

The Otago Peninsula

The Otago Peninsula draws many visitors every year to see the wildlife and enjoy the raw coastal scenery. The drive from Dunedin to the tip at Taiaroa Head runs through country that reminds us of the Yorkshire dells with fewer stone walls. It's about 25 or 30 kilometers from the city to the Head with some fine views and some fairly curvy roads.

It can be a bit confusing getting to the peninsula road. From the Octagon, get on Princes Street south, go about 1 kilometer, then turn left on Anderson's Bay Road. The road takes a sharp left, becoming Musselburgh Rise, then goes left again to become Ravelston Street. Soon after, at Silverton Street, turn right, and soon you should see a sign for Larnach Castle. Proceed. The tourist spots on the peninsula are signposted.

The first major attraction you come to is **Glenfalloch Gardens**, about 10 kilometers out of town at 430 Portobello Road. There are 30 acres of woodlands and gardens, with a licensed restaurant, the **Chalet Restaurant**. It's also a wine bar. Open for teas, lunches, dinners and some buffet dinners seven days. Moderate. ☎ *(03) 476-1006.*

Larnach's Castle in Dunedin is New Zealand's only castle.

Soon after is **Larnach Castle**, but it ain't really a castle, but more like a big, rambling Victorian mansion. The place does not live up to its descriptions. It's impressive enough, but for the $NZ10 charged per person to get in, not really worth it. It has 40,000 square feet of rooms, plus about 1000 acres of land. There is a verandah for light repast, and if you stay at the lodge, evening meals and breakfast are available in the castle. *It's open for a look from 9 a.m.–5 p.m.* The castle's ballroom is often used for public occasions. The castle folks have a couple of nice places to spend the night if you want to stay on the peninsula. The **Larnach Castle Lodge**, a re-created farm building, has better doubles with private bath starting at about $NZ140; shared facilities are $NZ55. There is also budget accommodation available. Castle tours, half price for guests. Information is available at the city visitors center or at the castle; ☎ *(03) 476-1616; FAX (03) 476-1574.*

For a look at the sealife that inhabits the Otago Peninsula area, stop in at the **Trust Bank Aquarium**, run by the Otago University Marine Research Station. Displays of marine life, touching pools, a tuatara. It's on a peninsula to the left past Larnach Castle. *Open weekends and holidays, noon–4:30 p.m.* Fee $NZ5. ☎ *(03) 478-1819.*

At the tip of the peninsula is the **Royal Albatross Colony**, where the huge seabirds have one of their few rookeries near civilization. Adults can fly 75 miles an hour, migrate more than 120,000 miles a year and have wingspans of nearly 11 feet. Entry permits, available at the colony's visitor center, are about $NZ15; reduced rates in the winter. The viewing season opens November 24, closes September 16 the next year. Information at the Trust Bank Royal Albatross Centre, ☎ *(03) 478-0499.*

Next to the colony is an old fort, which draws the curious to look at the **Armstrong Disappearing Gun**, an 1886 wonder that was aimed underground, raised to fire, then disappeared below again for a reload. It could fire a 100-pound shell five miles. Tours of the fort and the colony are often combined. Bookings through the Dunedin visitors center. Entry fee is $NZ10, or for both colony and fort, about $NZ20.

Adjacent to the royal albatross center at the head is a sanctuary where you can see southern fur seals and endangered yellow-eyed penguins. The last four hours of daylight are the best viewing hours for the birds. Bookings through the Dunedin Visitors Centre. Fee $NZ7.50.

Essentials

Getting There

Dunedin has regular air service from cities in the south, as well as the North Island. Daily service is offered by Air New Zealand from Auckland for about $NZ400 one way. Other prices: Wellington, $NZ270; Rotorua, $NZ370; Christchurch, $NZ190; Hokitika, $NZ230; and Invercargill, $NZ135. Train service is available on the Southerner Express from either Christchurch or Invercargill. The fare from Christchurch one way is about $NZ60; from Invercargill, about $NZ40. There is bus service to Queenstown, Timaru and Te Anau. The one-way fare to Queenstown is about $NZ50. The train/bus office is at *200 Cumberland Street; Mount Cook Line bus offices are at 67 Great King Street*.

Getting Around

Dunedin Taxis will take you around town, get you to the airport or, for about $NZ40 an hour, tour you around. They claim they will compete with airport shuttles. ☎ *(03) 777-777*.

Tours

Otago Harbour Cruises

This company has a couple of packages designed to show the full glories of the bay and the peninsula. You can cruise out to Taiaroa Head on the *M.V. Monarch* and bus back, or bus out and cruise back. The first plan is probably the best because the tour includes albatrosses and the penguins; the second stops at Larnach Castle. The cruise out/bus back is about $NZ60. It takes six hours. The bus out/cruise back is about $NZ40 and takes four hours. Other packages are available. Information: **Otago Harbour Cruises Office**, *corner Wharf and Fryatt streets*, ☎ *(03) 477-4276;* FAX *(03) 477-4216*.

Newtons Coachways offers peninsula **bus tours** with stops at most of the popular spots. The tour to the albatrosses and penguins is about $NZ35. *105 Melbourne Street;* ☎ *(03) 477-5577;* FAX *(03) 477-8147*.

A very nice **train trip** runs from the historic railroad station to the Taieri Gorge north of the city. Lots of canyons and scenery, often compared to the narrow-gauge trip in Durango, Colorado (which, incidentally, was built by one of the authors' great-grandfathers). The trip out and back runs about four hours September–April; limited service in the winter, May–August. There's wheelchair access and a bar/snack car. If you're camping, they'll drop you off and pick you up later. Tickets are available at the train station, the city visitor center or any InterCity booking office. The adult ticket is about $NZ40. *Information: Taieri Gorge Railway, Dunedin Railway Station*, ☎ *(03) 477-4449, FAX (03) 477-4953*.

Information

The **Dunedin Visitor Centre** is located in the Octagon. *Hours are 8:30 a.m.–5 p.m. weekdays, 9 a.m.–5 p.m., weekends.* ☎ *(03) 474-3300;* FAX *(03) 474-3311.* The **Department of Conservation** office is at *77 Lower Stuart Street,* ☎ *(03) 477-0677.* The **AA office** is located at *450 Moray Place,* ☎ *(03) 477-5945*.

Where to Stay

The city has for its size a remarkable number of good, basic hostelries and eateries for a wide range of purses. We like the Southern Cross because of its style and location, but some lodgings toward the peninsula and beaches are quite comfy as well. A number of good units are in the university area, which is shady and peaceful.

Southern Cross $NZ190–300   ★ ★ ★

Corner of High and Princes streets, close to the Octagon. ☎ *(03) 477-0752;* FAX *(03) 477-5776*.

Satellite TV, tea/coffee, dry cleaning/laundry service. Three restaurants, including the **Carlton** ★★★, à la carte gourmet, expensive; and the **Deli-Café**, open seven days, 24 hours; two bars. The hotel offers, would you believe, Scottish *haggis* ceremonies, the new rage in town. Suites with spa baths. Handicapped access. Gym, airport shuttle. Standard doubles in the high season are about $NZ190; spa suites about $NZ300.

Pacific Park Dunedin $NZ120–160 ★★★

21-24 Wallace Street. ☎ *(03) 477-3374; FAX (03) 477-1434.*
Hillside location overlooking the harbor, about a kilometer from city center. Honeymoon and deluxe suites, 2.5 acres of native bush, restaurant/bar, tennis courts, miniature golf, barbecue/picnic area, tea/coffee, minibars.

Quality Hotel Dunedin $NZ130–250 ★★★

Upper Moray Place, right on the Octagon. ☎ *(03) 477-6784; FAX (03) 474-0115.*
Minibars, tea/coffee, valet service, spa, sauna, restaurant/bar; good weekend deals.

Among the numerous two- or three-star motels around town are the following:

Abbey Lodge Motor Inn $NZ90–250 ★★★

900 Cumberland Street. ☎ *(03) 477-5380; FAX (03) 477-8715.*
Nice location near Otago University and the Botanical Gardens. Luxury and honeymoon suites, spas, indoor pool, sauna, laundry facilities, bar, restaurant, fridge, tea/coffee, some kitchens.

Cargill Motor Inn $NZ115–175 ★★★

678 George Street, close to the university and Otago Museum. ☎ *(03) 477-7983; FAX (03) 477-8098.*
Some luxury suites, garden courtyard, tour desk, spas, minibars, tea/coffee, laundry, bar/restaurant. Doubles about $NZ115; suites about $NZ175.

Skyline Leisure Lodge $NZ130–150 ★★★

30 Duke Street, university area. ☎ *(03) 477-5360; FAX (03) 477-5460.*
Original site of a brewery—stones from the old building were used in the bar, and the dining room is named after the oast house. Opposite the Botanical Gardens. Large landscaped garden, fine ambiance. One deluxe suite, some kitchenettes, family units, tea/coffee, laundry.

High Street Court Motel $NZ85–120 ★★

193 High Street, near the Octagon. ☎ *(03) 477-9315; FAX (03) 477-3366.*
Kitchens, laundry, gardens, breakfast available. One-, two- and three-bedroom units; a good bet.

Commodore Luxury Motel $NZ80–150 ★★

932 Cumberland Street, near the university and botanical gardens. ☎ *(03) 477-7766; FAX (03) 477-7750.*
One- and two-bedroom units with kitchens, courtesy van, pool, breakfast available, spa and sauna, car rentals, licensed restaurant.

Regal Court Motel $NZ80–130 ★★

755 George Street, near Otago Museum and university. ☎ *(03) 477-7729; FAX the same.*
One- and two-bedroom units and one "Persian" honeymoon suite. Kitchens, laundry, breakfasts available.

Alcala Motor Court $NZ85   ★★

George and David streets near city center. ☎ *(03) 477-9073; FAX the same.*
Rooftop units, executive and honeymoon suites, spa, laundry, microwaves, breakfast available.

Aberdeen Motel $NZ85   ★★

46 Bank Street, first motel off the northern motorway about 3 kilometers from town.
☎ *(03) 473-0133; FAX (03) 473-0131.*
Chalet units overlooking the Botanical Gardens, with kitchens, laundry, tea/coffee, morning paper, breakfast available.

Law Courts $NZ55–75   ★★

Corner Stuart and Cumberland streets. ☎ *(03) 477-8036; FAX the same.*
A favorite moderate-priced hotel. Funky Art Deco building with a Cobb & Company restaurant. Great staff, great urban neighborhood, comfortable bar, one of the Pub Hotel group. Private baths, coffee/tea.

Sahara Guesthouse and Motel $NZ65–75   ★★

619 George Street, about a kilometer from city center. ☎ *(03) 477-6662; FAX (03) 479-2551.*
B&B, laundry, motel and lodge units, some kitchens. A dozen guest-house doubles about $NZ75; motel doubles about $NZ65–75.

Leviathan Hotel $NZ80–115   ★★

65 Lower High Street. ☎ *(03) 477-3160; FAX (03) 477-2385.*
Private baths, house lounge/bar, laundry, minibars, restaurant, some rooms with rangettes; two suites with spas.

Castlewood B&B $NZ50–125

240 York Place ☎ *(03) 477-0526; FAX the same.*
The Tudor-style "gentleman's mansion" dates from 1913 and has what the owners see as a "subtle nautical theme," meaning portholes and the upstairs lounge with ship-like windows. New owners Peter and Donna Mitchell have added an extensive library, new feather duvets and numerous other cozy touches. Rooms are being redecorated and the gardens extended. Rooms include singles, doubles and queen rooms. Located near the city center.

Stafford Gables Hostel $NZ18–22

71 Stafford Street., five-minute walk to the Octagon. ☎ *(03) 474-1919; FAX the same.*
YHA facility close to a supermarket. Doubles, twins, triples and family rooms. Café open in summer. $NZ18 per person a night; nonmembers, $NZ22.

Aaron Lodge Motel and Holiday Park $NZ35–60

162 Kaikorai Valley Road, about 2.5 kilometers from town. ☎ *(03) 476-4725; FAX (03) 476-7925.*
Top 10 member. Kitchen, laundry units, spa pool, barbecue, linen rental. Tourist flats NZ$60 double; cabins $NZ35.

Where to Eat

Good hotel restaurants worth a try, in addition to the **Southern Cross** and the **Oast Room** at the Leisure Lodge, include the **Settlers Inn** at the Quality Inn, BYO, specializing in lamb, fish and steaks, moderate; **Cargill's Garden Restaurant**, located in the Cargill

Motor Inn, moderate to expensive; the moderately priced **Carvery** in the Wains Boutique Hotel at *310 Princes Street*, which has a reasonable Sunday smorgasbord, ☎ *(03) 477-1155*; the moderate **Abbey Motor Lodge restaurant**, which has a seafood and meat smorgasbord, weekends, and **Aggie's Restaurant** in the Pacific Park, which specializes in marvelously rich crayfish, moderate.

95 Filleul Street $$–$$$ ★★★

95 Filleul Street. ☎ *(03) 471-9265.*

Housed in an old pink Victorian house, it is one of the classiest places in Dunedin. Open fires, real china, ceiling fans, bare wooden floors. Menu changes with the seasons, but basically it's semi-wild and eclectic—for lack of a better term, Kiwi Soul Food, but very good (pork hocks, beetroot and sour cream strudel). Lots of fresh veggies. Very popular, reservations essential. Blues and jazz music while you dine. *Dinner Tues.–Sat. from 6:30 p.m.*

Blades $$ ★★★

450 George Street. ☎ *(03) 477-6548.*

Upstairs location over looking Knox Gardens; smoke free. Seafood to (ugghh) *haggis* tarts, actually edible and not bad. BYO, emphasis on fresh foods. Pacific Rim influence. *Mon.–Sat., from 6 p.m.*

Phoenix Chinese Restaurant $$ ★★★

434 George Street. ☎ *(03) 477-8433.*

Opposite the Knox Church and just the place to placate that tofu yearning—it's homemade here, along with a large variety of dishes prepared by a Hong Kong-trained chef. *Lunch daily from 11 a.m.; dinner from 6:30 p.m. daily.*

Palms Café $$ ★★

84 Lower High Street. ☎ *(03) 477-6534.*

Colonial furnishings, overlooking the Queen's Gardens. Nonsmoking restaurant. *Pasta specialities*, as well as vegetarian dishes and fish and lamb. *Dinner Mon.–Fri. from 5 p.m.; from 6 p.m. Sat.–Sun.*

Casa Italia $$–$$$ ★★

The Octagon in the historic Municipal Chambers. ☎ *(03) 474-1588.*

New Zealand and Italian wine list; Northern Italian cuisine, veal dishes, fresh pasta daily. Licensed and BYO. *Lunch noon–2 p.m. and dinner from 6 p.m. seven days.*

Bell Pepper Blues $$ ★★

474 Princes Street. ☎ *(03) 474-0973.*

Southwestern American motif. In the Prince of Wales Hotel. Very eclectic menu, from Mexican to seafood and venison. Reservations needed. *Lunch Wed.–Fri. noon–2 p.m.; dinner from 6:30 p.m. Mon.–Sat.*

Santa Fe $–$$ ★★

629 George Street. ☎ *(03) 477-0339.*

Tex-Mex with heavy doses of yippie-yi-oh decorations. Food runs from Mexican to Cajun, and it's not bad. It replaces the former Las Gatos and is the primo Mexican place in town. BYO. *Lunch noon Wed.–Mon.; dinner from 6 p.m. same days.*

Little India Restaurant   **$**   ★★
82 St. Andrew's Street. ☎ *(03) 477-6559.*
BYO. Tandori oven, vegetarian as well as saucy Indian meat dishes. *Lunch 11:30 a.m.–2 p.m., dinner from 6 p.m. Wed.–Mon.*

Stewart Coffee House   **$–$$**   ★★
Lower Octagon. ☎ *(03) 477-6687.*
The oldest coffee house in Dunedin, and wondrous it is if you like latte or cappuccino or fresh roasted coffee. Also has light meals. Popular hangout.

Bacchus   **$–$$**   ★★
On the Octagon. ☎ *(03) 474-0824.*
In an old bank building. With **Ombrellos**, two of the city's more popular-priced wine bars. Bacchus has a wide range of national wines and good blackboard menu. **Ombrellos**, *10 Clarendon Street,* is close to the university campus in two old buildings, with budget Italian/Mediterranean dishes. *Hours for Bacchus are 11 a.m.–late Mon.–Sat. Hours for Ombrellos, brunch and lunch Tues.–Sun.; dinner Tues.–Sat.*
☎ *(03) 477-8773.*

Captain Cook   **$**   ★★
Albany and Great Kings streets.
Garden bar, budget pub food. Where the university crowd hangs out. Very crowded. *Open for lunch noon–2 p.m.* Student prices.

North to Timaru

About 85 kilometers north of Dunedin are the famous **Moeraki Boulders**, a clutch of huge rock spheroids of special significance to the Maoris. The rocks, the legends say, are food baskets that washed ashore after one of the founding canoes of the first Maoris crashed onto an offshore reef. Just before the boulders, look for **Shag Point,** where from time to time you can spot fur seals. For eats and a place to stay near the Boulders, try **Mill House** on the main highway at Wainakarua. It's in an 1879 flour mill on the banks of a river. The house restaurant has set-price menus during the week, à la carte on the weekends. Mill House also has rooms for about $NZ75 double, and there is entertainment on weekends. Open for lunch and dinner seven nights. ☎ *(03) 439-5515.*

Roughly 60 miles north of Dunedin along the coast highway is the first major settlement, **Oamaru**, which is primarily known for the production of a creamy white limestone, that has been used in the construction of several notable New Zealand buildings, including the Town Hall in Auckland, Wellington's old Customs house and the cathedral in Christchurch. The town itself has a wealth of limestone buildings, so many, in fact, that efforts are underway to create a working Victorian town around what was the original trade center of the city. The old hulks are so attractive, they are becoming popular backdrops for motion pictures and music videos. Worth a look is the

Heading North

so-called **Victorian Street** *(Harbour and Tyne streets)*, where white stone buildings stand, a bit forlorn, as testimony to the once-thriving Gold Rush economy that flourished in the 1860s. The harbor here is artificial, constructed of the gravels that line the ocean bed close to shore. It was from Oamaru in the 1880s that the first shipments of refrigerated mutton and other sheep products were sent to England, creating a boom in the Kiwi farm business that lasted until England joined the European Common Market. If you're looking for a place to stay, try the **Brydone Hotel**, a member of the Pub Beds group. It's in a 100-year-old structure, and rooms have private bath and TV; restaurant and bar. Doubles are about $NZ70. It's at *115 Thames Street.* ☎ *(03) 434-9892; FAX (03) 434-5719.*

Oamaru is also the intersection of Highway 83, en route to Mount Cook and the Southern Alps. It is the commercial center of the fertile Waitaki River Valley where many fruits are grown. The area also produces some excellent cheeses; try the Whitestone cheddar. The river marks the boundary between the Otago and Canterbury districts. The city is also known for large colonies of blue penguins, the world's smallest species. There is a blind near shore where you can spot the wee birds in late afternoon. Information about the area is available from the **Oamaru Information Centre** at *No. 1 Thames Street,* ☎ *(03) 434-1656; FAX (03) 434-1657.* The **AA** office is at *273 Thames Street,* ☎ *(03) 434-9105.*

About 80 kilometers farther north is the city of **Timaru**, the agricultural center of South Canterbury. It has one famous son, Robert Fitzsimmons, the boxer. It is also the home of one of the most famous horses in history (at least in Australia and New Zealand), **Phar Lap**. The horse won almost every race he entered, so much so that the Aussies tried to get him banned from the Melbourne Cup. He was poisoned and died while on a trip to the United States. A very entertaining movie about the horse was made not long ago.

The heart of the city is **Caroline Bay**, where there is a very popular annual carnival held during the Christmas–New Year's holidays. The beach is described as "fine and sandy," but in early spring, we found it to be pretty muddy and not very attractive. It is a safe swimming spot, however, and very crowded in the summer. Like the other settlements along the east shore of the South Island, Timaru has a collection of old stone Victorians, including **St. Mary's Anglican Church**, made of local basaltic rock and limestone from Oamaru. The city's harbor is the central bulk handling area for the South Island, including facilities that reportedly can load 5000 sheep an hour onto transport—many, it is reported, headed for the dining rooms of Saudi Arabia. There is a huge DB brewery here (free tours) and what is billed as one of the largest tanneries in the world.

Timaru lies about halfway between Christchurch and Mount Cook, which is reached by taking Highway 8 east past Lake Tekapo and into the Alps. It's probably the best place to stop between Christchurch and Dunedin. While nothing fancy, there are some motels and good restaurants for those who want to haul in for the night. Information about the city, the region and some attractions (including some Maori rock paintings) is available from the **Timaru Information Centre**, *14 George Street;* ☎ *(03) 688-6163; FAX (03) 688-6162.* The **AA office** is at *26 Church Street,* ☎ *(03) 688-4189.*

Where to Stay

There are no major hotels in town, but it does have a clutch of two- or three-star motels, Among the choices:

Baywatch Motor Lodge   **$NZ80–95**   ★★★

7 Evans Street. ☎ *(03) 688-1886; FAX (03) 688-1171.*
Some suites with spa baths; kitchens, queen-size beds, laundry, cooked or continental breakfasts on request. No-smoking room.

Aaron Court Motel   **$NZ80**   ★★★

27 Evans Street. ☎ *(03) 688-0079.*
Close to Caroline Bay. Laundry, spa, kitchens, garages.

Aorangi Motel   **$NZ75**   ★★

400 Stafford Street. ☎ *(03) 688-0097; FAX the same.*
Overlooks Caroline Bay. Kitchens, laundry, breakfast available.

Cedar Motor Lodge   **$NZ80**   ★★

36 King Street. ☎ *(03) 684-4084.*
Kitchens, spa, laundry.

Selwyn Holiday Park   **$NZ22–55**   ★

Selwyn Street, north end of town. ☎ *(03) 684-7690; FAX (03) 688-1004.*
A Top 10 RV park. Kitchens, laundry, canteen. Tourist flats with rangettes and showers, $NZ55; cottages, $NZ30 double; cabins $NZ22 double.

Where to Eat

Casa Italia Restorante   **$$–$$$**   ★★★★

2 Strathallan Street. Grand old Customs House building. ☎ *(03) 684-5528.*
Homemade pastas, good Italian wine cellar. Award winner, and the pasta-seafood combos are excellent. Also steaks, red-wine sauces. *Lunch and dinner Tues.–Sat.*

(Bold As) Brasserie, The   **$$**   ★★★

335 Stafford Street. ☎ *(03) 688-3981.*
Good view; great seafood. Specialties are king prawns, mussels and scallops. *Lunch from 11:30 a.m.; dinner from 6 p.m. Mon.–Sat.*

Cheng's   **$$**   ★★

135 Stafford Street. ☎ *(03) 688-8888.*
Cantonese-style. Big servings, set menus, à la carte and Sun. smorgasbord. *Dinner from 5 p.m. nightly.*

Annette's Kitchen   **$$**   ★★

5 George Street. ☎ *(03) 688-4344.*

Heading North

Restaurant/café/wine bar combination. Varied menu, everything from lamb to tofu dishes. Lunch and dinner daily.

Dusty Miller Restaurant   **$–$$**   ★★

18 A Hobbs Street, in the Northtown Tavern. *(03) 688-0065.*
Family dining, bottle shop, budget pub food and moderate dinner menus.

Charlie's Coffee Shop   **$**   ★★

Stafford Mall. ☎ *(03) 688- 3955.*
A good place to stop for lunch on the road. Full menus or take-aways. Bargain daily specials. *Open 8:30 a.m.–5 p.m. Mon.–Thurs.; 9:30 a.m.–2 p.m. Sat., closed Sun.*

Mount Cook

Mount Cook National Park contains more than 20 peaks over 10,000 feet, including Mount Cook, the tallest mountain in Australasia.

If you're on the eastern side of the Southern Alps, it seems almost criminal not to go to Mount Cook, which has probably the most famous hotel in New Zealand (the Hermitage), and arguably one of the best views of the mountains on the whole South Island. As the crow flies, it's less than 10 miles from Mount Cook to Franz Josef, but the crow has to fly over 10,000-foot mountains and the glaciers. Mount Cook Village is the base of **Mount Cook National Park**, probably the most spectacular national park in the country, and one that rivals most scenery you'll see in the European Alps. The park, 270 square miles, contains more than 20 peaks over 10,000 feet, including, of course, Mount Cook, the tallest mountain in Australasia. The Maoris called it *Aorangi*—the Cloud Piercer. It also contains the world's longest temperate-zone glacier, the **Tasman**. The view from the village is such that Mount Cook is just one of a bunch of tall, snow-clad peaks, meaning the whole vista is spectacular.

Essentials

Getting There

There is daily air service to the Mount Cook airport, about five kilometers from the village, on Mount Cook Airlines. From Wellington, about a two-hour flight, the one-way fare is about $NZ390; from Rotorua, about $NZ500; from Auckland, about $NZ530. South Island fares are Queenstown, about $NZ200; Christchurch, about $NZ220; and from Nelson, about $NZ345. There is no direct air service between Fox Glacier, Franz Josef and Mount Cook, but charter flights can be booked. Bus service is available from the airport to the village. Note that the weather, particularly in the winter and shoulder seasons, can sock in the Mount Cook Airport, in which case, passengers are bused to Lake Tekapo.

Daily bus service is provided by both InterCity and Mount Cook Lines from Christchurch. The trip, about five hours on InterCity, costs about $NZ60 one way. There is daily Mount Cook Lines service to Queenstown for about $NZ55 and from Timaru for about NZ$45. When last we checked, there were no banking facilities at Mount Cook.

If you're driving from the south of the island, you turn at Oamaru onto Highway 8 and head west; coming down from Christchurch, either take Highway 79 from Geraldine to Fairlie then past Lake Tekapo. (Highway 8) or go south to Timaru and take Highway 8 from there. Whatever the route, stay on Highway 8 until you get to Twizel, then go about 55 kilometers north on Highway 80 along Lake Pukaki, formed by the Tasman River, itself formed by melt waters from the glaciers. The views of the mountains, especially Mount Cook, are splendid—provided the weather is decent. There are several vista spots to pull off along Highway 80.

If things are booked solid at the Hermitage and other park hostelries, you can probably find a room either at Lake Tekapo, about 100 kilometers from the park entrance, or at Twizel.

Lake Tekapo

The lake is gorgeous, and one of the best views on the South Island is standing next to the Church of the Good Shepherd and looking out across the lake at the Alps. If you don't have a camera, you'll kick yourself for a week. The church was dedicated in 1935 by the Duke of Gloucester and honors the pioneers of the area—called Mackenzie Country. Here we are confused. The area was apparently named after James McKenzie, he of sheep-stealing fame, but we can't find consistent spellings of that name used anywhere. Anyway, crime might not pay, but it does make you famous. Glacial melt waters turn the lake a lovely turquoise.

Among the places to stay:

Lake Tekapo Alpine Inn   **$NZ95–135**   ★ ★ ★

On the lake. *(03) 680-6848; FAX (03) 680-6873.*
Ground zero for beds and eats. It has four restaurants (Japanese to "Alpine") and a range of rooms from superior lakeview units to family rooms. Room and food packages available as well as multi-day packages. Pool, mountain bikes, fishing.

Chalet, The   **$NZ120**   ★ ★ ★

14 Pioneer Drive. ☎ *(03) 680-6774; FAX the same.*
Close to the Church of the Good Shepherd, very Alpinic in style and decor. Rooms are in separate units with kitchens and laundry. Great views, very quiet.

Lillybank Lodge   **$NZ1120**   ★ ★ ★ ★ ★

At the head of the lake. ☎ *(03) 680-6522; FAX (03) 680-6838.*
The most upscale digs in the area, sitting in a splendid location with great views of lake and mountains, all part of a large deer farm. The lodge, done in natural stone and timbers, has five suites with a king bed and three suites with two queen beds. There is a formal dining room; three meals are included in the tariff. The trophy room with dramatic views is all wood and leather. This is one of the finest lodges in the country.

For information about the Lake Tekapo area, stop in at the **Café Cassinia**, which serves good food and also serves as the town information center. ☎ *(03) 680-6861.*

Twizel

Just a hop and a skip from Mount Cook (about 35 miles), Twizel has several motels and cafés. The town airport serves as a backup in case the strip at Mount Cook gets weathered in—not an uncommon occurrence. There is a nearby rookery for black stilts, one of the world's most endangered birds, and the town is used as a base for heli-skiing. Information on Twizel is available from the visitors center on Wairepo Road ☎ *(03) 435-0802, FAX 435-0852.* Among the motels are **Mountain Chalets**, with cottage units from $NZ75 double ☎ *(03) 435-0785, FAX 435-0551;* the **Colonial Motel,** kitchen units from $NZ85 ☎ *(03) 435-0100, FAX 435-0499;* and the **High Country Holiday Lodge**, with a range of units from backpackers to motel-types, priced from $NZ15-70 ☎ *(03) 435-0671.* For food, try either the **Mackenzie Country Inn** or the **Hunter's Bar & Cafe**.

Mount Cook Village

In addition to the Hermitage and other accommodations choices, the Mount Cook village area also has a pub/bottle shop, grocery store and a gas station. By U.S. national park standards, it's pretty small potatoes, which makes it very nice, thank you. Information about the park is available at the

Mount Cook National Park Visitor Centre right next to the Hermitage. *It's open 8 a.m.–5 p.m. daily*, and for $NZ2, there's a 20-minute video on the park. During the summer, there are organized tours, illustrated talks and films. ☎ *(03) 435-1818; FAX (03) 435-1895.*

Activities

If you're a couch potato, just sit and stare at the mountains (provided, of course, the ever-changeable weather permits). For the more active:

Hiking

The activities desk at the Hermitage has daily guided walks, ranging from one to five hours; the one-hour treks are $NZ12 per person; five hours runs $NZ50 per person. If you want to go on your own, get maps and info at the park headquarters. There are several easy hikes, a few more strenuous. Suggestions:

Governor's Bush

The best easy trek which goes through a small beech forest. It's an hour-and-a-half trail that starts south of the park headquarters.

Kea Point

This three-hour walk starts at the Hermitage, and crosses a series of gravel deposits before heading up into a beech forest. It's a good trail to study many species of Mount Cook–area plants.

Hooker Valley

A bit more strenuous but good because it takes you up the Hooker River to the face of the Hooker Glacier, all the way to the beginning of the very tough Copland Pass track. It branches off from the Kea Point trail. At the Copland Pass trailhead, look for bunches of sassy keas in the area, and watch out for the famous Mount Cook lilies, in reality mountain buttercups. The petals are pure white. Allow about six–seven hours to go all the way to the Copland Pass trailhead and back.

For serious hikers, *Alpine Recreation Canterbury Ltd.*, based in Lake Tekapo, offers a three-day excursion across the mountains from Mount Cook village to Highway 6 on the Fox Glacier side.

The trek is done on the **Copland Track**, and it's not for amateurs. The best way is to take a guided trip over, which will require some fairly strenuous climbing and at least basic knowledge of ice work. The track connects the Hooker and Tasman valleys in the heart of the park. The company owns its own hut, and the route, while strenuous, is not technically difficult—the company says fit folks in their 60s and 70s have made it. The trip starts either at the Lake Tekapo bus stop or the visitors center at Mount Cook village. The trip, including the hut, all food, guides and equipment (such as boots if you wish), is about $NZ700 per person for the full three days. *Information: Alpine Recreation Canterbury Ltd., P.O. Box 75, Lake Tekapo;* ☎ *(03) 680-6736, FAX (03) 680-6765.*

In the village, **Alpine Guides** has a rental office, as well as guide services. The company offers everything from simple hikes to full-scale climbing expeditions to the top of Mount Cook itself. Some of these obviously require advanced mountaineering skills. The company also operates climbing schools. They aren't cheap, however. A guide for the day

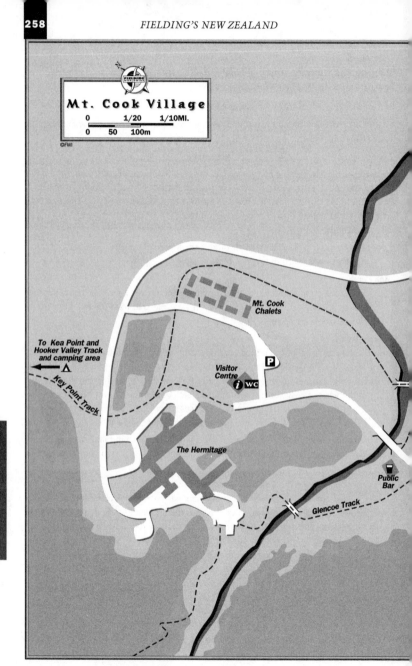

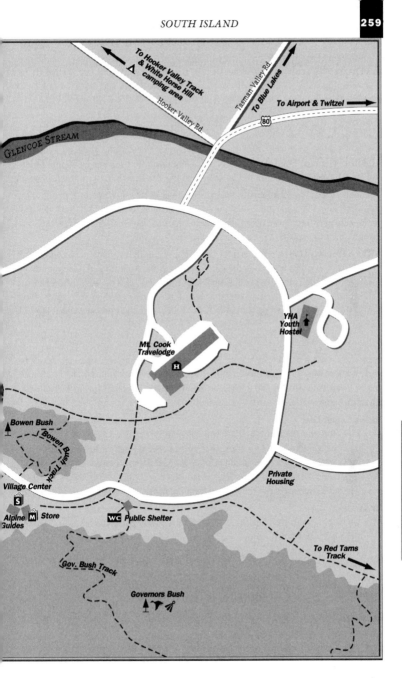

To Hooker Valley Track
& White Horse Hill
camping area

Hooker Valley Rd.

Tasman Valley Rd.

To Blue Lakes

To Airport & Twitzel ➡

80

GLENCOE STREAM

YHA
Youth
Hostel

Mt. Cook
Travelodge

H

Bowen Bush

Bowen Bush Track

Village Center

S

Alpine
Guides

M Store

WC Public Shelter

Private
Housing

To Red Tarns
Track

Gov. Bush Track

Governors Bush

runs about NZ$250; the climbing schools up to NZ$2000 per person and serious expeditions begin at about NZ$2500. Mount Cook, by the way, was first climbed on Christmas Day 1894. For about $NZ30 per person, the company offers an interpretive glacier tour, which includes a van ride with stops to look at local flora and fauna and a hike to the face of the Tasman Glacier.

Skiing

One of the more popular skiing trips in the South Island, for intermediates or experts, is to hop a ski-plane or helicopter and fly from Mount Cook to the Tasman Glacier and ski down. The trips from Mount Cook are a combination of services by **Alpine Guides and Mount Cook Line**. You should be at least an intermediate skier to try the Tasman.

The trip down the 27-kilometer-long glacier involves two ski runs, three flights and a gourmet lunch. Including guide fees, the cost per person is about $NZ550–600, depending on season (winter more expensive.) These trips can also commence in Queenstown. Ski equipment is available for rental in the Mount Cook village.

The Helicopter Line runs flights from Glentanner Park, about 15 miles south of Mount Cook Village. It offers essentially the same services as the Mount Cook Line, but drops skiers off in the Ben Ohau Range and the Neumann Range plus the Richardson Glacier. Three runs, four helicopter flights and a total vertical drop of 9800 feet. Price about $NZ500. *Helicopter Line:* ☎ *(03) 435-1890; FAX the same; or in Glentanner,* ☎ *(03) 435-1855.*

Flight-seeing

As we said when we were on the other side of the mountains, coming to the South Island and not doing a flight around, through and into the Alps is unforgivable. It doesn't matter much which side you do it from, because there are air services aplenty basically taking in the same territory.

The Helicopter Line

As noted, the company operates from Glentanner Park, and has trips that circumnavigate Mount Cook, look at the western and eastern glacier fields, do a snow landing and get you back in 45 minutes for about $NZ210 per person. A quick flight up to a landing on Richardson Glacier and down (30 minutes) is about $NZ140. There's a courtesy coach to take you from the Mount Cook village to Glentanner.

Air Safaris

Booked through the Helicopter Line, this fixed wing company flies in and around the Alps from Glentanner or Lake Tekapo for about $NZ110 an hour per person; a combination trip with a helicopter landing is about $NZ210. Mount Cook Line offers essentially the same services, including ski plane landings on the glaciers. An hour flight with landings will run about $NZ290.

Where to Stay

Hermitage, The   **$NZ170–280**   ★ ★ ★

☎ *(03) 435-1809; FAX (03) 435-1879.*
The third hotel of its name. The original was washed away in a flood in 1913; the second burned down in 1957. The new one, all picture windows and stone, is the

premier place to stay, but reservations long in advance are usually necessary in the summer. In early spring, late fall or winter, the weather is occasionally so lousy, about the only people who show up are bus tours and lost travelers, and getting a room is not hard. The multilevel hotel was formerly owned by the New Zealand government, but is now a member of the Southern Pacific Hotels group. There is a coffee shop, usually open all week from 9 a.m.–5 p.m. The **Panorama Room** ★ ★ ★ has great views of the mountains and is *open Oct.–May, 6 p.m.–9:30 p.m.* It specializes in alpine game and seafood from the South Island: things like chamois, hare, venison stews, mussel chowders, cod patties. It's expensive. The **Alpine Room** ★ ★ ★, the second restaurant, is *open all year, breakfast 6:30–9:30 a.m.; lunch 11:30 a.m.–2 p.m., and dinner 6–9:30 p.m.* It has a similar menu, with an emphasis on seafood, lamb and roast beef; very eclectic and generally quite good. It's moderate to expensive. There is also a licensed café/coffee shop for lighter budget snacks and meals. *In the summer, it's open seven days from 9 a.m.–6 p.m.; in the winter, from 10 a.m.–4:30 p.m.* Good soups, sandwiches, nothing great but good, filling portions. There is a large lobby bar with prime views the **Snowline Lounge**, *open in the summer from 11 a.m. until late; winter 4:30 p.m. until late.*

All rooms have baths and phones. The best rooms in the hotel are in the 800 Wing, all of which have balconies facing Mount Cook. The higher up the better, so try to get into a room between 830 and 839. The 800 Wing also has a laundromat and a small but usable hot tub and sauna. The deluxe rooms in the 800 Wing go for about $NZ280 double, and are very nice: hair dryers, great views, minibars, great beds. In the off-season, the rooms are about half the summer rate. We stayed once in the off-season and a deluxe was going for about $NZ170. Always ask.

Mount Cook Travelodge $NZ185   ★ ★
☎ *(03) 435-1809; FAX (03) 435-1879.*
A step down from the Hermitage, the Travelodge is a motel-style facility with about 60 rooms, located about a kilometer from the Hermitage. It's also a Southern Pacific hotel. Open only in the summer. B&B, tea/coffee, reservations also essential. The **Wakefield Restaurant** ★ ★ has budget to moderate buffet-style meals for lunch and dinner, with an emphasis again on seafood and lamb. There is also the **Chamois Bar**. *Open for breakfast 6:30–9:30 a.m.; lunch 11:30 a.m.–2 p.m; dinner 6–9:30 p.m.*

Mount Cook Chalets $NZ110   ★
☎ *(03) 435-1809; FAX (03) 435-1879.*
Also a Hermitage property. Basic cabin units down the hill from the Hermitage. Hot plates, fry pans, showers, fireplaces. Units are basic but not bad, and go for about $NZ100. Book through the Hermitage. Note: Guests staying at the chalets and the Travelodge are allowed to use Hermitage facilities.

YHA Mount Cook Youth Hostel $NZ18
☎ *(03) 435-1820.*
Corner of Bowen and Kitchener Drive. Pool table, food shop, central heating, sauna, shop, barbecue, handicapped facilities. Advance bookings needed in the summer. $NZ18 per person.

Heading North

Glentanner Park   **$NZ28–60**

☎ *(03) 435-1855; FAX (03) 435-1854.*

Outside the park, about 23 kilometers south of Mount Cook on the northwest shore of Lake Pukaki. Kitchen, laundry, camp store, café, tour desk, helipad, barbecue area. RV spots, tent sites. Tourist cabins are $NZ60 double; powered RV sites are $NZ8 per person, rudimentary cabins from $NZ30.

Top of the South

Te Pukatea Bay at Abel Tasman National Park offers campsites away from the crush of tourists around the huts.

Many visitors coming south miss much of the northern area of the South Island, opting usually to head for Christchurch or taking the Westport Highway toward the West Coast and the glaciers. *Area residents think Nelson, west of the Picton ferry dock, might be one of New Zealand's better-kept secrets* The sunsets around the area are justifiably famous, and Nelson has, on the average, more sunny days than any other part of the country. Nearby are the lovely fjords of the **Marlborough Sounds** country, which Captain James Cook used as his primary base during his explorations of New Zealand and the Antarctica region. Much of the area is now a **national maritime park**. The fjords are not technically fjords, but ocean-drowned river valleys. The Marl-

263

borough area between Picton and Christchurch is *the nation's third-largest wine-producing area,* home to the always good Montana line of wines and other vineyards scattered around Blenheim. In addition to huge catches of seafood and fish, the northern end of the island is also known for the production of fruits of various sorts.

Marlborough Sounds

The Sounds are a boater's and fisher's paradise with thousands of hidden and protected coves, miles of hiking trails, campgrounds and even some roads. But many of the special places are available only by boat, float plane or long hikes. Passengers on the **Interislander** ferries see only a piece of the whole picture, although **Queen Charlotte Sound**, used by the ferries, is one of the most beautiful of all the routes through the Sounds. One of the most gorgeous drives in the north part of the island runs between Nelson and Picton, the last stretch along the shores of Queen Charlotte Sound—a trip to die for. There are a number of adventure and recreational companies located in Picton or Havelock, the tiny settlement 10 miles west of Picton, that do various trips around the Sounds.

Included are **Charter Link** in Picton, with boats sailing all over the Sounds for about $NZ180 per day per vessel; ☎ *(03) 573-6591.* Or **Marlborough Sounds Charters** in Picton, with a variety of craft starting about $NZ100 a day; ☎ *(03) 573-7726.* Or **Portage Bay Charters** in Picton, with prices starting around $NZ90; ☎ *(03) 573-4445.* In addition, there are water taxis and a mail boat that you can hop aboard.

There are some fairly nice lodges stuck in remote areas, but the most famous place is probably **The Portage★★★**, on Kenepuru Sound across Queen Charlotte Sound and a peninsula from Picton. It can be reached by twisty dirt road, float plane or boat. It has a variety of watersports equipment available; a good bet for families and backpackers. It has a moderately priced restaurant, bar, pool, spa, gym and bunkrooms (no kitchen). Doubles are around $NZ90–100; four-person bunkrooms, about $NZ25 per person. ☎ *(03) 573-4309; FAX the same.*

Another good choice is the **Punga Cove Tourist Resort ★★★** on Endeavor Inlet, north of Queen Charlotte, also accessible by road (long drive), float plane or boat. It's a good spot located not far from Ship Cove, where Cook anchored and where there is a memorial to the famous captain. There are 10 self-contained chalets set in a bush environment with licensed restaurant, pool, sauna, shop, barbecue area, beach, fishing access and glowworms. The restaurant is open for lunch and dinner; continental breakfast baskets delivered to your room. Doubles are around $NZ100. ☎ *(03) 579-8561; FAX (03) 579-8080.*

The mail boat and water tours of the Picton area are available through **Beachcomber Cruises**, *8 London Quay in Picton*; a variety of cruises are offered in the $NZ40 range for two-hour jaunts. ☎ *(03) 573-6175; FAX (03) 573-6176.*

Information about other services, including dive shops, scooter rentals, air transport and tours, is available at the **Picton Visitor Information Centre** on the area of the bay called The Foreshore. ☎ *(03) 573-7477; FAX (03) 573-8362.* The **Department of Conservation** office is on the Foreshore, ☎ *(03) 573-7582; FAX (03) 573-8362.* **The Automobile Association** is reachable at ☎ *(03) 5736784.* **The Interisland Ferry Terminal** number is ☎ *(03) 573-8649.*

Ratimera Bay at Marlborough Sounds is a boating and fisherman's paradise.

Of interest on the harbor is the ancient hulk of the **Edwin Fox**, the oldest wooden merchant ship still afloat. It has a long and eventful history: Built in 1853, it's the last survivor of the Crimean War, the last surviving vessel that carried convicts to Australia, and the last surviving wooden sailing ship that brought settlers to New Zealand. Major efforts are under way to refurbish the old tub to its former glory. The ship and an adjacent visitors center are open seven days; $NZ4 for adults. ☎ *(03) 573-6868; FAX (03) 573-8414.* And on the Foreshore is a fishing and whaling museum worth a stop. It's open daily; $NZ3 for adults.

Where to Stay

For those wanting to haul in at **Picton**, especially if you're coming over on a late ferry, there are a number of reasonably priced motels, all in the two- to three-star range. Most have courtesy coaches, and most can be booked from Wellington or actually aboard one of the Interislander ferries.

Top of the South

Americano Motor Inn, The   **$NZ70–90**   ★★★

32 High Street, middle of the shopping area, near London Quay. ☎ *(03) 573-6398; FAX (03) 573-7892.*

Our favorite, probably because of the name. Kitchens, laundry, spa, bike and canoe rental, courtesy van. The motel **restaurant** serves all meals seven days a week; family style or candlelight, budget to moderate prices. Nice view of the harbor. Seafood, venison and Maori-style cooking.

Ancient Mariner   **$NZ95–160**   ★★★

Waikawa Road. ☎ *(03) 573-7002; FAX (03) 573-7727.*

Overlooks the sound. Spa, great pool, sauna, gym. Courtesy limo, handicapped facilities, the moderately priced **Edwin Fox Restaurant** ★★, laundry, barbecue, minibars.

Bellbird Motel   **$NZ60**   ★★

96 Waikawa Road. ☎ *(03) 573-6912; FAX the same.*

Fully contained units, laundry, courtesy van.

Best Western Koromiko Park Motel   **$NZ80**   ★★

Six kilometers south of town. ☎ *(03) 573-7350; FAX (03) 573-7988.*

Next to Picton Golf Course, kitchens, pool, spa, laundry, breakfast available, courtesy van.

Marineland Guest House   **$NZ70–95**   ★★★

26 Waikawa Road. ☎ *(03) 573-6429; FAX (03) 573-7634.*

Two-story home set in a garden. Pool, kitchen facilities, barbecue, some rooms with private baths, laundry. B&B doubles about $NZ80; motel-style units, NZ$70–95.

Admiral's Lodge   **$NZ80**   ★★

22 Waikawa Road. ☎ *(03) 573-6590; FAX (03) 573-8318.*

B&B with some motel-style units. Close to bus and train station. Fully cooked breakfast served in rooms. Courtesy pickup. Laundry, barbecue.

Tourist Court Motel   **$NZ55–70**   ★★

45 High Street. ☎ *(03) 573-6331; FAX the same.*

One- and two-bedroom units. Kitchens, laundry, tea/coffee, courtesy van.

Terminus Hotel   **$NZ60**   ★★

Corner London Quay and High Street. ☎ *(03) 573-6452; FAX (03) 573-6453.*

A Pub Beds facility. Overlooks the waterfront. Restaurant and three bars, tea/coffee, bottle shop, and entertainment some nights.

Gables B&B   **$NZ75–95**   ★★

20 Waikawa Road. ☎ *(03) 573-6772; FAX 573-8860.*

Housed in a 1920s-era house; three upstairs rooms with private baths. Big breakfasts; transport to and from the ferry. Laundry.

Wedgewood House   **$NZ15–20**   ★

10 Dublin Street, city center. ☎ *(03) 573-7797.*

YHA associate. Older-style guest house. Kitchens, laundry, some units with private baths. $NZ15; nonmembers, $NZ20.

Villa Backpackers   **$NZ18**   ★

34 Auckland Street. ☎ *(03) 573-6598; FAX the same.*

B&B. Log fires, spa, laundry, kitchens.

Blue Anchor Holiday Park   **$NZ30–70**   ★

78 Waikawa Road. ☎ *(03) 573-7212; FAX the same.*

Top 10 RV park. Laundry, pool, community kitchens. Motel unit doubles about
NZ$70; tourist flats NZ$55 double; cabins $NZ30 double.

Where to Eat

Marlborough Terranean   **$$$**   ★ ★ ★

31 High Street. ☎ *(03) 573-7122*

Probably the best restaurant in Picton; unfortunately, only open in the summer. Art
Deco interior, specializes in seafood, very creative dishes. Consistent high rating,
and excellent wine list. *Dinner from 6 p.m. Tues.–Sat.*

Fifth Bank   **$$$**   ★ ★ ★

33 Wellington Street. ☎ *(03) 573-6102.*

The name comes from the fifth BNZ bank opened in the country. Lace, linens, fireplace. Seafood, shellfish, steaks. *Open for dinner only.*

Ship Cove   **$$**   ★ ★

33 High Street. ☎ *(03) 573-7304.*

Specializes in seafood, steak and Marlborough wines. *Open at 5:30 p.m. seven days
for dinner.*

Toot-n-Whistle   **$**   ★

7 Auckland Street. ☎ *(03) 573-6086.*

Located in the restored train station. It's a bar and café for light meals, snacks and
take-aways. Outside deck dining. Open seven days lunch and dinner.

Nelson

Nelson, the city of sunsets, is the gateway to two fine preserves, **Northwest
Nelson Forest Park** and **Mount Richmond Forest Park**, as well as the very popu-
lar **Abel Tasman National Park**. Not far to the south is **Nelson Lakes National
Park**, an alpine area with hiking and many glacial lakes. It's a popular moun-
taineering area. In the Nelson Lakes area, check out the **Alpine Lodge ★ ★** at
St. Arnaud. It has a bar/restaurant, chalets, family and budget accommoda-
tions, pool and spa. Double budget chalets $NZ14–20 per person; family
units about $NZ115 double. ☎ *(03) 521-1869; FAX (03) 521-1868.* Or the
Top House ★ ★, an 1880s adobe hotel, with daily teas and meals. Dinner, bed
and breakfast is about $NZ100 double; shared facilities. ☎ *(03) 521-1848.*

The city dates its history back to the early 1840s and was a center for Ger-
man immigration to New Zealand. A local boy who made good was Nobel
laureate Ernest Rutherford, the noted atomic scientist. It's a popular sum-
mer vacation spot and has many gardens, art galleries and carnivals. The
beaches are crowded, and there are many outdoor activities available, includ-
ing watersports, caving, hiking and fishing. The centerpiece of the city is

Christ Church Cathedral, started in 1925 and finished in 1967, and is now officially called Nelson Cathedral on the Hill. Around town are a few stately old homes, including **Isel House** (1850), **Broadgreen House** (1855) and **Fellworth** (1880). For museum buffs, an excellent stop is the **Nelson Provincial Museum** in Isel Park of Hilliard Street. It houses one of the largest collections of historic photographs in the country, as well as a fine collection of Maori artifacts. *Hours are 10 a.m.–4 p.m. Tuesday–Friday, 2–5 p.m. Saturday and weekends.* Admission fee is $NZ2 for adults. ☎ *(03) 547-9740.*

Nelson is known as the city of sunsets and sailboats.

In addition to tourism, the area is dependent on fruits, fishing and forestry—and, with **Blenheim**, is becoming an important wine growing area. It is also known as an **artists' colony**. Information is available from the **Nelson Visitor Information Centre**, corner of Trafalgar and Halifax streets, ☎ *(03) 548-2304; FAX (03) 546-9008*. Information on the parks, including Marlborough Sounds, is available from the **Department of Conservation** office, *186 Bridge Street;* ☎ *(03) 546-9335*. The **AA** office is at *45 Halifax Street,* ☎ *(03) 548-8339*.

Nelson has regular air service to most of the major cities on both islands, using either Ansett or Air Nelson. One-way fares from Auckland are about $NZ250; from Wellington, $NZ130; from Christchurch, $NZ170; from Queenstown, $NZ405.

Regular train/bus service is also available from Christchurch (one-way fare about $NZ65), and there is also bus service to Dunedin and Invercargill to the south and Greymouth to the west. The bus terminal is behind the visitors information center.

Where to Stay

Quality Hotel Rutherford $NZ130–160   ★★★
Trafalgar Square. ☎ *(03) 548-2299; FAX (03) 546-3003.*
Rooms and suites, pool, spa, sauna, gym, three restaurants and bar, tea/coffee. Double/single rooms about $NZ130, suites $NZ160.

California House $NZ125–150   ★★★
29 Collingwood Street. ☎ *(03) 548-4173; FAX the same.*
Housed in a late 19th-century villa a five-minute walk from the city center. No-smoking facility, very good B&B cooked brekkie, tea/coffee, courtesy van.

Beachcomber Motor Inn $NZ100–145   ★★
23 Beach Road, Tahunanui, 4 kilometers from the city center, near the beach. ☎ *(03) 548-5985; FAX (03) 547-6371.*
Some kitchens, laundry, pool, tea/coffee, spa, restaurant and bar, courtesy coach.

Courtesy Court Hotel $NZ65–90   ★★
26-30 Golf Road, Tahunanui, near the beach. ☎ *(03) 548-5114; FAX the same.*
Best Western, kitchens, laundry, pool, spa, breakfast available.

AA Motor Lodge $NZ95   ★★
8 Ajax Street, on the banks of the Maitai River. ☎ *(03) 548-8214; FAX (03) 548-8219.*
Smoke-free, kitchens, honeymoon suite, laundry, breakfast available.

Wakatu Hotel $NZ70   ★★
Corner Bridge and Collingwood streets. ☎ *(03) 548-4299; FAX (03) 548-1419.*
Member of the Pub Beds group. Colonial hotel, with Cobb & Co. restaurant, bar.

Nelson YHA Hostel $NZ17
59 Rutherford St. ☎ *(03) 548-9988; fax 545-9989.*
A new facility downtown. Two kitchens, two dining rooms, laundry, handicapped facilities. $NZ17 for adults, $NZ9-12 for kids.

Tahuna Beach Holiday Park　　　　**$NZ18–80**

70 Beach Road, Tahunanui. ☎ *(03) 548-5159; FAX (03) 548-5294.*

Said to be the largest RV park in Australasia, capable of handling almost 5000 tourists a day. In addition to tent sites and RV pads, it has six kitchens, laundry, store, car wash, mini-golf and handicapped facilities. Motel units are about $NZ80 double; tourist flats $NZ50 double; cabins $NZ30–40 double; powered sites $NZ18 double.

Where to Eat

Junipers　　　　**$$$**　　　　★★★

144 Collingwood Street. ☎ *(03) 548-8832.*

Award winner. Fine dining in a century-old house, excellent service. Specialties include smoked snapper chowder, quail and venison, eels. Gooey and tasty desserts. *Dinner Tues.–Sat. from 6:30 p.m.*

Appleman's　　　　**$$$**　　　　★★★

38 Bridge Street. ☎ *(03) 546-8105.*

Pacific Rim/Continental with Kiwi overtones; chicken with spiced pickles, lamb goodies, and, especially, excellent seafood concoctions. *Dinner from 6 p.m. nightly.*

Ribbett's　　　　**$$$**　　　　★★★

20 Tahunani Drive. ☎ *(03) 548-6911.*

Rated as the best seafood restaurant in the area. Indoor or garden dining. Kiwi seafood with an eclectic flair (fish in tequila?). Good scampi and scallops, local venison dishes. BYO. *Dinner from 6 p.m, in the summer.*

Broccoli Row　　　　**$$–$$$**　　　　★★★

5 Buxton Square. ☎ *(03) 548-9621.*

Super vegetarian and seafood establishment, one of the best on the South Island if you like your veggies tasty and well-presented. It's BYO and *open for lunch and dinner Mon.–Sat.*

Ciao　　　　**$$–$$$**　　　　★★★

94 Collingwood Street. ☎ *(03) 548-9874.*

Hefty and very well prepared Italian fare, with interesting sauces and nice surroundings. The focaccia is quite good, as are some of the vegetable offerings. Veal is a specialty. It's BYO and *open for dinner Mon.–Sat.*

La Bonne Vie　　　　**$$**　　　　★★★

75 Bridge Street. ☎ *(03) 548-0270.*

One of the city's oldest buildings. Summer dining area, specializes in seafood; also great pâtés. BYO and licensed. Blackboard menu for deserts. *Lunch 11:30 a.m.–2 p.m. Mon.–Fri.; dinner, from 6 p.m. seven days.*

Boatshed Café　　　　**$$**　　　　★★★

350 Wakefield Quay. ☎ *(03) 546-9783.*

Good waterfront café, specializing in seafood. Good Kiwi wine list. Scallops always good. Probably the best fresh bread in town. Reservations needed because the café is small. A local favorite, always crowded. *Dinner from 6 p.m. nightly.*

Cobb & Co. Family Restaurant　　　　**$–$$**　　　　★

In the Wakatu Hotel, corner of Bridge and Collingwood streets. ☎ *(03) 548-4299.*

Usual family menus, senior discounts, specials. *Open 7:30 a.m.–10 p.m., seven days.*

Blenheim

The largest community in the Marlborough area, Blenheim is the capital of the South Island's growing wine industry. The industry began in the area in 1973 when Montana planted its first vines and is starting to rival the more famous wine areas on the North Island. (See "Wine Producing Regions" in "The Essential New Zealand" for specifics.) And as the wines become better known and more popular, the quality of inns and restaurants in the area is bound to get better. Besides, how can you go wrong—they grow a lot of garlic around here and harvest a lot of mussels—and that's most of the major food groups right in one spot.

You can reach Blenheim on the Coastal Pacific about a half-hour ride from Picton, or by bus. Information about the city and wine tours is available from the **Blenheim Information Centre**, *Forum Building on Queen Street; open 8:30 a.m.–6 p.m. seven days;* ☎ *(03) 578-9904, FAX (03) 578-6084.* The **Automobile Association** office is at *23 Maxwell Road;* ☎ *03) 578-3399.*

Where to Stay

Marlborough, The   **$NZ170–250**   ★★★★
20 Nelson Street. ☎ *(03) 577-7333; FAX (03) 577-7337.*
Probably the best place to stay in the Marlborough wine area. A smallish luxury hotel with restaurant and bar, close to golf, fishing, tennis and the local wineries. The restaurant, simply called the **Dining Room** ★★★★, is one of the best in the area, concentrating on fresh produce and seafood; menu changes daily. Expensive. The decor throughout the Marlborough is airy, all woods and wrought iron with contemporary art. Rooms come with large beds and minibars, and some suites have spa baths. The hotel offers a number of room packages that include excursions around the north end of the island, including sea kayaking, white-water rafting, a hike on the Queen Charlotte Walkway, plus wine tours and golf packages. Standard rooms are about $NZ170 double; suites are $NZ190–250.

Timara Lodge   **$NZ800**   ★★★★★
Dog Point Road, Renwick (west of town). ☎ *(03) 572-8276; FAX (03) 572-9191.*
Lovely estate, limited to eight guests at a time. The building sits next to a man-made lake in the heart of the wine country. There are extensive gardens, a pool and tennis courts. The tariff includes all meals. There are two twin-bed rooms and two double bedrooms, all with private bath.

Blenheim Country Lodge   **$NZ90–150**   ★★★
Seymour Square, corner of Alfred and Henry streets. ☎ *(03) 578-5079; FAX (03) 578-0337.*
Pool, minibars, restaurant and bar, tea/coffee, laundry. courtesy van. The restaurant, called **Seymour's** ★★★, is one of the better in the area, with entertainment

on Fri. and Sat. nights and a very nice Sun. smorgasbord; *it 's open noon–2 p.m. lunch, dinner from 6:30 p.m., seven days.* Moderate.

Bing's Motel $NZ70   ★★

Corner Maxwell Road and Seymour Street. ☎ *(03) 578-6199; FAX (03) 578-6159.*
Three acres of grounds, tennis courts, spas, pool, indoor bowling, kitchens, laundry, Chinese restaurant, handicapped facilities. Doubles about $NZ70.

Aorangi Lodge Motel $NZ75–95   ★★

193 High Street. ☎ *(03) 578-2022.*
One- and two-bedroom units, kitchens, laundry, pool, BBQ, handicapped facilities, courtesy van, breakfast available. Doubles about $NZ75–95.

Grove Bridge Family Holiday (RV) Park $NZ18–65

78 Grove Street, north end of town. ☎ *(03) 578-3667.*
On the way to Picton (Highway 1), next to a tavern/restaurant and store. Communal kitchens, pool, laundry, RV facilities. Tourist flats about $NZ50–65 double; cabins about $NZ40 double. Powered sites $NZ18.

Where to Eat

D'Urville $$ ★★★

52 Queen Street. ☎ *(03) 578-6940.*
Housed in an old civic building. Decor is modern and airy, and a great plus is a local wine list that features some hard to get but good wines. It's a brasserie, so the menu is pretty wide, but almost always good. The oxtail soup is wonderful. *Lunch noon– 2 p.m. Mon.–Fri.; dinner 6–10 p.m. seven days.*

Rocco's $$ ★★★

5 Dodson Street. ☎ *(03) 578-6940.*
Scampi, fresh fish, lamb, spit-cooking in the winter; Northern Italian fare. At least 85 Marlborough wines plus the requisite number of Italian offerings. *Lunch noon– 2 p.m. Wed.–Sat.; dinner from 5 p.m. Mon.–Sat.*

Hunter's Vintners $$–$$$ ★★★

Hunter's Vineyard, Rapaura Road. ☎ *(03) 572-8803.*
North of town off Highway 1. Try wine tasting, followed by one of the restaurant's excellent game meals, plus venison and lamb. Cheese board with local cheeses, good luncheon blackboard menu. *Afternoon teas 2:30-4:30 p.m. Lunch from noon seven days; dinner from 6 p.m. seven days.*

Abel Tasman Country

Heading northwest from Nelson, up along Tasman Bay, past Abel Tasman National Park and along Golden Bay, you'll see some of the finest country on the South Island. Highway 60, which runs inland from Nelson to Motueka and Takaka, passes caves, lush farmlands, coastal ranges and small communities.

The aerial view of Abel Tasman National Park is breathtaking.

The major draw in the area, in addition to the wine country near Nelson, is the national park. The hiking trails in the park are so scenic and so popular, they're giving their more famous relations in the Milford area a challenge. The two major trails are the Inland Track and the Coast Track.

The Inland Track is the roughest of the pair, passing through some fairly dense growth and up and over small ranges, with often spectacular views of the ocean to the east. There are three huts on the trek, which require either an annual pass or hut coupons; there is no guarantee you'll find room in a hut, even with permits. Rangers advise you carry a tent, and camping is in designated areas only. Huts do not have cooking facilities, but do have water. Allow 3-5 days to do a one-way hike.

The 51-kilometer Coast Track is one of the country's Great Walks, and is the most popular in the park as well as being the easiest. It's a combination of shady forests and wide-open beaches. It's normally done in 3-5 days, and there are five huts and 21 designated campgrounds. Note that special passes are required for any of the Great Walk trails in New Zealand; here, you'll need a $NZ6 Coast Track Hut and Camp Pass. The pass is available from DOC office, information centers, sporting goods stores and hostels.

Both trails start and end at the same spot, so many hikers do them both as a circle trip. Access from the south is at Marahau, about 70 kilometers north of Nelson. Or you can start at the north end of the trails by taking eastbound roads to Totaranui. It's not necessary to do the whole Coast Track because there are several spots along the way that have boat service.

Also, there are a number of short walks in the park. One of the easiest is the five-minute stroll from the Marahau information kiosk to the mouth of the

Marahau River; or try the 30-minute walk to Tinline Bay and follow the nature walk through a forest near the coast.

Note: Giardia has been found in park waters, so boil your drinking water. Giardia-free water supplies are available at the Totaranui campground, where there is also an information office, laundry facilities, cold showers and toilets. The Totaranui campground is so popular that applications to camp there between Dec. 20 and Jan. 31 are taken starting the previous July; contact the DOC office in Takaka for booking forms. There are a number of small hotels at Marahau, plus kayak rentals, boat services, RV parks and eateries.

Park information is available from the DOC office in Motueka, corner of King Edward and High Streets ☎ *(03) 528-9117* and from the DOC office at *1 Commercial Street, Takaka,* ☎ *(03) 525-8026.*

In addition to the campgrounds along the Coast Track, there are several small lodge-type facilities reached either by hoof or boat. One of the most popular is the **Awaroa Lodge and Cafe**, about two-thirds of the way north between Marahau and Totaranui. In addition to the lodge and cafe, there is a small landing strip and a swimming area. Just the place to get away from the office. Accommodation is either in shared quarters or doubles; doubles go for $NZ45–65; ☎ *(03) 528-8758.*

Boat service to the park is provided by a number of companies using large boats and water taxis. One of the best is the **Spirit of Golden Bay**, a high-speed catamaran that operates from Tarakohe Harbour northwest of the park (Golden Bay) to Nelson with stops all along the way. It leaves Golden Bay at 9 a.m. and arrives in Nelson at 12:30 p.m.; the return trip leaves Nelson at 1 p.m. and arrives back at Tarakohe Bay at 5:30 p.m. A one-way fare for the whole route is $NZ50 adult. The run from Nelson to the Awaroa Lodge is about 3.5 hours and costs $NZ35. Tickets and information on the boat are available from travel agencies in Nelson, Takaka or Motueka. Golden Bay Charters in Takaka: ☎ *fax and phone (03) 525-9135.*

Abel Tasman National Park Enterprises also runs several ferries along the coast. The company has bus service from Motueka and Nelson, connecting with launches at Kaiteriteri. The one-way boat fares are $NZ28 from Kaiteriteri to Totaranui (as far north as they go), or $NZ28 to the Awaroa Lodge. Information on all the company's services is available at the main office, Old Cedarman House, Main Road Riwaka, Motueka; ☎ *(03) 528-7801; FAX 528-6087.*

For bus service to the park, in addition to the National Park Enterprises vehicles, try buses operated by **Abel Tasman Express** ☎ *(03) 528-7014.* Buses run from the Nelson Information Centre to the information kiosk at the Motueka trailhead. The one-way fare to Motueka is about $NZ10 per person.

Top of the South

Motueka and Kaiteriteri

In addition to being a suburb of Nelson and the gateway to the national park, Motueka also serves as an agricultural center for the fertile river valleys in the area. The region grows green tea, hops, tobacco and kiwi fruit, plus vegetables. There are a couple of restaurants worthy of note. **The Gourmet ★★★**, *208 High Street*, started life as a joint project of the local Presbyterian and Methodist churches as a fund-raiser and is, in fact, housed in an old Methodist church. It has since been sold to private interests, but the food is still famous and the old church is a favorite restaurant for locals and in-the-know visitors. Great seafood; it's moderate to expensive. *Open for lunch an dinner from 11:30 a.m.-9:30 p.m. daily.* ☎ *(03) 528-6699.* The **Seafarers Restaurant ★★** is up the coast a hair at the port of Kaiteriteri, and is popular enough to require reservations. It's close to the beach and offers a very good menu specializing in seafood. Check for hours. ☎ *(03) 527-8114.*

In addition to the motels and lodges in Nelson and along the national park coast, there are also places in Motueka and at Marahau. A couple of suggestions are the **Kima Ora Health Resort** in Kaiteriteri and the **Abel Tasman Lodge** in Marahau. The health resort is an alcohol-free, smoke-free, health-conscious retreat with a vegetarian restaurant, and the expected range of athletic activities and spa treatments. Doubles are $NZ65-100 depending on season. ☎ *(03) 527-8027; FAX 527-8134.* The Abel Tasman Lodge is a short walk from the national park entrance, and has a restaurant/bar and laundry. Doubles are about $NZ100; off-season rates lower. ☎ *(03) 527-8250; FAX 527-8258.*

Golden Bay

Once in Motueka, unless you're going to the national park or continuing on up to Golden Bay, if you're heading west you should hang a left onto Highway 61 and head southwest to Highway 6. Heading north on Highway 60, there is no easy way to reach the main west coast cities; Highway 60 ends at Collingwood, northwest of the national park, but smaller roads continue all the way to **Farewell Spit**, a stretch of sand that forms the north edge of Golden Bay, and other roads cross over to the west coast. There is no great urge to make it easy to get to this part of the South Island—folks pretty much like it the way it is. And it is gorgeous.

The bay itself runs from the north edge of the national park to the Spit, and was first sighted by Abel Tasman in 1642; the Spit was named by Captain Cook in 1770. There are enough activities in the bay area to keep you busy for a week or more. One place not to miss is **Harwood's Lookout**, which is on a pass crossing over the hills outside Motueka—it has a splendid view of the bay.

Takaka is a one-street sort of town, but it is a noted center for artists, and of course serves as a fuel and food base for tourists. Just before reaching the city center, you'll come to a turnoff to the national park. The road hugs the

Top of the South

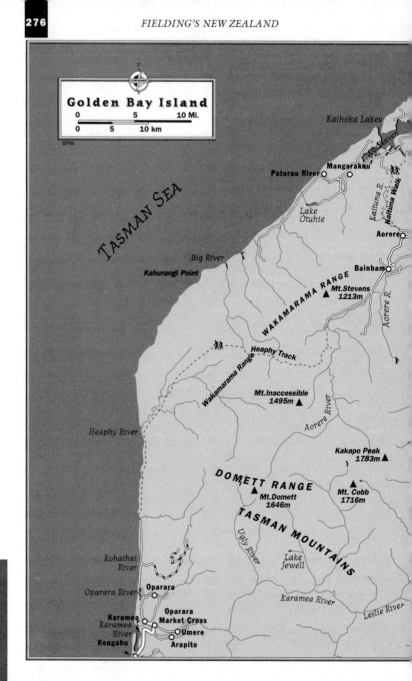

Golden Bay Island

0   5   10 Mi.

0   5   10 km

©FWI

Kaihoka Lakes

TASMAN SEA

Whakamarau

Paturau River

Mangarakau

Lake Otuhie

Kaituna R.

Kaituna Walk

Aorere

Big River

Kahurangi Point

Bainham

WAKAMARAMA RANGE

Mt. Stevens 1213m

Aorere R.

Heaphy Track

Wakamarama Range

Mt. Inaccessible 1495m

Aorere River

Heaphy River

Kakapo Peak 1783m

DOMETT RANGE

Mt. Cobb 1716m

Mt. Domett 1646m

TASMAN MOUNTAINS

Kohaihai River

Ugly River

Lake Jewell

Oparara River

Oparara

Karamea River

Leslie River

Karamea

Karamea River

Oparara Market Cross

Umere

Kongahu

Arapito

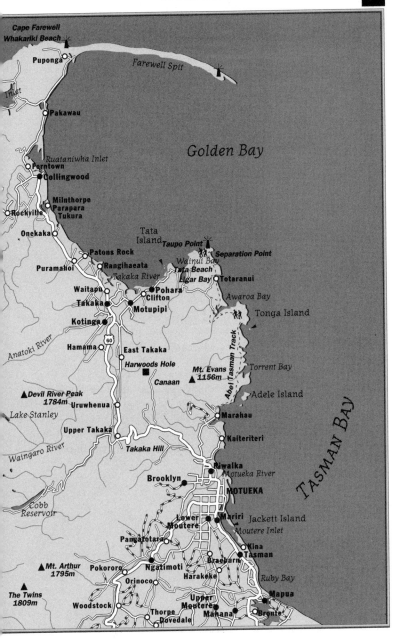

south shore of the bay and ends up at the campground at Totaranui. Along the way it passes **Pohara**, one of the most popular seaside resorts in the area. Just past Pohara is a monument to Abel Tasman, who had a really bad hair day here back in 1642—four of his crew were killed by Maori warriors and he never again set foot on New Zealand soil.

The Takaka visitors center is located on Commercial Street, as is a museum/gallery housed in the old post office—local arts and crafts displays, Maori historical items, old Golden Bay mementos. A bit north of town, look for a turnoff to the area's most famous attraction, the **Te Waikoropupu Springs** (aka the Pupu Springs), formed in the extensive limestone/marble formations in the area, which also has extensive cave systems. The springs are fed by local rivers seeping through the rocks. Not far away is the **Pupu Walkway**, which goes through beech forests and follows an aqueduct built during a gold rush at the turn of the century. It's quite a steep hike in places.

There are a few lodges and B&Bs between Takaka and Collingwood, including the **Tukurua Lodge**, situated about halfway between the towns on 10 acres next to the bay with a beach and rooms with private baths. Rooms are $NZ115; three-course dinners are $NZ30 per person including wine. ☎ *phone and FAX (03) 525-8644.*

In the settlement of Collingwood, you'll find a couple of companies that run treks up to Farewell Spit. The spit is 25 kilometers long, 800 meters wide, and is a bird sanctuary containing, among others, gannets, godwits, knots, Caspian terns and curlews. Some tours run along the south shore of the spit (beached whales not uncommon) and others run along the north side to the old lighthouse. Tour departure times are subject to tides. You can also get a cold beer or book a tour at the **Farewell Spit Cafe and Visitors Centre** at Puponga Point, just at the beginning of the spit ☎ *phone and FAX (03) 524-8454.* You can't get much farther north on the South Island. In Collingwood, check **Collingwood Safari Tours**, which does the run to the lighthouse on the spit for about $NZ50 per person; expect to spend a half-day at least ☎ *(03) 524-8257; FAX 524-8160.*

THE NORTH ISLAND

Prince of Wales Geyser, Whaka

A place of volcanic fire and history. Home to the nation's two largest cities, including the capital. Land of roaring geysers and bubbling thermal pools, with *some of the best soaking in this or any other world.* Land of easy sailing, great fishing—and the economic and population center of New Zealand. Not as pretty, we insist, as its southern sibling, but still managing to please the eye and placate the palate.

The North Islanders, being comparatively urbanized, sometimes look down on their bumpkin cousins down south as slow and perhaps a bit cloddish. The southerners, for their part, are quick to eschew the pressures and noise of living in the swirl of urban madness in Wellington and Auckland. But remember, this is New Zealand, so any fears about big-city tensions

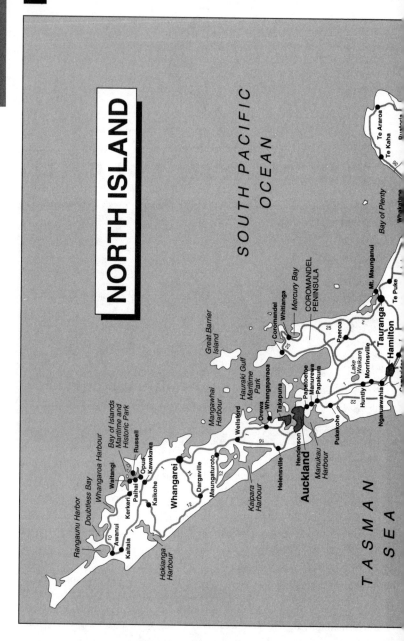

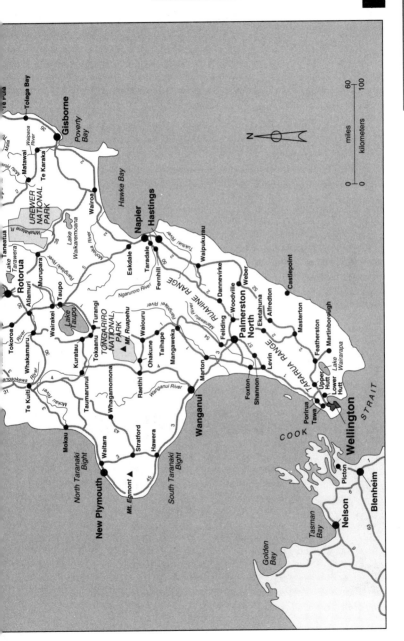

must be put into perspective. By North American standards, the two largest cities here are relatively small—Auckland's population is about 700,000, not counting suburbs; Wellington's is only about 325,000.

The metropolitan area of **Auckland**, lying to the north and south of the city center, has a population of close to a million, a full third of the country's population and, like Sydney, it is spread out all over the place. The tourism folks say the city and environs are more than 2155 square miles in area.

The influx of Polynesian peoples from other parts of the Pacific, combined with the native Maoris, have made Auckland the largest Polynesian city on earth. But once past these metropolitan spots, the open country of the North Island is every bit as rustic as the south.

Being closer to the equator, the North Island tends to be warmer than the south. But there are still skiing and other winter sports here, and it's not unusual to have a winter snowstorm block major north-south roads between Wellington and Auckland.

Wellington is the official capital of the country, but Auckland is the true center. The major international airport is here, so the first spot of Kiwi country most visitors see is Auckland. A nice enough place in its own right, Auckland is also close to some of the major attractions on the North Island, including the major thermal areas, the lovely Coromandel Peninsula and the Bay of Islands.

Herding sheep at Hawkes Bay

Auckland

The heart of Auckland is bustling Queen Street with Albert Park, the Auckland Domain and a large number of hotels, restaurants and shops.

In the early days before English colonial settlement started in earnest, the base of European operations was the **Bay of Islands** area near **Russell**, a whaling center and, in the early days, a raunchy settlement with an international bad-boy reputation. After the Treaty of Waitangi was signed in the early 1840s, the colonial administration decided to move the capital to a more central location, and picked a spot farther south on a narrow isthmus between two lovely bays. The English, à la Manhattan Island, bought the city site from the Maoris for about $US35. The new city was named in honor of Lord Auckland, a viceroy of India and mentor of the new colony's first governor, William Hobson. It did not start to develop into the largest urban center in New Zealand until well into this century. Other attractions, such as the **1860s gold rushes**, kept most of the interest and most of the population on the South Island. Eventually, better weather and better trade moved the population center to the Auckland area. In the early days, however, Auckland was far from the center of things and Wellington, closer to the South Island and endowed with an excellent—if windy—port was chosen to be the new capital in 1864.

The Auckland metropolitan area sits on and among more than 60 or so dormant or extinct volcanoes. **Rangitoto Island**, just to the northeast of the city center in the Hauraki Gulf, is believed to have last erupted about 800 years ago. In Maori times, the area was covered with *pas* (similar to forts), and one of the reasons the site was chosen by the English was the relative ease of interdicting Maori land movements. Only about five miles separate the Tasman Sea to the west and the Pacific Ocean to the east. For most of its history, Auckland grew south of Waitemata Harbour. Getting to the other side of the harbor—the North Shore—meant hopping a ferry or making a long detour around. It wasn't until 1959 that the new **Harbour Bridge** was built. As is true in many cases, the bridge was already too small when it was completed. Population on the North Shore grew in great leaps, and so did bridge traffic. (Something like 100,000 vehicles cross each day.) Congestion got so bad that in the end, the four-lane bridge was expanded by adding two lanes on each side. A Japanese firm did the work, and, of course, the new lanes became known as the "Nippon Clip-Ons." The bridge looks a little like the Coathanger—the Sydney Harbour Bridge—meaning a lot of people think it's pretty ugly. Auckland is definitely a water-oriented place, as befits its location. The official city boosters say it's New Zealand's most beautiful harbor city, which is, of course, a view not necessarily shared by some other Kiwi ports. *Auckland's official nickname is "The City of Sails."*

The heart of the city is bustling **Queen Street**, which runs uphill from the harbor to the area around Karangahape Road. Several large parks are scattered about, including the Auckland Domain and Albert Park at the city center. Many of the major hotels and restaurants are in the Queen Street area near the harbor, and Queen Street is lined with cafes, shops, shopping centers and office buildings. The central downtown area is compact enough to get around by foot.

Our best suggestion for seeing the city is to get above it all. If you're downtown, go to the observation deck atop the **Tower Shopping Centre** at *125 Queen Street*. For $NZ2, you can get a 360-degree look at the city and harbor areas. (Note: It's not really handicapped accessible, because at the end of the elevator ride up, there are two flights of steps to navigate.) Better, but windier, is to ascend one of the city's famous hills for a look. The hills are actually ancient volcanic cones. The sides of the cones still carry scars caused when

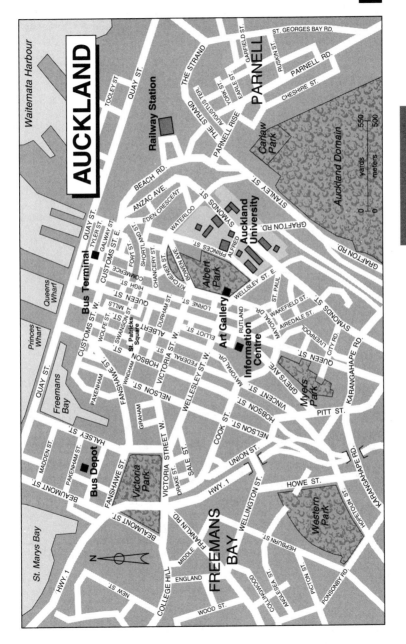

Auckland

early Maoris constructed extensive terraced fortifications. The highest spot in town (about 640 feet above sea level) is **Mt. Eden**, with a deep crater and a view that takes in the whole isthmus, both oceans and the lands to the north and south of the city—it's probably the best view in town. Another good spot (our favorite) is **One Tree Hill**, which was the largest Maori settlement in the area (estimates say around 4000 population or so). The hill was named after a huge native totara tree that once stood on its summit; it's been replaced by a big fir. Next to it is a tall obelisk honoring the Maori people. City buses go to both parks. If you're driving an RV, forget it— the road to the top of One Tree is very narrow and curvy, and parking at the top is tight and scarce. One Tree Domain is also the site of the **Auckland Observatory**, which has public programs *Tuesday and Thursday nights, 8–10 p.m.* The observatory has a 500mm telescope, the largest in the Southern Hemisphere, and also a shop with astronomical goods, *open Monday–Thursday 9 a.m.–3 p.m.* ☎ *(09) 625-6945*. Also at One Tree Domain is a very decent licensed restaurant, **Sorrento Cabaret** ★ ★ , *open Friday and Saturday for dinner 8 p.m.–1 a.m., plus a popular smorgasbord Sunday 6–10 p.m.* Moderate. ☎ *(09) 625-6012*.

The Auckland Museum has the country's best collection of Maori art.

The Essential Auckland

Activities

Auckland Domain
☎ *(09) 309-0443; FAX (09) 379-9956*.
In the Domain (park) is a small spring which, we are told, was used to raise the first rainbow trout in New Zealand. These trout—the Adams and Eves of the Kiwi rain-

bow world—were raised from eggs taken from the Russian River north of San Francisco. A popular attraction features enclosed areas with displays of plants from around the world. The Domain is also home to the **Auckland Museum**, which has probably the country's best collection of Maori art and artifacts. Included among the ground-floor displays are a meeting house, storage house and a magnificent 82-foot-long war canoe. On the first floor are displays of New Zealand arts and crafts, native animals and geology, and on the second floor is a war museum, which includes two Halls of Memory where the names of all those who died in the world wars and later are inscribed. *(Note: The Kiwis use the European system. What would be the first floor in the United States is called the ground floor, and our second floor is called the first floor, etc.)* Admission is free; donations welcome. *Hours are 10 a.m.–5 p.m. daily.* There are a gift shop and café.

Kelly Tarlton's Antarctic Encounter

23 Tamaki Drive, east across Waitemata Harbour from downtown. ☎ *(09) 528-0603; FAX (09) 528-5175.*
Even before it opened in mid-1994, this attraction was billing itself as "Auckland's and probably New Zealand's most exciting and unique entertainment experience." Well, maybe. The Encounter draws heavily on New Zealand's special relationship with Antarctica and lets visitors take a ride through a re-creation of the Frozen Continent, complete with real ice and snow, live penguins and a ride under the Antarctic ice pack. Visitors do the eight-minute ride aboard one of nine restored Snow Cats. Weather patterns and light conditions are controlled by computer and reflect actual conditions that day in Antarctica. At one point (à la Disney), a mock orca attacks mock seals right next to the cars. The best part of the facility, at least to us, is a faithful reproduction of the hut used by doomed explorer Robert Falcon Scott. The original still stands in Antarctica, and the replica is a remarkable living museum, complete with reproductions of canned goods, beds, scientific instruments, clothing and Scott's own private bedroom. The Encounter is tied in with Tarlton's Underwater World, for years one of the city's primo tourist stops. Tarlton, a famous Kiwi diver, created the walk-through aquarium (plastic tunnel) using what were once abandoned sewers near Waitemata Harbour. Sharks, sting rays, reef fish, a petting pond, great stuff for the kids. A ticket that combines both attractions is about $NZ20; *hours 9 a.m.–6 p.m.* Tarlton's is on the Auckland Explorer Bus route or the once-an-hour regular city buses. A taxi ride one-way will run about $NZ8. The Tarlton plot has spread—Underwater Worlds have opened in San Francisco and Minneapolis.

The Aotea Centre

☎ *(09) 307-5050.*
One of New Zealand's most famous citizens is Dame Kiri Te Kanawa, a Maori with international opera credits. She sang at Chuck and Di's wedding, and might be familiar to PBS viewers who saw her sing Paul McCartney's "Liverpool Oratorio" in 1991. She once announced that she would never sing opera in New Zealand until a decent opera house was built. Along came the Aotea Centre, opened in 1990. The 2500-seat theater has banquet facilities, meeting rooms and conference areas, and is

Auckland

Fielding NEW ZEALAND

RAIL AND GLACIER TOUR

Traveling from Auckland to Christchurch by train and ferry is a fun way to see New Zealand's most popular and scenic areas.

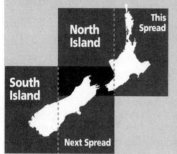

This Spread

North Island

South Island

Next Spread

ROTORUA

Rotorua is worth a stop to see the geysers and hot mud pools. The Whakarewarewa Thermal Reserve has the country's largest geyser.

TAUPO

Taupo boasts the country's largest lake and is popular for its trout fishing. The whole countryside is dotted with the remains of two giant craters as well as active geothermal areas.

PICTON

Take the Interislander ferry cruise through Marlborough Sounds to Picton.

LAKE TAUPO

NELSON

Nelson, the city of sunsets, is the gateway to two fine preserves, Northwest Nelson Forest Park and Mount Richmond Forest Park. Farther south is Nelson Lakes National Park, an alpine area with hiking and many glacial lakes.

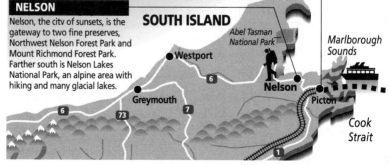

SOUTH ISLAND

Abel Tasman National Park

Westport

Nelson

Greymouth

Picton

Marlborough Sounds

6   73   7

6

Cook Strait

1

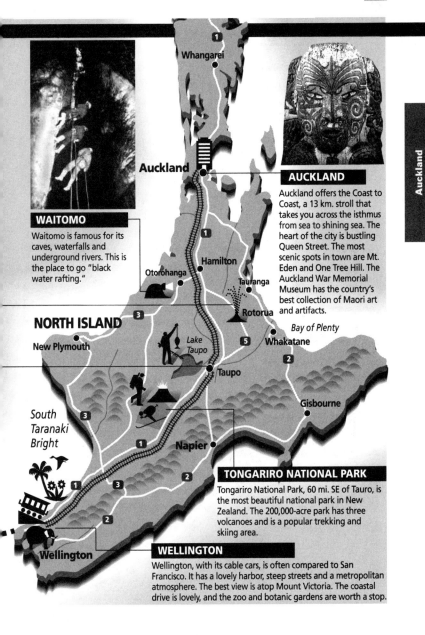

Whangarei

Auckland

WAITOMO

Waitomo is famous for its caves, waterfalls and underground rivers. This is the place to go "black water rafting."

Hamilton

Otorohanga

NORTH ISLAND

New Plymouth

Lake Taupo

Taupo

Tauranga

Rotorua

Bay of Plenty

Whakatane

Gisbourne

South Taranaki Bright

Napier

AUCKLAND

Auckland offers the Coast to Coast, a 13 km. stroll that takes you across the isthmus from sea to shining sea. The heart of the city is bustling Queen Street. The most scenic spots in town are Mt. Eden and One Tree Hill. The Auckland War Memorial Museum has the country's best collection of Maori art and artifacts.

TONGARIRO NATIONAL PARK

Tongariro National Park, 60 mi. SE of Tauro, is the most beautiful national park in New Zealand. The 200,000-acre park has three volcanoes and is a popular trekking and skiing area.

WELLINGTON

Wellington, with its cable cars, is often compared to San Francisco. It has a lovely harbor, steep streets and a metropolitan atmosphere. The best view is atop Mount Victoria. The coastal drive is lovely, and the zoo and botanic gardens are worth a stop.

Wellington

Auckland

Fielding NEW ZEALAND

RAIL AND GLACIER TOUR (continued)

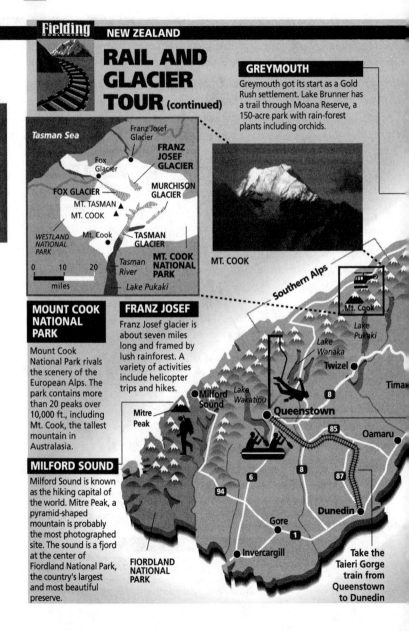

GREYMOUTH

Greymouth got its start as a Gold Rush settlement. Lake Brunner has a trail through Moana Reserve, a 150-acre park with rain-forest plants including orchids.

MT. COOK

Tasman Sea

Franz Josef Glacier

FRANZ JOSEF GLACIER

Fox Glacier

FOX GLACIER

MURCHISON GLACIER

MT. TASMAN ▲
MT. COOK ▲

WESTLAND NATIONAL PARK

Mt. Cook ●

TASMAN GLACIER

MT. COOK NATIONAL PARK

Tasman River

Lake Pukaki

0   10   20
miles

Southern Alps

Mt. Cook

Lake Pukaki

MOUNT COOK NATIONAL PARK

Mount Cook National Park rivals the scenery of the European Alps. The park contains more than 20 peaks over 10,000 ft., including Mt. Cook, the tallest mountain in Australasia.

FRANZ JOSEF

Franz Josef glacier is about seven miles long and framed by lush rainforest. A variety of activities include helicopter trips and hikes.

Lake Wanaka

Twizel ●

Lake Wakatipu

Queenstown

8

Timaru

85

Oamaru ●

MILFORD SOUND

Milford Sound is known as the hiking capital of the world. Mitre Peak, a pyramid-shaped mountain is probably the most photographed site. The sound is a fjord at the center of Fiordland National Park, the country's largest and most beautiful preserve.

● Milford Sound

Mitre Peak

94

6

8

87

Dunedin ●

Gore ●

1

FIORDLAND NATIONAL PARK

● Invercargill

Take the Taieri Gorge train from Queenstown to Dunedin

Auckland

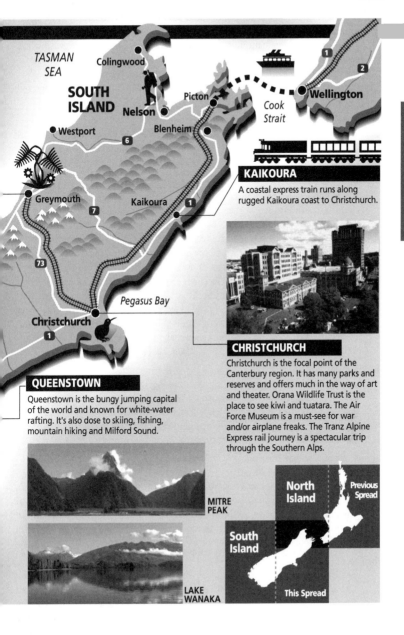

TASMAN SEA

SOUTH ISLAND

Colingwood

Nelson
Picton

Westport
Blenheim

6

Greymouth
Kaikoura

7

73

Pegasus Bay

Christchurch

1

Cook Strait

Wellington

1

2

Auckland

KAIKOURA

A coastal express train runs along rugged Kaikoura coast to Christchurch.

CHRISTCHURCH

Christchurch is the focal point of the Canterbury region. It has many parks and reserves and offers much in the way of art and theater. Orana Wildlife Trust is the place to see kiwi and tuatara. The Air Force Museum is a must-see for war and/or airplane freaks. The Tranz Alpine Express rail journey is a spectacular trip through the Southern Alps.

QUEENSTOWN

Queenstown is the bungy jumping capital of the world and known for white-water rafting. It's also dose to skiing, fishing, mountain hiking and Milford Sound.

MITRE PEAK

LAKE WANAKA

North Island

Previous Spread

South Island

This Spread

located on Queen Street in the center of the city. Kiri Te Kanawa proceeded to come back to New Zealand to sing opera, and how did they treat her? After a performance of *La Boheme*, the reviewer for a Wellington newspaper allowed as how "Te Kanawa was dramatically insipid but vocally rewarding." Anyway, now the country has a world-class performing arts center. There are walking tours available, but these almost never go into the main theater areas. If you want to take a look at the public areas, just go in by yourself. Check the ceilings for the huge abalone and the huge silver fern.

Albert Park

This is the closest park to downtown, just a few blocks off Queen Street. It was the site of barracks for imperial troops until the 1860s. Coming up Queen Street from the harbor, hang a left on Victoria Street.

SKY Tower and Casino

It was bound to happen, given the sudden rash of casinos in Australia and New Zealand, so it's no surprise that a big tower (1077 feet high) has come upon the Auckland skyline, complete with observation decks, hotel, restaurants, theaters and a convention center—plus Harrah's Sky City Casino. It's centrally located at the corner of Federal and Victoria, and the casino has 1000 poker machines and 100 table games. Hotel rooms in the tower are not cheap: about $NZ300 double for a standard room and $NZ400-500 for suites. The tower is taller than the Centrepoint structure in Sydney (998 feet) giving the Kiwis huge bragging rights. Others suggest it's an eyesore and if you go up, try to forget this is an earthquake area. Other casinos are planned for other cities including, would you believe, Hamilton and Dunedin. Anyway, if you want information about the tower complex from North America, call ☎ *(800) 427-7247; in Auckland, call* ☎ *(09) 912-6200.*

Auckland City Art Gallery

☎ *(09) 309-0831.*

This is one of the most important archives of New Zealand art in the country. Originally opened in 1888, the gallery is a center for research and exhibits of Kiwi artworks. Except for special exhibitions, admission is free. The gallery, located at the corner of Kitchener and Wellesley streets, is *open daily from 10 a.m.–4:30 p.m.*

Hobson Wharf Maritime Museum

☎ *(09) 358-1019; fax 377-6000.*

The museum is located on Quay Street next to Princes Wharf and is the country's most important sea-faring museum. Not to be missed is the huge (76-foot) Maori war canoe, plus displays on the country's role as a major whaling area and the importance of the fishing industry. Guided tours (partly on the water) are available; entry fee $NZ10. The museum is *open 9 a.m.–6 p.m. daily.*

The Zoo

☎ *(09) 378-1620.*

The 35-acre Auckland Zoological Park in Western Springs, a few kilometers from downtown, is your best bet to see some native New Zealand animals, including kiwis and tuataras. There's also the usual collection of beasts from around the world. There are café and picnic areas. Admission fee is about $NZ10. *Hours are 9:30 a.m.–5:30 p.m. daily; last admission at 4:15 p.m.*

Parnell Village is Auckland's most popular shopping area.

Parnell Village

A long block of Parnell Road, which runs just northeast of the Auckland Domain, has been turned into a restored Victorian-era maze of small shops, galleries, cafés, antique dealers and arts outlets. Parnell Village, as it's called, is one of the better places in Auckland to spend a morning shopping, finishing off with lunch. Our favorite spot is the **Iguacu**, a sidewalk café/beer garden serving breakfast and lunch. The eggs benedict are worth a trip to Auckland. Nearby is the **Black Olive** deli, also with great eats. Down an alley next to the deli is the **Elephant House**, where the works of more than 300 local artisans are on sale. Also in the village is a Maori tribal center and crafts shop. It's a fair hike from downtown, but the Village is on local bus routes—check at the Central Bus Terminal just off Quay Street next to the harbor. Or you can hop the Auckland Explorer Bus, which stops at the village once an hour. *Business hours are 9 a.m.–9 p.m. daily.*

Relics

You can't have a settlement in New Zealand without a stash of old buildings, and Auckland has its share. Among them are **Alberton** (1862), a mansion built from the proceeds of a gold fortune, located in the suburb of Mt. Albert; **Highwic** (1862), whose owner sired 21 children, located in Epsom; **Ewelme Cottage** (1863) in Parnell, made from kauri wood; and the **Kinder House** (1856), also in Parnell, which is a gallery and museum devoted to the works of clergyman/artist John Kinder.

North Head

Across the harbor from downtown is North Head, a military site first used for gun emplacements in the 1880s. It's now a park and offers excellent views of the city and the harbor area.

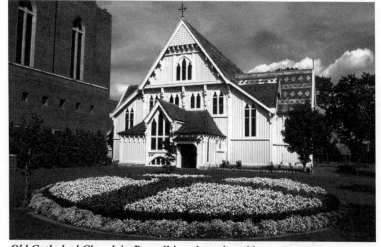

Old Cathedral Church in Parnell is a charming old structure.

Beaches

One of the reasons Aucklanders love to live where they do is the easy access to a number of good beaches on both coasts. *The best ones close to town are on the North Shore north of Devonport, easily reached by ferry or bus from the city center.* Among the more popular northern beaches are **Takapuna**, **Milford**, **Mairangi Bay** and **Browns Bay**. A popular beach for surfers (and thus not really good for swimming when the surf's up) is **Muriwai Beach** on the western shore about 30 miles northwest of the city off Highway 16; it's also home to a gannet colony. A bit farther out are the islands of the Hauraki Gulf, and about two hours from Auckland, the best of the lot, **Great Barrier Island**, always rated as having the best beaches in the area. The islands can be reached using a number of charter boat companies which can be booked through city tourism offices. Or you can fly over to Great Barrier Island in about a half-hour. Accommodation on the island ranges from backpacker to resort. See (TOURS) a bit later on.

Golf

As we noted, New Zealanders are crazy about golf so it's no secret that the City of Sails has a bunch. Among the ones in the Auckland area you might want to check out are the **Pukekohe Golf Course** in the suburb of the same name southwest of the city; the **North Shore Golf Club** in Auckland; the **Manakau Golf Club** in Auckland; the **Grange Golf Club** southeast of the city; the **Titirangi Golf Club** in Auckland; or the **Whitford Country Club** in Auckland.

Climate

Auckland, the country's northernmost major urban area, is generally fairly pleasant, with winter highs in the 60s, lows in the 50s. In the summer, highs will normally be in the upper 70s, with a fair amount of humidity. Annual rainfall hovers around 50 inches.

Nights, even in summer, tend to be cool. In a winter rainstorm, it can get downright chilly. New Zealand, being close to the South Pole, does have a problem with the ozone layer, as does Australia. The threat of skin cancer led two Canterbury-area farmwives to develop a line of swimming wear for children called Ozone Swimsuits, which cover the kids from neck to knees. Take the hint —if you're in the sun, use high-protection ointments.

Information

The Auckland Visitor Centre is the central tourism office, located on Aotea Square near the intersection of Queen and Wellesley streets *(299 Queen Street). Hours are 8:30 a.m.–5:30 p.m., Monday–Friday and 9 a.m.–4 p.m. on weekends and holidays.* ☎ *(09) 366-6888; FAX (09) 358-4684.* There is also a visitors center at the international airport terminal, open 24 hours a day. ☎ *(09) 275-6467; FAX (09) 256-1742.* The U.S. Consulate is at the corner of Shortland and O'Connell streets; ☎ *(09) 303-2724.*

For information about the South Island:

South Island Information and Travel, *Endean Building, 2 Queen Street; open 8:30 a.m.–5:30 p.m. Monday–Friday,* ☎ *(09) 303-0473.* Handicapped information is available from the Disabilities Resource Centre, ☎ *(0800) 801-981.*

For details on regional parks:

Parks Information Service, *Ferry Buildings on Quay Street downtown. Hours are 8:15 a.m.–4:30 p.m. weekdays,* ☎ *(09) 366-2166.* On weekends and holidays, ☎ *(09) 817-7134.* Another useful source for area facilities, as well as national parks around the country, is the **Department of Conservation Centre**, also in the Ferry Buildings, *open weekdays, 1–4:30 p.m.* ☎ *(09) 366-2166.*

The Auckland City Council also has a computerized data base listing 10,000 organizations and clubs in the city, both tourist and other businesses. You can contact the library by calling ☎ *(09) 377-0209.*

If you're planning to hit the beaches or just do some touring on the North Shore, contact the **North Shore Information Centre**, *Hurstmere Road, Takapuna;* ☎ *(09) 486-0060.*

The central post office is on Queen Elizabeth II Square near Quay Street. *Hours are 8 a.m.–5 p.m., Monday–Friday.* ☎ *(09) 302-1059.*

The **Automobile Association** office is located at *99 Albert Street. Hours are 8:30 a.m.–5 p.m.;* ☎ *(09) 377-4660; FAX (09) 309-4563.* For emergency road service, call the AA at ☎ *(0800) 500-222.*

Telephone

The telephone area code for Auckland is (09).

Getting There

If Auckland is not your entry point in New Zealand, you can reach the city by air or ground transportation from anywhere in the country. *Air New Zealand* and *Ansett* have daily service from Wellington for about $NZ240 one way. From Christchurch, daily service is about $NZ320. From elsewhere in the South Island (Invercargill, Dunedin,

Queenstown), expect to pay between $NZ400 and $NZ500. It'll cost about $NZ200 to fly to the northern parts of the North Island from Auckland. In addition to North American carriers, Auckland is served by most of the major South Pacific airlines, as well as JAL, UTA, Thai International, Garuda, Singapore and British Airways.

By train, there are two choices from Wellington. **The Silver Fern**, which has rail car service, runs Monday–Saturday and takes about 12 hours. The one-way passenger fare is about $NZ110. The fare includes complimentary lunch. There is bar service; it's a nonsmoking train. It leaves Wellington around 8:30 a.m., arriving in Auckland at 6:30 p.m.

Overnight service Sunday–Friday is available on the **Northerner Express**, which has no sleepers. Refreshment and snacks are available, but no alcohol. Smoking seats are available and a video is shown each night. The train leaves Wellington at 8 p.m., arriving in Auckland at 6:50 a.m. One-way fare is about $NZ75. Daily bus service from Wellington is offered by InterCity and Newman's. The one-way fare is about $NZ90 and takes about 11 hours.

Intercity buses arrive at the **Downtown Airline Terminal** on Quay Street. Trains arrive at the Auckland Central Railway Station on Beach Street. The central station for inner-city buses is behind the central post office.

Getting Around

The airport is a ways out of town (about 13 miles). A taxi ride will run about $NZ35 (no tipping). The *Airbus Service* runs daily every half hour from 6:30 a.m.–8 p.m. from the airport, and from 6:10 a.m.–8:20 p.m. from the city to the airport. It stops at most— but not all—major hotels and at major bus stops and takes about 40 minutes one way. The one-way fare is about $NZ10 per person. ☎ *(09) 275-7685* or ☎ *(09) 275-9396; FAX (09) 275-9394.* There are also several shuttle bus companies offering door-to-door service for around $NZ15. These can be booked at information counters at the airport.

Taxis can be hailed, but it's better to look for a taxi rank or go to a major hotel. For information, contact **Auckland Co-Op Taxis** at ☎ *(09) 300-3000;* they also has limos.

Buses around town or suburban, contact **Buz A Bus**, the city's bus information service. *Hours are 7 a.m.–7 p.m., Monday–Saturday;* ☎ *(09) 366-6400.* The city also has a bus information counter at the corner of Victoria Street West and Hobson Street; *hours are 8:15 a.m.–5 p.m. Mon.–Fri.* And there is an information kiosk at the downtown bus terminal *(off Quay Street near the harbor); hours are 7 a.m.–6:30 p.m. Mon.–Sat., 9 a.m.–5 p.m. Sun.* For $NZ10, you can buy a **BusAbout** pass, good for one-day unlimited travel on the bus system *(after 9 a.m.)*; purchase it from the driver. ☎ *(09) 358-1149.* A good way to see the sights is to buy a pass on the **Explorer Bus**, which for $NZ15 lets you stop and get on at the various tourist spots around town. Among stops are Kelly Tarlton's, Parnell Village and the Victoria Park Market. ☎ *(09) 360-0033; FAX (09) 360-0305.* Many shuttles and buses leave from the Downtown Airline Terminal Building on Quay Street near Albert Street.

Ferries to the North Shore run every hour on the hour from the Ferry Buildings and cost about $NZ7 per person one-way. Information from Fuller's, ☎ *(09) 367-9102* or ☎ *(09) 367-9111.*

Banks

Auckland banks are open Monday–Friday 9 a.m.–4:30 p.m. Most have currency exchanges, and there is a currency exchange office at the airport.

Tours

Using Auckland as a base, you can easily arrange a tour to nearby attractions. A number of options are available, such as:

Gray Line New Zealand, with an Auckland tour that includes admission to Kelly Tarlton's Underwater World and the Antarctic Encounter. The tour leaves the Downtown Airline Terminal at 9:15 a.m. and costs about $NZ35 per person. ☎ *(09) 377-0904.*

A free harbor cruise, which is part of a full-day bus tour of the city offered by **ABC Tours.** The company also has *half-day trips*. The full day is about $NZ60; the half-day trips go around the city in the morning, coast to coast in the afternoon. ☎ *(09) 302-1100.*

Farther afield, Gray Line also has a *day trip to Rotorua*, which takes in the thermal attractions, plus a stop at the *New Zealand Agrodome* for a 60-minute show on sheep. An optional luncheon cruise is also offered. The trips cost about $NZ120 per person and leave the Downtown Airline Terminal at 8:15 a.m. and return at 8:40 p.m.

Scenic Tours has a similar package for about the same price. In addition, you can book longer trips, such as a two-day affair that goes to the *Waitomo Glowworm Caves*, lets you feast at a Maori hangi, takes you trout fishing, puts you up in a hotel in Rotorua and tours the thermal areas for about $NZ350 per person, all meals included. *A one-day trip to the glowworm caves* is about $NZ110 per person. Similar trips are offered by **Vanway Tours Ltd.**, *15A Scotstoun Place, Glen Eden;* ☎ *(09) 817-8046.* Or try **Thrifty Tours**, ☎ *(09) 478-3550*, which has essentially the same itineraries.

If water is your taste, there are several companies offering tours and cruises around **Waitemata Harbour**. One of the most extensive is **Fuller's**, which operates the ferries to the North Shore. It has an hourlong tour at noon that hits the East Coast bays and goes around **Rangitoto Island**, a volcano that erupted 800 years ago. The cost, including lunch, is about $NZ35 per person. The company also has longer trips to such destinations as **Great Barrier Island** and **Waiheke Island**. A good idea is to get the company's special five-day activity pass, available for about $NZ50, which allows visits to the Hobson Wharf museum, Underwater World and the Antarctic Encounter, discounts on the Waiheke Island and Great Barrier Island boats, a tour of the city and a glass of beer here and there. The Waiheke Island boat, along with a winery tour or a bush walk, is $NZ35. The Barrier Island trip alone is about $NZ70 adult. ☎ *(09) 367-9111.*

If hoofing it is an option, try a trek with **Auckland Walking Tours,** which has several city tours, including one that combines a ferry ride. The tours all start from the Ferry Buildings and last about two hours. Tickets can be purchased at the Outdoor Adventure Company at the Ferry Buildings or from guides. Adults tickets are between $NZ10 and $NZ15; kids less. The company has an information hotline, ☎ *(09) 309-9060.*

It stands to reason that Auckland, the City of Sails, would be ready to entice you onto the water. Several companies offer "hands-on" sailing, which gives you a chance to pay them while you do all the work—raising sails, manning the helm, getting blisters hauling in the sheets. No sailing experience is needed, and rates run around $NZ50 per person for a five-hour jaunt. Most of the companies involved also offer intensive sailing lessons for higher fees. Try **Performance Yacht Charters**, ☎ *(0800) 653-753*, or the **Rangitoto Sailing Centre**, ☎ *(09) 358-2324*.

Less-strenuous trips are offered by the sailing vessels of the Pride of Auckland company, which operates luncheon and dinner cruises around the harbor. The three-hour dinner cruise is about $NZ70 per person, and can be booked at the Downtown Airline Terminal or at ☎ *(09) 373-4557*. Several of the land tour companies offer **Pride of Auckland excursions** in some of their itineraries.

Shopping

O'Connell Street, a couple of blocks east of Queen Street, and the streets leading off O'Connell, is a maze of small arcades filled with boutiques, eateries, pubs and specialty shops.

Vulcan Lane, with a cobbled street, is our favorite, but explore and pick your own spot. Great for shopping or people-watching. The lane is about two blocks long off Queen Street between Wyndham and Swanson streets. Fine area for a cappuccino. Once upon a time, there was a tract of land that had a garbage disposal plant, power station, stables and a blacksmith shop—all gone now except a 38-meter-high chimney.

Victoria Park Market, open seven days, is full of stores, an international food hall, licensed restaurants, Rick's Café Americain (neon, Art Deco, photos of Bogie) and a McDonald's. The market, located on Victoria Street West, is a regular stop on the Auckland Explorer bus route. The *markets are open 9 a.m.–7 p.m. daily*. There is also a free bus that leaves the Downtown Airline Terminal weekends and public holidays starting at 10 a.m., then every 15 minutes until 2:45 p.m. *Market information:* ☎ *(09) 309-6911*.

The China Oriental Markets on the waterfront are housed in an old railway warehouse and offer 140 stalls, Asian foods and Kiwi products. The warehouse is at the corner of Britomart Place and Quay Street, not far from the bus terminal. *The markets are open daily from 10 a.m.–6 p.m.* Karangahape Road—known around town simply as *K Road*—is at the opposite end of Queen Street from the harbor and is the Polynesian center of the city. It's within walking distance of the Sheraton Hotel, and offers a wide variety of South Pacific goods. Check out the Polynesian Bookstore at *3 K Road*, where you can get books, posters, music and Maori dictionaries. ☎ *(09) 302-0678*.

A good spot on the North Shore:

Compendium Gallery at the corner of Clarence and Victoria streets in Devonport has a nice supply of greenstone and other artworks.

There are scads of places selling sheepskin products. Many of the larger places will ship the fleeces home, and you don't have to pay the general sales tax. Try **Breen's** at *8 Quay*

Street on the waterfront. Or if you can forgive the name, **Woolywood** at *94 Quay Street* next to the Travelodge. There are several places in the Ferry Building, which also has a number of other stores and eateries.

The antique center of the city is out near the airport on Manukau Road in Epsom. There are about 20 stores within walking distance of each other. Start at the corner of Manukau and Arcadia; check out **Yvonne Sanders and Chatham Antiques**. Another antique complex is in Remuera, a few miles southeast of the city center. Called the **Market Road Antique Centre**, it's a group of seven shops open six days a week. Other shopping opportunities are **Breen's Sheepskin Specialists**, *8 Quay Street*; **Made in New Zealand**, *75 Queen Street*; **Downtown Shopping Centre**, *corner of Queen and Quay streets*; **Queen's Arcade**, *corner of Queen and Customs Street West*; and **Lyle & Scott**, *Lower Albert and Quay streets*. There are also many duty-free shops all along Queen and Albert streets.

Where to Stay

Note that all prices we quote for hotels do not usually include an added GST (general services tax), currently running at 12.5 percent.

Stamford Plaza $NZ340–1500 ★★★★★

Corner of Albert and Swanson streets. ☎ *(09) 309-8888; FAX (09) 357-9215.*
The city's premier hotel, the Plaza is an 11-story building with harbor views. It has several restaurants and bars, rooftop swimming pool, health club, luxury suites, spa, courtesy coach, tea/coffee, two nonsmoking floors. More than 300 rooms, with doubles starting around $NZ300–350. There are complimentary shuttles to the central business district; when new owners took it over in 1996, it was renovated. Suites start at $NZ700, deluxe rooms at $NZ365.

Carlton Hotel $NZ320–1800 ★★★★★

Corner of Mayoral Drive and Vincent Street. ☎ *(09) 366-3000; FAX (09) 366-0121.*
Although it's a popular spot for business types, the former Pan Pacific, now the Singapore-owned Carlton, is also a very good location for ordinary tourists and one major draw is its marvelous views of the city. It sits behind the Aotea Centre within easy walking distance of Queen Street. It has a lovely atrium and outdoor elevator, plus three very good restaurants and two executive floors. Valet parking, business center, tennis courts, fitness center and nearby pool. Doubles start at $NZ320; the royal suite (fireplace, grand piano), $NZ1800. All rooms have minibars, two phones, TV and very nice bathrooms.

Centra $NZ250 ★★★★

128 Albert Street. ☎ *(09) 302-1111; FAX (09) 302-3111.*
Located in the center of the business and shopping area, the newest hotel in town. Monolithic and undistinguished on the outside, but quite nice rooms inside. Good location. The casual and moderately expensive **Gantry Restaurant** ★★★ is always popular, and there is a lobby bar; suites available.

Hyatt Auckland $NZ275–330 ★★★★

Corner of Princes Street and Waterloo Quadrant near Auckland University. ☎ *(09) 366-1234; FAX (09) 303-2932.*

Located on a steep hill with harbor view; easy walk down, a hike back up. Luxury suites available. Two restaurants, including the expensive **Top of the Town** ★★★, an award winner; also a very nice bar, the **Champs**.

Sheraton Auckland Hotel and Towers   **$NZ250–350**   ★★★★

83 Symonds Street, near Karangahape Road. ☎ *(09) 379-5132; FAX (09) 377-9367.* Excellent view of the city looking toward the harbor, supposedly the largest hotel in New Zealand. Two restaurants, three bars, pool, spa, laundry, health club, minibars, handicapped facilities, luxury suites, breakfast included. Doubles about $NZ250, suites start at $NZ350.

Auckland Novotel   **$NZ230**   ★★★

Corner of Queen and Customs streets. ☎ *(09) 377-8920; FAX (09) 307-3739.* Purchased by the Novotel Group in 1994. Nice central downtown location, close to shopping. Some rooms overlook the harbor. Two restaurants, including rooftop bar and brasserie.

Auckland City Travelodge   **$NZ220**   ★★★

96-100 Quay Street on the waterfront. ☎ *(09) 377-0349; FAX (09) 307-8159.* Two restaurants, a bar, underground parking, spa, baby-sitting.

Quality Hotel Airport   **$NZ200**   ★★★

Corner of Ascot and Kirkbride roads about 5 kilometers from the airport. ☎ *(09) 275-7029; FAX (09) 275-3322.* Restaurant/bar, pool, spa, sauna, handicapped facilities, coffee/tea.

Auckland Quality Inn Anzac   **$NZ200**   ★★★

150 Anzac Avenue, close to the railroad station. ☎ *(09) 379-8509; FAX (09) 379-8582.* Some harbor views, some suites. Restaurant/bar, live entertainment, sauna, tea/coffee.

Quality Hotel Rose Park   **$NZ180**   ★★★

100 Gladstone Road, Parnell, across from the Parnell Rose Garden. ☎ *(09) 377-3619; FAX (09) 303-3716.* On bus route to city. Some villas (self-contained units with kitchens). Restaurant/bar, pool, spa, tea/coffee.

White Heron Hotel   **$NZ165–250**   ★★★

138 St. Stephens Avenue, Parnell. ☎ *(09) 379-6860; FAX (09) 309-1540.* On a hill with great harbor views. Standard rooms and apartments. Three restaurants, poolside grill and bar. Pool, Japanese bathhouse, business center, tea/coffee, courtesy van. Doubles about $NZ165; apartments from $NZ250.

Abby's Boutique Hotel   **$NZ160**   ★★

Corner of Wellesley and Albert streets. ☎ *(09) 303-4799; FAX (09) 302-1451.* Recently renovated, good central downtown location. Restaurant, bar and the very popular **Honkytonk Bar & Café** on the ground floor.

Barrycourt Motor Inn   **$NZ125**   ★★

10-20 Gladstone Road, Parnell. ☎ *(09) 303-3789; FAX (09) 377-3309.* Restaurants, bar, kitchen units, tennis, four private spas, some harbor views. Laundry.

Park Towers Hotel   **$NZ90–135**   ★★

3 Scotia Place, off Queen Street downtown. ☎ *(09) 309-2800; FAX (09) 302-1964.*

Brasserie/bar, laundry, tea/coffee, courtesy van, minibars, handicapped facilities. Some rooms with shared baths.

Aachen House   **$NZ55–85**   ★★

39 Market Road, Remuera. ☎ *(09) 520-2329; FAX (09) 524-2898.*
Near One Tree Hill close to the train station, a restored Victorian (1905) B&B. Large rooms, scenic views, expansive grounds, no smoking. Coffee/tea, courtesy van, dinners available.

Albion Hotel   **$NZ70–75**   ★★

Corner Wellesley and Hobson streets downtown. ☎ *(09) 379-4900; FAX (09) 379-4901.*
A restored 1870 hotel, all rooms with private bath. Licensed restaurant and bars, laundry, minibars, tea/coffee, breakfast available. Special rate on airport shuttle.

Bavaria B&B Guest House   **$NZ95**   ★★

83 Valley Road, Mt. Eden. ☎ *(09) 638-9641; FAX (09) 638-9665.*
A B&B about three kilometers from city center and close to a bus stop. Parking, tea/coffee, all rooms with private baths. They speak German.

Auckland Central Backpackers   **$NZ20**

9 Fort Street near Queen Street. ☎ *(09) 358-4877; FAX (09) 358-4872.*
Supposedly New Zealand's largest backpackers hostel. In-house movies, restaurant, laundry, rooftop bar, travel service, free transport from airport, open 24 hours. Doubles with shared bath start at $NZ20 per person.

Pub Beds   **$NZ140**

☎ *(09) 445-4400; FAX 445-1010.*
There are five of these budget-style accommodations in Auckland, part of a group of pub hotels all over New Zealand. The intent is to let you mingle with the locals and see the Kiwis in a relaxed state. The first time out, you must make bookings directly with member hotels, but afterward, each hotel can make reservations at other members for you. In the Auckland area, we suggest the comparatively expensive **Esplanade Hotel ★★**, sitting on the waterfront in **Devonport** not far from the ferry wharf. Elegant old heap; doubles with bath starting at $NZ140 per person. ☎ *(09) 445-1291; FAX 445-1999.*

Farm and home stays   **$NZ55–120**

There are more than two dozen of these B&B-style places in the Auckland area, offering everything from private beaches, pools, bush hiking to small houses with pastoral settings. Rates can be as low as $NZ50 double. For information, contact the Auckland Visitor Centre or the AA travel offices. Two worth considering are the Devonport Villa Inn and Badger's of Devonport.

Devonport Villa Bed and Breakfast Inn   **$NZ150–195**   ★★★

46 Tainui Road, Devonport, Auckland. ☎ *(09) 445-8397; FAX: (09)445-9766*
Situated just a two minute walk from beautiful Cheltenham Beach, this Edwardian villa with Queen Anne turret offers five distinctively decorated spacious rooms, two elegant suites and a cottage. The lounge features stained-glass windows, antiques, an extensive library and complementary tea and coffee. Leisurely breakfasts (included in the rate) are served in the dining room or guests' rooms.

Badger's of Devonport $NZ89–119   ★★★

30 Summer Street, Devonport, Auckland. ☎ *(09) 445-2099; FAX: (09) 445-0231*
Built in 1908, this villa has been completely renovated combining all modern conveniences such as ensuites and private baths while retaining the ambience of a bygone era. The attentive and friendly owners pamper guests with sumptuous breakfasts, an inviting guest lounge and personalized tours of New Zealand. Special requests such as mystery weekends to surprise a spouse are their specialty.

Remuera Motor Lodge
and Camping Ground $NZ18–85

16 Minto Road, Remuera. ☎ *(09) 524-5126; FAX (09) 524-5639.*
One of the Top 10 group. The closest RV park to the city. Laundry, kitchens, close to shops and restaurants. Pool, laundry, kitchen facilities, barbecue. Tent sites, motel units. Motel doubles about $NZ65–85; RV sites $NZ18.

Where to Eat

A reminder: We have rated restaurants not only from a quality standpoint, but from a monetary one, as well. To simplify things, we have three levels of cost: budget, moderate and expensive. These ratings apply to basic meals, and do not include wines or other meal extras. Budget means a meal for two persons in the $NZ15–40 range; moderate is $NZ40–90, and expensive is from $NZ90 up.

The trend around New Zealand these days is to get away from what they call "fine dining" establishments, meaning linen napkins, silver and china, and dress codes. Once, Auckland had dozens of such places; now, there are only a few. The emphasis now is on relaxed informality and cuisine with a definite infusion of Pacific Rim flavors. *We should also point out that restaurant hours are also coming of age. In the past, few restaurants were open Sundays; this is changing, so the hours we list might be different by the time you get to Auckland. Also, many places were once only BYO and did not have full liquor licenses; this also is changing.* Some of the best places to eat in the city are in hotels:

Partington's $$$ ★★★★★

In the Sheraton Hotel. ☎ *(09) 379-5532.*
Perhaps the most elegant venue in Auckland, with French tapestries, multistory levels, white-linen service. Herbs aplenty, saucy meat dishes, seafood, decadent desserts. The real aim is to make the most of local game and produce with a French flair. A real treat. *Dinner 6:30–10 p.m. seven days.*

Catlin's $$$ ★★★★

In the Carlton Hotel on Mayoral Drive. ☎ *(09) 366-3000.*
A great example of the new wave in Kiwi cuisine, Catlin's is an intimate, very popular restaurant with emphasis on taste and presentation. Deer medallions (excuse us, *cervena*) with braised baby leeks and grilled boccocini, boned stuffed quail with spinach and kumara, sashimi of beef with lemon soya. *Open Tues.–Sat. for dinner, 6:30 p.m.* Reservations a necessity.

Keyaki $$$ ★★★★

Also in the Carlton. ☎ *(09) 366-3000.*

On everybody's list of the best Japanese restaurants in New Zealand. It has a sushi bar and also a teppanyaki dining area; impeccable service, kimono-clad waitresses. Try the combination plate, which is a delicious guided tour through things Japanese. Thursday is buffet night. *Dinner seven nights.*

Brasserie at the Plaza $$$ ★★★★
☎ *(09) 309-8888.*
Ground floor of the Stamford Plaza, with floor-to-ceiling glass windows. Excellent food, but you pay for the privilege: tequila-cured salmon, roasted venison, honey brule. *Breakfast 6–11:30 a.m., lunch 11:30 a.m.–6:30 p.m., dinner 6:30–11 p.m.*

Delmonico's $$ ★★
In the Hotel De Brett, corner of Shortland and High streets. ☎ *(09) 303-2389.*
Nice Art Deco decor, plus a very good wine bar. Sunday brunches. Call for hours.

Brasserie, The $$ ★★
In the Albion Hotel, corner of Wellesley and Hobson streets. ☎ *(09) 379-4900.*
A meat-and-potatoes sort of place, some ethnic foods, large quantities. *Open seven days; breakfast 7–9 a.m., lunch noon–2:30, dinner 5:30–9:30 p.m.*

Some good bets around town include the following:

Cin Cin on Quay $$ ★★★
99 Quay Street. ☎ *(09) 307-6966 or 6967.*
One of the in spots for the luncheon crowd, but also popular for dinner. Located in the historic Ferry Building. Happy hour (very popular) from 5–7 p.m. *Good lunches, specializing in seafood and grilled fish, but also offering ethnic foods.* Outdoor dining in the summer. Probably a good idea to call ahead for dinner because seating is limited. *Open seven days, 11 a.m.–1 a.m. weekdays; weekends 8 a.m.–1 a.m.*

Harbourside Bar & Grill $$
☎ *(09) 307-0556.*
Next door to Cin Cin, this restaurant features nice stained glass, a fish tank and deck seating with a view of the harbor. *Open daily 11:30 a.m.–11 p.m.*

Fisherman's Wharf Restaurant $$ ★★★
2 Queen Street, Northcote Point across the Harbour Bridge. ☎ *(09) 418-3955.*
Best view in town, overlooking Waitemata Harbour. Shellfish, fresh fish, steaks, poultry. *Lunch noon–2:30 p.m. Mon.–Fri. in the summer; dinner seven days from 6–10:30 p.m.*

Antoine's $$$ ★★★
333 Parnell Road. ☎ *(09) 379-8756.*
New Zealand cuisine with French overtones, winner of many awards. It's in a restored house in Parnell Village, complete with brass doorbell. Intimate dining areas. Extensive wine list. *Lunch noon–2 p.m. Mon.–Fri.; dinner from 6 p.m. Mon.–Sat.*

Kermadec $$$ ★★★★
Viaduct Quay, Lower Hobson and Quay streets. ☎ *(09) 309-0412.*
An art-choked complex of several restaurants, including the main Ocean Fresh Restaurant, plus two Japanese venues. It's housed in an old utilities building, and has

an Asian/Polynesian motif throughout. The emphasis is on Japanese-style seafoods, plus New Zealand standards. Shellfish dishes are a specialty, as are the whole grilled crayfish. Excellent service and presentation. Very popular with the locals. *Open daily for lunch noon–2:30 p.m. and dinner from 6 p.m.*

Jurgen's Restaurant $$$ ★★★
12 Wyndham Street. ☎ *(09) 309-6651.*
Classy old former printing building, specializing in seafood, especially crayfish and whitebait and a marvelous house pâté or the squid with herbs, ouzo and red wine. Also European fare with flambé at your table. *Lunch from noon Mon.–Fri.; dinner 6–11 p.m. Mon.–Sat.*

Hunting Lodge $$$ ★★★★
Waikoukou Valley Road, Waimauku, about 30 minutes west of the city in the winery area. ☎ *(09) 411-8259.*
Part of the Matua Valley Winery, set in a 19th-century homestead. Excellent wines, of course, with open fire, outside dining in the summer. Award-winner, with such goodies as stilton-Guinness soup, aged venison with roasted garlic and sherry glaze, carrot and walnut cake with ricotta icing. The place for Yorkshire pudding. *Open lunch noon–5 p.m. weekends; dinner Thurs.–Sun. from 6 p.m.*

Sails Restaurant $$$ ★★★
The Anchorage on Westhaven Road. ☎ *(09) 378-9890.*
Yachting ambience near the Westhaven Marina and Yacht Club. Nice setting, specializing in seafood and lamb. Licensed. *Lunch noon–2 p.m. Mon.–Fri.; dinner Mon.–Sat. 6:30–10:30 p.m.*

Union Fish Company $$ ★★★
16 Quay Street. ☎ *(09) 379-6593.*
Housed in an old warehouse, with the bar in a boat tied to the dock. Crayfish tank to pick your own. Japanese goodies and delectable seafood menu. Licensed, reservations. *Lunch noon–2:30 Mon.–Fri. Dinner 6–10:30 p.m. seven days.*

Alhambra Restaurant $$ ★★★
3 Lamps Plaza, 283 Ponsonby Road. ☎ *(09) 376-2430.*
One of our favorites, situated in an old movie theater where you can catch live jazz and blues, plus a great view of the harbor. Good seafood (especially the mussels), good cellar, excellent lamb. Open from 11 a.m. Sunday brunch. Closed Mon.

Corfu $$ ★★
44 Ponsonby Road. ☎ *(09) 378-8676.*
The smells alone will stop you in your tracks. Great Greek goodies, great place for lunch. Live music and dancing. *Lunch Mon.–Sat., noon–midnight; Sun. 5 p.m. until late.*

Hammerheads $$ ★★
19 Tamaki Drive, Mission Bay near Kelly Tarlton's. ☎ *(09) 521-4400.*
On the waterfront, with great scenery and seafood to match. Oyster bar, fish with pasta and a great Sunday brunch. *Daily from 11 a.m. until late.*

Mekong $$ ★★
295 Queen Street, next to Aotea Square, fourth floor. ☎ *(09) 379-7591.*

Very popular and excellent Vietnamese fare. Good lunch buffet (finger foods, soup, etc.) for about \$NZ10. Many seafood specialties. *Lunch noon–2 p.m. Mon.–Fri.; dinner from 6 p.m. seven nights.* Licensed but you can BYO wine.

Ramses Bar & Grill $$$ ★★
435 Kyber Pass Road. ☎ *(09) 522-0619.*
Relaxed, casual atmosphere, highlighted by huge floor-to-ceiling windows, Egyptian decor. Usually four fish specials daily, char-grilled vegetables, pastas; happy hour 5–7 p.m. *Lunch noon–3 p.m. Mon.–Fri.; dinner nightly 6–11 p.m.*

Tony's ★★
The original is at 27 Wellesley Street West; others on Manukau Road on the way to the airport and at Mission Bay on Tamaki Drive. ☎ *(09) 373-4196.*
A chain of good steakhouses. Huge steaks for moderate prices. *Lunch Mon.–Fri. noon–2 p.m; dinner nightly 5:30–10 p.m.*

Mexican Café $ ★★★
67 Victoria Street West. ☎ *(09) 373-2311.*
Mexican food, taped Mexican music. The best Mexican food in town, basically Tex-Mex. Very popular with the after-work crowd. Margaritas a specialty at happy hour, 5–7 p.m. *Lunch noon–2:30 p.m. Mon.–Fri.; dinner nightly from 5 p.m.*

Rick's Café Americain $–$$ ★★
Victoria Park Market. ☎ *(09) 309-9074.*
The place for American-style brekkie. Blackboard lunch menu. *Hours 7:30–12:30 a.m. Mon.–Fri.; 9 a.m.–midnight weekends.* Budget breakfast (two eggs, bacon, toast \$NZ2.95), moderate otherwise.

Shakespeare Tavern $ ★
Corner of Albert and Wyndham streets. ☎ *(09) 373-5396.*
Probably our favorite lunch or post-shopping spot in the city. It is housed in a pink building and is the city's oldest private brewery, with a wide selection of brews and some very good counter meals, including steamed mussels. If you drink enough of their product (and can still walk), they give you a certificate. Live music and poetry readings on occasion. If the owner, Peter Barraclough, is around, tell him we said howdy. Beer and a daily lunch special *(11 a.m.–3 p.m. Mon.–Fri.)* is about \$NZ5.

Nightspots

The Customhouse Glato's
Customs Street near the harbor. ☎ *(09) 358-2185.*
Live music and disco Tues. through Sat.; live jazz Fri. noon.

Abby's
Corner of Wellesley and Albert streets. ☎ *(09) 303-4799.*
Live music Thurs., Fri., Sat., 8–11 p.m.

Burgundy's
289 Parnell Road. ☎ *(09) 309-5112.*
Cabaret and smorgasbord restaurant, dancing. Reservations required. *Open Thurs. through Sat.* Call for hours.

Auckland

Kestral Ferryboat

☎ *(09) 377-1771.*

The Kestral, an old ferry, runs from the ferry building to Devonport and back, offering dinner cruises and live music by the Riverboat Ramblers. *It normally sails starting at 7 p.m. Fri.* and Sat. nights. Also check with *Fuller's,* which runs dinner cruises.

The Coromandel Peninsula

About 120 kilometers by road from Auckland (and directly east as the crow flies) is one of the North Island's better-kept secrets—at least for many foreign visitors. Most folks around Auckland, as well as other parts of New Zealand, know the secret. It's called the Coromandel Peninsula.

Coromandel has many inviting swimming holes.

The peninsula juts northeast into the sea, separating the Bay of Plenty to the south from the Hauraki Gulf on the north, and creating the Firth of Thames directly to the west. In Maori legend, the peninsula is a giant canoe with the prow at Cape Colville and its stern at Te Aroha. *It is one of the North Island's most popular vacation spots, containing several excellent beaches, some great bush walks, lots of scenery and an assortment of places to stay.* It's roughly

100 kilometers long, and is crisscrossed by roads, some good, some pretty rough. (See "Road Conditions" later in this chapter.)

It's an easy drive from Auckland to Thames, the so-called "gateway" to the peninsula. *Note: The area code for the peninsula (and Thames) is (07).*

Captain James Cook came calling in the area in the 1770s at a place now called *Mercury Bay* on the peninsula's east coast. There is evidence to suggest that the area was one of the first settled by the Maoris who immigrated from the South Pacific more than 1000 years ago, and there are several *pa* sites that date back to around 750 A.D. European history in the peninsula began in earnest during a gold rush in the 1860s. At the peak, it is estimated that more than 70 mines were operating and according to official estimates more than 2 million ounces of gold were pulled from the ground during the mining era. At one point, Thames was the largest city in New Zealand, with 18,000 population, 100 hotels and three theaters. The peninsula was also at one time covered with kauri trees, which were all but wiped out by eager lumberjacks.

These days, Thames has a population of 6500 and large chunks of the peninsula are part of forest preserves and parks. The rugged scenery and excellent beaches make both sides of the peninsula a great place to spend a few days.

Getting to Thames and beyond is easy if you're driving. The motorway south of Auckland (Highway 1) is four-lane all the way to the peninsula turnoff (Highways 2 and 25). Figure a maximum three-hour drive. To really do the Coromandel area, you need a vehicle, but there are a number of companies offering trips from Auckland.

In Auckland, **Bush and Beach Ltd.** has a one-day tour from the city that hits the major spots on both sides of the peninsula, including a picnic lunch, for about $NZ150 per person. The more extensive two-day tour costs about $NZ350, which includes accommodations, meals and entertainment. *Bush and Beach,* ☎ *(09) 478-2882.*

Bus Service

If you want to try it on your own, there is good bus service from Auckland, Rotorua and other cities. Four companies cooperate for Coromandel service. Routes normally take you to Thames, where you then pick up shuttle bus service to major settlements around the peninsula. The service runs several times a day, seven days a week in the summer and six days during the winter. Buses in Auckland will either pick you up from your hotel or from the Downtown Rail Station. Normal service runs from 7:45 a.m. to 6 p.m. There is also direct afternoon service from Auckland to Paeroa and Waihi at the southern end of the peninsula. Return service normally runs from 10 a.m. to 9 p.m. Note that route times vary depending on which of the four carriers you use. Shuttle service around the peninsula runs daily during the

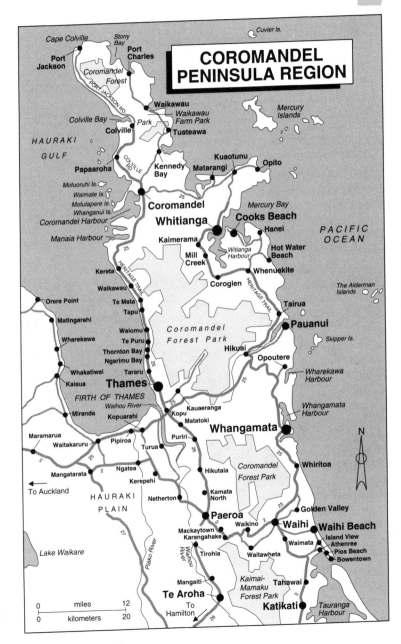

COROMANDEL PENINSULA REGION

Cuvier Is.

Cape Colville
Stony Bay
Port Charles
Port Jackson

Coromandel Forest

PORT JACKSON RD

Waikawau
Waikawau Farm Park

Colville Bay
Colville

Park

Tuateawa

Mercury Islands

HAURAKI GULF

Papaaroha

COLVILLE RD

Kennedy Bay

Kuaotunu

Matarangi

Opito

Motuoruhi Is.
Waimate Is.
Motutapere Is.
Whanganui Is.
Coromandel Harbour

Coromandel

25

Whitianga

Cooks Beach

Mercury Bay

Hanei

PACIFIC OCEAN

Manaia Harbour

Kaimerama

Mill Creek

Witianga Harbour

Hot Water Beach

HERITAGE TRAIL

Kereta

Whenuakite

Waikawau

Coroglen

The Alderman Islands

Te Mata

HERITAGE TRAIL

Tairua

Orere Point

Tapu

Pauanui

Matingarahi

Waiomu

Coromandel Forest Park

Skipper Is.

Wharekawa

Te Puru

Thornton Bay

Hikuai

Whakatiwai

Ngarimu Bay

25

Opoutere

Wharekawa Harbour

Kaiaua

Tararu

Thames

FIRTH OF THAMES

Waihou River

Kauaeranga

Whangamata Harbour

Miranda

Kopuarahi

Kopu

28

Matatoki

Whangamata

Maramarua

Pipiroa

Puriri

Waitakaruru

2

25

Turua

26

Coromandel Forest Park

Whiritoa

Mangatarata

2

Ngatea

Hikutaia

N

Kerepehi

Kamata North

To Auckland

HAURAKI PLAIN

Netherton

Paeroa

Golden Valley

27

Waikino

2

Waihi

Waihi Beach

Lake Waikare

Mackaytown
Karangahake

2

Waimata

Island View
Athenree
Pios Beach
Bowentown

Piako River

Tirohia

Waitawheta

Waihou River

Mangaiti

Kaimai-Mamaku Forest Park

Tahawai

Te Aroha

To Hamilton

28

Katikati

Tauranga Harbour

0 miles 12
0 kilometers 20

The Coromandel Peninsula

summer, Sunday–Friday in the winter. A Coromandel pass, which includes service from Auckland to the peninsula and back, is available for about $NZ75 per person; good for three months. General information about all services and reservations is available from **Murphy Buses** in Thames ☎ *(07) 868-6265*, or from the Auckland Visitors Centre. There is also a Thames area information center in the town at *405 Queen Street,* ☎ *(07) 868-7284; FAX (07) 868-7584.* **InterCity**, the nationwide bus/train/ferry service, provides regional service to Thames; information in Thames, ☎ *(07) 868-7251*; in Auckland, *(09) 357-8400*. Budget bus service information for backpackers is available at the visitors center. *For further information on peninsula bus services, contact Sunkist Lodge, 506 Brown Street, Thames,* ☎ *(07) 868-8808.*

You can also fly from Auckland to almost any place on the peninsula on **Air Coromandel** for about $NZ150 per person round-trip. It's a 30-minute flight, twice a day, seven days. The company also does scenic flights around the peninsula for $NZ25. *Information:* ☎ *(07) 866-4016; fax 866-4017.* Helicopter service is available through **Peninsula Helicopters** in Pauanui; ☎ *(07) 864-7099.*

The Coromandel Peninsula

Coromandel Peninsula features excellent beaches.

Most transportation and accommodations information is available at the Auckland information centers. To help you find your way around, there are several visitor centers scattered around the peninsula. They include Coromandel, on Kapanga Road, ☎ *(07) 866-8598*; Whitianga, on Albert Street ☎ *(07) 866-5555, FAX (07) 866-2222*; Whangamata, on Port Road, ☎ *(07) 865-8340*; Pauanui, at the shopping center, ☎ *(07) 864-7101*; Paeroa, on Belmont Road, ☎ *(07) 862-8636*, and Tairua, shopping center, main road,

☎ *(07) 864-7055.* The **AA office** in Thames is at *424 Pollen Street,* ☎ *(07) 868-8358.*

Around the Peninsula

Thames got its name from James Cook, who looked at the Waihou River nearby and thought it looked like the Thames River back in London. If you go to the part where there are a lot of mud flats, you might see his point. Modern Thames is your basic small New Zealand town with a few extra places to stay and eat because of the tourist boom. Nothing very special.

Visit a Gold Mine

If you're interested in the *mining history* of the town, go to the Thames Gold Mine and Stamper Battery complex at the north end of town across from the Cable Price Foundry. The complex, part of the original Thames goldfields, offers *underground tours* of some mines plus a look at the stamping machinery used to crush the ore. The tours, operated by the Hauraki Prospectors Association, take about 45 minutes and cost about $NZ5 per person. Call for hours. ☎ *(07) 868-7448.*

The best part of a Coromandel Peninsula tour will be the drive from Thames up along the east coast to the village of Coromandel. The road (Highway 25) hugs steep cliffs as it goes along the beach-ridden coastline, past small settlements, RV parks, hiking areas and often dense bush. The road lies at the base of the **Coromandel Range**, a line of peaks running down the spine of the peninsula, now mostly part of the **Coromandel Forest Park**. The park, about 185,000 acres, contains groves of protected kauri trees, as well as other indigenous trees and plants. Near Waiomu, on Highway 25 about 10 miles north of Thames, is the **Waiomu Kauri Grove**, the largest stand of trees on the peninsula. East of Tapu, a few miles farther on, is the famous **Square Kauri Tree**, one of the oldest in the area, estimated to be 1200 years old. You reach the tree by taking the Tapu-Coroglen road about 30 kilometers east.

For campers, hikers or just folks who want to get out into the open country, the best first stop on the peninsula is the **Department of Conservation** office at Kauaeranga, reached by taking the Kauaeranga Valley Road southeast from Thames. The DOC has maps and information about hiking, camping, off-road vehicles, camping huts and horse-riding areas. At the headquarters is a theater where you can see a film about the history of kauri logging in the area. *It's open daily 8 a.m.–4 p.m.;* ☎ *(07) 868-6381.*

Road Conditions

Most rental car agencies in New Zealand void insurance if vehicles travel on unpaved roads, which has been a problem getting around the peninsula in the past. Budget, after extensive discussions with tourism officials, finally dropped most of its ban on the peninsula *(a few of the really rugged roads are still off-limits: Highway 309, plus the road from Tapu to Coroglen, the road from Kuaotuna to Opito, and all roads north of Colville).* Other rental companies might have different exclusions; please ask. Half of all international visitors to the peninsula are in some form of rental vehicle.

By the Sea

Coromandel is a small village with a few old Victorians left over, and it gets pretty active during the tourist season. It also serves as an artists colony. From Coromandel, you can either go northwest to Long Bay and the excellent beach at **Oamaru Bay**, or northeast to **Kennedy Bay**, a popular crayfishing and yachtie harbor, or take the 309 road to Whitianga. The paved portion of the highway ends near Coromandel, starting again at Kaimarama. The road between is washboarded in places, but basically good. You will pass lots of pine forests, as well as ranch land and some nice beaches at Whangapoua Harbour and Kuaotunu Bay.

A Hahei Explorer *is a good way to see Cathedral Cove, Coromandel.*

The Whitianga area around Mercury Bay is probably the best beach area on the peninsula, as is the small headland opposite which contains **Cook's Beach**, **Cathedral Cove** and **Hahei**. The locals say it's the best scenery in New Zealand, and they're not far wrong. *The rugged seacoast is worth a stop, but it is hard to get to.* There are roads that go to Hahei, generally considered to be the best beach on the peninsula, from a point about halfway between Coroglen and Whenuakite on Highway 25 southeast of Whitianga. Also at this point is the road to the famous **Hot Water Beach**, where there are thermal streams just below the beach sand—just dig a hole, sit down, voilà: instant hot tub. **Whitianga** has a permanent population of around 3000, which rises to as much as 25,000 during the school holiday period. You can also reach the Cook's Bay/Cathedral Cove area by ferry from Whitianga. The ferry runs from 7:30 a.m. to noon and from 1–6:30 p.m. During school holidays, it runs from 7:30 a.m.–7:30 p.m. The fare is about $NZ2 round-trip. You can also reach Cook's Bay by hiking from Hahei, about a 40-minute jaunt.

For our money, the best spot to hang your hat on the east coast of Coromandel (maybe the whole peninsula, for that matter) is **Pauanui**, located on Tairua Harbour south of the Hot Water beach. The village cum retirement/ summer vacation spot is not easy to get to by regular bus service, as it's more than 10 kilometers off the main highway. Services in town are confined to a small shopping center, and nightlife is mostly absent. But the beach is great, the scenery superb and it's the location of our favorite Coromandel accommodations, the **Puka Park Lodge ★★★★**. (See "Where to Stay.") Across the harbor is Pauanui's twin settlement, **Tairua**, connected by a regular ferry service. Tairua is older and has more to offer in the way of services, accommodation, banks and restaurants, plus it's on the main highway. (In Tairua, try the **Pacific Harbour Motor Lodge ★★** in the middle of town; motel and Polynesian-style chalets, spa, kitchens. Doubles are $NZ100-135, depending on season. ☎ *and FAX (07) 864-8581.* Next door is the **Shell House ★★** restaurant, moderately priced South Pacific dining featuring fresh local seafood. *Open seven nights from 6 p.m.* ☎ *(07) 864-8811.* Both settlements have golf courses, fishing charters, Outback tours, and the beaches are probably the easiest to get to on the coast. Dominating the harbor between the two is **Paku**, a twin-coned Maori *pa* site; there's a trail to the top from Tairua. The Pauanui shopping center has a grocery store, several coffee shops, a library, medical center and a visitors center, *open seven days from 10 a.m.–4 p.m.* Here also is a well-known and popular restaurant, **Keith's ★★**. *It's open for lunch only in January; dinner all year from 6:30 p.m.–midnight Wednesday–Sunday.* Moderate. ☎ *(07) 864-8825.*

The hills in back of the Pauanui area are covered in dense virgin forest, and there are several good tracks to hike (check with the visitors center). Sharon Johansen runs tours all year to glowworm caves, gold mines, kauri forests and offshore islands. Give her a call at ☎ *and FAX (07) 864-8731.*

The same rugged scenery is what makes the **Puka Park Lodge ★★★★** so special. The lodge, one of the best in New Zealand, sits on 25 acres of lush bush amid native trees and ferns. The lodge's modern chalets are semi-rustic in decor, with wood furnishings, decks and (it's the bush, remember) mosquito netting. (Puka Park advertises a heated swimming pool—we tried it and froze. Maybe "heated" is relative.) The lodge offers two dining venues: the moderately priced **Café Puka ★★**, casual dress and a blackboard menu, and the main and expensive **Puka Park Restaurant ★ ★ ★**, semi-dress code and silver service. The café offers a range, from salads and soups to lamb shanks with white beans and rosemary and chicken with red wine and mushrooms. The main restaurant has a slightly more urbane menu: fresh grilled grouper, smoked salmon with artichoke hearts, filet of beef with peppercorns and cheese. Both restaurants have an excellent wine list, and the cheese and fruit plate dessert at both is also excellent, almost a meal in itself. The lodge can arrange many activities, including Harley motorcycle rides, luxury boat charters for fishing, parasailing or scuba, skeet shooting, helicopter rides, champagne picnics and tennis. If you want to be decadent, try a helicopter trip to nearby Slipper Island, a private island with a silver-sand beach, complete with gourmet picnic hamper and champagne ($NZ660 per couple). You can reach the lodge by helicopter or through Air Coromandel. Summer rates start at around $NZ300 standard double; suites up to $NZ1500. *Reservations and information:* ☎ *(07) 864-8088; FAX (07) 864-8112.*

Tours

There are a wide variety of activities on the peninsula, and a number of companies offer tours to satisfy most appetites. Among your choices:

Coromandel Connection

☎ *(07) 866-8468; FAX (07) 868-9760.*

This Coromandel company has the Coromandel Peninsula Pass, a three-day adventure excursion that takes you to the Hot Water Beach and Fletchers Bay, plus wine tasting, a half-day fishing trip, a visit to a mussel farm and hiking treks. If you're staying at a hotel in Auckland, the company will even pick you up there. The price of $NZ110 does not include accommodation or meals. Note: The company says its activities are "adventurous," and that they might "involve some element of danger." But there are also more genteel day tours from $NZ35–40.

Rangihau Ranch

Located about halfway between Whitianga and Tairua. ☎ *(07) 866-3875.*

It sits near Coroglen on the east coast. Here's your chance to horse around on the peninsula. The ranch has a herd of 30 steeds ready to take you on one- to three-hour rides through farmland, native bush and some great scenery. One-hour rides go for about $NZ20 per person, three-hour for $NZ40; there are also overnighters for $NZ80 (meals included). The rides follow 1800s-era pack horse trails; there are also trails for kids.

Aotearoa Tours & Adventures

147 Cook Dr. Whitianga. ☎ *(07) 866-2807; FAX the same.*

The company specializes in tours of the peninsula and the East Coast. The tours have a maximum of 16 persons, but most are in the 4-8 person range. The price of the tours includes door-to-door pickup in Auckland. Coromandel one-day tours can be tailored to special interests; look for a price of around $NZ80 per person including lunch.

Where to Stay

Thames

Brian Boru Hotel · $NZ90–350 · ★ ★ ★

200 Richmond Street, downtown. ☎ *(07) 868-6523; FAX (07) 868-9760.*
Built in 1868, the hotel is home to popular *mystery weekend packages* (30 guests, eight actors spend the weekend solving a crime). Call the hotel for mystery weekend dates. Licensed restaurant, bar, courtesy van. Normal doubles are $NZ90. The mystery package, which includes two nights' accommodations, a tour of the peninsula, a fancy dress dinner and the mystery, is about $NZ350 per person.

The bulk of the other accommodations on the Peninsula are motels and B&B units, almost all in the two- to three-star range. Among the Thames offerings are the following:

Avalon Motel · $NZ75–100

Jellicoe Crescent, south of Thames. ☎ *(07) 868-7755; FAX the same.*
Kitchens, executive spa suite, pool and sauna, BBQ, laundry, breakfast available.

Crescent Motel · $NZ75–85 · ★

100 Fenton Street, corner of Jellicoe south of Thames. ☎ *(07) 868- 6506; FAX (07) 868-8050.*
Best Western, kitchens, BBQ, courtesy van, spa pool, laundry, breakfast available.

Rolleston Motel · $NZ85

105 Rolleston Street, 1 kilometer from city center. ☎ *(07) 868-8091.*
Pool, spa, tour desk, courtesy van, BBQ, breakfast available.

Coastal Motor Lodge · $NZ90–110 · ★ ★

Highway 25, 2 kilometers north of Thames. ☎ *(07) 868-6843; FAX (07) 868-6520.*
Chalets with sea view, spa, laundry, rangettes, handicapped facilities, close to restaurant.

Sunset Motel · $NZ75

Highway 25, 4 kilometers north of town. ☎ *(07) 868-8573.*
Kitchens, laundry, spa, tea/coffee, courtesy van, breakfast available.

Dickson Holiday Park · $NZ12–70

Off Highway 25, 3.5 kilometers north of Thames on Victoria Street. ☎ *(07) 868-7308; FAX the same.*
Pool, linen rental, kitchen, courtesy van, barbecue, sports equipment, laundry. On-site RVs, $NZ35-45 double; tourist flats, $NZ55-70 double; cabins, $NZ40-50 double; dorm beds, $NZ12 per person; RV sites, $NZ18.

Waiomu Bay Holiday (RV) Park · $NZ10–75 · ★ ★

Off Highway 25, 13 kilometers north of Thames. ☎ *(07) 868-2777.*
A Top 10 park. Kitchen, recreation hall, laundry, beach, pool. Motel units about $NZ75 double; tourist flats $NZ55; cabins $NZ40; RV sites $NZ10 per person.

Sunkist Backpacker's Lodge · $NZ15–40

506 Brown Street, north Thames. ☎ *(07) 868-8808; FAX (07) 868-7426.*
Maybe the only hostel in New Zealand with a ghost. The lodge was built in 1868. Doubles and dorm rooms. Laundry, bike rental, courtesy van.

The Coromandel Peninsula

On the Peninsula

Angler's Lodge Motel and Camp Park   **$NZ80–95**

Amodeo Bay, about 18 kilometers north of Coromandel. ☎ *(07) 866-8584.*
Some one- and two-bedroom units plus RV and tent sites. Pool, spa, laundry, camp store, tennis, dinghy rental. Motel doubles $NZ95; cabins, $NZ80.

Coromandel Colonial Cottages   **$NZ85**   ★★

Rings Road, 2 kilometers from Coromandel town center. ☎ *(07) 866-8857; FAX the same.*
The units are two-bedroom cottages, fully equipped. Pool, laundry, spa, handi-capped facilities. Four-wheel-drive rentals.

Coromandel Hotel   **$NZ25**

Kapanga Road, Coromandel city center. ☎ *(07) 866-8760; FAX (07) 866-8241.*
Historic 19th-century pub. À la carte restaurant/bar, tea/coffee, breakfast available.

Tui Lodge   **$NZ14–35**

600 Whangapoua Road, on Highway 25 just east of Coromandel. ☎ *(07) 866-8237.*
A hostel set in an orchard, with rooms in a chalet and a dorm. Bus service, bike rental, laundry, courtesy van, friendly folks. $NZ35 double; dorm beds $NZ14 per person; chalets $NZ25 per person.

Mercury Bay Beachfront Resort   **$NZ75–165**   ★★

111-113 Buffalo Beach Road, Whitianga. ☎ *(07) 866-5637; FAX (07) 866-4524.*
Safe beach, kitchens, courtesy van, restaurant. Spa, BBQ, catamaran, fishing and golf equipment. Doubles about $NZ75–165, depending on season and unit.

Homestead Park Resort   **$NZ90–200**   ★★

Purangi Road, Flaxmill Bay. ☎ *(07) 866-5595; FAX the same.*
At the ferry landing near Cook's Beach across from Whitianga. Better cottages on a secluded beach, tanning rooms, windsurfers and dinghies for rent, courtesy van, spa. Doubles about $NZ90–200.

Buffalo Beach Tourist Resort
(also the Marlin Motor Lodge)   **$NZ20–75**   ★★★

13 Buffalo Beach Road, corner of Eyre Street, Whitianga. ☎ *(07) 866-5854; FAX the same.*
Top 10 facility, *probably the best on the peninsula*. Seven acres of park, within walk-ing distance of seven beaches. Waterfront motel units, Champagne Hot Springs thermal pool, cold pool, backpackers lodge, kitchen, laundry. Close to restaurants and wharf. Motel units, $NZ40–75 double; backpacker's lodge $NZ30 double. RV sites $NZ20.

Hahei Holiday Resort   **$NZ30–70**

Harsant Avenue, Hahei Beach, near Cook's Beach across from Whitianga. ☎ *(07) 866-3889; FAX the same.*
Part of the Kiwihost group. On the beach, laundry, BBQ, close to restaurants. Tent and RV sites. Cabins, $NZ45 double; tourist flats, $NZ60-70 double. Backpackers lodge $NZ30-35.

Aotearoa Lodge   **$NZ75–230**   ★★★

Highway 1, 17 kilometers south of Whitianga near Coroglen. ☎ *(07) 866-3808.*
An upscale B&B lodge offering a variety of packages, including fishing, rafting, bush treks, diving and hunting. Tea/coffee, courtesy van. Rates are about $NZ75

per person a night; dinner by arrangement. A three-day adventure package with various options is about $NZ230 per person, including meals and accommodation.

Cedarwood Motor Hotel $NZ95–110
Port Road, Whangamata. ☎ *(07) 865-9211; FAX the same.*
Licensed seven-day restaurant, tennis, pool, spa, sauna, kitchens, tea/coffee. Some two-bedroom units. Doubles about $NZ95–110.

Whangamata Motel $NZ65–85
106 Barbara Avenue. ☎ *(07) 865-8250; FAX the same.*
One- and two-bedroom units. Close to beach. Pool, spa, kitchens, doubles from $NZ65–85.

Whangamata Backpackers $NZ16
227 Beverley Terrace. ☎ *(07) 865-8323.*
Close to town and beach. Kitchen, lounge, laundry, tour bookings. $NZ16 per bed.

Whangamata Motor Camp $NZ8–35
Barbara Avenue, close to beach. ☎ *(07) 865-9128.*
Kitchen, laundry, BBQ, dairy store. Cabins $NZ35 double. RV and tent sites $NZ8 per person.

Where to Eat

In Thames

Old Thames Restaurant $$ ★★
704 Pollen Street. ☎ *(07) 868-7207.*
Natural wood paneling with photos of the good old days, lots of machinery hanging around. Menu outside the door (very civilized), specializing in seafood and lamb, but also family-style offerings such as satays and steak. *Lunch noon–2 p.m., dinner 5 p.m.–midnight, seven days.*

Brian Boru Hotel Restaurant $$ ★★
Corner of Richmond and Pollen streets. ☎ *(07) 868-6523.*
À la carte, buffets and set menus. *Lunch noon–2 p.m., dinner 6–10 p.m.*

Cotswold Cottage $$ ★★
Maramarahi Road. ☎ *(07) 868-6306.*
Set menus on Sunday; popular, so call ahead. Seafood, lamb and chicken specialties. *Lunch Wed. through Fri., noon–2 p.m.; dinner from 6 p.m. Tues. through Sun.*

Regency Room $ ★★
Hotel Imperial, 476 Pollen Street. ☎ *(07) 868-6200.*
Bistro bar, good Sunday night carvery. *Dinner 5:30–9:30 p.m.*

Bakery Coffee Lounge, The $ ★
326 Pollen Street. ☎ *(07) 868-6719.*
The place for breakfast; fresh baked goods. Also meat pies and other take-aways. *Hours 7:30 a.m.–4 p.m. seven days.*

On the Peninsula

Te Puru Coast View Lodge Restaurant $$ ★★
Te Puru, Highway 25, 14 kilometers north of Thames. ☎ *(07) 868-2326.*

The Coromandel Peninsula

Lovely white Spanish adobe-style building on a hill, (*specializing in Tex-Mex*, but also seafood). BYO. Limited seating, call ahead. *Lunch noon–2 p.m.; dinner 6–9 p.m.*

Coromandel Hotel $$ ★★★

Kapanga Road, city center. ☎ *(07) 866-8760.*
Good selection of fresh seafood, especially mussels and exquisite scallops. Bistro as well as à la carte. Reservations necessary. *Lunch noon–1:30 p.m.; dinner 6–8:30 p.m. Mon.–Sat.; Sun. summer only.* Bottle shop.

Kingfisher Restaurant $$ ★★

37 Albert Street, Whitianga. ☎ *(07) 866-4010.*
Licensed, à la carte, specializing in Mercury Bay seafood. Call for hours.

Doyle's $$ ★★

21 Esplanade, Whitianga. ☎ *(07) 866-5209.*
Nice views of Buffalo Beach. Seafood a specialty: oysters, chowders, smoked salmon, whitebait; also pasta and steaks. *Open seven days, breakfast 7:30–10:30 a.m.; lunch only in the summer, 11:30 a.m.–2:30 p.m., dinner from 5:30 p.m.*

Snapper Jacks $$ ★★

Corner Albert and Monk streets, Whitianga. ☎ *(07) 866-5482.*
Another seafood place, but also has take-away fish and chips and such. The specialty is the Seafood Bazaar, using whatever's fresh that day. *Lunch 11:30 a.m.–2 p.m.; dinner from 6 p.m.; open seven days.*

Port City Restaurant $ ★★

606 Port Road in DJ's Mall, Whangamata. ☎ *(07) 865-9121.*
Cantonese BYO and take-aways. Very popular. *Lunch noon–2 p.m. Mon.–Sat.; dinner (reservations required) from 6 p.m. seven nights.*

Whangamata Hotel ★★

Highway 25, 3 kilometers north of town. ☎ *(07) 865-8521.*
Family fare; dining in the garden in the summer. Pub food but also lots of seafood. Bottle shop and live entertainment some nights.

Rotorua

The green and white terraces of Waiotapu in Rotorua are spectacular.

We don't like Rotorua much, because it is over-touristed, commercial and fairly unattractive, but there's no denying its popularity as a major draw for visitors coming to New Zealand, as the rows of tour buses will attest. In fairness, it is worth a short stop to see the geysers and hot mud pools, but we think, for enjoyment of the North Island's geothermal wonders, there are better places.

Rotorua is about 220 miles southeast of Auckland, and sits in the middle of what is called the **Taupo Volcanic Zone**, which goes from northeast to southwest across the North Island. The area has long been a popular spa area, and the locals make use of the hot steam that rises to the surface for heating their homes, cooking and building their own private hot pools. (You smell the city

319

long before you get to it.) Over the years, the amount of thermal activity has slowed. Some of the blame is put on all the homes and hotels and pools that have tapped into the hot underground water and steam sources, but a large part of the reduction is often blamed on the big geothermal power plant at Wairakei near Taupo, one of the largest geothermal power plants in the world. At least one other plant on the volcanic zone is planned, adding to fears that the golden goose might be in danger.

Rotorua offers a Maori cultural center where you can see dancing or watch Maori artists at work.

The usual focus for all 600,000 or so tourists who visit the city each year is the **Whakarewarewa Thermal Reserve**, which has the country's largest geyser, **the Pohutu**, which goes off with no set schedule and sprays anywhere from a half hour to several hours. It shoots water 100 feet or so into the air and is fairly spectacular. Also within the reserve are mud pools, hot springs and mineral pools. The reserve is also a **Maori cultural center**, where you can see dancing or watch Maori artists carving and creating other artifacts. The front door of the reserve is an elaborately carved Maori gateway, and there is a replica of a Maori *pa* on view where you can see food cooked in thermal springs and other activities. There is also a nocturnal house where you can spot a kiwi or two. Daily concerts at the *pa* are given at 12:15 p.m. November–April and during school holidays. Guided tours of the **New Zealand Maori Arts and Crafts Institute** on the grounds are run hourly from 9 a.m.–4 p.m. daily. The tour takes about two hours, and you get to see works in progress, as well as finished pieces. There is a gift store. *The reserve is about 3 kilometers south of the city on Highway 5 (Fenton Street). Hours are 8:30–4:30 p.m. daily;* admission

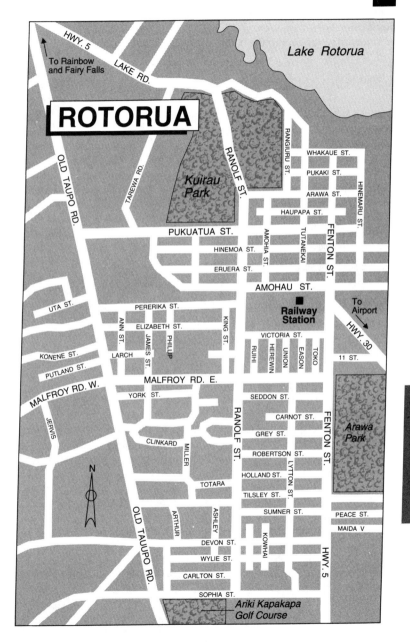

is about $NZ10 per person, which includes the crafts center tour. The concert is extra. For information, ☎ *(07) 348-9047.* By the way, don't bend your teeth trying to pronounce the name—the locals just call it "Whaka."

Thermal Pools

The country's largest geyser, Pohutu, shoots water 100 feet or more in the air at Whakarewarewa Thermal Reserve.

Being a spa city, Rotorua has a number of places where you can plunk your body into thermal waters. The biggest and probably most popular are the **Polynesian Pools**, dating from 1882, situated near the Government Gardens. There are several famous springs here—including **Priest** and **Radium**—all having different mineral content and alleged to aid in your health. Priest and Radium are acidic springs and change temperature and turbidity according to geothermal activity (kids not allowed); the temperatures range between 92 and 110 degrees Fahrenheit. Most of the public pools are soft water with alkaline content, usually about 100 degrees Fahrenheit. There are also about 30 private and family pools available, as well as massage and hydrotherapy services. The large public pools (kids okay) cost about $NZ6.50 per person for a half-hour; the private pools about $NZ7.50 per person for a half-hour; Priest and Radium are $NZ6.50 per person a half-hour. Massage by appointment is $NZ35. Towels, security lockers and suits can be rented for about $NZ2 each. The small private pools are about the size of a large walk-in closet, with changing rooms and an open ceiling. *Facility hours are 6:30 a.m.–10 p.m. daily.* Souvenir shop and restaurant. ☎ *(07) 348-1328.*

A bit farther afield, another popular Rotorua-area spa is at **Waikite**, about 35 kilometers south on Highway 5. Boiling hot water is cooled by three cascading pools into the main pool, which is set in a parklike area. There is a private pool and a kids' pool. Light refreshments are available. *Hours are 10 a.m.–10 p.m. daily;* admission is about $NZ5.

If you didn't get your fill of thermal activity at Whaka, another popular spot is the **Waimangu Volcanic Valley** southeast of the city about 30 kilometers. Take Highway 5 south, then turn left onto Waimangu Road. Entry to the valley costs about $NZ10.

Among the attractions is the **Waimangu Caldron**, supposedly the *world's largest boiling lake*, and the Inferno Crater, a lake that rises and falls about 30 feet a month. For another $NZ15, you can take a launch trip on **Lakes Rotomahana** and **Tarawera**. The launch passes the site of the once-famous **Pink and White Terraces**, two huge silica ledges on the shores of Lake Rotomahana, which drew visitors from around the world. But on June 10, 1886, nearby Mt. Tarawera, supposedly an extinct volcano, erupted, burying the terraces and also the nearby village of **Te Wairoa**. The village, reached by a second launch, has a small museum with photos taken before and after the eruption. *The valley is open 8:30 a.m.–5 p.m. seven days.* ☎ *(07) 366-6137.*

The New Zealand Maori Arts and Crafts Institute has an impressive display of Maori carvings.

A Peek Inside a Crater

It's possible to take a trip to the top of the mountain to look into the crater, 700 feet deep, five miles long. The trip, combining a boat trip with four-wheel drive up the mountain, can be booked with several companies through the city information center. If you have your own vehicle, drive south on Highway 5 to Highway 38 toward Lake Rerewhakaaitu, turn left on Rerewha-

Rotorua

kaaitu Road, left on Bretts Road to Ash Pit Road, then turn right, following the signs to a parking lot. The summit is about two hours up. Wear a jacket because it can get really cold on top, and carry water. It's not difficult, just a good hike. The view is incredible. The mountain is Maori trust land, so you need permission first from the Te Arawa Trust Board on Pukuatua Street. ☎ *(07) 348-9498.* Four-wheel-drive tours are available for about $NZ65 per person from **Mount Te Arawa FourWD Tours**. The price includes pickup from your hotel and morning/afternoon teas. ☎ *(07) 357-4026.*

Excavated Village

With your own vehicle, you can also drive to the **Buried Village**, going past Blue and Green Lakes. The village, covered by more than six feet of mud and debris from the blast, has been partially excavated; work continues. There is a café and souvenir shop, and bush walks around the village take in waterfalls and streams. Take Highway 30 east from town, then turn onto Tarawera Road about 3 kilometers from the city. You can catch the launch here for the trip over to the Pink and White Terraces, as well. There is also a trail up to Mt. Tarawera on the narrow neck of land you walk over to get from launch to launch. *Open 8:30 a.m.–5 p.m. seven days.* Admission to the village is about $NZ10. ☎ *(07) 362-8287.*

Another popular geyser is the **Lady Knox**, which, like Old Faithful, erupts regularly—in this case, at 10:15 a.m. The geyser is part of the Wai-o-Tapu thermal area about 30 kilometers south of town off Highway 5 (the name means "Sacred Waters" in Maori). Other attractions are the **Champagne Pool** (hot springs), the **Primrose Terraces**, which give a good idea of what the pink and white terraces were like before they were buried in 1886, and **Bridal Veil Falls**. Entry to the area, definitely worth a trip, costs about $NZ10. *It's open from 8:30 a.m. to dusk all year.* ☎ *(07) 348-5637.*

Finally, for some lively thermal activity (sorry, no geysers), try **Hell's Gate**, a small but very interesting thermal area about 15 kilometers east of town on Highway 30. Smaller and more intimate than Whakarewarewa, it's also not as crowded but just as fascinating; self-guided tour. *Hours are 9 a.m.–5 p.m. daily;* admission is about $NZ10. ☎ *(07) 345-3151.*

If you like things a bit less sedate, do please try the two-day safaris offered by **Tamaki Tours** in Rotorua. For about $NZ250 per person, you will climb down into the Mt. Tarawera crater, do a horseback trek through virgin forest, camp alongside the Whakatane River, have a bush dinner, raft some white-water rapids on the Rangitaiki River, soak in a hot-water stream in the bush and be dropped off back at your hotel. A definite hoot. ☎ *(07) 346-2823.*

Another good tour is the one-day outing offered through **Tourism Rotorua**. For about $NZ120, you get free hotel pickup, a visit to Wai-o-Tapu and the Lady Knox geyser, a hot stream swim, picnic lunch, a tour of the Waimangu

Valley and a four-wheel-drive trip to Mt. Tarawera. ☎ *(07) 347-1199* (24 hours).

Tourists take a lunch break at Lake Okataina, Rotorua.

On the Water

Rotorua is set amid a number of lakes, so there are plenty of water-oriented activities for visitors. One popular set of excursions is aboard the **Lakeland Queen**, a paddle-wheeler with a number of day and evening cruises, some with snacks or dinner; prices $NZ15–40. There are about four trips a day. ☎ *(07) 348-6634.*

Several cruises are available on Lake Tarawera through the **Lake Tarawera Launch Service**. There's a daily 2.5-hour cruise to the volcano, and arrangements can be made for fishing, barbecues and other activities. The cruise is about $NZ25. ☎ *(07) 362-8595.*

Within short driving distances from Rotorua are a number of white-water rivers, and several companies in town offer trips from amateur to hair-curling. A popular choice is **Huka Jets**, which does the Waikato River. The company, owned by the widely respected Shotover Jet company in Queenstown, charges about $NZ65 for the half-day trip. ☎ *(07) 348-5179.* Also try the **River Rats** (six rivers) at ☎ *(07) 347-8068*, or **Longridge Jet** at ☎ *(07) 533-1515.*

Air Tours

One way to see many of the volcanic sites of the North Island quickly is by plane, such as flights offered by **White Island Airways** in Rotorua. The company's offerings range from short jaunts over Mt. Tarawera (about $NZ110 per person) to flights to White Island and then along the Taupo Fault Zone

Rotorua

(about $NZ225). The company also operates biplanes and does aerobatic flights. ☎ *(07) 345-9832.*

Other companies offer helicopter or float plane trips—try **Tarawera Helicopters**, ☎ *(07) 348-1223*; **Volcanic Air Safaris**, ☎ *(07) 348-9984;* or **Marine Helicopters**, ☎ *(07) 357-2512.* Prices and itineraries vary.

Trout Fishing

The Rotorua area, combined with Lake Taupo to the south, is one of the finest trout fishing regions in the world. If you don't bring your own equipment, there are many guides in the area who can supply gear, boats and licenses. As a rule, the guides will run you about $US30 an hour for stream fishing (usually a minimum of two hours) or about $US35 an hour for lake trolling (also two-hour minimum). Licenses, if not issued by the guides, are available at the Department of Conservation office or at sporting goods stores. A couple of guides to check with are **Bryan Colman**, *32 Kiwi Street in Rotorua*, ☎ *(07) 348-7766,* and **Ray Dodunski**, ☎ *(07) 349-2555.* Other guide services are available through the city information center.

If you want your fishing with a little upscale relaxation, there are several excellent lodges in the Rotorua area that can set up fishing trips or other activities. Non-fishers can just enjoy the high-quality service and cuisine. Our favorite is the **Moose Lodge ★ ★ ★ ★ ★**, on Lake Rotoiti about 15 kilometers east of town on Highway 30. The lodge was built as a getaway home for a very rich contractor, Noel Cole, and has been visited by all manner of swells, including Queen Elizabeth and Charles and Diana. The 100-acre site includes golf, tennis facilities, and the lodge has its own bubbling thermal pool. It's a very special place and has a fishing boat of its own. Reservations should be made at least two months in advance; during the Christmas period, more like two years ahead. Rates for full board (all meals) are about $NZ441–702. One of the top resort lodges in New Zealand. Occasionally the lodge will have room for dinner even if you're not staying there; give 'em a call as far in advance as possible. ☎ *(07) 362-7823; FAX (07) 362-7677.*

A couple of other lodges, for fine service or for use as a fishing base, are the **Solitaire Lodge ★ ★ ★ ★**, a secluded place on the shores of Lake Tarawera. The tariff of about $NZ980-1500 per couple includes all meals and liquor. It's smoke-free. ☎ *(07) 362-8208; FAX (07) 362-8445.* The **Muriaroha Lodge ★ ★ ★ ★**, located in Rotorua on Old Taupo Road, features private garden suites. The price of about $NZ600 per couple includes most meals and liquor. ☎ *(07) 346-1220; FAX (07) 346-1338.*

Much closer to what most of us fly fishers expect in an angling camp can be found at the **Ohau Channel Lodge ★ ★** on the northeast shore of Lake Rotorua. It's basically motel-style, but the emphasis is definitely on fishing. It has boat and equipment rental, cleaning facilities, a smokehouse and guides.

The lodge is also headquarters for the Rotorua District Trout Fishing School. Rates at the lodge, which also has RV and tent sites, are about $NZ60 double; all units have cooking equipment and dishes; linen can be rented. ☎ *and FAX (07) 362-4761.*

Museums

The main museum area in town is at the so-called **Tudor Towers**, an old hulk that used to house the Government Bath House but now is home to the **Rotorua District Museum** and the **Rotorua Art Gallery**. The museum has a good display about the Pink and White Terraces, plus a re-creation of the old mud baths that used to draw the crowds. The gallery houses an extensive collection of national art, including some fine studies of Maori life. *The two facilities are open 10 a.m.–4:30 p.m. daily.* Admission $NZ4. Tudor Towers is situated in the Government Gardens, a 100-acre preserve. On most sunny afternoons, the grounds are crawling with lawn bowlers. ☎ *(07) 349-8334.*

More Sheep

One Rotorua attraction that should be hokey but manages to pull it off anyway is the **Agrodome**, where you can get a really good look at how the New Zealand sheep business operates. There are three shows a day (9:15 and 11 a.m. and 2:30 p.m.), and you'll get to see sheepdogs do their thing, plus watch a champion shearer in action. The facility is about five miles north of town on Highway 5. Tickets are about $NZ10. You can also ride horses and milk a cow, if you're really bored. There's a store selling sheepskin and other souvenirs. ☎ *(07) 357-4350.*

For those who like to look at fish but not necessarily catch them, there are several *trout springs* around town, full of some truly humongous fish. The best is probably **Rainbow Springs**, a couple of miles north on Highway 5. There is also an aviary, as well as a nocturnal kiwi house, tuataras and some Cap'n Cookers. For the kids, there's a bunch of farm pets and some deer. *Hours are 8 a.m.–5 p.m.*; admission is about $NZ10. Across the road is the **The Rainbow Farm Show**, another sheep epic, which costs about $NZ8 but isn't as good as the Agrodome. Show times are 10:30 a.m., 1 and 2:30 p.m. It has a restaurant. Information for the farm show, ☎ *(07) 347-8104*; the Springs, ☎ *(07) 347-9301.*

Next door to the Rainbow facilities is the **Skyline Skyrides**, a gondola that goes up Aorangi Peak with views of the city and the lakes. There's a licensed restaurant on top. If you're absolutely mad, you can try the so-called "luge track," a kilometer-long sidewalk you ride down on little blue cars with handlebars, a dandy way to scrape your nose and bang your butt. It's very popular, however. The round-trip on the gondola is about $NZ10; the luge rides are $NZ5 a pop. *Open seven days from 10 a.m.* ☎ *(07) 347-0027.*

Rotorua

Golf

There are four golf courses in the city, three of which are 18-holers. The Rotorua Golf Club course, with the wholly daunting name of **Arikikapakapa**, is 18 holes. The clubhouse and bar facilities are open seven days, and electric carts and rental clubs are available. ☎ *(07) 348-4051.* Springfield offers the same amenities. ☎ *(07) 348-2748.* The Lake View Golf Club has great views of the lake. Information, ☎ *(07) 357-4675.*

A Maori storehouse at Whakarewarewa

Maori Visits

A very popular reason for coming to Rotorua is the large number of *hangi* feasts and Maori concerts held at local hotels and Maori villages. *Hangi* means "cooking pot" in Maori, but the basic idea is the same as a luau. One of the things they'll force on you is the traditional *hongi*, the Maori nose-to-nose greeting, plus maybe a try at a *haka* or two—the war dance of greeting. The food will be traditional Maori: sweet potatoes, mussels, pork, lamb, venison, and it'll fill you up. Everybody in town seems to have a favorite place to do the *hangi*, but your best bet is the nightly party at the **THC Rotorua International** at the corner of Tryon and Froude streets off Highway 5 near the Whaka thermal area. The tab for the *hangi* and the entertainment is about $NZ45 per person and might be the best you'll see in New Zealand. Doors open at 6 p.m., the Maori concert starts at 8 p.m. *Reservations* and *transport information:* ☎ *(07) 348-1189.* There are also *hangi*/concerts at the **Sheraton**, nightly from 7 p.m., concert at 8:30 p.m., ☎ *(07) 348-7139*; the **Quality Resort Hotel**, nightly from 7:30 p.m., concert at 8:30 p.m., ☎ *(07) 347-1234*; the **Lake Plaza Hotel**, nightly from 6:45 p.m., concert at 8:30 p.m.,

☎ *(07) 348-1174.* In addition, there is a *hangi* at the restaurant in the Tudor Towers; daily at 7 p.m. during the summer (meal not mandatory). Check with the hotels for prices; most will be around $NZ40–55 per person.

A Maori sculpture made from jade

You can also just take in Maori concerts without the food. In addition to the noontime show at Whakarewarewa, there are evening concerts at the Maori Cultural Theatre in the Civic Theatre Building on Haupapa Street at 7 p.m. daily, or at the Tamatekapua Meeting House. These concerts will run you about $NZ10-15 and can be booked at the visitors center. **Carey's Sightseeing** offers a trip to a Maori settlement south of town for the Te Maori Encounter, a *hangi*/concert at the Tumunui Cultural Centre. Pickup from Rotorua during the summer is at 6 p.m.; winter 5:30 p.m. The $NZ45 cost includes transportation.

If you really want to do the Maori bit in style, try one of the overnight stays at a Maori settlement near Rotorua. At **Waka Hikoi**, on the shores of Lake Rotoiti, you can have a concert, a *hangi*, a soak in a secluded hot spring, a nature walk and breakfast. You spend the night sleeping on the floor of a traditional *marae* (meeting house). The price is about $NZ125 per person. Waka Hikoi also has longer stays, which include kayak trips, bush walks and visits to thermal sites. ☎ *(07) 362-7878*. A similar experience is offered by the **Te Arawa Tangata Maoris**. The overnight stay runs about $NZ95 and includes a hangi and concert; the concert and feast alone are about $NZ45. Information: ☎ *(07) 332-3446*.

The Essential Rotorua

Information

The Tourism Rotorua Centre is the city's new and comprehensive visitor information facility, located at *67 Fenton Street* near Government Gardens. Opened in 1993 by Prime Minister Jim Bolger, it incorporates two restored historic buildings, a post office and the old tourist bureau. Services include visitors information, a café, baggage storage, gift shop, shower facilities, transportation and tour booking services, a map shop, and "Visions of New Zealand," a $NZ2.50 audiovisual show in the building's theater. A new sight-seeing shuttle service starts from the center and runs to most of the city's tourist spots (hotel pickup by arrangement). The cost is $NZ14 for a half-day pass, $NZ20 for a full day. The Department of Conservation offices are also here. *Open seven days 8 a.m.–5:30 p.m. Center information,* ☎ *(07) 348-5179; FAX (07) 348-6044*.

The Automobile Association office is at *59 Amohau Street. Hours are 8:30 a.m.–5 p.m. Mon.–Fri.; 24 hour service.* ☎ *(07) 348-3069, after hours* ☎ *(0800) 807-766*.

The Forestry Corporation of New Zealand office in the Whakarewarewa State Forest Park is a little tough getting to, but it's on the same road you take to get to the Buried Village. Go on Highway 5 to the Sheraton, turn east onto Sala Street, go to Te Ngae Road, turn right to Tarawera Road, then right again to Long Mile Road and another right. *It's open 9 a.m.–5 p.m. Mon.–Fri. and 10 a.m.–4 p.m. weekends.* ☎ *(07) 346-2082*.

Banks

Most of the major banks are located along Hinemoa Street (two blocks south of the tourist information office). *Banking hours are from 9 a.m.–4:30 p.m., Mon.–Fri.*

Post Office

The Rotorua GPO is also on Hinemoa Street, corner of Tutanekai Street. *Hours are 8:30 a.m.–4:30 p.m. Mon.–Thurs.; Fri. 8:30 a.m.–5 p.m.* ☎ *(07) 347-7851*.

How to Get There

Mt. Cook Airlines flies several flights from Auckland to Rotorua for about $NZ180 one way. The airline also flies from Christchurch ($NZ290); Wellington ($NZ200); Queenstown ($NZ525), plus other cities. Ansett also has similar flights.

Rotorua

Regular Bus service is available on both Newman's and InterCity buses with connections to most North Island cities. The fare from Auckland is about $NZ45 one way; from Wellington, about $NZ75. The Auckland-Rotorua trip is about four hours, and it's about eight hours from Wellington. The InterCity terminal is on Amohau Street (Highway 5) near the Air New Zealand office in the center of town; ☎ *(07) 348-1039,* after hours, ☎ *(07) 379-9020.* Newman's is in the information center at the Corner of Fenton and Haupapa streets near Government Gardens; ☎ *(07) 348-0999.* All these buses stop at the information center, which also can book the trips for you.

Getting Around

There is regular Reesby's bus service that hits most of the major tourist spots, from Whaka to the Rainbow Farm. There is a one-day, unlimited pass for about $NZ10 you can buy from the driver. The depot is on Marguerita Street. Information: ☎ *(07) 347-0098.*

Taxis can be obtained 24 hours by calling ☎ *(07) 348-5079.* Mount Cook Landline operates a half-day tour of the city, including stops at Whaka, the Agrodome and Rainbow and Fairy Springs. The fare is about $NZ40 per person. The Mount Cook office is on Amohau Street next to the Air New Zealand office. ☎ *(07) 347-7451.* The fare from the airport is about $NZ15. Shuttles are about $NZ10 for two people.

Where to Stay

Moose Lodge   **$NZ441–702**   ★ ★ ★ ★ ★

SH 30, R.D. 4, Lake Rotoiti. ☎ *(07) 362-7823; FAX: (07) 362-7677.*
Spread over 100 acres, this luxury lodge overlooking Lake Rotoiti and surrounded by magnificent gardens, also features a golf course, tennis court, helipad, boathouse and mineral baths. Twenty suites are available including four deluxe suites with private spa baths. The lodge features a large restaurant and conference facilities. Royalty, heads of state and celebrities have enjoyed Moose Lodge as an elegant refuge.In and around the lodge, you can go fishing, hunting, horseback riding, boating, walk in the bush or soak in thermal pools. The attractions of Rotorua are 15 minutes away.

Sheraton   **$NZ205–300**   ★ ★ ★

Corner of Fenton and Sala streets near the Whaka thermal area. ☎ *(07) 349-5200.*
Rooms include eight suites with private spas and balconies. Three restaurants, bar, pool, health center, thermal facilities, handicapped facilities, minibars, coffee/tea. Standard doubles, $NZ205; suites with spas $NZ300 and up.

Lake Plaza   **$NZ155–225**   ★ ★ ★

6 Eruera. ☎ *(07) 348-1174; FAX (07) 346-0238.*
Heated indoor/outdoor swimming pool, private spas, restaurant/bar, minibars, coffee/tea equipment, laundry, business center. Standard rooms have shower only; superior have bath and shower. Standard doubles start at $NZ155; suites $NZ225.

Quality Resort Lake Rotorua   **$NZ180**   ★ ★

Hinemaru Street near the lakeshore and the Polynesian Pools. ☎ *(07) 347-1234; FAX (07) 348-1234.*
Restaurant, bar, coffee/tea, handicapped facilities, heated pool, health center.

Rotorua

Quality Hotel Rotorua   **$NZ160**   ★★

Corner of Fenton and Maida Vale streets near the Sheraton. ☎ *(07) 348-0199; FAX (07) 346-1973.*
Pool, spa, sauna, restaurant/bar, lighted tennis court, gym, tea/coffee.

Regal Geyserland Hotel   **$NZ125–140**   ★★

Fenton Street next to the Whakarewarewa thermal area. ☎ *(07) 348-2039; FAX (07) 348-2033.*
Heated outdoor pool, spa, sauna, gym, restaurant/bar, children's activities, dancing weekends; close to 18-hole golf course.

THC Rotorua International   **$NZ95–120**   ★★

Corner Tryon and Froude streets next to the Whaka thermal area. ☎ *(07) 348-1189; FAX (07) 347-1620.*
Standard rooms plus villa apartments. Pool, spa, tea/coffee, two restaurants, bar, kitchens in villas, baby-sitting.

Wylie Court Motor Lodge   **$NZ125–145**   ★★

345 Fenton Street. ☎ *(07) 347-7879; FAX (07) 346-1494.*
Two-acre site. Each unit has a private hot pool plus heated swimming pool. Restaurant/bar, laundry, tea/coffee, courtesy van, breakfast available.

Ambassador Thermal Hotel   **$NZ90**   ★★

Corner Whakaue and Hinemaru streets downtown. ☎ *(07) 347-9581; FAX 348-5281.*
Best Western. Heated pool, spa, thermal pools, kitchens, laundry, some two-bedroom units, new executive suites.

Heritage Rotorua Motor Inn   **$NZ110–190**   ★★

349 Fenton Street. ☎ *(07) 347-7686; FAX (07) 346-3347.*
Some rooms with private spas. Restaurant/bar, pools, kitchens, tea/coffee, BBQ area, tennis courts, courtesy van.

Grand Establishment Hotel   **$NZ60**   ★

Hinemoa Street, city center. ☎ *(07) 348-2089; FAX (07) 346-3219.*
One of the nationwide Pub Hotel group. Cobb & Co. restaurant, two bars, sauna, tea/coffee.

Eaton Hall Guesthouse   **$NZ65**

39 Hinemaru Street. ☎ *(07) 347-0366; FAX the same.*
Eighty-year-old, thermally heated B&B. Thermal pool, tea/coffee, laundry, dinner available.

Rotorua YHA   **$NZ18**

Corner Eruera and Hinemaru streets downtown. ☎ *(07) 347-6810; FAX (07) 349-1426.*
YHA facility. Thermal pool, some family rooms, kitchen, tour desk, bike hire.

Rotorua Thermal Holiday Park and Lodge   **$NZ18–55**

Old Taupo Road near the Whaka thermal area. ☎ *(07) 346-3140; FAX (07) 346-1324.*
Kiwi Kamp facility. Several active mud pools on site. About 45 acres, with pool, kitchens, laundry, store, linen hire, BBQ. Next to golf course. B&B tourist flats $NZ55 double; log cabins and regular cabins from $NZ35; bunk rooms $NZ18 per person; lodge bunks including breakfast $NZ18 per person.

Holden's Bay Holiday Park   **$NZ25–75**

21 Robinson Avenue, off Highway 30 near the airport. ☎ *(07) 345-9925; FAX the same.*
Top 10 facility, close to Lake Rotorua and the best RV/tent site in the area. Pool,
private hot pools, laundry, linen hire, tour desk, store. One- or two-bedroom Tourist flats $NZ55–75 double; cabins $NZ25–45. RV and tent sites $NZ20.

Where to Eat

Landmark   **$$$**   ★★★★

Fenton and Meade streets, overlooking the Whaka thermal area. ☎ *(07) 348-9376.*
French/New Zealand fusion cuisine in an old robber baron's Edwardian mansion
complete with turrets. Four separate dining rooms, all china, crystal and chande-
liers. Licensed but you can BYO wine. Reservations. *Dinner 6–10 p.m.*

Aorangi Peak Restaurant   **$$$**   ★★★★

Atop Aorangi Peak. Tough to find but great view. ☎ *(07) 347-0046.*
Go north on Highway 5 to the traffic lights at Clayton Road. Go left on Clayton to
Mountain Road, turn right and climb to the top. Specialties include lamb and ven-
ison and Bay of Plenty scallops in season. Large wine selection plus imported beers.
*Open seven days; cocktail lounge opens at 5:30 p.m. Lunch noon–2 p.m.; dinner
from 6:30 p.m.*

Poppy's Villa Restaurant   **$$$**   ★★★

4 Marguerita Street, a few blocks north of the Quality Hotel Rotorua. ☎ *(07) 347-1700.*
Award-winning seafood restaurant housed in an old Edwardian villa amid a land-
scaped garden. Also specializes in game dishes, omelets and lamb. *Dinner 6–10
p.m., seven nights.*

Rumours   **$$**   ★★★

81 Pukuatua Street, near the Kuirau Park. ☎ *(07) 347-7277.*
Red decor from the neon down, musical motif, casual and comfortable. Eclectic but
rich food: scampi, filets of crocodile, steak with wine-glazed fungi and decadent desserts. *Dinner Tues.–Sat. from 6 p.m.*

Skyline Restaurant   **$$**   ★★

On Aorangi Peak, not to be confused with the Aorangi Peak Restaurant. ☎ *(07) 347-
0027.*
Café and dinner service. Evening meals include the gondola ticket. *Lunch noon–2
p.m.; dinner from 6:30 p.m., seven days.*

Lewishams   **$$**   ★★

115 Tutanekai downtown, one block west of Fenton Street. ☎ *(07) 348-1786.*
One of the oldest buildings in town, furnished in antiques with brick fireplace and
courtyard dining in the summer, open fire in winter. Austrian influence, with seafood and spicy meat stews using lamb, veal and venison. Rich desserts. *Small and
popular. BYO. Open for lunch Mon., Wed.–Fri. 11:45 a.m.–2 p.m.; dinner Wed.–
Mon. 6–10 p.m.*

Alzac's Café and Bar   **$**   ★★

135 Tutanekai Street. ☎ *(07) 347-2127.*

Casual and light-hearted decor, vaguely Mediterranean cuisine, blackened fish, smoked eel, pastas, also Cajun offerings. *Open Mon.–Fri. 10 a.m. until late; Sat. and Sun., 8 a.m. until late.*

Gazebo $ ★★

45 Pukuatua Street. ☎ *(07) 348-1911.*
BYO. European decor, interesting blend of cuisines with such goodies as warm chicken liver salad and venison and lamb dishes; also Asian noodle dishes. Popular with the locals. *Lunch from noon–2 p.m. Tues.–Fri.; dinner 6 p.m. Tues.–Sat.*

Heritage $$ ★★

349 Fenton Street. ☎ *(07) 347-7686.*
In the Heritage Motor Inn. Popular bar, English-flavor restaurant, a far cut above normal motel eateries. Game dishes, seafood specials. *Open early morning until around 9 p.m. daily.*

Cobb & Co. $ ★

Grand Establishment Hotel on Hinemoa Street. ☎ *(07) 348-2089.*
Senior discounts, family dining, two bars, no-smoking section. *Open seven days 7:30 a.m.–10 p.m.*

Zanelli's $ ★★★

23 A Amohia Street. ☎ *(07) 348-4908.*
Good basic Italian fare, à la carte and blackboard menus; also seafood (good mussels), pastas, lamb. BYO. *Dinner from 6 p.m. seven days.*

Tour coach north of Punakaiki

Central North Island

The Bay of Plenty

Captain Cook named this bay after he sailed in and, to his delight, found friendly natives and lots of food to replenish his stores. The Bay area is still supplying stores today, especially kiwi fruit, but also citrus fruit, apples, strawberries and macadamia nuts. The region is also becoming a popular tourist area, with several excellent beaches.

The best way to get to the bay from Auckland is to take Highway 2 just south of Bombay and head toward Waihi Beach on the coast. Near the turnoff on Highway 1 is the **Franklin Information Centre**, *open 8:30 a.m.–5 p.m. seven days.* ☎ *(09) 236-0670; FAX (09) 236-0580.* About 10 kilometers east of the Auckland turnoff is the village of Pokeno. Look for Lyons Road and a rural road turnoff to a popular getaway and conference spot, the **Hotel du Vin** ★★★. While not actually in a major wine-growing area, the hotel does have vineyards and fairly upscale food and lodging with a variety of house-produced wines bottled under the De Redcliffe Estate label. Try the cabernet merlot Franc 1992. Rooms are bungalows/condo style, with ceiling fans and decks, and depending on your location, subject to early morning harassment from a herd of nearby cows. It offers a "sojourn package," which includes a five-course meal, breakfast and a night's lodging for $NZ195 per person. Executive suites are $NZ345; deluxe suites $NZ295. We found it a bit sterile and fairly boring, but it does have an excellent pool/sauna area, three tennis courts and a friendly bar. Transport available from the Auckland airport. ☎ *(09) 233-6314; FAX (09) 233-6215.*

Just past the town of **Paeroa**, Highway 2 enters a very scenic area, the **Karangahake Gorge**, with several excellent trails, one of which goes over a bridge and returns through an abandoned 1000-meter railway tunnel. Halfway through the gorge is a track to the Owharoa Falls Scenic Reserve, with wildflowers and a picnic/swimming area. Gold mines in the gorge produced millions of dollars worth of gold at the turn of the century. From palm-bedecked Waihi, going toward Tauranga, you pass bay views, vineyards and vegetable plots. Plan a stop south of **Katikati** at the **Morton Estate Winery**, a Spanish-style winery with tastings and a restaurant. The town also has a lot of crafts and pottery stores. The major center of activity at the north end of Bay of Plenty is at **Tauranga**, about an hour's drive northwest of Rotorua on Highways 33 and 2. The city is built on a peninsula with bays on either side, and is a game-fishing and recreation center. Tauranga is also New Zealand's largest export port, handling produce, timber and dairy goods. Probably the biggest local draw is the **Tauranga Historic Village** at the south end of town. The village is full of period buildings and re-created shops and an 1877 steam locomotive. Some days everybody is in period clothing. *Hours are 9 a.m.–6 p.m. daily in summer; 9 a.m.–5 p.m. in winter.* ☎ *(07) 578-1302.* Also in town is **Gate Pa**, where a bloody battle was fought in 1864 between English soldiers and Maori warriors. The best beach in the area, one of the best on the North Island, is along another peninsula to the east, Mt. Maunganui. There's a trail to the top of the small 700-foot peak, which gives views of the harbor area and the beaches. **Mt. Maunganui Beach** ambles east for about three miles, running into another good beach area at Papamoa. The **Mt. Maunganui Information Centre** is on Salisbury Avenue; *open 8:30 a.m.–7 p.m. Monday–Friday; 8:30 a.m.–12:30 p.m. Saturdays.* ☎ *(07) 575-5099; FAX 578-1090.* Also in the area is the Mt. Maunganui Golf Club, home of the New Zealand PGA tournament. Information on the area is available from the **Tauranga Information Centre, The Strand**. *Open 8 a.m.–5 p.m. daily; 8 a.m.–2 p.m. weekends.* ☎ *(07) 578-8103; FAX 577-1090.*

South of Tauranga is the beach town of **Te Puke**, which proclaims itself to the be *the kiwi fruit capital of the world*, and, if you're interested, you can call in at **Kiwifruit Country**, an orchard/factory/showroom about six kilometers east of Te Puke on Highway 2. Look for the giant sliced kiwi fruit sign. They'll haul you around the orchards on little kiwi fruit cars, let you have some kiwi fruit wine and generally tell you more about kiwi fruit than you'll ever remember. ☎ *(07) 573-6340.* Tickets are about $NZ8. But there's more to Te Puke than Chinese gooseberries. It is also home to several very good beaches and is a fishing and hunting center.

Highway 2 skirts the sea all the way south to the bay's second major tourist center, Whakatane. The main draw here is the excellent beach at nearby **Ohope**. Offshore a few miles is **White Island**, an active volcano known for its dense plumes of smoke. Boat and air tours to the island are available. The *Island Princess* will run you to the island and back for about $NZ60, lunch included, and, for an extra 10 bucks, you can go ashore and get close to the volcano. The company also does dive and supper cruises, ☎ *(07) 312-4236.* Information about the area is available from the **Whakatane Visitor Informa-tion Centre** on Boon Street ☎ *(07) 308-6058; FAX 308-6058.* The Depart-ment of Conservation office is at *28 Commerce Street.* ☎ *(07) 308-7213.*

Taupo

Southwest of Rotorua, almost in the center of the North Island, you find one of the most beautiful parts of New Zealand: the area around Lake Taupo and the Tongariro National Park to the southwest. Here is the showcase of the North Island's fiery volcanic history. **Lake Taupo** itself is the remains of two giant craters, and the whole countryside is dotted with old cones, as well as active geothermal areas. A few miles north along the **Waikato River**, feeding into the lake, is the **Wairakei Natural Thermal Valley** and, alongside, a large geothermal power station. Part of Taupo's popularity is the lake's trout fishing, widely acknowledged to be some of the finest in the world. It's not unusual to hook into a 10-pound rainbow, and the lake's pure water seems to be a perfect en-vironment for the fish. At 230 square miles, it is also the country's largest lake. Still, there are times it's tough getting to the shore because fishermen are lined up elbow to elbow.

Base of Exploration

The Taupo area is so attractive, in fact, that we suggest you use this as the base for your explorations of the central North Island. You're about an hour from Rotorua, a couple of hours from the winery areas of Hawkes Bay and, as not-ed, next door to one of the finest national parks in New Zealand. The view across the lake at the volcanoes in the park is worth the price of admission.

Compared to Rotorua, Taupo is pretty low-key, and there's nothing around town to compare with either Whakarewarewa or Hell's Gate for geo-thermal wonders. But there are a few places worth a look and, not far away, a great place to take the waters.

You can take a look at the **geothermal power plant** at Wairakei, about 10 ki-lometers north of town on Highway 5. There's an information center with displays and an audiovisual program, and a nearby lookout area where you can see the plant operating. Guided tours can be arranged. The center, on the west side of the road just before you get to the plant, is *open daily 9 a.m.– noon and 1–4:30 p.m.* The plant generates about 200,000 kilowatts, roughly 5 percent of the country's electric power.

Just north past the information center (over the bridge) is a road going west to the **Wairakei Natural Thermal Valley**, a region of sulphurous fumes and mud pools, a geyser or two and lots of steam. There's a small RV park and tent camp. Entry is about $NZ5. Critics point to this area when they talk

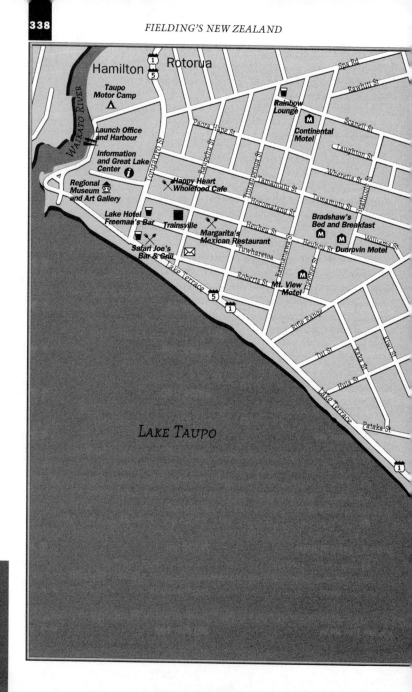

Gee Dub's
Cafe and Spa Bakery

Taupo Cabins

Berkenhoff Lounge

Taupo

0   1/8   1/4 Mi.

0   125   250m

©FWI

Rifle Range

Brice St

Crown Rd

Invergarry Rd

Turangi

Napier

about the effects of the power plant. Once, the valley supposedly had dozens of geysers; now only a couple of fairly tame spurters remain, the rest the victim of steam being drawn off for the power plant. Near the geothermal information center is the 18-hole **Wairakei International Golf Course**, *one of the best in the country and one with an international reputation.* There's also a nine-hole facility nearby. Clubs and carts are available for hire; nonmembers welcome. *For fees and information:* ☎ *(07) 374-8152; FAX 374-8289.*

North of Wairakei is what used to be one of the best-kept thermal secrets in the country, a marvelous little place called **Orakei Korako**. There are silica terraces that look like the White and Pink Terraces at Rotorua before the volcano buried them. There are caves. There's a sacred Maori pool. There are geysers and mud pools. The area sits next to the Upper Waikato River near a lake created by a **hydroelectric** dam. There is a **tearoom**, souvenir shop, boat hire, gas station and picnic area. *It might be the prettiest thermal area in the country.* Admission is about $NZ12. There are cabins for rent (about $NZ20-40) and a camping area. To get there, take Highway 1 north from Taupo to Tutukau Road about 15 kilometers north, then go east. *The valley is open 8:30 a.m.–4:30 p.m. (4 p.m. in the winter).* ☎ *(07) 378-3131 in Taupo.*

Blue-Green River

Another popular spot near Taupo is **Huka Falls**, where the Waikato River plunges over an 80-foot cliff. *Here you can see the blue-green color of the river at its best.* There's a footbridge across the river near the falls. One semi-touristy way to get close to the falls is aboard the ***African Queen*** (yup), a vintage (1908) riverboat that does a variety of cruises on the Waikato River. In addition to the falls, the *Queen* will take you to visit a prawn farm (with tastings), or stage a moonlight falls trip with glowworms thrown in. A daytime falls cruise with barbecue is about $NZ35. ☎ *(07) 374-8338.* Hunting, fishing and river-rafting services are available.

About 300 yards upstream from the falls is what many travelers think is *the best accommodation in all of New Zealand,* the **Huka Lodge** ★★★★★. Set among 17 acres of trees, lawns and garden next to the river, the lodge has 17 luxury suites set in private chalets. In the old days before it was extensively remodeled, the lodge was home to such visitors as Charles Lindbergh and James Michener. It is often used as the Camp David of New Zealand. The dining is elegant, the service up to international standards, the furnishings of the rooms and main buildings superb. There are tennis courts, a spa pool, library and a helipad. The summer tariff of about $NZ1300 for two persons a day includes breakfast and a five-course dinner, cocktails, airport transfers from Taupo, use of the fishing boat and kayaks. Winter rates are about $NZ1115 double. The fly fishing right in front of the lodge is often excellent, and, in addition, the lodge offers many other activities, including bungy jumping, horseback rides, golf and white-water rafting. The activities prices are commensurate with the lodge tariffs. ☎ *(07) 378-5791; FAX (07) 378-0427.*

If you want to try a **lake cruise**, there is the slow and ancient (but interesting) **Ernest Kemp**, an old steam ferry that does two-hour scenic cruises around the lake and also can be hired for picnics and meals. It also does dinner cruises in the summer. The tour fare is about $NZ20. *In the summer, there are trips at 10 a.m. and 2 p.m.; in the winter at 2 p.m. only.* Tickets and information are available at the city information office or by calling ☎ *(07) 378-3444* or ☎ *(07) 378-6136.*

If you're keen to try for a trout or two, there are a number of guide services operating from Taupo and also from Turangi at the south end of the lake. A good bet is to contact the Taupo Commercial Launchmen's Association Inc. in Taupo, which represents more than a dozen skippers. Guide fees run about $US25 an hour for rivers and streams, minimum of two hours; trolling around $US30 an hour, minimum of two hours. Most guides supply tackle and can sell licenses. The association can be reached at ☎ *(07) 378-3444* (24 hours).

Fishing Packages

Lake Taupo fishing packages can be booked ahead from North America. For example, a five-day fishing trip, using Taupo as a base, will run about $US600 and includes two days with a professional guide, breakfast and dinner, transfers from the airport, and accommodation in a motel. (No international or internal airfare is included.) Upscale, staying at the Huka Lodge (and all the amenities), a five-day trip will run about $US1800. Packages can be booked through the **Best of New Zealand Fly Fishing,** *2817 Wilshire Boulevard, Santa Monica, CA 90403;* ☎ *(800) 528-6129 or (310) 998-5880; FAX (310) 829-9221.*

Thermal Pools

As for soaking the tired bod in the waters, there are essentially two places: the **A.C. Thermal Pools**, in town, and **DeBrett's**, about three kilometers from town.

The A.C. is so named because the Armed Constabulary used to come for a dip in colonial times. It has one large pool—the Lido —which is not actually a mineral pool but Lake Taupo water treated and heated to about 95 degrees F. There are some private mineral pools where the water is kept at 40 degrees C—104 degrees F. There's a sauna, waterslide for the kids plus picnic and barbecue areas. *Open 8 a.m.–9 p.m.* Admission is about $NZ5. ☎ *(07) 378-7321.*

DeBrett's is our favorite soaking spot on the North Island, not only for the pools but also for the hotel/restaurant and RV park complex available. There are two large pools, one about 104 degrees F, the other about 97 degrees F. The pools are in a wooded area downhill from the hotel complex, and, at night, with steam rising to blot out the stars, the spot is about as relaxed as it gets. There are also a number of private pools, which come in varying degrees of heat. *Open 8 a.m.–9 p.m.*; general admission is about $NZ5. ☎ *(07) 378-8559.*

Tours

For a spectacular look at the Taupo area, try a flight with Taupo Air Services that goes down the lake, around Tongariro National Park and back for about $NZ120. ☎ *(07) 378-5325.* Or DeBrett's Aviation, ☎ *(07) 378-8559.* Ten- to 90-minute flights, $NZ25 to $NZ150.

If you want to tour around, contact *Paradise Tours*, which operates mini-van trips around the immediate area and also runs to Rotorua. The Taupo-area trip is about $NZ30. ☎ *(07) 378-9955.* Tours can also be booked through the city information center.

There is no direct major air service to Taupo, the nearest service being to Rotorua, where you can catch a bus to Taupo for about $NZ20. At present, there are three daily buses, leaving at 9 a.m., 11 a.m. and 1:30 p.m., arriving in Taupo about an hour later. The fare from Wellington is about $NZ70; from Auckland, about $NZ50.

Information

The Taupo Information Centre is located at *13 Tongariro Street* near the waterfront, and is *open from 8:30 a.m.–5 p.m.* ☎ *(07) 378-9000; FAX (07) 378-9003.* The Turangi Information Centre is on *Ngwaka Place.* ☎ *(07) 386-8999; FAX (07) 386-0074.* The Taupo AA office is at *93 Tongariro Street.* ☎ *(07) 378-6000.*

Where to Stay

Huka Village Estate $NZ115–420   ★★★

Huka Falls Road next to the Historic Huka Village. ☎ *(07) 378-5326; FAX (07) 378-5333.*

Very nice colonial-style units set in a fruit orchard. Restaurant/bar, pool, spa, kitchens, tea/coffee, courtesy van, tennis court, horseback riding. Studio units, some suites with spa bath. Studios are $NZ115 double; one- or two-bedroom suites, $NZ135–195; executive suite, $NZ420.

Cascades Motor Inn $NZ90–280   ★★★

Highway 1, on Lake Terrace. ☎ *(07) 378-3774; FAX (07) 378-0372.*
Units have private patios, suites with spa bath and waterfront views. Heated pool, kitchens, tea/coffee, courtesy van. Studios for $NZ90–120; suites from $NZ130–280.

Wairakei Hotel Resort $NZ140–230   ★★★

Five miles from Taupo, Highway 1 just across from the Geothermal Information Centre, close to the golf course. ☎ *(07) 374-8021; FAX (07) 374-8485.*
Two pools, spa, two tennis courts, some kitchen units, handicapped facilities. Bar/restaurant, tea/coffee. Doubles start about $NZ140; family units, $NZ185–220, suites from $NZ230.

Karaka Tree Hotel   **$NZ100–195**   ★★★
216 Lake Terrace, residential area northeast of the harbor. ☎ *(07) 378-2432; FAX (07) 378-0216.*
Each unit has a private mineral spa. Kitchens, spa, courtesy van, coffee/tea. Studio, one- and two-bedroom units, handicapped facilities. Laundry, breakfast available. Doubles about $NZ100–120; two-bedroom units $NZ120–195.

DeBrett's Thermal Hotel   **$NZ30–90**   ★★
Highway 5, the Taupo-Napier road, about a kilometer from the lake. For the hotel, ☎ *(07) 378-7080; FAX (07) 378-4174. For the other units,* ☎ *(07) 378- 8559.*
Our choice when we haven't sold a kid or two to pay for a room at the Huka Lodge. The century-old DeBrett's hotel has tons of class and creaky floors, nice bar, and free access to the thermal pools. Bar/restaurant. Also a motel and RV park. The hotel rooms are about $NZ90 double; reservations recommended. Motel units are $NZ65 double, cabins $NZ50 double, and budget rooms $NZ30 double.

Lakeland Motor Inn   **$NZ105**   ★★
Highway 1, on Two Mile Bay. ☎ *(07) 378-3893; FAX (07) 378-3891.*
Two licensed restaurants, bar, minibars, laundry, handicapped facilities.

Sunseeker Motel   **$NZ85–105**   ★★
Taharepa Road, just off the lakefront. ☎ *(07) 378-9020.*
Laundry, spa, tea/coffee, breakfast available.

Loretta's Quality Guest House   **$NZ60–100**   ★★
135 Heu Heu Street, center of town. ☎ *(07) 378-4927; FAX the same.*
B&B, laundry, BBQ, tea/coffee, dinner available (Italian a specialty).

Suncourt Motor Hotel   **$NZ70–85**   ★★
14 Northcroft Street, near lakefront. ☎ *(07) 378-8265; FAX (07) 378-0809.*
Pool, spa, some kitchenettes and spa baths. Rooms and motel units. Restaurant/bar.

Lake Establishment   **$NZ50**   ★★
Corner of Tongariro and Tuwharetoa streets, downtown. ☎ *(07) 378-6165; FAX (07) 377-0150.*
A pub/hotel member housing the country's original Cobb & Co. Restaurant. Two bars and a bottle shop. Some rooms without baths, some with balconies; tea/coffee.

Rainbow Lodge Backpackers   **$NZ15–40**
99 Titiraupenga Street, downtown. ☎ *(07) 378-5754; FAX (07) 377-1568.*
Popular, friendly spot; book ahead. Kitchen, dining room, sauna, laundry, BBQ, courtesy van, tour bookings. Bunk rooms $NZ15 per person; doubles $NZ30–40.

Where to Eat

Truffles   **$$$**   ★★★
116 Lake Terrace. ☎ *(07) 378-7856.*
Set in a 70-year-old cottage, fireside dining and dandy views. Terrace dining in the summer. "Fine dining" establishment. Salmon-spinach terrines, lamb with lavender sauce, Austrian cheesecake. Bring your trout, they'll fix it. *Lunch in summer, noon– 2 p.m. Fri.–Sun.; dinner from 6:30 p.m. Tues.–Sun.*

Finch's   **$$**   ★★★
64 Tuwharetoa. ☎ *(07) 377-2425.*

A real comer and award-winner, it has two lounge areas, open fireplace and outside dining. Great scallops, venison, lamb, Japanese dishes, yummy desserts. Very popular. *Lunch noon–2 p.m. Mon.–Fri.; dinner from 6 p.m. nightly.*

Edgewater Room   **$$$**   ★★★

In Manuel's Resort Hotel on the lakeshore. ☎ *(07) 378-5110.*
One of the best in town with great lake views and award-winning cuisine, specializing in fresh fish and classic French fare. Superb view. *Dinner 6:30–10 p.m. nightly.*

Graham Room, The   **$$**   ★★

In the Wairakei Hotel. ☎ *(07) 374-8021.*
The place to bring those trout you caught—they'll fix 'em up. Venison, lamb, seafood. *Breakfast 7–10 a.m.; lunch noon–2:30 p.m., dinner 6–10 p.m. Open seven days.*

Echo Cliff   **$$**   ★★

Tongariro Street near the visitors center. ☎ *(07) 378-8539.*
One of our favorites, also with nice lake views and friendly staff. No reservations taken. Casual, great views. Licensed or BYO wine, good seafood. *Lunch noon–2 p.m. Mon.–Fri.; dinner from 5:30 p.m. nightly.*

Nonnie's   **$**   ★★

Corner of Lake Terrace and Tongariro. ☎ *(07) 378-6894.*
A café by day, Italian restaurant by night. Fairly plain decor, good Italian. Licensed. *Breakfast and lunch 7 a.m.–3 p.m.; dinner Mon.–Sat. from 6 p.m.*

Safari Joe's   **$$**   ★★

17 Tongariro Street. ☎ *(07) 378-3302.*
Popular bar and restaurant, full of noisy but friendly locals chowing down on huge slabs of beef, chicken, venison and lamb. Licensed. *Dinner from 5 p.m. seven days.*

Freeman's Café & Bar   **$**   ★★

Tuwharetoa Street, next to the Lake Establishment Hotel.
Live music (often country/western) on Fri. and Sat. nights. Sandwiches, burgers and their own really good pub beer, Waikato Bitter. *Open from noon on; closed Sun.*

Tongariro

The oldest national park in New Zealand—and one of the most beautiful—is Tongariro, less than 60 miles southeast of Taupo. The park, about 200,000 acres, has three active/dormant volcanoes. It is a popular tramping area in the summer and, in the winter, a major skiing area. It was established in 1887, about the same time as Yosemite National Park in California and Glacier and Yoho national parks in Canada. It's a **World Heritage area**.

The volcanoes continue to cause problems—and deaths—right up to the present day. The upper slopes of the cones are spattered with hot rocks and mud from time to time, and **Mt. Ruapehu** (at about 9200 feet, the tallest mountain on the North Island) is still very active. In 1995 and 1996, it erupted in a series of spectacular blasts, scattering tourists and skiers and forcing evacuations from area villages. It's still rumbling as you read this. Its sister peak, **Ngauruhoe**, has had several major eruptions as well. The third peak, **Mt. Tongariro**, has not erupted recently.

The park is a contrast in ecosystems. On the eastern side, the area is a near desert. On the west, which gets heavy precipitation, there are lush forests. The park contains about 500 species of native plants, from conifer forests to orchids to wildflowers and vast areas of tussock.

The park is reached by driving south on Highway 1 to Turangi, then taking on Highway 47 to Highway 48. At the end of the highway (the so-called "Bruce Road") are the park headquarters, the **Château Tongariro** and a number of chalets and lodges belonging to ski clubs. (For ski information, see the "Skiing" section in "The Perfect Vacation" chapter.) The settlement here is called **Whakapapa Village**. It's also possible to take a train to the park area. Both the Silver Fern and Northerner trains stop at National Park, a small settlement about 15 kilometers from the park headquarters. The Fern leaves Auckland at 8:30 a.m. Monday–Saturday and arrives at National Park about 1:30 p.m. From Wellington, trains leave about 6:30 a.m., arriving at National Park around 1:15 p.m. The fare is about $NZ80 from Wellington, $NZ50 from Auckland. From National Park, there is fairly regular bus service to Whakapapa.

Using a series of sealed state highways, it's possible to drive completely around the park, although some roads might be blocked in the winter. But the real draw in the summer is hiking. *One of the most interesting treks is to the crater lake near the summit of Mt. Ruapehu.* The lake, warmed by subterranean steam, is not suitable for swimming, but the scenery from the area is tremendous—if the volcano hasn't closed down the trips. **The lake can be deadly**, however. In 1953, the lake level rose because mud and lava blocked its exit down the mountain. When it finally broke through, the flood rushed down the slopes and swept a passenger train off the tracks at Waiouru at the south end of the park, killing 153 people. The trip to the lake and back can be made in a day—check with park headquarters about conditions and necessary equipment. There are a number of shorter walks as well, including one that goes to the spectacular Taranaki Falls east of the village. Information is also available at Turangi.

Most trails start at Whakapapa Village. Maps and other information are available from the park headquarters, located behind the château. There are a limited number of camping huts located on the trails around the park. The Whakapapa Visitors Center in the village has accommodation and activities information; *open seven days 8 a.m.–5 p.m.* ☎ *(07) 892-3729; FAX (07) 892-3814.*

Château Tongariro is one of the country's oldest hotels and offers top-notch accommodations and restaurants.

Château Tongariro

The park is the site of one of the country's old premier hotels, the **Château Tongariro** ★★★, which is of the same ilk as the grander Hermitage at Mt. Cook. The château, built in the 1920s, offers pretty good accommodation and decent food in several restaurants, including a moderately priced cafeteria. Rooms at the Château during the winter are between $NZ160 and $NZ250 (single or double, same price). In the summer, rooms are in the $NZ110–160 a night double range. It has a pool, spa and sauna and ski-drying area. The mailing address for the hotel, as well as other places in the village, is actually Mt. Ruapehu. ☎ *(07) 892-3809; FAX (0800) 733-955.* There is also the **Skotel** ★★, which has a range of rooms from plain to fancy, with prices from about $NZ40 hostel double to around $NZ110 for the chalets. It has a spa, restaurant/bar and some chalets with kitchens. ☎ *(07) 892-3719; FAX (07) 892-3777.* Finally, there is the **Whakapapa Holiday Park**, a Top 10 facility which has cabins for about $NZ35 and tourist flats for about $NZ50. There are also tent sites and backpackers units in the summer. ☎ *(07) 892-3897; FAX the same.*

Information on the park is available in Taupo, as well as ranger offices in Ohakune and Turangi. Turangi info is at ☎ *(07) 386-8999; FAX (07) 386-0074.* The Department of Conservation in Turangi is ☎ *(07) 386-8607; FAX (07) 386-7086.*

Hawkes Bay

One of the country's premier wine-growing areas lies along Hawkes Bay, running from the Mahia Peninsula to the Napier/Hastings area. The bay also has a fair number of good beaches and the Mediterranean-like weather makes it a popular, but still underexposed tourist area. There are more than a dozen small-to-medium wineries in the area, specializing in cabernets, sauvignon blanc and some good reds. These **wineries**, combined with those further to the north in the Gisborne area, are a major source of New Zealand wines, producing more than a third of the total output. (See "Wine Producing Regions" in "The Essential New Zealand" chapter.) Toward the end of October, the vintners in the area hold a charity wine weekend, with wine tastings, tours, horse racing, music, auctions, and a gala/buffet dinner. The event raises around $NZ80,000. *Information: Hawkes Bay Vintners Charity Wine Auction, P.O. Box 7095, Taradale, New Zealand;* ☎ *(06) 844-2053.*

The major base for exploring the wine region is **Napier**, the self-proclaimed *Art Deco capital of the world* (look out, Miami Beach). And the town does have a large selection of Art Deco buildings, all courtesy of a devastating 7.9 earthquake that hit the city in 1931. More than 250 people died, the city was leveled, and a huge chunk of marsh and swamp area (nearly 8500 acres) was raised above sea level, in some places as much as six feet. The town was rebuilt in the style of the times, creating a living museum of Art Deco architecture. The city airport, by the way, is built on the earthquake-raised land. There are also some nice Art Deco structures in **Hastings**, 20 kilometers south, also rebuilt after the town was destroyed by the quake.

The city is so proud of its collection, in fact, that in February it holds an Art Deco weekend, when visitors are urged to wear vintage costumes, try a tea dance or two, take walking tours of the city and sample some regional wines. This is all part of the activities of the **Art Deco Trust**, a Napier organization that tries to keep the old relics ship-shape and attractive for the growing tourist trade. *Information:* ☎ *(06) 835-0022.* And every Sunday throughout the year, there are walking tours of the city with emphasis on the Art Deco, as well as looking at the remains of the earthquake damage. The tours leave the Desco Centre, *163 Tennyson Street*, at 2 p.m. Wednesdays and weekends and cost about $NZ6.50

The museum—full name **Hawkes Bay Art Gallery and Museum**—is located on Marine Parade at the waterfront, and is well worth a stop. In addition to a before-and-after audiovisual show about the earthquake, the museum houses an excellent collection of Maori art—in this case, a display designed and placed by the Maoris themselves. *It's open 10 a.m.–4:30 daily.* Admission is about $NZ3. ☎ *(06) 835-7781.*

Another good spot to stop on Marine Parade is the **Hawkes Bay Aquarium**, said to be the largest in the Southern Hemisphere. In addition to the usual fishy features, you can see **tuataras**. Feeding time is 3:15 p.m.; *hours are 9 a.m.–5 p.m. daily*. Admission is about $NZ8. In conjunction with the aquarium is Marineland of New Zealand, with trained dolphins and sea lions. There are shows at 10:30 a.m. and 2 p.m. daily. *It's open from 10 a.m.–4:30 p.m. daily*. Admission is about $NZ10. ☎ *(06) 835-7579*. A good spot to hole up in the area is at the **Napier Travel Inn ★★**, *311 Marine Parade* on the beach. Bar, restaurant, pool. Doubles start at $NZ125; weekend specials. ☎ *(06) 835-3237; FAX (06) 835-6602.*

And if you haven't met a **kiwi** yet, the **Nocturnal House** at the north end of the Parade is a good bet, particularly because, in this case, you get to actually touch one of the beaky critters; *it's the only place we know of in New Zealand that allows people to get that close to them*. Hit the exhibit at 1 p.m. for the tactile program. Feeding time is at 2 p.m. *The Nocturnal House is open from 11 a.m.–3 p.m. daily*. Admission is about $NZ5. If you've lain awake nights trying to figure out how they create those incredibly soft sheepskins they're always trying to make you buy, check out the Classic Sheepskins tannery tour in Napier, where you can take a tour at 11 a.m. and 2 p.m. seven days a week. (Of course, there's a store.) ☎ *(06) 835-9662.*

Gannet Colony

One of the major tourist attractions in the Napier/Hastings area is the large colony of gannets that arrive every July to nest at **Cape Kidnappers**, a point of land about 20 miles west of the two cities. The sanctuary is closed between July and October while the birds mate and nest, but is open the rest of the year. There are usually around 3000 pairs of birds, and the best time to see them is between November and February.

There are several companies in Napier and Hastings that do **gannet tours**, which can be booked through the city information offices. Alternatively, you can drive as far as **Clifton**, then hike to the sanctuary. Or you can take a tractor-pulled trailer guided tour. *The hike is a bit strenuous, five miles each way, and must be done only at low tide.* Tide tables are available at the city information offices; you have to start the trek no later than three hours after high tide and return no later than an hour or so after low tide. Carry water and wear good boots or hiking shoes. There are a toilet and drinking water near the gannet beach. The normal time to do the round-trip is about five hours. You get a free permit and tide tables at Clifton where you park your car.

The easy way is to take the trailer from Burden's Motor Camp at Te Awanga, about 20 kilometers from Napier. For about $NZ15, you get a guided 4-hour trip. The trip departs daily between October and April. Another way to get there is to take a four-wheel drive tour with **Gannet Safaris** from Summerlee Station near Te Awanga. The trip goes over land, rather than along the ocean. The daily trips from October through April depart at 1:30 p.m. The cost is about $NZ40. ☎ *(06) 875-0511.*

Fantasyland

The big draw in Hastings is **Fantasyland**, especially if you have younger children along. The park, a sort of miniature Disneyland, has rides, amusements, ice cream parlors—the usual. It's on Grove Road south of Highway 2. The park is open daily. Entrance fee is about $NZ3.

Information on the Hawkes Bay area is available from the **Napier Visitor Information Centre**, *Marine Parade*, ☎ *(06) 834-4161; FAX (06) 835-7219;* or from the **Hastings Visitor Information Centre**, *Russell Street*, ☎ *(06) 878-0510; FAX (06) 878-0512.* The Department of Conservation office is located in the Courthouse on Marine Parade in Napier. *Open 9 a.m.–4 p.m. Monday–Friday.* ☎ *(06) 835-0415.* The AA office in Napier is at *164 Dickens Street.* ☎ *(06) 835-6889;* in Hastings, the AA is at *337 Heretaunga Street.* ☎ *(06) 878-4101.*

Napier/Hastings is served by regular air service from Auckland and Wellington, as well as major South Island cities. The one-way fare from Auckland is about $NZ190; from Wellington, about $NZ170; from Christchurch, about $NZ260. The **Bay Express** train runs from Wellington to Hastings and Napier for about $NZ65. It leaves Wellington at 8 a.m., arriving in Napier at 1:30 p.m. There are some very interesting stretches along the line as it cuts through the mountains, using a series of bridges and tunnels. Meal service is offered. Daily bus service is available to Taupo ($NZ35); Rotorua ($NZ55), and Auckland ($NZ75).

Where to Stay

Napier

The accommodations available in Napier are all motel units in the two- to three-star category, plus some B&Bs and backpackers units. Among the choices:

Tennyson Motor Inn　　　　　　**$NZ95–135**　　　　　　★★
Corner Tennyson and Clive Square, city center. ☎ *(06) 835-3373; FAX (06) 835-8500.*
Restaurant/bar, tea/coffee, courtesy airport van.

Fountain Court Motel　　　　　　**$NZ90–120**　　　　　　★★
411 Hastings Street. ☎ *(06) 835-7387; FAX (06) 835-0323.*
Best Western. Some suites with spas, handicapped facilities, pool, some kitchens, coffee/tea, breakfast available.

Marewa Lodge Motel　　　　　　**$NZ80–120**
42 Taradale Road. ☎ *(06) 843-5839; FAX (06) 843-3232.*
Studio units, laundry, barbecue, kitchens, spa, pool.

Master's Lodge　　　　　　**$NZ140–220**　　　　　　★★
10 Elizabeth Road, Bluff Hill, Napier. ☎ *(06) 834-1946; FAX: (06) 834-1947*

Eight months of extensive renovations have transformed the former residence of tobacco pioneer Gerhard Husheer into an upscale lodge catering to four guests at a time.Carefully collected antiques and elaborate filigree woodwork were retained from the original decor. Swiss cuisine is served to guests who prefer to dine in. The lodge is in walking distance of the city center and views from each suite are unique. Children and pets are prohibited.

Masonic Hotel $NZ55–85

Tennyson and Marine Parade. ☎ *(06) 835-8689; FAX (06) 835-2297.*
A Pub Beds Art Deco structure with a Cobb and Co. restaurant. A bit run-down, but hanging in there.

Pinehaven Travel Hotel B&B $NZ70   ★★★

259 Marine Parade. ☎ *(06) 835-5575; FAX the same.*
No-smoking B&B in a grand old house converted into a hotel. Laundry, courtesy car, shared baths, tea/coffee.

Napier Hostel $NZ18

277 Marine Parade. ☎ *(06) 835-7039.*
YHA in an old guest house. Mostly twin and family units. Kitchen, dining room, bike rental, Open 24 hours.

Criterion Backpackers Inn $NZ15–18   ★★

48 Emerson Street. ☎ *(06) 835-2059.*
Former hotel, accommodations upstairs. Downstairs is a bar, café and pizza parlor. Balconies and a spa. Dorm and twin rooms.

Kennedy Park Motor Park and Motels $NZ75   ★★

Storkey Street on the Kennedy Road, northeast of city center. ☎ *(06) 843-9126; FAX (06) 843-6113.*
Top 10 group. Kitchen, laundry, pool, store, licensed restaurant. Tourist flats $NZ55 double; motel units with kitchens, coffee/tea.

Hastings

As in Napier, your choices of accommodations are limited to motel-type units, two- to three-star quality. Among them:

Fantasyland Motel $NZ80   ★★

Corner Sylvan Road and Jervois Street, opposite Fantasyland Leisure Park. ☎ *(06) 876-8159; FAX (06) 876-2616.*
Kitchens, pool, spa, tea/coffee, courtesy van.

Town Lodge Motel $NZ75–95   ★★

911 Heretaunga Street East, close to Fantasyland. ☎ *(06) 876-5065; FAX (06) 876-9058.*
Best Western. Some kitchens, tea/coffee, courtesy van.

Angus Inn Motor Hotel $NZ70–150   ★★★

Railway Road. ☎ *(06) 878-8177; FAX (06) 878-7496.*
Some kitchen units. Restaurant, pool, sauna, spa, in-house movies.

Where to Eat

Napier

Bayswater Restaurant $$$ ★★★

Hardinge Road. ☎ *(06) 835-8517.*
Waterfront locale with outside dining. Monthly menu changes, but expect quality seafood, as well as crocodile, kangaroo, lamb and venison. Homemade breads and desserts. Excellent Hawkes Bay wine list. Sunday brunch in the summer. *Open lunch noon–2 p.m.; dinner 6 p.m.–1 a.m. Closed in winter Sun., Mon., Tues.*

Beaches Restaurant $$ ★★★

War Memorial Building, Marine Parade. ☎ *(06) 835-8180.*
Award-winning cuisine featuring lamb, venison and seafood. On the waterfront with a good view of the Bay. *Lunch noon–2 p.m.; dinner from 6 p.m., closed Sun.*

Tennyson Restaurant $$ ★★

Corner Tennyson and Clive Square. ☎ *(06) 835-3373.*
Seafood, steaks, venison, lamb. Cocktail bar. *Breakfast 6:30–9 a.m.; lunch noon–2 p.m.; dinner 6:30–9:30 p.m. Open seven days.*

Harston's Café $ ★★

17 Hastings Street. ☎ *(06) 835-0478.*
Cowboy tucker: huge burgers, ribs, steaks. Old license plates, pix of Hollywood stars. Noisy and big portions. BYO. *Lunch noon–1:30 p.m. Tues.–Fri.; dinner from 6 p.m., Sat.–Mon.*

Cobb & Co. $ ★

☎ *(06) 835-8689.*
In the Masonic Hotel. Family dining, senior discounts. *Open 7:30 a.m.–10 p.m. seven days.*

Hastings

Vidal Winery Brasserie $$ ★★★

At Vidal of Hawkes Bay winery, 913 St. Aubyn Street East. ☎ *(06) 876-8105.*
One of the best in the area, housed in a classy building with stained glass, oak decor and fireplace. Giant wine barrels abound, with wooden tables and metal chairs. Big fireplace and open kitchen and glass conservatory. A blackboard menu with seasonal specials. In the summer, eat outside. Lamb and seafood specialties. *Open for lunch and dinner from noon until late daily; Sunday brunch from 10:30 a.m.*

McGenty's Licensed Restaurant $$ ★★

Anvil Court Motor Lodge, 1408 Karamu Road North. ☎ *(06) 876-4122.*
Also BYO wine. Specializing in Hawkes Bay seafood. Good wine list. *Lunch noon–2 p.m.; dinner 6 p.m.–midnight.*

St. Vinees $ ★★

108 Market Street South. ☎ *(06) 878-8596.*
Wine bar and casual dining, a popular local hangout for low-cost meals and a good range of local wines. *Lunch and dinner from 11 a.m.–11 p.m. Tues.–Sat.; 11 a.m.–7 p.m. Sun. and Mon.*

Rush Munro's Ice Cream Garden   **$**   ★

704 Heretaunga Street West, as you enter Hastings from Napier.
A legend since 1926, this spot is a pilgrimage for some New Zealanders. (Also has a branch in Wellington.) Specializes in "homemade" ice cream using local fruit. A secret recipe, of course. *(In the summer, it's open from noon to around 9 p.m.)*

Taranaki Area

If you ever get to **New Plymouth**, at the central western bulge of the North Island, you'll always remember the gracious, snow-covered cone of Mt. Egmont, or in Maori, Mt. Taranaki. The 8261-foot-high peak is New Zealand's Mt. Fuji, and was named by Captain Cook. The mountain is almost a perfect cone, marred just a bit by a subsidiary cone about two kilometers south of the main peak. Egmont is officially classed as a dormant volcano, having last erupted in the 1630s.

Surrounding the peak is **Egmont National Park**, an 82,000-acre national park that was the second established in the country. Much of it is lush bush, which like the excellent farmlands in the vicinity, owes its robust existence to Taranaki's volcanic ash eruptions. There are more than 320 kilometers of paths and tracks in the park, including a trail to the top of the peak. The weather on the mountain is extremely changeable and subject to frequent rain—in fact, it's one of the wettest places in the country. For that reason, inexperienced hikers should not try the peak climb alone. *The North Egmont Visitors Centre in the park is open 9 a.m.–5 p.m. seven days in the summer; 9:30 a.m.–4:30 p.m. Monday–Thursday in the winter.* ☎ *(06) 756-8710.*

Information about the national park is available at Department of Conservation offices on Devon Street in New Plymouth. *Open 8 a.m.–4:30 p.m. Monday–Friday.* ☎ *(06) 758-0430.* Information is also available at ranger stations in the park itself; at the conservation office at Stratford on Highway 3 east of the park, and at the New Plymouth visitors center. If you're serious about doing some hiking on the mountain and in the park, pick up a brochure on what is called *the Round the Mountain Trek,* which details three- or five-day hikes, with details on mountain huts, trail information and cautions. The rangers rank the hikes right up there with Milford Sound or Routebourne on the South Island. *Hut passes are available from the Stratford information office, Broadway and Miranda streets;* ☎ *(06) 765-6708; FAX (06) 765-7500.*

The Stratford Aero Club will fly you over and around the mountain; a 45-minute flight runs about $NZ50 a seat. ☎ *(06) 765-6628.*

The **New Plymouth area** is one of the major dairy regions in the country, and the Port of New Plymouth ships more cheese out of the country than any other. For a taste, try the **New Zealand Rennet Co.,** in the town of Eltham southeast of New Plymouth. Gift shop with wide selections of area cheeses, and a tasting bar. *Open weekdays 8:30 a.m.–5 p.m.* ☎ *(06) 764-8008.* If your palate runs to fruit wines, check out Cottage Wines in New Plymouth, which has a selection including elderberry, plum, apricot, passion fruit and honey mead. *Hours are 9 a.m.–6:30 p.m. daily.* ☎ *(06) 758-6910.* The New Plymouth area is also the center of the nation's fossil fuel reserves. There have been oil fields worked in the area, but they dwindled. But a huge offshore natural gas field was discovered in 1969, and the energy industry is expanding again around the area. And, just in case you care, in the town of Hawera on the Tasman coast southeast of New Plymouth is the Elvis Presley Memorial Room (records, souvenirs, Elvis sightings). Call ahead ☎ *(06) 278-7624.*

The coast north of New Plymouth has some of the best seascapes in New Zealand, and looks like a twin to some stretches of the Pacific Coast Highway north of San Francisco. Lots of sea stacks, towering cliffs, marvelous ocean views. Many of the beaches in the area are made of black iron—you can actually pick them up with a magnet. The entire coastline from Wanganui to Waitara is dotted with hiking trails and scenic overlooks. There is an excellent patrolled surfing/swimming beach at Oakura off Highway 3 southwest of New Plymouth.

The New Plymouth Information Centre is at *81 Liardet Street. Hours are 8:30 a.m.–5 p.m. weekdays; 10 a.m.–3 p.m. weekends and holidays.* ☎ *(06) 759-6080; FAX (06) 759-6073.* The Automobile Association is at *49 Powderham Street.* ☎ *(06) 757-5646.*

Where to Stay

Again, a selection of one- and two-star motel units:

Amber Court Motel **$NZ75–100** ★★
61 Eliot Street, main highway, New Plymouth. ☎ *(06) 758-0922; FAX (06) 758-6559.*
Best Western. Indoor heated pool, spa, waterbeds, breakfast available. AA discounts.

Saddle & Sulky Motel **$NZ85–100** ★
188 Coronation Avenue, New Plymouth. ☎ *(06) 757-5763; FAX the same.*
Next to the Pukekura Raceway & Park. Kitchenettes, spa, laundry, off-street jogging track, meals by arrangement.

Dawson Falls Tourist Lodge **$NZ105–125** ★★
Manaia Road, Stratford. ☎ *(06) 765-5457; FAX the same.*
About 22.5 kilometers from town on a paved road, sits on the slopes of Mt. Egmont. Established 1896. Swiss-style with bar and restaurant open seven days; four-course table d'hote meal runs about $NZ35. Gym, pool, sauna. Honeymoon suites.

Regan Lodge Motel **$NZ75** ★
16 Regan Street, Stratford. ☎ *(06) 765-7379; FAX the same.*
One- and two-bedroom units, some with with kitchens; laundry, spa, tennis court, indoor heated pool, dinner by arrangement.

Where to Eat

Gareth's   **$$**   ★★★

182 Devon Street. New Plymouth. ☎ *(06) 758-5104.*
Popular with the locals. Earth tones, candles, French touches here and there and
basically very good offerings. Escargot, lamb, seasonal specials. Good wine list.
Lunch from noon Mon.–Fri.; dinner from 6 p.m. seven nights.

Portofino   **$$**   ★★★

14 Gill Street, New Plymouth. ☎ *(06) 757-8686.*
Across from shopping center, the only Italian spot in town. Pastas and the rest, with
the occasional house special using local foods. Licensed bar. *Lunch noon–2:30 p.m.
Fri.; dinner 5–11 p.m. seven nights.*

Waitomo

It's on almost every tour itinerary of the North Island, maybe as famous as
the geysers around Rotorua, *easily the most popular insect attraction in New
Zealand*: the **Glowworm Grotto**, also known as **Waitomo Cave**, one of three
caves open to the public in a largely unexplored underground cavern area
about 100 kilometers west of Rotorua.

*There are glowworm colonies in many spots around New Zealand, but the
caves at Waitomo are the biggest and the best.* The main cave, somewhat dark
and slippery in spots, is fairly standard issue until you get on a flat-bottom
boat and slide out onto an underground river and look up. It's a sort of
greenish Milky Way, dotted with thousands of lights from the insects clinging to the cave roof. The worms—actually the larval stage of a fly—emit light
to attract other insects to sticky filaments they dangle to snare their food. We
love the little devils: Their favorite food is mosquitoes. At one dry spot in the
cave is a wide chamber used for performances. Among the famous folks who
have sung here are Dame Kiri Te Kanawa, the Vienna Boys Choir and Glen
Campbell. Weddings are held here as well as church services. (No indication
of how the worms feel about all this noise.) There are two other caves in the
area as well, Ruakuri and Aranui. Ruakuri is the largest, Aranui the prettiest.
Tours of the Glowworm Grotto run every half hour from 9–4:30 daily and
cost about NZ$15. Smoking and photography (including video) are not al-
lowed. The grotto is so popular that often there are a half-dozen boats
thumping around inside the cave and you might have to stand in line a long
time, especially when the tour buses arrive. The rangers told us the best time
to hit the cave is the first tour at 9 in the morning. **Aranui Cave** tours run from
10 a.m.–3 p.m. It's about three kilometers from the grotto. Tickets about
$NZ15. A ticket for both caves is $NZ25, and lunch and one cave is about
$NZ30. *For reservations and information: Museum of Caves Information
Centre, Main Street, about a half-kilometer before the caves, open 8:30 a.m.-5
p.m., later in summer.* ☎ *(07) 878-7640, FAX (07) 878-6184.*

In recent years, the most popular way to do the caving experience is what is called "black water rafting." After a lesson or two on the nearby river, you are given a wet suit, a hard hat with lamp and an inner tube and taken below ground on a three-hour journey through the darkness of **Ruakuri Cave**. You climb over waterfalls, glide along underground rivers and see a cave like you've never seen before. At the end of the trip, you get a hot shower and some hot soup. It's a marvelous trip, but not for folks who don't like dark, confined spaces. Tours cost about $NZ50 and can be booked at the Waitomo Museum of Caves. The trips are so popular, you'd better book ahead. Or check with the **Outdoor Adventure Company** at the Ferry Buildings in Auckland, ☎ *(09) 358-5868,* or **Waitomo Down Under** in Waitomo, ☎ *(07) 878-6577.*

There is bus service to the caves from Auckland. The bus leaves Auckland at 9:15 a.m., arriving in Waitomo at 1:30 p.m. A bus from Rotorua leaves at 9:30 a.m., also arriving at the caves at 1:30 p.m. Various combinations of excursions between the three points are available. Check with an InterCity agent.

If you plan an overnight at the caves, there is the very good **Waitomo Caves Hotel ★★★**, with some budget rooms, as well as premium rooms and suites. The hotel is a white wooden structure with gardens. It has the best food in town, laundry and a cocktail bar. It's old enough but in good enough condition to hover somewhere between quaint and scruffy. The bar is sometimes populated by ale-loving wasps, and one of us (the wimp) ran screaming from the room holding his beer. Rooms run from $NZ40 to $NZ135; suites about $NZ280. ☎ *(07) 878-8227; FAX (07) 878-8858.* There are also several motels, including the **Waitomo Guest Lodge ★**, about 100 yards from the museum and grotto entrance, self-contained units with bath about $NZ30 per person, ☎ *(07) 878-7641;* **Caves Motor Inn ★★** at the caves turnoff, about $NZ65–75 double, backpackers $NZ13, ☎ *(07) 873-8109;* and the **Glowworm Motel ★★**, also at the turnoff, doubles about $NZ55–75, ☎ *(07) 873-8882; FAX 873-8856.* North of the turnoff to the caves on Highway 3 at Otorohanga is the Kiwi House and Native Bird Park. It is supposedly the country's largest walk-through aviary, and also home to tuataras. The nonprofit park guarantees you will see the kiwis. *Open daily 10 a.m.–5 p.m.; winter closes at 4 p.m.* Entry fee about $NZ10. ☎ *(07) 873-7391.*

Wellington

Wellington

Wellington's cable cars offer hilltop views.

If you ever catch a real San Franciscan with his guard down, you soon discover that a lot of that haughty civic pride the city is so well known for is partly bluff. Sure, he'll rave about the culture, the history, the scenic beauty, Golden Gate and all that tourism office stuff. But way down deep, he also hates the place for the steep streets that ruin his brakes and tear out his transmission, an impossible city to find a parking place (especially in front of his house), insane drivers, streets choked with tourists, high prices and the lousy weather. Damp, foggy, and a never-ending wind. San Franciscans say they love the murky weather, and especially love the wind because it keeps the skies clear of the ugly smog they claim covers the rest of the state.

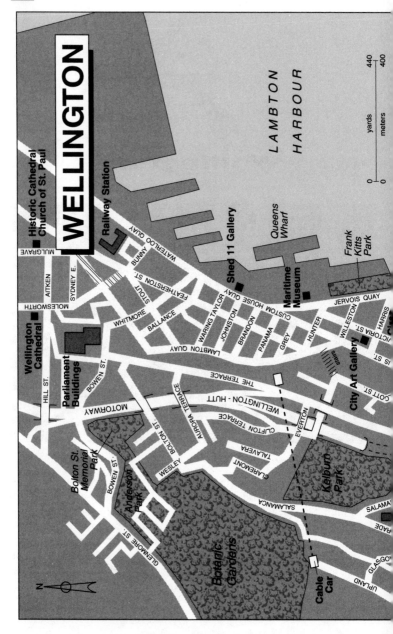

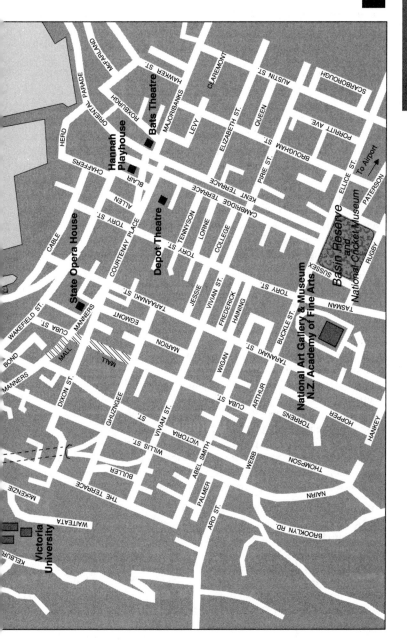

Yeah. We heard the same sort of rumblings in Wellington, a town often compared to San Francisco. Lovely harbor, steep streets that ruin your brakes and tear out your transmission, a never-ending wind, metropolitan atmosphere, no place to park—the sort of things that make civic boosters swell their chests and sing out loud. Also—and this is something few residents of either city will say out loud—there is among both sets of citizens that continual, deep-seated, back-of-the-brain tingle of fear about "The Big One." Both cities, you see, are sitting right on top of some very serious earthquake faults, and one of these days....

A big chunk of downtown Wellington is built on land uplifted in a huge earthquake in 1855. In fact, if you walk down the main business street—**Lambton Quay**—you're walking along the original shoreline. We can only hope that this big chunk of reclaimed land is not composed of the same sort of fill that was used in San Francisco, upon which was visited most of the damage in the big 1989 quake. But, like the citizens by the Bay, the Wellingtonians say most of the buildings around town are earthquake-proof, an interesting concept depending on the magnitude of the quake in question.

Despite the cosmetic similarities, it's a bit of a stretch to call them sister cities, because they have, after all, different cultures and are really miles apart in attitude. But on one thing we can agree. The weather in both cities is basically lousy.

Smog in Wellington? Never. The city's location might have been selected with clean air in mind. The only problem is that the clean air is moving past at about 50 miles an hour, courtesy of the Roaring Forties. Wellington sits on the edge of the **Cook Strait**, a channel of water that takes those mighty southern winds and funnels them right down the middle of town. Add a little rain (which can happen any minute), and you have cause to understand why folks who live in calmer parts of the country get in and out of Wellington as fast as they can. The local papers keep track of the high wind speeds the same way the *Minneapolis Star Tribune* keeps track of the wind chill index. It's not uncommon to have 70- or 80-mile-an-hour air (clean and nuclear-free) raging down the waterfront, blowing unwary tourists into the drink.

We'll be blunt right up front and tell you that Wellington is not our favorite New Zealand city. It doesn't have the energy of Auckland or the class of Christchurch. It's a pain to get around in because of the maze of one-way streets, and a major pain getting to and out of. In truth, one of the major reasons to go to Wellington—unless you work for the New Zealand government—is to get to someplace else. In fact, a lot of folks, both domestic and foreign, miss most of Wellington because the Picton ferry dock is several miles from downtown. They hop in their cars and RVs and head for Taupo or Rotorua.

Having said that, we must also say that parts of the city are very nice indeed, especially the harbor. **Port Nicholson**, as it was originally named, is the remnant of an ancient and huge volcano that collapsed and was filled by the sea. The harbor, now lined by corporate and governmental high-rises, lies at the base of low hills that terrace back into residential areas, which are themselves a blend of old and new, fairly jumbly like the neighborhoods of San Francisco but still having a distinctly New Zealand look. The downtown area for the most part is 20th-century eclectic, not particularly attractive but efficient and relatively clean.

Wellington has been the capital of New Zealand since 1865, picked as a compromise of sorts. Auckland, even then starting to flex its muscles, was thought to be too far away from the South Island. There were loud grumblings and threats coming down south about proclaiming a separate colony, and it was thought that putting the capital nearer the South Island would stop the secessionist plots, which it did. (It has not stopped the southerners from casting long glances down their noses toward the north, of course.) Auckland finds itself in much the same position as New York City—the largest city in the country, the main financial base, but playing second fiddle to a smaller and bureaucrat-ridden city to the south.

Wellington is the site of the Parliament, a number of museums, a zoo, plus numerous shops and gardens.

The major tourist target for New Zealanders (and for those from abroad who like to look at buildings) is the **Parliament**. There are, in fact, several other interesting buildings parked around the seat of government, which is located at the end of The Terrace, just north of Lambton Quay. The place where the legislators actually meet is an English-style marble edifice whose interior is bedecked with native woods. It was designed with two houses of Parliament in mind, but one hall is no longer in regular use because New Zealand's government became unicameral in the 1950s. The building was completed in 1922. Nearby is the **Beehive**, the executive quarters of the government. The name comes from the shape of the building, a truncated cone of glass and metal, which was built in 1981. This is where the prime minister and his/her cabinet do their thing. In the complex of buildings also is the **General Assembly Library**, a Gothic-style heap built in 1897. The library serves as a research facility for the Parliament, as well as a sort of Library of Congress for the country. Free conducted tours of the Parliament are available on weekdays. They run hourly from 9 a.m.–3:30 p.m. ☎ *(04) 471-9999.*

Across Lambton Quay from the government center is what is said to be *the second-largest all-wood structure in the world,* the **Government Building**. If you ever wondered where all those kauri trees went, here's part of the answer. The Italianate structure, completed in 1876, used more than a million board feet of kauri and other native hardwoods. Wood was chosen because it was supposedly earthquake resistant. The huge building (about 30,000 square feet) was built on land reclaimed after the 1855 quake. It's in the process of being restored after a 1992 fire.

On Mulgrave Street, a few blocks to the south of the government center, stands one of the prettiest churches in New Zealand, **Old St. Paul's**. This building, too, is all wood and was built as a temporary cathedral until a bigger stone structure could be erected. Over the years, there were attempts to tear it down or remodel it, which fortunately came to naught, and the church today is a fine example of what Gothic looks like when it's made from native New Zealand wood. *The church is open from 10 a.m.–4:30 p.m. Monday through Saturday; Sunday, 1–4:30 p.m.*

Wellington is best seen from on high, and the usual place to see the city is from atop **Mount Victoria**, which rises about 640 feet above the city on a peninsula at the southeast end of the city harbor. The view is the best in town. Be prepared for wind. You can either drive to the top or take a No. 20 bus from the downtown Railway Station Terminal on Waterloo Quay.

Another very popular vantage point is in **Kelburn** at the end of a cable-car run, yet another tie to San Francisco. It's pretty tame by Frisco standards, but almost a million people a year ride it up the hills. The total run is about half a mile. The **cable cars** are relatively new, having been installed in 1979. They replaced earlier cable cars first installed in 1902, and which were disassembled shortly before the new Swiss-designed system was opened. Catch it by walking along Lambton Quay to Cable Car Lane, about a half mile south of the Parliament buildings. A ride to the top costs about a buck. *The cars* *run from 7 a.m.–10 p.m. Monday–Friday; 9:20 a.m.–6 p.m. Saturdays, and 10:30 a.m.–6 p.m. Sundays and holidays.*

Once there, you can shop (there's a shopping center about half-mile to the left down Upland Road) or walk back down through the **Botanic Gardens**. The gardens, about 60 acres, are known for their tulips, begonias and the Lady Norwood Rose Garden, a 100-bed display, each bed with a different variety of rose. There is also the Dell, where outdoor concerts are given. The botanical gardens date from 1869.

Oriental Bay is a popular beach area in Wellington.

The best way to do the oceanside thing in Wellington is to take the highway around the beaches south and east of the harbor. The road, which has a variety of names, starts at Courtenay Place and Cambridge Terrace. Turn onto Oriental Parade and just keep hugging the coast. Along the way, you pass **Oriental Bay**, a popular swimming area; Freyberg Swimming Pool, named after a hero of World War I; the Wellington International Airport; and **Shelley Bay**. Then around the tip of the Miramar Peninsula to Scorching Bay, a small fishing beach, you'll pass by **Worser Bay**, another popular beach; around past Breaker Bay and Moa Point to **Lyall Bay**, a popular surfing beach; Houghton Bay to Island Bay, where the fishing fleet hangs out, then back down The Parade to Adelaide Road and downtown once again. The entire circle is about 25 or 30 miles or so.

If you still haven't seen a **kiwi** by now, there is a nocturnal house at the **Wellington Zoo** in Newtown, about 2.5 miles from downtown. *The kiwi house is open from 10 a.m.–4 p.m. daily; the zoo itself, which has a collection of animals from around the world, is open from 8:30 a.m.–5 p.m. daily;* admission is about $NZ7. Take a bus from downtown—it will be marked "Newtown Park Zoo."

For an excellent day trip, and a chance to see the harbor up close, take one of the ferries that go from Queen's Wharf to Days Bay east across the harbor. The high-speed catamaran takes about 25 minutes to cross the harbor and costs about $NZ6 per person; there are several trips a day and hours vary. **Trust Bank Ferries**, ☎ *(04) 499-1273.* Once across, there is a good restaurant (At Bay), beaches and a park.

If you'd like a more leisurely cruise, try **Bluefin Launches**, which has coffee and lunch cruises. Coffee cruises are $NZ20; luncheon cruises for about $NZ30, or a sight-seeing cruise for about $NZ20. ☎ *(04) 569-8203.*

If you're a literary buff, you can visit the home of Kiwi writer Katherine Mansfield *(The Doll's House, The Garden Party)*. The house where Kathleen Beauchamp (her real name) was born in 1888 is on Tinakori Street near the U.S. Embassy. *It's open 10 a.m.–4 p.m. daily;* $NZ4 admission charge. In a park next to the embassy is a memorial placed there by her father.

On Buckle Street near Basin Reserve Park is a large park area where the **National Museum** and the **National Art Gallery** are located. The museum is one of the better places to see what Captain Cook was all about. Included in the displays are part of the collection his two on-board botanists made on his epic first voyage, as well as the figurehead from his ship, *Resolution*, which he used to explore New Zealand. There is also a large Maori collection, including a carved meeting house. In the art gallery above the museum is a large collection of mostly European and New Zealand works. There are cafés and a souvenir shop—plus the skeletal remains of old **Phar Lap**, the poisoned pony. *The complex is free and is open from 9 a.m.–5 p.m. daily.*

Next to the museum building is the **National War Memorial** with a hall of memories and carillon. Another museum worth a look is the **Maritime Museum**, which houses boat models, displays of the harbor and paintings and photographs. The facility is located back of Queens Wharf on Jervois Quay. *The museum is open from 9:30 a.m.–4 p.m. Monday–Friday, and from 1–4:30 p.m. weekends and holidays.* Small admission fee.

The Essential Wellington

Climate

Aside from the strong winds, Wellington has almost the same summertime climate as Christchurch, meaning fairly mild. Highs will run around 70, lows around 60. Rainfall will average about 50 inches or so a year, but it's fairly unpredictable. In the winter, highs will be around 60, lows around 40.

Marina at Whangarei City

Band rotunda, Rotorua Gardens

Oriental Bay in Wellington

Fitzroy Beach at sunset, New Plymouth

Mt Cook National Park extends from the Cook River to Fiordland.

Downtown Auckland is compact enough to tour on foot.

Information

The Wellington Visitor Information Centre is at the Civic Square, corner of Victoria and Wakefield streets. *It's open every day from 9 a.m.–5 p.m.* ☎ *(04) 801-4000; FAX (04) 801-3030.*

The Automobile Association office is at *342 Lambton Quay;* ☎ *(04) 473-8738.* The main post office is on Waterloo Quay near the railway station.

The Department of Conservation office is located at *59 Boulcott Street. Open 8:30 a.m.– 4:30 p.m. Mon.–Fri.* ☎ *(04) 471-0726.*

Getting There

As noted elsewhere, Wellington has an international airport for Australia, as well as service by internal airlines. In addition to flights to major New Zealand cities on both islands, there are flights to Napier/Hastings and the Nelson area. The fare to Auckland is about $NZ235; to Christchurch, about $NZ180; to Queenstown, about $NZ400, and to Rotorua, about $NZ200.

Wellington is the terminus for two major train services:

Northerner Express and the **Silver Fern**. The Northerner runs Sunday through Friday, departing Wellington at 8:45 p.m. and arriving in Auckland around 7 a.m. Sleeper chairs, bar and light meal service. The fare is about $NZ90. The Monday–Saturday Silver Fern leaves Wellington at 8:20 a.m., arriving in Auckland at 6:30 p.m. The service includes complimentary morning and afternoon tea and lunch. The fare is about $NZ110. Information is available from the InterCity office on Bunny Street off Waterloo Quay near the Government Buildings and the central post office. *Hours are 7:30 a.m.–6:15 p.m. Mon.–Fri. and 7:30–11 a.m. weekends.* ☎ *(04) 498-3190* or ☎ *(04) 498-3199* after hours.

Daily **bus service** is available to Auckland, Hastings, Taupo, Rotorua and other cities on the North Island. The fare to Auckland is about $NZ110; to Rotorua, about $NZ75, and to Taupo about $NZ70. InterCity buses arrive at the railway station; Mt. Cook and Newman's depart from the city bus terminal on Stout Street up from the InterCity office and the railway station.

Cook Strait ferry service runs from Wellington to Picton. Free buses leave from the railway station to go to the Aotea Quay north of the city center about 35 minutes before each sailing time. For information on ferry service, contact the Arahura Ferry Information Centre, ☎ *(04) 498-2130, FAX (04) 498-3676,* or the Aratika Ferry Information Centre, ☎ *(04) 498-2805, FAX (04) 498-3676.* Both are located on the third floor of the Wellington Rail Station.

Getting Around

The Big Red service—Wellington City Transport buses operate downtown and to the suburbs. The fares for a hop around downtown are about a dollar. There are two passes as well. The Day Rover lets you ride suburban trains, as well as all buses for $NZ15 a day from 9 a.m.–4 p.m. and from 6 p.m. to midnight. A Day Tripper lets you ride any city or suburban bus for $NZ6.50 after 9 a.m. on weekdays and all day on weekends. The passes can be purchased at ticket offices at the railway station and Courtenay Place; the Day Tripper can also be purchased on any bus.

The WCT also operates a 2.5-hour **tour of the city** starting at 2 p.m. daily. The tour, which costs about $NZ30, takes in all the major spots and as an added bonus, they pick you up and return you to your hotel. The tour can also be picked up at the city information center. ☎ *(04) 385-9955.*

There are two **shuttle bus** services from the airport to hotels and back on a 24-hour basis for about $NZ10. Try **Shuttle Express**, ☎ *(04) 384-7654,* or **Super Shuttle**, ☎ *(04) 387-8787.* A taxi ride in will cost about $NZ15. Taxis don't cruise, so find a taxi rank, a big hotel or call. **Capital City Cabs** is ☎ *(04) 388-4884*; **Gold & Black** is ☎ *(04) 388-8888.*

Information about all local transportation, including the Picton ferry, is available by calling **Ridewell** at ☎ *(04) 801-7000.* It's operated by the Wellington Regional Council.

Shopping

Lambton Quay is lined with stores, in just about all sizes and tastes. One good guide, found at the tourist information center, is the free paper, *Capital Times,* which has listings of many crafts stores and other outlets, as well as current information on shows, plays and other entertainment.

The best-known leather shop in town is probably **Skin Things** at the corner of Cuba and Manners streets next to the Cuba Street pedestrian mall, which is also a major shopping area. Another popular shopping area is the underground mall at the **BNZ Centre** on Willis Street near Lambton Quay.

Where to Stay

Note: Many hotels in Wellington have special weekend rates; always call and ask.

Plaza International Hotel   **$NZ275–450**   ★★★★

148-176 Wakefield Street. ☎ *(04) 473-3900; FAX (04) 473-3929.*
Our favorite digs in Wellington for the top service, proving there are still some places that treat hotel guests as guests and not chunks of cold meatloaf. Airy lobby, minibars, large bright rooms. Rooms include 17 suites; some harbor views. Two bars, two restaurants. Tea/coffee, handicapped facilities, courtesy van.

James Cook Hotel   **$NZ255–550**   ★★★★

147 The Terrace, near the business district. ☎ *(04) 499-9500; FAX (04) 499-9800.*
Restaurant, piano bar. Autographs of the famous who have stayed there are on display, good view of the city and harbor. Tea/coffee. Some suites.

Wellington Parkroyal   **$NZ295–355**   ★★★★

Corner of Grey and Featherston streets, city center. ☎ *(04) 472-2722; FAX (04) 472-4724.*
Two restaurants, two bars. Pool, spa, sauna, health center, tea/coffee, courtesy van. Some suites.

Terrace Regency   **$NZ155–200**   ★★★

345 The Terrace. ☎ *(04) 385-9829; FAX (04) 385-2119.*

Hillside location. Restaurant/cocktail lounge. Indoor pool, sauna, health club, tea/coffee, courtesy airport van; special rates on weekends.

Quality Inn Plimmer Towers   **$NZ160**   ★★★
Corner of Boulcott and Gilmer. ☎ *(04) 473-3750; FAX (04) 473-6329.*
Restaurant, two bars. Tea/coffee, sauna, handicapped facilities, courtesy van.

Quality Inn Oriental Bay   **$NZ170–230**   ★★★
73 Roxburgh Street, Mt. Victoria, northeast of the city. ☎ *(04) 385-0279; FAX (04) 384-5324.*
Close to golf courses, harbor views, 15 minutes from the airport. Indoor pool, sauna, restaurant/bar, tea/coffee.

Motel 747   **$NZ90**   ★★
80 Kilbirnie Crescent, near the airport. ☎ *(04) 387-3184; FAX the same.*
About 3 kilometers from the airport. Handicapped facilities, coffee/tea, courtesy van, breakfast available.

Sharella Motor Inn   **$NZ85–140**   ★★
20 Glenmore Street, opposite the Botanic Gardens. ☎ *(04) 472-3823; FAX (04) 472-3887.*
Restaurant/bar, tea/coffee, courtesy van, minibars, laundry.

West Plaza Hotel   **$NZ180**   ★★
110-116 Wakefield Street. ☎ *(04) 473-1440.*
Restaurant/bar, coffee/tea.

Harbour City Motor Inn   **$NZ125–145**   ★★
92-96 Webb Street. ☎ *(04) 384-9809; FAX (04) 384-9806.*
Studio units and suites. Restaurant/bar, kitchens, tea/coffee, handicapped facilities.

St. George Hotel   **$NZ60**   ★
Corner of Willis and Boulcott streets. ☎ *(04) 473-9139.*
Art Deco building. Restaurant, two bars. Tea/coffee.

Able Tasman City Hotel   **$NZ80–115**   ★
Corner of Willis and Dixon streets. ☎ *(04) 385-1304; FAX (04) 385-8416.*
Restaurant, tea/coffee; weekend specials.

Trekker's Motel   **$NZ16–100**   ★
213 Upper Cuba Street. ☎ *(04) 385-2153; FAX (04) 382-8873.*
One- and two-bedroom motel units. Restaurant and café, house bar, spa, sauna, laundry, tea/coffee. Doubles from $NZ100. Also available are budget rooms with or without baths starting at $NZ60, plus backpackers accommodations starting at $NZ16 per person. Linen rental and breakfast available.

Academy Motor Lodge   **$NZ90–110**   ★
327 Adelaide Road, south of the city center. ☎ *(04) 389-6166; FAX (04) 389-1761.*
One- and two-bedroom units. Kitchens, spa, laundry.

Capital Hill Apartments   **$NZ110–135**   ★
54 Hill Road, off Main North Motorway 3 near Parliament. ☎ *(04) 472-3716; FAX (04) 472-3887.*
Family and executive suites. Short- and long-term rentals. Kitchens, tea/coffee, courtesy van to restaurant.

Flanagan's Hotel $NZ45–60 ★

8 Kent Terrace, south of Oriental Parade. ☎ *(04) 385-0216; FAX (04) 384-4500.*
Café/bar, kitchenettes available, most rooms with shared baths. Breakfast available.

Port Nicholson YHA Hostel $NZ18

Corner Cambridge Terrace and Wakefield. ☎ *(04) 801-7280; FAX (04) 801-7278.*
Central city, close to transport services. Some rooms with baths; kitchen, laundries,
travel services, shop.

Where to Eat

Petit Lyon $$$ ★★★

8 Courtenay Place. ☎ *(04) 384-9402.*
Romantic dining with white linen and the trimmings. Very upscale Continental
New Zealand cuisine, where for a hefty price, you can create your own menu with a
little help from the staff. Great for anniversaries or special events. *Open dinner from
6 p.m. Mon.–Sat.*

Tinakori Bistro $$ ★★★

328 Tinakori Road. ☎ *(04) 499-0567.*
Popular and small, located in a colonial house, specializing in lamb, seafood and prime
cuts. Also a BYO. *Lunch noon–2 p.m. Mon.–Fri.; dinner from 6 p.m. Mon.–Sat.*

Café Laffite $$ ★★

232 Oriental Parade. ☎ *(04) 385-1779.*
New Orleans–style creole restaurant on the bay. Very popular, almost always
crowded. Woody and airy. Also many menu items using Kiwi lamb and seafood.
BYO and licensed. *Open daily 10 a.m. until late; Sunday brunch.*

City Bistro $$ ★★

101 Wakefield Street, Civic Square. ☎ *(04) 801-8828.*
As close to California cuisine as you'll find in the city—chili, roasted peppers, eggplant salad, game dishes, lamb. Very eclectic, very crowded. Stone tables and
exposed pipes. Easy and casual dining. *Lunch 12–2:30 p.m. daily; dinner from 5:30
p.m. daily.*

Armadillo Bar & Grill $$ ★★

129 Willis Street. ☎ *(04) 385-8221.*
Howdy, buckaroos. Yup, barbecues, steaks, ribs and other Wild West fare, even a
house beer and private label steak sauce. Very popular, stand-in-line place. Licensed.
Dinner from 6 p.m. seven days.

Angkor Restaurant $$ ★★

43 Dixon Street. ☎ *(04) 384-9423.*
Cambodian food, maybe the best of all the Asian cuisines. Coconut chicken curries,
excellent noodle dishes, fish in a different way, finger rolls. Take-away. Licensed.
Lunch noon–2:30 p.m. Mon.–Fri.; dinner from 6 p.m. seven days.

Piero's Il Cavallino $$ ★★

13 Pirie Street. ☎ *(04) 384-9040.*
Italian songs and dances some nights. Nice decor with fountain and grand piano in
the dining room. BYO and licensed. Pastas, some Italian wines. Garden patio bar

Wellington

open in the summer. Huge portions, some blackboard specials. *Lunch noon–2:30 p.m. Mon.–Fri.; dinner from 6 p.m. Tues.–Sat.*

Mexican Cantina $ ★★

19 Edward Street, just north of Dixon Street. ☎ *(04) 385-9711.*

Located in an old warehouse in central Wellington. The usual Mexican fare plus vegetarian dishes and take-aways. Licensed and BYO. *Lunch noon–2 p.m. Mon.–Fri.; dinner 6–10 p.m. Mon.–Sat.*

Cathay Restaurant $ ★★

14-16 Courtenay Place. ☎ *(04) 384-8513.*

Wellington has more Chinese restaurants than any other city in New Zealand, many along Courtenay Place. The fare is basically Cantonese; nothing special. The Cathay is a BYO with special Hong Kong–style lunches. Open noon until late seven days. A few others are the **Ping On**, **Uncle Cheng's** and the **Casablanca**. The Ping On is at *125 Manners Street* (Courtenay Place runs into Manners). The Casablanca, Cuba and Manners streets, has a *smorgasbord lunch noon–2 p.m. Mon.–Fri.*, and Uncle Cheng's, *70 Courtenay Place*, also has Szechuan. All budget.

Greek Taverna $ ★★

97 Willis Street. ☎ *(04) 472-4538.*

One of only a few Greek restaurants in town, it sits on two levels. Standard but very good Hellenic cuisine. Good value, good price. Bar. *Lunch noon–2 p.m. Mon.–Fri.; dinner from 5:30 p.m. nightly.*

Baxter's Restaurant and Wine Bar $ ★★

22 Brandon Street. ☎ *(04) 473-4608.*

The main draw here is the extensive cellar of New Zealand wines by the glass or by the bottle, but you can also nibble on some tasty snacks while sipping the grapes. Or you can get light meals. *Hours are 11 a.m. to late.*

Cuba Cuba $ ★★

179 Cuba Street. ☎ *(04) 801-8017.*

Here's an odd combination of game arcade, dance floor and café. Noisy and popular. Licensed. Sandwiches and meat/potato dishes plus breakfasts. Dance floor, live music on the weekends. *Hours 9 a.m.–3 a.m. Mon.–Sat.; Sun. 11 a.m.–1 a.m.*

Hotel Dining

Kimble Bent's Restaurant $$$ ★★★★

Parkroyal Hotel, Featherston and Grey streets. ☎ *(04) 472-2722.*

Maybe the best in town. Classic French with lots of lamb and an extensive wine list. *Lunch Mon.–Sat. noon–2:30 p.m., dinner 6–10:30 p.m.*

Panama Street Brasserie $$ ★★

Also in the Parkroyal.

A lively spot done in Italian decor with colorful banners, open kitchen, inlaid-tile floor and casual atmosphere. Grilled meats the speciality. *Open 6:30 a.m.–1 a.m.*

Burbury's $$$ ★★★★

Plaza International, 148 Wakefield Street. ☎ *(04) 473-3900.*

Glass elevator leading to the best view in town. Complimentary champagne and nibblies to start. Impressive wine list, Pacific Rim cuisine, salmon tartare, pan-fried wild boar, cashew nut crust lamb, nice desserts. *Dinner 6:30 p.m.–midnight Tues.–Sat.*

Joseph Banks $$$ ★★★
James Cook Hotel, 147 The Terrace. ☎ *(04) 499-9500.*
Nouvelle French and California style cuisine, menu changes daily. Reservations necessary. *Dinner 7–11 p.m. Mon.–Sat.*

Atrium Restaurant $$ ★★
Quality Plimmer Towers, off Lambton Quay. ☎ *(04) 473-3750.*
Light and airy decor overlooking Plimmer Lane. Brasserie with a Kiwi touch. *Breakfast 7–10 a.m.; lunch noon–2 p.m., and dinner 6–10 p.m.*

Flanagan's Brasserie $$ ★★
Flanagan's Hotel, 8 Kent Terrace. ☎ *(04) 385-0216.*
Seafood sausages, shrimp sauces, huge charcoaled steaks. *Lunch noon–2:30 p.m.; dinner 6–11:30 p.m.*

Plantation Café $$ ★★
West Plaza Hotel, 110 Wakefield Street. ☎ *(04) 473-1440.*
Dining in a plant-shrouded hotel foyer. Vegetarian dishes, lamb and chicken. *Open seven days: breakfast 7–10 a.m.; lunch 11:30 a.m.–2:30 p.m.; dinner 6–9:30 p.m.*

Crab and Coconut Bistro $ ★★
Trekker's Hotel, 213 Cuba Street. ☎ *(04) 385-2150.*
Good quantity for the price, with a varied blackboard menu. Popular with the budget crowd. Also take-aways. *Lunch 11:30 a.m.–2 p.m.; dinner from 6 p.m.*

The Winterless North

Ie Werahi Beach, Cape Reinga is a worthwhile day trip.

The northern tip of New Zealand stretches northwest of Auckland into the relatively balmy climate of the subtropics.

The gentle climate, lack of population, magnificent beaches and unspoiled bush country make this spot a popular vacation target for New Zealanders, especially those interested in watersports.

It was in this piece of the country that European settlers first established a beachhead on New Zealand soil, and it was here that the Treaty of Waitangi was signed, ceding control of the country to the British Empire. Away from major population centers (the largest city north of Auckland is Whangarei, with 45,000 people), the region generally has the same laid-back, pastoral feel you get on the South Island. In the winter, when the kids are in school, the roads up north are every bit as deserted as they are in the south.

The major tourist destination for Kiwis, as well as for foreign visitors, is probably the **Bay of Islands**, a lovely harbor area with good diving, a booming yacht-charter business and a growing deep-sea fishing trade. It also attracts visitors for historic reasons, as the Waitangi treaty was signed there. The major industry in the north is agriculture, although there is also a growing industrial base with a major oil refinery and other industries at Whangarei.

Way, way up north is the **Ninety Mile Beach** area, one of the best day trips in New Zealand, and at the extreme tip is **Cape Reinga**, a popular tourist spot but also a place of special significance to the Maoris.

Driving to the north is fairly straightforward, and if you have the time, you can do the area in a wide-circle trip. Our choice is to take Highway 1 to Wellsford, then go east to Whangarei, up to the Bay of Islands, up through Kerikeri to Ninety Mile Beach, and then back down Highway 12 along the west coast back to Auckland. Or you can reverse directions.

Whangarei

The city, which calls itself the "Gateway to the North," sits next to one of the deepest protected harbors in the country. It serves as the commercial and shipping center of the region. But the primary lure of the area is not the city, but the **beaches** that lie at the ocean edge of the harbor, 40 kilometers to the east.

The area, called **Whangarei Heads**, has some quite good beaches, and the drive out to the heads follows the jagged ridge of the **Manaia mountain range**. A favorite track goes to the top of **Mt. Manaia** (about 1400 feet high), with a lovely view of the area. The road out to the heads passes several good beaches before it turns inland to cut across the headlands to the exposed length of **Ocean Beach**, a primo surfing area. Another popular trip is to take the heads road to Pataua South Road, which leads to the nice little settlements of Pataua and Pataua South, which also have great beaches.

A popular attraction for many Kiwis is the Marsden Point oil refinery, which can be seen from many vantage points in the area. Refineries not being high on our list, we suggest you head instead to one of the most photogenic waterfalls in New Zealand, **Whangarei Falls**, which drops about 80 feet into a pool surrounded by a park area. The falls are on the Ngunguru/Tutukaka road leading from downtown (Bank Street, then Mill Road). The site is about five kilometers north of the city center.

Another attraction is the **Northland Regional Museum** southwest of the city center. The museum is actually a big homestead with displays of farm animals, a historical center, a steam train, lumberjack contests and other delights. The major reason to go is the **nocturnal kiwi house**, where the wee birds are on display. To get to the museum, take State Highway 14 (Maunu Road) to Dargaville. *The displays are open daily,* admission about $NZ10.

Scuba Diving, Poor Knights Islands

North of the city on the coast about 30 kilometers is the fishing port of **Tutukaka**, which is becoming important as a base for fishing and diving trips to **Poor Knights Islands**, a volcanic amalgam of caves, tunnels, arches and other bizarre formations, completely surrounded by herds of sea creatures. The islands are reputed to be the best diving in New Zealand and, if you listen to the Kiwis, maybe the best in the world. The islands are part of the **Hauraki Gulf Maritime Park** and are protected. There are companies in both Whangarei and Tutukaka that can arrange diving, fishing or sightseeing trips. Visitor information is available at the Whangarei Visitors Bureau in Tarewa Park on Highway 1 south of the city center. *Open 8:30 a.m.–5 p.m daily.* ☎ *(09) 438-1079; FAX (09) 438-2943.* There is also an information office at the corner of Rust Road and Water Street (take Maunu Road east from Highway 1; it becomes Water Street). There is a Department of Conservation office at *154 Bank Street* (the main drag) that has information about the Poor Knights Islands and other sites, ☎ *(09) 438-0299.*

Northland Coastal Adventures ☎ *(09) 436-0139* offers day trips for up to six people featuring kayaking, fishing, bush walks, snorkeling and boogie boarding. Explore historic whaling stations or walk the coastal track to uninhabited bays.

There are several good 18-hole golf courses in the area: the **Sherwood Park Golf Club** and the **Whangarei Golf Club**, both in Whangarei, and the **Northland Golf Club** in the suburb of Kamo.

The Bay of Islands

Opua Harbour, Bay of Islands

If you're a sailor, The Bay of Islands is one of those places, like the Greek islands, where the sailing is so easy and the scenery is so grand, you think you've died and gone to wherever it is that old salts go.

There are something like 150 islands in the bay, which sits between two headlands with a ragged coastline of about 500 miles.

In history, the Bay of Islands has seen both the pious and the profane. Early Christian missionaries arrived here in 1814, when the Rev. Samuel Marsden held the first church service in the country. Marsden, whose reputation in Australia was so bad he was called the Whipping Parson because of his treatment of convicts, was a bit kinder in New Zealand, and established missions in the area in the early 1800s. About 1820, another settlement came along, this one at a place called Kororareka, which came to be called Russell, a hangout for whalers, whores, brigands, thieves and other riffraff. Russell, after a time, came to be called the "Hellhole of the Pacific," and was a source of much mumbling from the Christian communities nearby.

Before major settlements grew up farther south on both islands, the Bay of Islands was the center of European settlement in New Zealand, and it was at Waitangi, across a harbor from Russell, that the English and the Maoris signed the treaty that started modern New Zealand history.

One of the biggest industries in the area is deep-sea fishing. Thousands of fishers come every year to try for marlin and billfish. The area was a favorite hangout for American author Zane Grey, who set down his impressions of the bay in *Tales of the Angler's El Dorado*. The bay is also noted for excellent diving.

A fisherman displays his prize catch at the Bay of Islands.

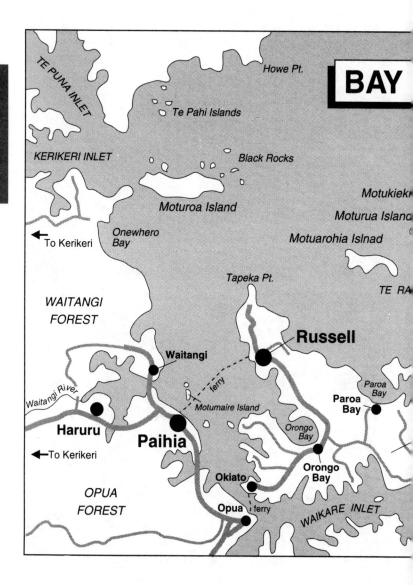

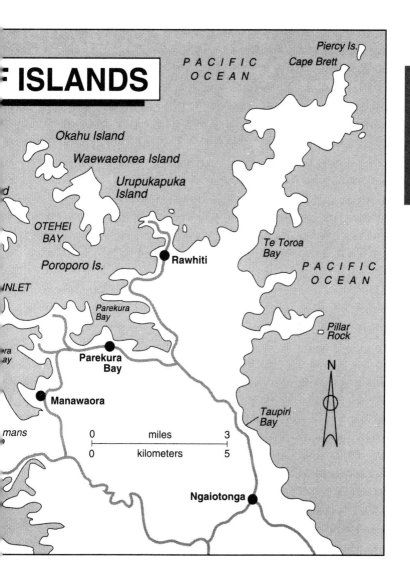

F ISLANDS

PACIFIC OCEAN

Piercy Is.

Cape Brett

Okahu Island

Waewaetorea Island

Urupukapuka Island

OTEHEI BAY

Poroporo Is.

Rawhiti

INLET

Te Toroa Bay

PACIFIC OCEAN

Parekura Bay

Pillar Rock

ra ay

Parekura Bay

Manawaora

Taupiri Bay

mans

0	miles	3
0	kilometers	5

N

Ngaiotonga

Paihia

Paihia, which started life as a mission station, is the tourist center of the Bay of Islands. The ideal time to visit the area is in March or April, when the town is almost deserted and you can literally walk into any hotel or motel and get a bed. The main information offices, as well as ferry services and fishing boat offices, are located in the Maritime Building on the waterfront downtown. From here, you catch the small ferry boats that make regular runs across the bay to Russell. The Bay of Islands Information Centre on Marsden Road has the lowdown on almost any activity you want, and it can book tours; ☎ *(09) 402-7547, FAX 402-7314*. As befits its role in life, the city of 1750 population has a large number of motels, holiday apartments, RV parks and restaurants. The other good news is that in the off-season, room rates drop as much as $NZ30 a night.

One of the most popular trips, nationally famous, is the so-called "**Cream Trip**," operated by the Fullers company. The launch for years served as a mail and provision boat for folks scattered in remote settlements around the Bay of Islands, and today the five-hour excursion is probably the best single experience in the area—unless, of course, you're on your own sailboat.

The trips leave from the Maritime Building in Paihia at 10 a.m. daily from November through May, and at 10 a.m. on Mondays, Wednesdays, Thursdays and Saturdays from June to October. If you're staying at Russell, the launch stops there at about 10:15 a.m. The boat then returns to Russell at 3:15 p.m., arriving back at Paihia at 3:30. The tour includes a stopover at **Otehei Bay** on Urupukapuka Island, where Western author Zane Grey had a marlin-fishing camp. Here you can sunbathe, swim or take a ride on a 30-passenger underwater-viewing boat over reefs, caves and the ocean floor. Or you can chow down at the local eatery—the **Zane Grey Restaurant** (what else?). The boat has bar service, running commentary on the sights and, on a sunny day, provides a wonderful view of the bay. The price is about $NZ50 per person (lunch not included), and the excursion can be booked at the Fullers office at the Maritime Building.

Fullers also has a trip out to the scenic **Hole in the Rock**, a water-carved rock at **Cape Brett**, the southeastern headland of the Bay of Islands. The four-hour trip also stops at Otehei Bay. There are two daily trips. From November–May, the catamaran leaves Paihia at 9 a.m., Russell at 9:10 a.m., and then goes back to Russell at 12:50 p.m., and Paihi at 1 p.m. From June to October, the trip is only three hours, with no stops at Otehei Bay. The fare is about $NZ50. ☎ *(09) 402-7421*. The company also offers one-, two- and three-day trips around the bay starting in Auckland. The three-day, with stops at the Treaty House, a night in Paihia, a run up to Cape Reinga and a cruise around the islands, runs about $NZ435 per person including some meals. In Auckland, call ☎ *(09) 358-0259.*

Just across a causeway north of town is the road that leads to the **Waitangi Treaty House** and the **Waitangi National Reserve**. As noted in "The Maori" chapter, this is not a place to be on February 6 if you don't like crowds. Here is where New Zealand's national day is celebrated with pomp and circumstance, much pressing of noses and many *hakas* (war dances). The queen shows up from time to time, and there are usually thousands of Maoris to either protest or support the anniversary of the treaty. In less frantic times, the reserve and historic building afford an opportunity for a nice stroll through grassy lawns and hikes through the bush surrounding the area.

The place to start is the visitors center, where you can view an audiovisual program on the treaty, as well as see copies of the document written in both English and Maori. There is a souvenir shop with some nice Maori carvings. **The Treaty House** (actually the home of James Busby, the British official who signed the treaty) is one of the oldest surviving colonial buildings in the country. It was prefabricated in Australia, then shipped to New Zealand in 1833. The rooms in the buildings have been restored and furnished in colonial style.

Outside, across a wide sweep of lawn, are a flagpole and plaque marking the spot where the treaty was signed, and to the side is the beautiful carved Maori meeting house, one of the finest in the country. (Take your shoes off when entering.) A path from the treaty house leads to **Hobsons Beach** and the **Canoe House**, which contains the largest war canoe in the world, a Maori craft with the ungodly name of Ngatokimatawhaorua. The canoe, 123 feet long, was crafted from two kauri trees. The bow and stern pieces came from a chunk of tree three meters across. The boat was built for the 1940 centennial of the treaty signing and carries 80 warriors. It is launched every February 6. Trails around the preserve go on a coastal walk, through mangrove swamps and native bush, an area of about 1250 acres in all. It costs about $NZ5 to enter the preserve, *open 9 a.m.–5 p.m.* ☎ *(09) 402-7308.*

Where to Stay

Paihia

The accommodations scene is mostly two- to three-star motels. Among the possibilities:

Abel Tasman Lodge	**$NZ70–175**	★★

Marsden Road, on the waterfront. ☎ *(09) 402-7521; FAX (09) 402-7576.*
Kitchens, coffee/tea, spa, courtesy van, laundry.

Ala Moana Motel	**$NZ65–125**	★★

52 Marsden Rd. Waterfront. ☎ *(09) 402-7745; FAX the same.*
Kitchens, tea/coffee, spa, laundry, courtesy van.

Autolodge Motor Inn $NZ130–180   ★★★

Marsden Road, close to the beach. ☎ *(09) 402-7416; FAX (09) 402-8348.*
Bar/restaurant, spas in suites, tea/coffee, pool, spa, sauna, games room, complimentary bikes and dinghy, laundry. Suites are one bedroom with kitchenettes.

Swiss Chalet Lodge $NZ75–195   ★★★

3 Bayview Road, close to beach. ☎ *(09) 402-7615; FAX (09) 402-7609.*
Kitchens, one- and two-bedroom units, tea/coffee, handicapped facilities, spa, BBQ, boat and windsurfer hire, courtesy van, breakfast available.

Cook's Lookout Motel $NZ55–120   ★★

Causeway Road off Yorke Road, Haruru Falls. ☎ *(09) 402-7409; FAX the same.*
Take the Kerikeri road, a few miles out of town. Great view of the bay. Kitchens, studio units, tea/coffee, pool, spa, BBQ, laundry, breakfast available.

Casa Bella Motel $NZ75–160   ★★

3 McMurray Road. ☎ *(09) 402-7387 ; FAX (09) 402-7166.*
Spanish-style units with kitchens, some suites. Restaurant/bar, tea/coffee, tour desk, laundry, tennis, pool, spa, courtesy van, breakfasts available.

Paihia Pacific Resort Hotel $NZ115–150   ★★★

27 Kings Road. ☎ *(09) 402-8221; FAX (09) 402-8490.*
Units in landscaped garden. Restaurant, pool, spa, bar, handicapped facilities.

Mayfair Lodge $NZ15

7 Puketona Road, end of Marsden Road. ☎ *(09) 402-7471.*
Dorms and doubles. Open 24 hours, kitchen, BBQ, spa, tour desk. $NZ15 per person and up.

Lodge Eleven $NZ15

Corner McMurray and Kings roads. ☎ *(09) 402-7487.*
Dorms and doubles with baths, linen rental, open 24 hours, kitchen, BBQ, tour desk, courtesy van.

Panorama Motor Lodge and Caravan Park $NZ10–80   ★★

Old Wharf Road, Haruru Falls off Puketona Road. ☎ *(09) 402-7525.*
Our choice, for rooms or RVers. The facility sits on a lake near the falls. Very friendly managers, good food, very tranquil spot. Studio and family units, spa, swimming pool, bar/restaurant, BBQ, laundry, charter boat for fishing, dinghy and paddleboat rental, courtesy van. Doubles from $NZ50–80. RV spaces are $NZ10 per person.

Waitangi

Quality Resort Waitangi $NZ115–250   ★★★

Just across the bridge from Paihia. ☎ *(09) 402-7411; FAX (09) 402-8200.*
Two restaurants and the Zane Grey Bar. Adjacent to golf course. New wing has better units. Boardwalk to Haruru Falls, pool, tea/coffee, courtesy van. The main restaurant is the moderately priced Waitangi Room ★★, featuring Bay of Islands seafood, plus lamb and venison. *Dinner 6:30–10 p.m. Mon.–Sat.* The hotel also has **Waitangi Backpackers** with single and double rooms, some with private baths. Tavern, bistro, Sunday smorgasbords. $NZ24 per person with bath.

Where to Eat

Bistro 40   **$$**   ★★★
40 Marsden Road, in an old house across from the waterfront. ☎ *(09) 402-7444.*
Indoor and outdoor dining. Blackboard menu, specializing in bay goodies, including Russell oysters, prawn chowder and crayfish, game dishes; also award-winning lamb dishes. *Dinner from 6 p.m. Mon.–Sat.*

La Scala   **$$**   ★★★
Selwyn Road. ☎ *(09) 402-7031.*
Seafoods with a European influence, steaks. Lounge bar. Specialty of the house is The Extravaganza, a selection of seafood—$NZ85 a couple. Reservations necessary, extensive wine list. *Dinner 6:30–10:30 p.m.*

Ferryman's Restaurant and Bar   **$$**   ★★★
Opua Store Wharf, 6 kilometers south of town. ☎ *(09) 402-7515.*
Housed in an old sailing bark with a window in the floor to watch the fishies swimming by. If you're in Paihia without wheels, there is a water taxi to the restaurant. Blackboard menu, as well as à la carte. The special here is The Fish Kettle—scallops, mussels, oysters, prawns, squid and fish cooked in a cream chowder and baked in an iron pot. $NZ60 a couple. Also lamb and venison. *Open 10 a.m.–10 p.m. daily.*

Tides Restaurant   **$$**   ★★★
13 Williams Road. ☎ *(09) 402-7557.*
Perennial award winner for its menu. Seafood, beefalo (the bison-beef mix) and venison, discounts for early birds (before 7 p.m.). *Dinner from 6 p.m. daily. Closed Sundays during the winter.*

Alby's Bistro   **$**   ★★
Lighthouse Tavern, second floor. ☎ *(09) 402-8324.*
Licensed, light meals such as Thai chili lamb and nachos. Daily specials. *Lunch noon–2 p.m.; dinner from 6 p.m.*

Café Over the Bay   **$**   ★★
Waterfront opposite the Maritime Building. ☎ *(09) 402-8147.*
Country cooking with an Italian tilt plus American-style appetizers. Light meals all day, daily specials. *Open 8 a.m. until late seven days.*

Russell

There ain't much to Russell, but, as Spencer Tracy used to say, what there is, is "cherce." It's a little bayside village with a couple of good hotels, a nice waterfront, lovely scenery and a sort of Bahamian away-from-it-all atmosphere. The bad attitude types who hung around here in the 1820s wouldn't recognize the place today and probably wouldn't hang around, either. Russell makes its living off the day-trippers who come across on the ferry from Paihia and the eager fishermen who come down to pursue the wily marlin.

The Strand, or waterfront, once had more than 20 hotels, and stacks of grog shops and bawdy houses. There are still a few good hotels and groggeries around, including the venerable old **Duke of Marlborough Hotel**, which lays claim to holding the oldest liquor license in New Zealand (July 14, 1840). The beach in front of town is not very good, but if you walk about a kilometer over the hill behind town, you come to a really nice stretch of sand, **Long Beach** on Oneroa Bay.

If you walk out the front door of the Duke of Wellington and turn right, you will come to Wellington Street. Take that to the top of Maiki Hill, where one of our favorite Maoris did his thing. The hill is also called **Flagstaff Hill**, and thereby hangs a tale.

In the middle 1840s, there was in the Russell area a Maori notable named Hone Heke. The local British administration, always ready to make a buck, enacted a port duty, which caused ships not to visit so often, cutting into the revenue given by ships' captains to the local Maoris. Heke put up with this loss for a few years, and then one day he marched to the top of Maiki Hill and chopped down the flagstaff, British flag and all. The Brits, having noticed what unpopular taxes had led to in Boston, rescinded the order and the flagpole was replaced. Legend has it that an American living in the village persuaded Heke that such acts of independence against the British were noble, indeed, so the lad chopped down the flagstaff again. The English retaliated by placing guards around the staff, but Heke snuck in and chopped it down a third time. The flagpole was replaced and, just in case, wrapped with iron to stop would-be axers from attacking. But Heke managed to hack it down a fourth time, after which he and his tribe attacked the town, chased the residents out to sea, and proceeded to relieve the grog shops of most of their stores. From that day on, Russell faded into obscurity until tourism came along to revive it.

At the south edge of town is the **Pompallier House**, which started life in the 1840s as a printing plant for a Catholic mission, and which still carries musket-ball holes from Heke's attack. The house, one of the oldest in the country, now houses a small museum and is open daily; admission about $NZ4. More bullet holes are also evident in the walls of **Christ Church**, the oldest church in New Zealand. In the church cemetery are the graves of several seamen killed in Heke's 1845 attack. Most of the town was destroyed, by the way, by naval bombardment from offshore English ships.

Also in town is the small **Captain Cook Memorial Museum**, with some interesting exhibits of the great explorer's voyages. *It's open from 10 a.m.–4 p.m. daily;* admission $NZ2. Next to the museum is the **Bay of Islands Park Information Centre**. The park, which encompasses many of the islands plus onshore areas, has hiking trails, huts, camping areas and wildlife walks. The center has maps and other information about activities. It has an audiovisual program and is *open daily 9 a.m.–5 p.m.* ☎ *(09) 403-7685.*

The main information office for Russell is on the boat dock where the ferries tie up, and there is a Fullers office near The Strand.

If you don't want to walk to see the sights of Russell, you can take a van tour with **Russell Mini Tours**. The one-hour tour costs about $NZ10 and hits all the high spots. The vans depart from the wharf and can be booked at the Fullers offices in Paihia or Russell. ☎ *(09) 403-7891.*

If you want to take a car or camper to Russell, you should take the car ferry from Opua, south of Paihia. There is a road to Russell, but it's rough and long. The ferry runs every 10 minutes, starting at 6:50 a.m. and ending at around 9 p.m. It lands at Okiato, about 10 minutes by car from Russell.

The passenger ferry from Paihia (there are actually two companies) runs about every half hour starting at 7 a.m., last trip at around 10 p.m. The Waimarie charges $NZ3 one-way; Fullers Bay Belle is $NZ2.50. Both can be booked at the Maritime Building.

As noted earlier, it's possible to book a wide range of fishing activities while staying in the Russell area. But you can also arrange Bay of Islands fishing trips from North America through Shoreline International, a California-based, New Zealand–owned company.

For example, a five-day trip starts in Kerikeri and offers three days of big game fishing and two days of light saltwater tackle. Luxury accommodation is in a resort hotel, as well as aboard the sportfishing boat, and includes most meals and all equipment. The trip runs about $US1200. Also includes a rental car. More and less expensive packages are available.

Where to Stay

Russell has two upscale lodges to supplement the old **Duke of Marlborough**, which is starting to sag a touch.

Okaito Lodge   **$NZ620–1180**   ★★★★★

☎ *(09) 403-7948; FAX (09) 403-7515.*
Probably the premier lodge in the north country, with limited accommodations (four double suites) and excellent meals. Beautiful location on a bluff overlooking the ocean with spectacular views, and close to a forest of rare kauri trees. It has an indoor/outdoor spa pool and a menu featuring lamb and New Zealand seafood. The nightly rate includes two meals, including a four-course dinner, wine, liquor and transfers from the airport at Kerikeri. Limousine service is available from Auckland; it's about three hours one way. A very elegant place. Doubles are about $NZ620; suites up to $NZ1180.

Kimberley Lodge   **$NZ400–500**   ★★★★★

☎ *(09) 403-7090; FAX (09) 403-7239.*
A white mansion sitting atop a hill not far from downtown. It was built in 1989, using lots of kauri wood. It's relatively small (four double rooms and a studio), and comes with all the goodies you'd expect from a world-class hideaway. It has a pool/

spa on a deck overlooking the ocean, and some of the rooms have spa pools as well. There are gardens, a lounge with a grand piano, and a family-style dining room with huge kauri-wood table and chandelier. It also has a fireplace, video equipment and a courtesy van. Full breakfasts are included in the tariff, and you can opt for a five-course formal dinner or a more casual feast. Tariffs include morning and afternoon tea and refreshments; lunch and dinner optional; off-season rates.

Others

Duke of Marlborough   **$NZ75–200**   ★★★

The Strand. ☎ *(09) 403-7829; FAX (09) 403-7828.*

As noted, a little long in the tooth. The rooms are small, and, if you have a choice, make sure you get an ocean view. We give it three stars mostly for the feel. The bar almost makes up for the whole hotel—it's elegant and comfy. **Somersets Restaurant**, overlooking the harbor, is a favorite dining spot. The hotel will be full most of the summer, especially when the marlin are running between Dec. and Apr. Rooms, all of which have baths, range from budget to suites. Doubles start about $NZ50–100; suites $NZ140.

Te Maiki Villas   **$NZ145–185**   ★★★

Flagstaff Hill. ☎ *(09) 403-7046; FAX 403-7106.*

Nine villas, two- and three-bedroom units. Units have dining rooms, outdoor decks, great views. Spa, laundry, coffee/tea, courtesy van.

Commodore's Lodge   **$NZ65–170**   ★★

Next door to the Duke of Marlborough. ☎ *(09) 403-7899; FAX (09) 403-7289.*

Once part of the Duke, this motel-style unit is now under separate management. Good views of the bay. Kitchens, pool, sauna, gardens, BBQ, laundry, breakfast available.

Russell Lodge   **$NZ50–90**   ★★

Corner Chapel and Beresford streets, near the post office. ☎ *(09) 403-7640; FAX (09) 403-7641.*

Family units and cabins, some with kitchens, all with private bath. Tea/coffee, BBQ, pool, laundry. Doubles range from $NZ50-90 per person; backpackers $NZ12.50 per person.

Orongo Bay Lodge and Holiday Park   **$NZ15–30**

On the road between Russell and the Opua/Okiato ferry dock. ☎ *(09) 403-7704; FAX the same.*

YHA accommodations, as well as cabins, tent sites and RV sites. Kitchen, pool, BBQ, bike rental, laundry, tour bookings, camp store, linen rental. Backpackers $NZ15 per person; cabins $NZ30 double.

Russell Holiday Park   **$NZ18–90**

Long Beach Road, up Wellington Street east of The Strand. ☎ *(09) 403-7826; FAX (09) 403-7221.*

A Top 10. Kitchens, laundry, store, BBQ, linen rental. Tourist flats $NZ90 double; tent and RV sites are $NZ18.

Where to Eat

Gables, The $$$ ★★★★

On The Strand. ☎ *(09) 403-7618.*
Probably the best restaurant in the bay area. Located in a house built in 1847 with whalebone as foundation and pit-sawn kauri throughout the interior. It creaks and tilts, but it's elegant. Seafood, steaks, daily menu. Check out the asparagus pancakes or white chocolate cheesecake. *Dinner from 7 p.m. seven days during the summer; closed Mon.–Tues. in winter.* Check for hours during off-season. Call for reservations.

Somersets $$ ★★

In the Duke. ☎ *(09) 403-7829.*
Excellent views, formal dining. Seafood, lamb and beef. *Lunch 11:30 a.m.–2:30 p.m.; dinner 6:30–9:30 p.m. Open seven days.*

Quarter Deck $$ ★★

The Strand. ☎ *(09) 403-7761.*
Outside dining in the summer. Fresh seafood, salad bar, steaks. *Dinner from 6 p.m.*

Duke of Marlborough Tavern $ ★

Behind the Duke hotel.
The pub is pretty seedy, but the family dining room is separate and the food is good and basic. *Lunch noon–2 p.m.; dinner from 6 p.m.*

Kerikeri

The Stone Store in Kerikeri is the oldest stone building in the country.

Kerikeri is an agricultural base at the north end of the Bay of Islands. It's a big kiwi fruit producing area, and you can buy them by the ton for cheap when the harvest is on in May and June. There's not much to do, but the town is a good base for exploring the area. And the Bay of Islands airport is here with daily service from the rest of the country.

Of some note is the **Stone Store**, the oldest stone building in the country, dating from 1835. Kerikeri was the site of the second mission station in the bay area, dating from 1819. The store was used by missionaries to store goods. It was purchased by the New Zealand Historic Trust in 1975, and still is operated as a store. There's a small museum on the second floor. The small wharf next to the river is hip deep in ravenous ducks. Across the bridge from the store is a reproduction of a Maori village, called **Rewah's**, with displays of plants and buildings. There's a small admission fee. Next to the store is the **Kemp House**, built in 1821, the oldest surviving building in New Zealand. You can take a tour from 10 a.m.–12:30 p.m. and 1:30–4:30 p.m. for $NZ3.50.

Information about the Kerikeri area is available at the information center in Paihia. Mt. Cook Airlines flies daily to Kerikeri from Auckland for about $NZ200 one way. There are also flights to Wellington ($NZ440), Christchurch ($NZ490), and Rotorua ($NZ290), as well as to several other cities. For golf in the area, try the 18-hole courses at the **Kerikeri Golf Club** in Kerikeri or the **Waitangi Golf Club** near the treaty site.

Among the Bay of Islands tours available are those offered by **Vanway Tours** in Auckland. A two-day tour, which includes the Waitangi Reserve, Russell, the Cape Brett boat trip, breakfasts and accommodation, is about $NZ240 per person double. A three-day tour adds a trip to **Cape Reinga**. The tours pick you up and return you to your hotel in Auckland. *Information: Vanway Tours, 15a Scotsdoun Place, Glen Eden, Auckland;* ☎ *(09) 817-8046.*

Or you can take a shuttle bus that leaves Auckland Tuesdays, Thursdays and Sundays and that has door-to-door service between your Auckland address and your hotel in Russell, Paihia or Kerikeri. The shuttle leaves Auckland at 6:45 a.m., returns from Kerikeri at 3:30 p.m. The round-trip fare is about $NZ70. ☎ *(09) 366-3566 in Auckland.*

From Paihia or Kerikeri, you can also organize a day trip to Cape Reinga and Ninety Mile Beach. The trip, which includes lunch, is about NZ$70 from both towns. The trip can be booked in Paihia, Russell, Kaitaia or Mangonui.

Where to Stay

Villa Maria $NZ95–130   ★ ★ ★

Inlet Road, Kerikeri. ☎ *(09) 407-9311; FAX the same.*
Three very nice bungalows set in tropical gardens, very Spanish in motif. Nice views, with saltwater swimming pool and cooked breakfasts. Airy and spacious rooms.

Colonial House Lodge   **$NZ95–130**   ★★

178 Kerikeri Road between the Stone Store and town. ☎ *(09) 407-9106; FAX (09) 407-9038.*
Kitchens, saltwater pool, spa, laundry, games room, BBQ, tour desk, handicapped facilities, courtesy van.

Abilene Motel   **$NZ75–85**   ★★

136 Kerikeri Road. ☎ *(09) 407-9203; FAX (09) 407-8608.*
Studio and one- and two-bedroom units, kitchens, private patios, spas, pool, tour desk, tea/coffee.

Kerikeri YHA Hostel   **$NZ15–18**

Close to Stone Store. ☎ *(09) 407-9391.*
Kitchen, laundry, store, tour desk, bike rental, hot meals available. $NZ15, $NZ18 nonmembers.

Aranga Holiday Park   **$NZ18–60**

Banks of the Puketotara River, close to town. ☎ *(09) 407-9326; FAX the same.*
Top 10 facility. Kitchen, laundry, BBQ, canoe rental. Cabins $NZ30 double; tourist flats, $NZ60 double; backpackers bunkroom, $NZ15 per person; powered sites $NZ18.

Where to Eat

Adam and Eve Restaurant   **$$**   ★★★

Waipapa Road, off State Highway 310. ☎ *(09) 407-8094.*
French cuisine in a spacious garden setting. Seafood, steaks, lamb. Licensed. *Dinner from 6 p.m. Wed. through Sun.*

Taylor's Restaurant   **$$**   ★★

State Highway 10. ☎ *(09) 407-8664.*
Olde English decor. Fireside dining, poolside in the summer. Chicken, lamb, fish, venison, steaks. *Dinner Tues.–Sun. from 6 p.m.*

Stone Store Tearooms and Restaurant   **$**   ★

Across from the Stone Store.
Indoor and outdoor seating. Beware duck attacks. *Open from 9 a.m.– 9 p.m.*

The Winterless North

Top of the North

The Tararua Range is a challenge for hikers.

Cape Reinga is not actually the northernmost point in New Zealand; that honor falls to North Cape, across the tip of the country to the east. But Reinga is the easiest to get to and has the added advantage of being next to Ninety Mile Beach. At the cape, there is a lighthouse and small souvenir shop. From the base of the lighthouse, you can look out and see a swirling mass of water where the currents of the Pacific Ocean and the Tasman Sea collide. It's a windy vantage point and one of the prettiest in the country.

The tip of the cape is also of religious significance to the Maoris. Here stands a gnarled old pohutukawa tree which, according to Maori legend, is the place departing souls leave New Zealand. The spirit goes down the roots of the tree to the seabed, rises again on one of the offshore **Three Kings Is-**

389

lands, says goodbye to New Zealand and then heads for the ancient Maori homeland of Hawaiki. The tree is supposedly 800 years old.

Tours of the **Cape Reinga** area normally start in the Paihia area and go up the center of the island to Kaitaia, then on to the cape. Depending on tides, the tour buses either go up the road and down **Ninety Mile Beach** or vice versa.

A lot of the land in the extreme north is reclaimed sand dunes. In fact, when Cook sailed by on his first voyage, he described the area as a desert. Once there was a huge kauri forest here, but successive ice ages raised and lowered the sea level and the area was inundated several times, killing the trees and creating vast expanses of sand. The few trees that survived were almost wiped out by loggers after colonization began. The government has planted thousands of fast-growing pine trees and flame trees to stabilize the dunes. The tour also takes you through the remains of the gum fields— which further destroyed the land. The gum, a resin that accumulated at the base of kauri trees, was used as a varnish and, for years, extracting it was a major industry. But to get the resin, the ground had to be torn up, and there are still vast areas that haven't recovered.

The top of the North Island is predominantly agricultural, with banana plantations, macadamia nut groves, avocados and a growing cultured mussel industry. You'll also see sheep and cattle and wild turkeys. A popular stopping place on the tour is at **Houhora Heads**, at the head of a bay on the east side of the island. Located here is the **Wagener Museum**, an eclectic collection of New Zealand antiques, Maori war clubs, chamber pots and stuffed possums (including stuffed baby possums). There's also a Maori war canoe at the bayshore if you want to try your hand at paddling.

Along the way, you also pass Great Exhibition Bay, so named by Captain Cook because of the display put on for *Endeavor* by a pod of dolphins. This is a major nesting area for migrating birds, especially godwits. There are also shellfish farms in the area, especially for abalone.

Once at the cape, you'll notice that here the wind tends to blow a lot. This is the spot on tours where you are given a box lunch, and the trick is to find someplace out of the wind to eat. It's only a small hike to the lighthouse, where you get wonderful views of **Cape Marie van Dieman** to the west and, off in the distance, **Abel Tasman's Three King Islands**. Close to the concession stand, there is also a hill that offers great views.

Ninety Mile Beach is not, of course. We got estimates of between 56.6 miles and 69.4 miles, depending on where you start measuring. But whatever, it's a great drive. Whichever direction you're going, try to sit on the ocean side; the windows on the land side tend to get covered with sand and saltwater.

The beach is a clammer's haven. No commercial fishermen are allowed within 1.5 miles of the low-tide mark, but the public can take up to 150 clams a day each, so it's a popular area. The traditional method is to wiggle your toes in the sand to find them.

The bus drivers generally drive straight down the beach but swerve from time to time to miss wet spots. It's not really smart—or legal—to drive a rental car onto the beach. The tour buses pass the remains of several cars that have bogged down and had to be abandoned. If you lose a car that way, you pay for the whole car. The tour starts by going down a quicksand-ridden stream bed on the **Te Paki River**, a scene right out of *Dune*. It's hard to tell you're in clean, green New Zealand. As noted, you can book Cape Reinga tours in Auckland or the Bay of Islands area, as well as Kaitaia. During the summer, there are special nighttime drives with barbecues and trips to glow-worm areas. If you stay up north, the tour buses will stop and pick you up.

If tour buses are a bit too calm for you, try one of the four-wheel-drive trips  offered by **Sand Safaris in Kaitaia**. The vehicles get off the beaten path and go to kauri forests, look for wild horses, go over and around huge sand dunes, and generally spend the day getting away from it all. The trips are about $NZ50 per person, a real deal, and light lunch is included. Booking information: ☎ *(09) 408-1778, 24* hours. Information on the Far North area is available from the Northland Information Centre in Jaycee Park on South Road in Kaitaia. ☎ *(09) 408-0879; FAX the same.*

At Cape Reinga lighthouse, you can view the currents where the Pacific Ocean and Tasman Sea collide.

Where to Stay
Kaitaia
Accommodation in the Kaitaia area is limited to a few two- or three-star motels and backpackers units. Among those available:

Orana Motor Inn   **$NZ60–70**   ★★
> *238 Commerce Street.* ☎ *(09) 408-1510 FAX (09) 408-1512.*
> Bar/restaurant, pool, laundry, close to shops, tea/coffee.

Best Western Wayfarer Motel   **$NZ70–80**   ★★★
> *231 Commerce Street.* ☎ *(09) 408-2600; FAX (09) 408-2601.*
> Kitchens, tea/coffee, pool, spa, tour desk, courtesy van, breakfast available.

Sierra Court   **$NZ65–120**   ★★★
> *65 North Road.* ☎ *(09) 408-1461; FAX (09) 408-1436.*
> Studio and family-size units with kitchens, laundry, pool, tour desk, BBQ, courtesy van, all meals available. Doubles about $NZ65–80, family unit $NZ120.

Kaitaia Motor Lodge   **$NZ50–70**   ★★
> *118 North Road.* ☎ *(09) 408-1910; fax 408-1911.*
> Fishing trips arranged, spa, pool, laundry, kitchens, BBQ.

Main Street Hostel   **$NZ12**   ★
> *235 Commerce Street.* ☎ *(09) 408-1275.*
> Kitchen, laundry, camp gear and sand sports equipment for rent, tour bookings. $NZ12 per person.

Farther North
Park, The/Ninety Mile Beach   **$NZ30–50**
> *At the Waipapakauri Ramp entrance to the beach, 18 kilometers north of Kaitaia.* ☎ *(09) 406-7298; FAX (09) 406-7477.*
> Restaurant/bar, kitchen, laundry, shop, nice family service. Tourist and budget cabins, some with with baths. Food at the restaurant on demand; just let them know. The specialty is lamb on a spit. Many tour buses stop here for morning and afternoon teas.

Houhora Heads Campgrounds   **$NZ8**   ★
> *Next to the Wagener Museum.* ☎ *(09) 409-8850.*
> RV park only, no power, no hot water. Toilets, BBQ, showers, boat ramp. There is a snack bar at the museum. $NZ8 per person.

Houhora Chalets Motel   **$NZ65–75**   ★★
> *45 kilometers north of Kaitaia.* ☎ *(09) 409-8860; FAX the same.*
> Overlooks Wagener Park. Two A-frame units with kitchens, sleep two–six people. Pool, laundry, BBQ, fishing and golf arranged.

Pukenui Lodge Motel and Hostel   **$NZ15–900**   ★★★
> *On the Aupouri Peninsula 45 kilometers north of Kaitaia near Houhora Heads.* ☎ *(09) 409-8837; FAX (09) 409-8704.*
> Kitchen, laundry, tourist flats, backpackers bunkhouse, pool, room service, motel units $NZ90 double; bunkhouse, $NZ15 per person.

Where to Eat

Beachcomber   **$$**   ★★

222 Commerce Street, Kaitaia. ☎ *(09) 408-2010.*
Licensed and BYO wine only. Salad bar, daily specials. Local oysters and scallops, as
well as lamb and venison. *Lunch 11:30 a.m.–2:30 p.m. Mon.–Fri.; dinner from 5
p.m. Closed Sun.*

Garden Restaurant   **$$**   ★★

185 Commerce Street. ☎ *(09) 408-0910.*
As the name suggests, candlelight dinners in a garden setting. Avocado shrimp a
specialty. *Dinner 6–9 p.m.*

Top of the North

HOTEL INDEX

RESTAURANT INDEX

INDEX

NEW FIELDINGWEAR!

Now that you own a Fielding travel guide, you have graduated from being a tourist to full-fledged traveler! Celebrate your elevated position by proudly wearing a heavy-duty, all-cotton shirt or cap, selected by our authors for their comfort and durability (and their ability to hide dirt).

Important Note: Fielding authors have field-tested these shirts and have found that they can be swapped for much more than their purchase price in free drinks at some of the world's hottest clubs and in-spots. They also make great gifts.

WORLD TOUR

Hit the hard road with a travel fashion statement for our times. Visit all 35 of Mr. D.P.'s favorite nasty spots (listed on the back), or just look like you're going to. This is the real McCoy, worn by mujahadeen, mercenaries, UN peacekeepers and the authors of Fielding's *The World's Most Dangerous Places*. Black, **XL**, heavy-duty 100% cotton. Made in the USA. $18.00.

LIVE DANGEROUSLY

A shirt that tells the world that within that high-mileage, overly educated body beats the heart of a true party animal. Only for adrenaline junkies, hardcore travelers and seekers of knowledge. Black, **XL**, heavy-duty 100% cotton. Made in the USA. $18.00.

MR. DP CAP

Fielding authors have field-tested the Mr. DP cap and found it can be swapped for much more than its purchase price in free drinks at some of the world's hottest clubs. Guaranteed to turn heads wherever you go. Made in U.S.A. washable cotton, sturdy bill, embroidered logo, one size fits all. $14.95.

Name:

Address:

City:

State: Zip:

Telephone:
Shirt Name:
Quantity:

For each item, add $4 shipping and handling. California residents add $1.50 sales tax.
Allow 2 to 4 weeks for delivery.
Send check or money order with your order form to:
Fielding Worldwide, Inc.
308 South Catalina Avenue
Redondo Beach, CA 90277

or order your shirts by phone,:
1-800-FW-2-GUIDE
Visa, MC, AMex accepted

International Conversions

TEMPERATURE

To convert °F to °C, subtract 32 and divide by 1.8. To convert °C to °F, multiply by 1.8 and add 32.

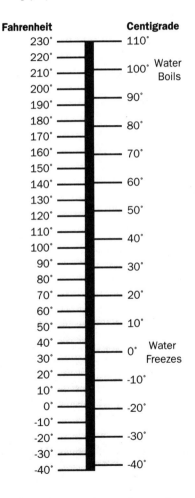

Fahrenheit   **Centigrade**

230° — 110°
220° —
210° — 100° Water Boils
200° —
190° — 90°
180° — 80°
170° —
160° — 70°
150° —
140° — 60°
130° —
120° — 50°
110° —
100° — 40°
90° — 30°
80° —
70° — 20°
60° —
50° — 10°
40° —
30° — 0° Water Freezes
20° — -10°
10° —
0° — -20°
-10° —
-20° — -30°
-30° —
-40° — -40°

WEIGHTS & MEASURES

LENGTH

1 km	=	0.62 miles
1 mile	=	1.609 km
1 meter	=	1.0936 yards
1 meter	=	3.28 feet
1 yard	=	0.9144 meters
1 yard	=	3 feet
1 foot	=	30.48 centimeters
1 centimeter	=	0.39 inch
1 inch	=	2.54 centimeters

AREA

1 square km	=	0.3861 square miles
1 square mile	=	2.590 square km
1 hectare	=	2.47 acres
1 acre	=	0.405 hectare

VOLUME

1 cubic meter	=	1.307 cubic yards
1 cubic yard	=	0.765 cubic meter
1 cubic yard	=	27 cubic feet
1 cubic foot	=	0.028 cubic meter
1 cubic centimeter	=	0.061 cubic inch
1 cubic inch	=	16.387 cubic centimeters

CAPACITY

1 gallon	=	3.785 liters
1 quart	=	0.94635 liters
1 liter	=	1.057 quarts
1 pint	=	473 milliliters
1 fluid ounce	=	29.573 milliliters

MASS and WEIGHT

1 metric ton	=	1.102 short tons
1 metric ton	=	1000 kilograms
1 short ton	=	.90718 metric ton
1 long ton	=	1.016 metric tons
1 long ton	=	2240 pounds
1 pound	=	0.4536 kilograms
1 kilogram	=	2.2046 pounds
1 ounce	=	28.35 grams
1 gram	=	0.035 ounce
1 milligram	=	0.015 grain

cm 0 1 2 3 4 5 6 7 8 9 10

Inch 0 1 2 3 4

Order Your Guide to Travel and Adventure

Title	Price	Title	Price
Fielding's Alaska Cruises and the Inside Passage	$18.95	Fielding's Indiana Jones Adventure and Survival Guide™	$15.95
Fielding's America West	$19.95	Fielding's Italy	$18.95
Fielding's Asia's Top Dive Sites	$19.95	Fielding's Kenya	$19.95
Fielding's Australia	$18.95	Fielding's Las Vegas Agenda	$16.95
Fielding's Bahamas	$16.95	Fielding's London Agenda	$14.95
Fielding's Baja California	$18.95	Fielding's Los Angeles	$16.95
Fielding's Bermuda	$16.95	Fielding's Mexico	$18.95
Fielding's Best and Worst	$19.95	Fielding's New Orleans Agenda	$16.95
Fielding's Birding Indonesia	$19.95	Fielding's New York Agenda	$16.95
Fielding's Borneo	$18.95	Fielding's New Zealand	$17.95
Fielding's Budget Europe	$18.95	Fielding's Paradors, Pousadas and Charming Villages of Spain and Portugal	$18.95
Fielding's Caribbean	$19.95	Fielding's Paris Agenda	$14.95
Fielding's Caribbean Cruises	$18.95	Fielding's Portugal	$16.95
Fielding's Caribbean on a Budget	$18.95	Fielding's Rome Agenda	$16.95
Fielding's Diving Australia	$19.95	Fielding's San Diego Agenda	$14.95
Fielding's Diving Indonesia	$19.95	Fielding's Southeast Asia	$18.95
Fielding's Eastern Caribbean	$17.95	Fielding's Southern California Theme Parks	$18.95
Fielding's England including Ireland, Scotland and Wales	$18.95	Fielding's Southern Vietnam on Two Wheels	$15.95
Fielding's Europe	$19.95	Fielding's Spain	$18.95
Fielding's Europe 50th Anniversary	$24.95	Fielding's Surfing Australia	$19.95
Fielding's European Cruises	$18.95	Fielding's Surfing Indonesia	$19.95
Fielding's Far East	$18.95	Fielding's Sydney Agenda	$16.95
Fielding's France	$18.95	Fielding's Thailand, Cambodia, Laos and Myanmar	$18.95
Fielding's France: Loire Valley, Burgundy and the Best of French Culture	$16.95	Fielding's Travel Tool™	$15.95
Fielding's France: Normandy & Brittany	$16.95	Fielding's Vietnam including Cambodia and Laos	$19.95
Fielding's France: Provence and the Mediterranean	$16.95	Fielding's Walt Disney World and Orlando Area Theme Parks	$18.95
Fielding's Freewheelin' USA	$18.95	Fielding's Western Caribbean	$18.95
Fielding's Hawaii	$18.95	Fielding's The World's Most Dangerous Places™	$21.95
Fielding's Hot Spots: Travel in Harm's Way	$15.95	Fielding's Worldwide Cruises	$21.95

To place an order: call toll-free 1-800-FW-2-GUIDE
(VISA, MasterCard and American Express accepted)
or send your check or money order to:
Fielding Worldwide, Inc., 308 S. Catalina Avenue, Redondo Beach, CA 90277
http://www.fieldingtravel.com
Add $4.00 per book for shipping & handling (sorry, no COD's), allow 2–6 weeks for delivery